Saidie May

Pioneer of Early 20th Century Collecting

Enjoy!

Susan Helen Adler

Susan Helen Adler

www.saidiemay.com

FIRST EDITION

Book Design: Stonehouse Design

ISBN 078-0-615-46653-8

Table of Contents

Preface

During the late nineteenth and early twentieth centuries, many great private collections of art and antiquities were amassed in America with wealth created as a result of the industrial revolution. Two such collectors, Saidie Adler May and Blanche Adler, were sisters, born in the last decade of the nineteenth century in Baltimore into a German Jewish immigrant family which made its fortune in shoe manufacturing and sales. Their legacy reaches into the twenty-first century through the Modern paintings, sculptures and prints that they gave to museums throughout the United States.

Not much has been written about the Adler sisters. The more famous collecting sisters from Baltimore were the Cones, Dr. Claribel (1864–1929) and Miss Etta (1870–1949). They acquired works by Renoir, van Gogh, Gauguin and a large number painted by Matisse. The Cones were ten years older than Saidie and Blanche, and started their collections earlier. The story of the Cone sisters' lives has been documented by the Baltimore Museum of Art as well as in a few recent nonfiction works.

Saidie and Blanche's story has remained totally in the shadows, only occasionally mentioned in small articles about their collections in museum magazines when an exhibit includes their works. Brief biographical information about Saidie Adler May exists in the book, *André Masson, Les Années Surréalistes, Correspondance, 1916–1942*, by Françiose Levaillant, and in the few letters of correspondence between Saidie and Masson. The only other work that I am aware of that includes Saidie Adler May was a dissertation written by Doris Birmingham in 1978, *André Masson in America: The Artist's Achievement in Exile 1941–1945*, again only with a brief mention of Saidie Adler May.

As I started to comb through books on the subject of Surrealist Art and expatriates in France from the 1920s through the 1940s, the only time I found mention of Saidie Adler May was in occasional references as a donor of a work of art by a well-known artist to a museum. She was never mentioned as a "player" in the world of the elite collectors of the twentieth century. Like some other young women born into affluence during the Victorian age, Saidie Adler May was a world traveler and fluent in three languages, but she was years ahead of her peers. Twice married and divorced by 1929, Saidie traveled throughout Europe with a South American-born painter, Alfred Jensen, who was almost the same age as her son. Jensen was her lover and traveling companion until she died in 1950. She had a keen eye and an inquisitive mind, and she and Al painted with the best young European artists of the time. Saidie understood their *raison d'être* and formed collections of their work, many purchased off their easels before they were even dry. I don't believe that, were she alive today, the same collecting opportunities would be available to her as they were from the 1920s through the 1940s.

As the great-great-niece of these two remarkable people, I grew up surrounded by competent, artistically energetic women, and I followed in that tradition. Some of the artworks from the sisters' collections were displayed in my family's homes. The study of art history came naturally to me, and there was a special closeness that I felt toward many of the famous Modern artists whom I studied in art school. I never quite understood that unique attraction, but just took it for granted that their work appealed to me.

After art school, I volunteered at a few local historical museums, feeling a special affinity to these sites, and enjoying the excitement visitors felt when I conveyed my love of Maryland history and tradition to them. I especially liked working with touring school groups.

When I became pregnant with my first child, I studied my family's roots back to Germany. I stayed at home with my two children until they were in school for the full day, and then my intellectual desires lured me back to the museums. This time, a friend who worked at the Baltimore Museum of Art (BMA) enticed me to come and research my great-great-aunt's involvement with that institution. They had given so much over the years and had all but been forgotten.

Ms. Carol Murray, registrar at the Baltimore Museum of Art, kindly granted me access to the Saidie A. May Archives and Blanche Adler Papers at the museum. For five years I sorted through hundreds of letters, a process that was, at times, challenging, as the letters had not been archived or put into chronological order, and many were in old-style French, which had to be translated before I could work with them. Mr. James Archer was kind enough to volunteer his time to perform this task for me. Some of the correspondence was on onionskin paper, typed on both sides, almost illegible. Especially helpful were the canceled checks for the purchase of paintings that Saidie bought directly from the artists, with signatures on the backs that matched those on the canvases hanging on the gallery walls only a few yards away!

There were also letters from gallery owners: prestigious galleries in New York and many from Paris, citing such painters as Picasso, Chagall, Léger, Vlaminck, and Bonnard, as well as more obscure artists. There were many colorful postcards from all over Europe, describing the beautiful cities and the purchases the sisters had made in these exotic places. It was a staggering find! I couldn't believe the amount of material that had been hidden from the public since my great-great aunts had died and left their collections and personal effects to the museum. The only things that were missing were their toiletries and underwear!

I then sought out additional documents, biographies and archival materials from the other museums that the sisters had dealt with: the Museum of Modern Art (MOMA)and the Metropolitan Museum of New York, the San Diego Art Museum, the Walters Art Museum, the Nelson Adkins Museum in Kansas City, the Carnegie Museum of Pittsburgh and the Montclair Art Museum in New Jersey. I also looked for anyone related to the sisters, or others involved in the museums who might remember them or have written about them. I read interviews with past curators and spent much time on the internet search engines researching all of the interesting characters who passed through their lives. I read books on the artists and gallery dealers with whom Saidie and Blanche dealt and met distant relatives I had never known about. It was a journey that I had not been prepared for, but slowly I began piecing this important story together: the story of two modern, energetic, forward-thinking risk-takers, who had timeless vision. Energetic women who, rather than clinging to their traditional and proper Edwardian roots, devoted their lives to promoting the forward-thinking values of art education and accessibility of Modern art to the public.

Regrettably, I was denied access to the diary kept by Saidie Adler May during her collection career. Her niece, my aunt, has possession of this treasure. I was also unable to convince the widow of Alfred Jensen, Saidie's "companion" of 20 years, to tell me the real story of their relationship. However, we emailed for several months and I was given "bits and pieces" of answers to my questions. I was unable to get any information on Saidie's only son, Murray, who was institutionalized as a boy for mental retardation. In spite of these obstacles, I believe that I have composed as complete a portrait of these two women as possible, based on the materials available. Theirs is a story of perseverance and faith in their instincts to better humanity's appreciation of artistic expression through the ages.

Acknowledgements

This work is dedicated to Mr. Stanley Leonard Cahn, my maternal grandfather, who steadfastly believed in my abilities and helped to shape the artist, writer and person I am today.

I would like to thank many past and present members of the staff of the Baltimore Museum of Art who helped make my research possible. They include: Carol Murray, former Registrar; Melaine Harwood, Senior Registrar; George Chang, Assistant Registrar; Emily Rafferty, Associate Librarian and Archivist; Susan Dackerman, former Curator of Prints and Drawings; Katie Rothkopf, Curator of French Painting; Anita Jones, Curator of Textiles; Brianna Bedigan, Rights and Reproductions; and Barbara Baxter, former Director of Docents. Jay McLean Fisher, Deputy Director of the Museum, was especially supportive and generous with the collection.

Mr. James Archer spent long hours translating many letters in colloquial French to and from Mrs. May, which were crucial to the understanding of her relationships with gallery owners and artists from that country.

Thanks go to Susan Melnick, Archivist at the Heinz History Center, as well as Martha Berg, Archivist at Rodef Shalom Congregation, for their patience and dedication to helping me long-distance with Mrs. May's twenty-year Pittsburgh connection.

Without the guidance and support of author Gilbert Sandler and Bill Johnston, Director of the Walters Museum, I would have had a more difficult time navigating through this process.

With citing others who have assisted me over the years, I have undoubtedly overlooked some, and to them I extend apologies, for it had taken over ten years to see this project to fruition. As is often the case with a long-term project, family and friends can support the author during difficulties. Not surprisingly, those with the most influence have been women. I want to especially thank Clare Baer, Ellen Lehman and Phyllis Meyerhoff.

Introduction

Saidie Adler lived in Pittsburgh as Mrs. Albert C. Lehman for over twenty years. She was socially and philanthropically active within the Jewish community and at the Carnegie Museum of Art. Suddenly, she divorced her husband and, within one year married another wealthy Jewish businessman in that town. They quickly moved to New York, with no trace of their status change recorded in the local newspapers…Curious!

The obstacles in gaining access to the most private details of Saidie's life indicate that our society still perceives independence in a female as a negative quality. Saidie's son's illness reflects on society's former difficulty accepting those with mental problems, "putting them away," so as not to have to deal with them. This inspired me to search out other reliable sources to fully understand Saidie's story.

The Adler sisters were "obsessed" with art, artists, collecting and philanthropy. One could liken them to Peggy Guggenheim, whom Saidie knew through art circles in New York and her gallery, Art of This Century. Another contemporary, a few years their elder, was Katherine Dreyer from Connecticut. She was an avid Modern art collector and founder of the Société Anonyme, the first museum of Modern art in the United States. Dreyer also spent many years living with the European artist Marcel Duchamp as her "companion." These women had an incredible eye for talent, and worked to understand the Modern art they sought out. Both Saidie Adler May and Blanche Adler had these same talents, but were never recognized for it.

The Adler sisters helped to make it possible for the American public to experience the new and exciting art being created in Europe during the 1930s and 1940s. Most of the young French artists of this time period were relatively unknown in the United States. A benefit of the sisters' fluency in French and German was their ability to communicate directly with the artists whose work they purchased. Saidie and Blanche brought their fresh new work across the Atlantic to expose Americans to the exciting art and ideas being created in Europe. Almost everything they purchased was shipped directly to the museums.

The two sisters amassed a formidable collection of Modern paintings, sculpture, textiles, works on paper, antiquities and curios—the bulk of which was left to the Baltimore Museum of Art (BMA). They were passionate about making fine art available to the public without charge and sought to help museums educate the public and provide a pleasant environment for enjoying and learning about art.

Saidie's commitment to art was not limited to acquisitions. During the Second World War, she was an active member of the American Rescue Committee, which expedited the smuggling of blacklisted individuals out of France. Her most notable achievement was helping two very prominent European artists (targeted as "dissidents" by Hitler's Nazi regime) to escape to the United States during 1940. These were the Russian-born Jewish painter, Marc Chagall, and the French Surrealist artist, André Masson, both of whom had significant influence on the development of Modern art in early-twentieth-century Europe, and then in America on the Abstract Expressionist movement from the late 1940s through the 1960s.

Saidie was an avid collector and devotee of André Masson's work, and insisted on paying full passage for him and his entire family to be smuggled out of France (his wife and family were Jewish). She arranged housing for them for their five-year stay in the United States during the war, and expedited Masson's first lecture and gallery showing at the Baltimore Museum of Art. Masson's work was shown extensively in the United States while he resided here.

The exile's influence on the young American artists living in New York was invaluable. As a result, painters such as Jackson Pollock, Bill Baziotes, and Robert Motherwell had the unique opportunity to study his work firsthand and learn about his thoughts and techniques through his lectures and involvement in the New York "art scene." Thus, Saidie Adler May helped to facilitate an environment where the new Abstract Expressionist movement could flourish.

Saidie donated the first Picasso to the Museum of Modern Art (MOMA) (also the first of his work to be in a museum collection in the United States). She was involved in the art scenes in New York and Paris, where she knew the owners of the foremost galleries of that time on a first-name basis. Often, those gallery owners would write to her about an artist's work, even before his show was installed in their gallery. She would have her pick of the paintings before the general public even got to see them.

Saidie's collecting career was unique in that she was trained as an artist, and studied with the best art teachers available at the time. She understood their work, and as a savvy negotiator, she dealt both with purchasing from the artist directly as well as from gallery owners. She understood the "collecting game," and held her own in negotiations with museum directors and curators, many of whom did not understand the foreign works, or put restrictions on the acceptance of her gifts. This book gives a special insight into those dealings, especially with the eccentric Alfred Barr of the Museum of Modern Art in New York.

(l–r) Luis Masson, Diego Masson, Alexander Calder, André Masson, and Mrs. Mario Pedrosa, Roxbury, Connecticut, 1944. Courtesy Calder Foundation.

Saidie traveled in intellectual circles which kept her abreast of the latest trends in art, allowing her to take advantage of her keen eye in spotting fresh, young talent. She lived a bohemian lifestyle after 1929, keeping no permanent address. She and Al Jensen moved from one hotel or rented home to another until her death. They spent many hours visiting artists' studios and personally learning about their individual work. Saidie and Al read voraciously, everything from the Greek philosophers to the latest works of nonfiction.

Interestingly, although Saidie collected avidly, she did not keep anything that she purchased, but sent it directly to a museum for the general public to enjoy and learn from. She was dedicated to helping that public understand art and personal expression—especially children—and she planned and executed one of the first museums dedicated to children. Moreover, in 1949, Saidie designed an addition to the Baltimore Museum of Art which housed her collection and had studios for the creation of art. The idea was that pieces from her collection could be displayed in the galleries of the wing and used as teaching tools for students to work with, in order to

Saidie working on a painting (which she later donated to the San Diego Museum of Art) in her winter studio in Charleston, South Carolina, 1949. Reprinted with permission of the *Baltimore Sun* Media Group. All Rights Reserved.

understand what they were about to create. The wing embodied state-of-the-art museum storage and studio space, a radical idea for its time. (Unfortunately the studios are now abandoned, and the wing is just extra gallery space and staff offices for the BMA.)

Blanche Adler was involved with the Baltimore Museum of Art from its inception, and was instrumental in many aspects of its growth. She was the driving force behind the creation of the Department of Prints and Drawings at the museum, funding and donating an extensive portion of the collection, as well as volunteering hundreds of hours toward getting the entire collection catalogued and accessible to the public. She helped convince other important collectors to contribute their collections as well. The BMA's Print and Drawing Department is one of the largest of its kind in this country.

The Adlers' collection spanned art from Egyptian times through the middle of the twentieth century. Many of the Surrealist works which Saidie collected are considered among the finest examples of those artists' works. She was one of the few individuals to purchase the portfolio *VVV*, a unique compilation of Surrealist writings and artwork, created by André Breton during World War II, with the artists who were exiled in the United States. Saidie convinced Etta Cone to buy the series as well. Both were left to the Baltimore Museum of Art, the only institution in the world to possess two complete sets, one for public viewing and the other archived for future use.

At Saidie's death in 1950, the public was not ready to understand the significance of the gifts these sisters had given the city of Baltimore. Unfortunately, over the years the capital left by them was not sufficient to totally pay for the upkeep of the Wing and the other amenities given by Saidie (a Members' Room, Children's Museum and Renaissance Room), and these ideas were abandoned and taken over by other necessities within the museum. The sisters have been all but forgotten!

This biography contributes important new information on the history of art and collecting in the United States. It takes the reader into the world of these first-generation females at the turn of the twentieth century, and helps one understand what led them to the pursuit of collecting art specifically for a museum. Their relationship with the museum and its staff was a unique partnership, where they worked together to build a collection. Many if not most other collectors of their day were more interested in amassing a collection for their homes or to attract and/or impress others. The Adler sisters thought differently: their aim was to collect for the public, and their home was a public one.

The story of Saidie A. May and Blanche Adler adds another piece in the puzzle to the history of the American art scene, painting a portrait of two women who represented the modernity of the twentieth century. By intervening for European artists, they risked their lives and fortunes for the public good. Their story is unique because of the time in which they lived. The legacy of Saidie May and Blanche Adler lives on through their important collections, and the story of how they thoughtfully put them together.

The pictures in this book have been intentionally printed in black and white. It is not possible to give an adequate reproduction of the play of colors that conveys the excitement and intensity of these artworks. One must see these treasures in person to truly experience them. Saidie and Blanche invite you to see their collections.

Passage from Marseilles

Waiting. Waiting silently, breathlessly for the hour to come. Finally night fell, the bleak, steel-gray afternoon sky gently faded into shades of soft mauve tones, eventually succumbing to blue-black. It became dark quickly, street lights were scarcely utilized. There was a subtle orange glow coming from some of the windows along the tiny streets where rows of houses protected their inhabitants from winter's grip. The icy cobblestone streets reflected the glow like a misty sea. The port town of Marseilles was preparing for another long night of chilling cold. The life had been sucked out of this prosperous port city due to the bad weather, and as night's silence fell on it, one could feel the stinging cold engulfing its being.

Four figures walked silently through the winding streets, attempting not to think about how cold they were. Finally, the long, tedious months of waiting would end. Relieving them from the bitter, crackled cold of winter with too little food or wood for heat. Among the four fugitives was painter André Masson. Masson could feel his heart pulsing in his throat. He felt a combination of fear, excitement and sadness about leaving his native land, his beloved France, but it had become too difficult to remain in France. As a Jewish family, during the Nazi occupation, they were no longer safe; the stakes had become too overwhelming. Finally, he had to put his family first. His sweet supportive wife, Rose, and their precious young sons, Luis and Diego, deserved to be in a safe place, away from any possibility of being arrested and sent away to one of those dreadful camps in Germany which Masson had read about.

The danger was too great for him to overcome. As Jews, Rose and the boys were in danger. Masson had made a name for himself as a rebel—one of the Surrealists, a group known for political dissent and rowdiness. He and his compatriots had been blacklisted by

Left: View of a major intersection in Marseilles, France 1940–1941. Collection of the United States Holocaust Museum, courtesy of Hiram Bingham.

the Nazis, and it was only a matter of time until the cold-faced soldiers would come for him. Luck had favored him until now, but that luck was running out, and the family had to leave.

It was the last day of the month of March, 1941. He had recently been introduced to Varian Fry. This tall, lanky American was the leader of the American Rescue Committee, a group which helped intellectuals stranded in Nazi-occupied Europe to escape.[1] Just this morning, Fry had contacted him with the good news: he and his family would be leaving after nightfall on one of the last cargo ships out of Marseilles, bound for Martinique and safety. The escape had been made possible by Saidie Adler May from Baltimore, Maryland, Masson's close friend and patron. She had generously paid the American Rescue Committee to get the Masson family out of France. Masson had initially been against this idea, but concern for his family's safety prevailed.

Recently, Masson's best friend, philosopher André Breton, who spearheaded the Surrealist movement, had been smuggled out with his wife and daughter. Before departing, Breton and Masson vowed to meet again, hoping to settle in another part of the world where they could express their ideas freely.

They would be allowed to take only one small bag per person, plus the clothes that they were wearing. Masson had to leave behind all of his unfinished work in his painting studio. His personal item was a portfolio filled with as much of his artwork as he could stuff into it. This was all that mattered to him. The rest of the domestic minutiae could be sacrificed. However, there was always that nagging thought that Masson could not get control of—what if they were all caught? What would be their fate? It was too much for him to dwell on.

This evening would be treacherous; they would have to sneak down to the wharf, avoid being detected and board the ship quietly and carefully. The craggy cobblestone streets were icy and slippery, and German soldiers were patrolling the area, watchful for refugees. The four carefully made their way down the dimly lit street to their destination, a rooming house in town (the "safe house," one of several used by Fry for those awaiting passage).

They found the house and made their way up the three flights of creaky steps, lit by a solitary bulb hanging by a cord from the ceiling. On the third landing, Masson knocked carefully on a worn oak door. A woman quietly opened the door, admitting the four to a small, dimly lit apartment. Masson found several people waiting there, and looked around, silently nodding to two other men. All were silent. One man sat with his family on a sofa at the other side of the room, quietly stroking the heads of his sleeping children. It had been their mother who opened the door.

The four newcomers seated themselves at a table in another corner of the room. A lone window was covered with a dark piece of cloth, concealing them. After a while, Luis and Diego, exhausted, crossed their arms on the table and laid their heads down to sleep. Rose stroked Diego's hair.

The Carimaré cargo vessel of Compagnie Générale Transatlantique. Collection French Lines.

Later, a young woman emerged from behind a door, her eyes reddened and swollen from crying. Masson watched her walk over toward a table in the center of the room where a large woven basket covered with a blue-and-white-striped cloth held food for a meager meal: strips of dried meat, a few loaves of stale bread and four bottles of wine. Placed next to the basket were faded blue napkins and a number of small, chipped wine glasses, some clear, others clouded with faded names of local cafés. Masson was familiar with the names—places where he had spent countless hours discussing philosophy, politics, science and art. Cafés where he drank and sang and argued life's trials with friends old and new. Places where he felt at home, but which he would be leaving, perhaps never to return.

A woman's voice brought Masson out of his reverie. "We need to eat now," the young woman whispered to the group in colloquial French. The adults gathered around the table as she divided the food and laid the portions onto each napkin. Children who had been dozing sat up to see what was going on. One of the men poured the wine and another man said a prayer for the meal. Everyone ate in silence. Masson felt sick from the memories and could only force the wine down. He gave his food to the boys, who eagerly accepted.

After the meal, the group went back to waiting. Masson wished he could light a cigarette to calm his nerves, but he feared that someone outside might smell the smoke and discover them. Sitting, waiting, sitting, waiting some more. When would this torture end? Finally, just before midnight, there was a soft tap-tap on the entrance door. The woman who had admitted them earlier went to answer it. Everyone watched as the door was opened and light shone into the room from the staircase outside. There in the doorway stood Varian Fry, tall and statuesque, his person backlit, casting a long, dark shadow into the tense room. Fry was their deliverer and had come to free these captives from their prison. Masson sighed in relief. He knew he would have to keep his wits about him, as their journey was just beginning.

Masson's sons had been sleeping, and Rose woke them gently. At the same time, Fry encouraged the group to ready themselves: "This is it, everything is ready, and the boat is waiting for you." He said in a low voice, "Follow me as quickly and quietly as you can—keep the children close, and do not look at anyone as you proceed. When we get to the wharf, we will board the ship—be careful to watch where you are walking, the gangplank is somewhat narrow, and we don't want any accidents or noise."

The group gathered their belongings and followed Fry down the stairs. Once outside, they walked in pairs, with parents concealing children under their coats. Their breath came out in the crisp coldness like small, icy clouds.

They made their way down towards the wharf. In the distance a single light post stood at the entrance, beckoning them to enter. Once they passed that point, they would be free—the wharf's darkness wrapping around them. When their feet touched the wharf, they could feel the difference between the cold, hard, crooked cobblestones and the smoother, softer wood. They would just have to be careful of any icy patches. It was so dark now: a sliver of a moon hanging over the horizon was all they had to light their way.

Up to the left was a large, dark object, gently swaying as a small wave licked the pilings of the wharf. As they got closer, they could see that it was an old, dilapidated cargo ship. A dark figure was standing near it on the pier, waving the group towards him. Fry walked faster to meet him first. The rest hustled along, on the verge of pushing their children in their anticipation. On the bow of this Portuguese boat was a weathered, rectangular brass plaque engraved with the name "Carimaré."

As they got closer, they could see Fry whispering to a bearded man, waving the group onboard. As he had indicated, the gangplank was narrow, and one by one the group boarded. Two other refugees whom Masson knew were already onboard, sitting on crude benches at the other side of the boat. Even through the cold, as Masson breathed, there was an acidy stench from the boat that made him feel queasy. Rose was relieved to be there, and anxious to get moving. Fry boarded the boat, leaving the bearded man on the wharf. The group waited for him before sitting. Again, this tall man hovered over them as he briefly gave them their itinerary and bade them goodbye and Godspeed. It would take a few months, but the plan was for them to eventually go to America.

Fry went down the gangplank and disappeared into the darkness. Rose and the children found a place to sit together on a bench, and Masson watched the bearded man undo the large ropes from the tall pilings on the wharf, and then he pushed the boat away from the dock. As it moved, he could see thin, white, rippling lines in the dark water, reflected by the sliver of the moon. Now he heard the engine start up with a low groan, and the boat maneuvered out into the harbor, occasionally coming into contact with a piece of floating ice which crunched beneath its hull.

Masson finally lit a much-needed cigarette, and as its smoke filled his lungs, he stood watching the fading skyline turn into darkness as the boat headed out to sea. Though he and his family had made it through this crisis, their adventure was just beginning—a new life in a new land. America.

Notes

1 Varian Fry, *Surrender on Demand* (New York: Random House, 1945), preface, x.

The Patron's Roots

Flight from Germany

Eighty-five years earlier in 1856, from the same country whose dictator was terrorizing the rest of Europe (forcing the Massons to flee), Calman Adler, a very ambitious young man of 16, living in the small town of Niedenstein, contemplated the same journey. His voyage to America would also be to escape the persecution of Jews. He was born Calman Adler in December of 1839, the eldest child of Sussman and Malchen Adler. He would become the father of Saidie Adler May, the woman who paid the American Rescue Committee to have the Massons smuggled out of France to save their lives.

After Calman, the Adlers had two daughters, Berta and Karoline, and another son, Michael. They rented a small house in Niedenstein, a tiny rural town near Cassel, in the German state of Hesse-Nassau, composed of a few simple homes built along a lush, rolling hillside. The family lived simply, although the Adler children were sent to the local public school to be educated in Fritzlar, a larger, more sophisticated town. The family walked along dirt roads from Niedenstein into the old walled city of Fritzlar, situated on the Eder River, dating back to the Middle Ages. A colorful place of tall, brightly painted buildings.[1]

The Adlers were poor, and, being Jewish, Sussman was restricted by law as to how he could earn a living to support his family. He worked as a baker in Fritzlar, while Malchen raised their family. Thanks to his job, there was enough food to go around, but little else. All of the children wore hand-me-down clothes until they were either too small or had too many holes in them. By the mid-1850s, the villages of Hesse-Nassau were financially depressed, making it even harder for Sussman to make ends meet for his growing family. Calman had finished school and was now old enough to work, and he became a baker like his father.[2]

By the summer of 1856, at age 15, the handsome Calman had had enough of this bitter life. He informed his family that he was leaving them. His father was angry that he was

Left: Postcard of Fritzlar, Germany c.1915. Collection of the author.

losing the extra income, but one of his daughters was now old enough to do domestic work, and the other one was right behind her. There was no way for him to prevent Calman from going. Soon the son bid his family goodbye, leaving his small village to head for the coast. He carried only the clothes on his back, two meals his mother had packed for him, and all of the determination that had been pent up for over a year.

He planned to walk the entire distance, and occasionally was lucky enough to hitch a ride with anyone who would be kind enough to help him. Usually it would be on the back of a wagon, laden with goods, and he would be expected to help unload them at the owner's final destination. Calman worked any odd jobs he could find to feed himself and slept wherever he could find a place to lie down, sometimes in a dry ditch on the side of the road. If it was a lucky day, while walking he would pass a tree with fruit, or find berries in the bushes along the way, anything to help fill his aching stomach.

Like Calman, there were many other poor German Jewish men who were fleeing this desperate situation for the chance for freedom and a new life. Soon Calman was befriended by Asher Rosenmeyer, another ambitious Jewish boy of 16 from Cassel. The two liked each other and got along well, so they decided to join forces. They helped each other and looked out for one another, giving moral and emotional support when times were tough. Calman felt much less anxious about how he would take care of himself with Asher by his side. They had approximately 250 miles to cover to reach the port of Bremen on the Elbe River, on the way to the North Sea. But the weather had been fair, which helped enormously—they could sleep anywhere without being cold. Along the way, people were kind to them and they were able to manage well enough. It took the two strong young men about three weeks to cover that enormous distance.

The boys finally reached the port town of Bremen. Now they had to find work to acquire enough money to purchase their tickets to sail to America. They worked all of the odd jobs they could find. Once they had made some money, they found an inexpensive boarding house to stay in, continuing to work long, hard hours to earn as much money as they could. The town was filled with other young men doing the same thing. As a result, fights would break out over jobs or food, anything of value to these men who were desperate. It was not an easy time, and the boys tried to stay focused on their goal. It would take them a full year to earn enough money for the voyage.

They were also at the mercy of the weather—their transportation would be on a three-masted, "barque-rigged" sailing ship, weighing several tons, which could leave only when the tides and winds were favorable. Due to the enormous costs of the journey, the boat had to be filled with passengers to make it profitable to venture across the ocean.[5]

By the beginning of September, the two young men had saved enough money to purchase the tickets and supplies they would need for their voyage to America. They had to have a rodent-proof

Right: Postcard of Rotschilds Stammhaus in Frankfurt, Germany. Collection of the author.

metal provision box, cooking and eating utensils, and enough food to last them for the entire voyage, since nothing would be provided for the passengers during the trip.[6] They were booked on the *Hammonia*.

The Voyage

The day had finally come for the two to leave Germany. Early in the morning, they headed towards the dock where the ship was tied up. It was a crisp fall morning with a bright sun shining—hopefully, an omen of a safe voyage. Already, a long line was forming at the foot of the dock. There were German emigrants of all ages, from all over the country, many Jewish, some Christian, all anxious to leave and all looking forward to a better life in America. Most people only had with them what they could carry; everything else was either left behind or sold to pay for the voyage. Mothers carried their babes in their arms, little children sat at their feet next to bundles packed with the family's provisions. The air was buzzing with voices as the boys got in the queue.

They all waited as the crew members boarded first, burly men, each carrying a large duffle slung over their massive shoulders. Behind them were loaded wagons. As the crew boarded, large rope slings filled with supplies for the boat were hoisted onto the back of the deck. Then wooden barrels filled with fresh water were rolled up by workers and loaded on. Calman and Asher knew this routine well. Often they had jealously observed this scene as ships prepared to depart for foreign lands.

Ship's Passage

Once the ship was readied, the passengers were allowed to board slowly. They headed up the wooden ramp, onto the boat and into the steerage deck through heavy wooden hatches, the only source of ventilation for that living area.[7] Eventually the long line shrunk until Calman and Asher could board. They headed up the ramp and made their way through the hatch together.

Inside, the dark, overcrowded steerage deck was stuffy, with low ceilings. There would be no privacy in this noisy environment. Each passenger was assigned their own small, hard wooden berth, where they would try to catch some sleep whenever they could. The two managed to find their assigned berths and stowed their personal belongings there, headed back up to the top deck to watch the ship leave. As it was finally pushed away from the dock, the boys, filled with excitement, found themselves a bit scared, having only left home a year ago, never venturing out of their homeland before. They missed their families, but they had each other and were confident in themselves and their ability to succeed.

Day and night, the cramped steerage deck teemed with the all of the activities of daily life. Women cooked meals as best they could on cast-iron stoves, working with dried ingredients or cured meats. They had to be careful with fire on this vessel, for fear of burning the wooden hull. Any light they had came through the open hatch during the day. Candles or oil-burning lamps were used at night or in bad weather. For long periods each day, families prayed, hoping for calm seas and a safe passage.[8]

At best, the sanitation facilities were crude. To make matters worse, if the weather was bad or the seas rough, light and air would be cut off when the hatches were closed to prevent seawater from pouring into the cabin. The stench could be unbearable. However, on a good day, if the seas were calm, the passengers could sit out on the deck of the boat and get some much-needed fresh air and sunshine.

Some of the other boys were rough and hardened, stealing and provoking fights. Such boys had been forced out of their homes because of their behavior. Calman and Asher had to be careful around them, and kept to themselves. They would play games with other boys whom they could trust, and listened to stories told by other passengers. They slept when they could, but there was always noise, children crying, people talking, someone sick and moaning, and just the noise of the boat creaking as it rolled up and down on the active seas. Everyone became anxious to see land and get off the ship. This mostly unpleasant voyage took two full weeks.[9]

The ship finally arrived at the coast of the United States and proudly sailed up the Hudson River to get to the port of New York. The water was much calmer in the river, and the sun was shining, which made for a pleasant end to their voyage. It was September 18, 1857. They were finally in America! New York was one of the largest port cities in the United States where a large percentage of the German immigrants landed. Exhausted, dirty and hungry, the boys were anxious to see their new home.

New York

The boat slowly sailed up towards the landing pier. No one was there to greet them except for a team of officials and a local doctor, waiting to board the boat to check each passenger before he was allowed to disembark. It seemed to take forever for the boat to reach the dock and tie up. Again, a long wait. Everyone had to have a physical examination by the doctor and then have their travel papers verified and signed in order for them to leave.

Eventually, Asher and Calman had their physical examinations. Neither boy spoke any English and so they were unable to communicate. Luckily, both boys were healthy and had not caught anything on the voyage over. When it was time for their travel papers to be signed, Calman's first name became Anglicized, changing it to Charles. He would be known as Charles Adler for the rest of his life, and have subsequent heirs bear his name. Asher was able to keep the German-Jewish name that he had been given at birth.

Once they were allowed off of the ship, the passengers scattered in many different directions. Some looked for housing; others met relatives who were waiting for them, anxious to embrace them into their Americanized lives. Still others searched for transportation out of New York to other parts of the state or country.

The port was very busy, loading and unloading the ships which arrived daily. Once the hold of the *Hammonia* was cleaned from its passengers' use, it was loaded up with hogsheads of tobacco that were shipped back to Germany for the Europeans' ever-growing desire to smoke. These leaves (worth their weight in gold), would be processed into cigarettes and pipe tobacco in Europe for local consumption. This was a very profitable business for the German shipping lines: transporting immigrants to America and returning with a full load of tobacco for the German and European markets.

America

Once in New York, the young men again took any odd jobs they could find, as well as taking a room in a boarding house. After work, their free time was spent with other young German immigrants, comparing experiences and learning about this new country and what it had to offer. They tried to learn English as quickly as they could. New York was noisy and crowded, not unlike the town of Bremen, where they had spent the last year. Neither one wanted to stay there for very long. The most popular and profitable jobs available to young Jewish men were garment-sewing or peddling. The boys decided to become peddlers, and worked for others until they could each afford to purchase a large backpack. They would stock it with approximately 80 pounds of household goods or special trinkets, like inexpensive jewelry or gifts.[10] According to those already in the business, the best opportunities to earn money were in the outlying rural areas, where the residents did not have easy access to goods readily available in the big port cities. That would work out perfectly for them, since they did not like being in this city.

Settlement in Maryland

As soon as Charles and Asher accumulated all of the goods they could carry, they left New York and headed south towards Washington, D.C. Traveling by foot, they stopped to peddle their wares at small hamlets similar to the villages they had left behind in Germany. The two worked to save as much of the money they earned as possible, spending only what was necessary to eat and spend the night at the cheapest lodging. They continued working their way south through Pennsylvania and Delaware, and spent some time in the larger towns along the way, restocking their heavy backpacks. Once they reached Maryland, they visited Baltimore (the largest port in the country at the time) and stocked up on the more exotic goods which could not be found in other cities. They continued to work their way west, along the well-traveled Rolling Road. They peddled their way to Frederick, Maryland, and then headed southward, following the Potomac River until they reached the small rural hamlet called Germantown, started by a group of proud German immigrants. It felt very much like their homeland where they could converse in their native tongue, so they decided to stay.

Germantown comprised a few one-room log houses when the boys arrived. These houses were dark, lucky if they had one glass window for light. The walls were thick, with rough-hewn horizontal logs stuffed in between with mud and stones. Most of the residents lived self-sufficient lives, since the nearest large town was a day's ride away. This meant that families had their own livestock to care for, and their children were as responsible for the chores as the parents. Most people bartered for the goods they needed, having little money.

Even under these circumstances, Germantown was able to support a general store, owned by a Mr. Lowe. By the time Charles and Asher reached Germantown, Mr. Lowe had passed away, and soon they were able to purchase the store as partners with the money they had saved.[11] Charles was now his own boss, and enjoyed the freedom of making all the decisions about his new life and career. He answered to no one.

People in this town worked hard during the week, but on the weekend they relaxed and had a good time. Everyone would participate in barn dances at the local mill with lively music and singing. Weddings, country fairs and harvesting parties also kept the community involved.[12] Charles and Asher felt at home here and were starting a good life. However, their freedom was to change due to problems arising from the beginnings of the Civil War, and the unrest in the area near their business.

The War

Being of military age but not involved in the politics surrounding the war, Charles took advantage of the legally available custom of that day. When he was drafted into the army, he ran an advertisement in the local newspaper for a substitute to fight for him, at a predetermined sum. This way he could continue to run the store.[13] Germantown was situated close to the Potomac River, and was particularly vulnerable to the movement of soldiers and mobs of sympathizers from both the Union and Confederate sides. These groups would antagonize each other, and occasionally the residents of the town would get caught in the middle of the conflict. Unfortunately, this happened to Charles and Asher.

No major battles were fought in Germantown, even though historic records reflect disorder there. Armies marched through the area on their way to and from battles in Virginia, western Maryland and Pennsylvania.[14] It is not known for certain whether the mobs of hoodlums creating havoc in the Germantown area were Southerners or just rowdy men, but a group ran through town on the night of August 21, 1863, and ransacked their store, burning it to the ground.[15] It was reported the next day in the local Germantown newspaper, the *Sentinel*, that the "Vagabonds" took $700 and cleaned out the store.[16]

A New Life in Baltimore

At the age of 22, Charles was devastated and penniless again. Frustrated, he decided to leave Germantown, having no ties there other than his good friend, Asher. After Charles had left Germany, his younger brother Michael loyally wrote to him, wanting the same opportunity. In 1860, he also came to America (at the age of 13) and had gotten a job in Baltimore with the H. Frank & Company shoe manufacturers. By 1862, he became one of their salesmen. He continued to correspond with Charles, and hearing of his loss, he begged him to come to Baltimore and work with him. Charles left his first home in America and traveled back to Baltimore, the prosperous port where there was a large, well-established community of German Jews with whom he hoped to find a good, secure job. Now with his own experience in managing a successful business, Charles joined his brother to work for the Franks as a clerk.

It was in Baltimore that Charles finally settled down and made his fortune. He took a job working with Henry (Haymann, or "Haym") Frank, a German Jew who had started the shoe manufacturing business H. Frank & Co. after immigrating to America some time after February of 1837. Henry and his oldest son, Solomon, ran the business. Baltimore was the perfect place for this endeavor, the busiest port in the country. Baltimore, like New York, drew immigrants from all over Eastern Europe, ready to work. Many had valuable skills they had learned in their native countries, and they were also eager to "make it" in this new land of freedom.

Charles moved in with his younger red-headed brother, Mike, in the German Jewish community of Old Town. This was in a poorer part of Baltimore, one mile north of the port of Fells Point, where all of the new immigrants started out when they came to Baltimore. One had only to walk down Broadway, the main street, to hear people talking in every imaginable language and dialect. But this place was different from New York. It was smaller, with a slower pace, and Charles liked that. It was so good to be with Mike. He had really missed his family, and it meant so much to be reconnected with his brother. When Charles arrived in Baltimore, the shoe business was booming, and Charles' strong character, good business sense and gregarious personality enabled him to fit in well. He quickly became an integral part of that business. Situated in Maryland, on the Mason-Dixon Line, they were able to sell shoes to the Union and Confederate soldiers at the same time. They were making a fortune!

He was well liked by the Frank family and started courting one of Frank's daughters, Caroline, who was 2 1/2 years younger than he. Soon they were married, guaranteeing success for Charles, and, by 1867, they had their first son, Simon Adler. Two years later, they had another son, Abraham, followed by a third son, Harry.

By the 1870s, the manufacture of shoes and boots were at their peak—a lucrative business— approximately one-half of the substantial monetary value of the men's clothing industry in Baltimore. There was strong demand for shoes in the South and newly discovered Western part

Left: Charles Adler from *Tercentenary History of Maryland Illustrated*, Vol. III, 1925. Right: Caroline Frank Adler by Bachrach Photographic Art Gallery, Baltimore, Md. Collection of the author.

of this country, and the combination of the nearby location of leather tanners, along with the improvements in power machinery, created an ideal environment.[17]

In 1873, at the age of 33, Charles Adler and Henry and Solomon Frank became partners and changed the name to the "Frank & Adler Shoe Company." The business moved from a small shop at 242 Lexington Street to the more prestigious location at the corner of Lexington and 212 & 214 West Baltimore Street. They purchased a large, handsome five-story iron-front warehouse, "stacked with case upon case of goods in the line of boots, shoes and rubbers of all kinds." They had a large force of men working in the building, as well as a staff of eighteen traveling salesmen representing the house on the road.[18]

Within a decade, production decreased in Baltimore, and New England became the center for the industry. So, under Charles' direction, Frank & Adler changed to boot and shoe wholesaling and jobbing merchandising, selling footwear by the thousands of pairs. They negotiated contracts to supply shoes for large corporations such as the Baltimore and Ohio Railroad. Their firm was also among the organizers of the Baltimore Shoe and Leather Board of Trade.[19] Charles could do no wrong. With hard work he had found his dream in America!

Over the years, there was some confusion about a story concerning the statement that Charles Adler had invented the "elevated shoe." This is untrue. All of the patents designed for the Frank & Adler Shoe Company were held by an Abraham Adler from an unrelated family, (Adler was a fairly common surname in Bavaria.) Abraham Adler developed and patented the "elevator heel" as well as many other patents related to shoe manufacturing.[20]

ALL CLAIMS MUST BE MADE WITHIN 5 DAYS AFTER RECEIPT OF GOODS.
AFTER SHIPPING GOODS AND GETTING A RECEIPT FOR THEM IN GOOD ORDER OUR RESPONSIBILITY CEASES.

Baltimore, Oct 9 1882

BOUGHT OF

FRANK & ADLER

314 & 316 W. BALTIMORE ST.

WHOLESALE DEALERS IN BOOTS & SHOES.

BETWEEN LIBERTY & HOWARD.

Terms 30%

Traveling Agents, without special written authority from us are not authorized to collect money on our account.

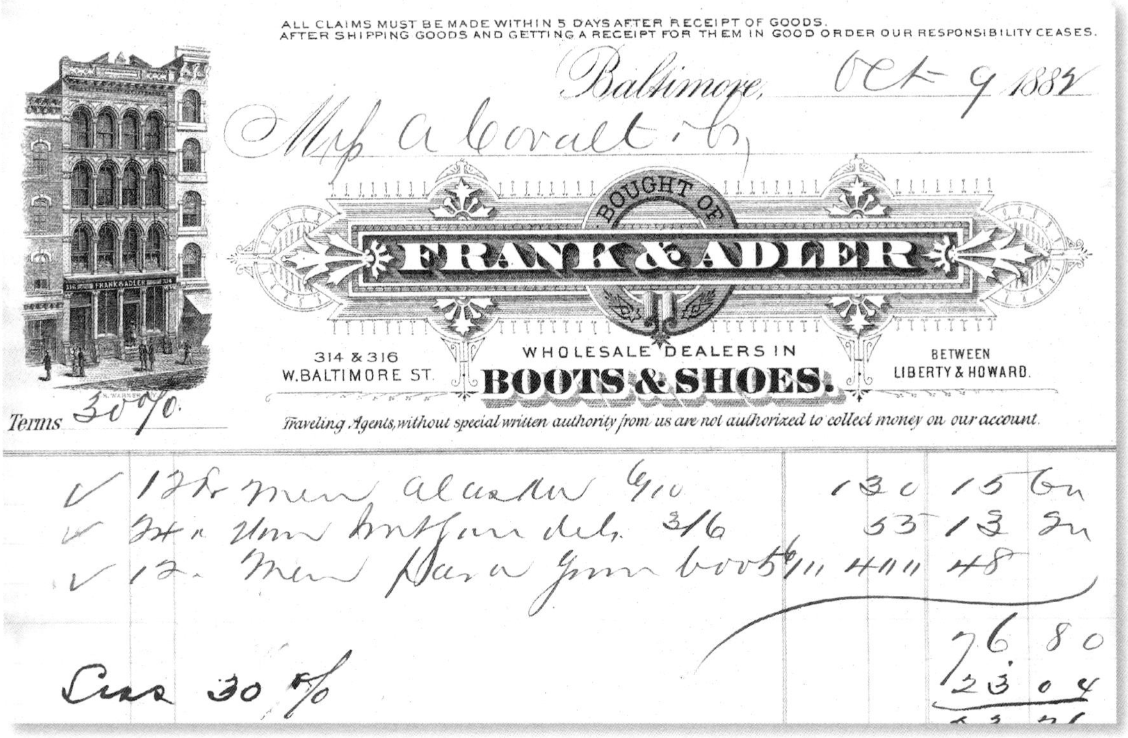

Billhead from Frank & Adler Shoe Company, 1882. Collection of the author.

Notes

1 G & C. Merrian & Co. *Webster's Geographical Dictionary* (Wisconsin: Collegiate Press, 1959), 405.

2 Ira A. Glazier & P. William Filby eds., *Germans to America: Lists of Passengers Arriving at U. S. Ports*, Vol. 11: April – November, 1857 (Wilmington, DE: Scholarly Resources, 1988).

3 John F. Flynn, *German Revolution of 1848 and Historiography in the German Democratic Republic, Encyclopedia of Revolutions of 1848*, 2005 James Chastain Chastain@www.cats.ohiou.edu.

4 Anton Gill, *Art Lover, a Biography of Peggy Guggenheim* (New York: Harper Collins, 2001), 17.

5 Philip Kahn Jr., *Uncommon Threads: Threads that Wove the Fabric of Baltimore Jewish Life* (Baltimore: Pecan Publications, 1996), 7.

6 *Ibid.*, 8.

7 Anton Gill, *Art Lover, a Biography of Peggy Guggenheim* (New York: Harper Collins, 2001), 17.

8 *Ibid.*

9   Philip Kahn Jr., *Uncommon Threads: Threads that Wove the Fabric of Baltimore Jewish Life* (Baltimore: Pecan Publications, 1996), 8.

10 Philip Kahn Jr., *Uncommon Threads: Threads that Wove the Fabric of Baltimore Jewish Life* (Baltimore: Pecan Publications, 1996), 14.

11 Susan Soderberg, *A History of Germantown, Maryland* (Germantown, MD: privately published, 1988), 74.

12 *Ibid.*, 76.

13 Philip Kahn Jr., *Uncommon Threads: Threads that Wove the Fabric of Baltimore Jewish Life* (Baltimore: Pecan Publications, 1996), 37.

14 Susan Soderberg, *A History of Germantown, Maryland* (Germantown, MD: privately published, 1988), 117.

15 *Ibid.*, 118.

16 "More Robberies," *Sentinel*, Montgomery County, MD., August 22, 1863.

17 Philip Kahn Jr., *A Stitch in Time, The Four Seasons of Baltimore's Needle Trades* (Baltimore: Maryland Historical Society, 1989), 111.

18 *Baltimore, the Gateway to the South* (Baltimore: Mercantile Advancement Co., 1898), 167.

19 Philip Kahn Jr., *A Stitch in Time, The Four Seasons of Baltimore's Needle Trades* (Baltimore: Maryland Historical Society, 1989), 111.

20 Patent, Abraham Adler, *Official Gazette of the United States Patent Office*, Vol. XVI, 1879 (Government Printing Office, Washington D.C. 1880), 698.

Jewish Geography, 1884–1890

Charles Adler and his wife, Caroline, lived a good life in Baltimore. They had six children during their marriage, three sons—Simon, Harry and Abraham—and three daughters—Helen, Blanche and Saidie. Charles' brother Mike remained a bachelor and lived with them, too. By 1884, Charles had established himself as a partner at Frank and Adler. He was now able to move into "high society" and purchased a handsome, large brick townhouse in fashionable Bolton Hill. This elite community, where many "well-to-do" German Jews resided, sat on a hillside overlooking downtown Baltimore, removed from the dirt and noise of the city. This was one of the most exclusive neighborhoods in Baltimore, where the intellectual elites, doctors, lawyers, bankers and well-to-do merchants resided.

Bolton Hill was planned after the lavish neighborhood communities in Paris and New York. Many styles of grand townhouses were arranged in rows along broad, hilly streets.[1] There was a laid-back Southern feel to this quiet neighborhood.[2] Imposing houses of worship anchored the blocks at the corners. Across the street from the Adlers' home on Eutaw Place, the Hopkins University provided a showy mansion for their president, Daniel Coit Gilman. This block was referred to as the "highest point of land and possibly of prestige in town."[3]

Situated just 1 1/2 miles north, the 500-acre Druid Hill Park drew residents from Bolton Hill, where they could enjoy a leisurely drive through the park in their carriages before breakfast, or ride horses hired from the riding school estate, "Bolton."[4] This serene park had its own miniature steam train, a zoo, and a lake used for boating in the summer and skating when it froze over in the winter.[5] A shepherd lived on the property with his flock of sheep, lazily manicuring the massive lawn. In the summer, when the weather became too sultry, nearby residents would arrive with their sheets and pillows to spend the night sleeping out of doors in the coolness under large shade trees in the park. It was always bustling with people who came to the park by way of a streetcar line that ran up Eutaw Place from downtown.

Left: Postcard of Eutaw Place Temple, Baltimore, Md. Collection of the author.

This was the perfect place for Charles Adler to raise his family in the proper manner. The large redbrick townhouse with its wide white marble steps was typical of the "Baltimore Style"—a statement of his new wealth. One entered the home through imposingly tall, carved, Eastlake-style double doors with etched-glass panels. Inside, the oak-paneled foyer had a cold, black and white inlaid-marble floor. From the second floor, a heavy dark walnut staircase wound its way down, ending with an elegantly carved post.

To the right were two parlors for entertaining and showcasing the family's good taste. From the high ceilings hung massively heavy crystal gas-burning chandeliers. On the opposite walls, each room had ornately carved marble fireplaces, topped with tall, framed, beveled mirrors, reflecting light in the room. Each parlor could be separated by a set of enormous walnut paneled pocket doors, pulled out from the sides like massive, secret stone tablets. Striped oak floors had elegant dark inlays around their perimeter. Overtop were soft oriental carpets filled with flowers, triangles, squares and stripes in shades of gold, garnet, dark green, azure blue and cream. A French gilded bronze mantle clock proudly dominated the center of one of the pink marble mantles. Its measured tick-tock broke the silence of the dense furnishings and, on the hour, a deep chime reverberated throughout the first floor.

The focal points of each of these showy rooms were two large oil paintings, each encased in wide, gold gilded frames—a true luxury. The scenes were serene landscapes of the homeland, the German countryside—an idealized reminiscence of Charles' birthplace. Rolling hillsides with large trees dominated the foreground, while animals grazed on lush green grass as peasants worked in the fields.

Each parlor room had its "suite" of furniture, stiffly horsehair-stuffed and covered in heavily tufted dark green velvet. Eight matching high-backed side chairs sat in the corners of the rooms, poised for activity. The symmetrical layout of these parlors denoted the owner's "good taste" in design. These two rooms were proudly saved for company or special occasions, the only time the children would be allowed in. As a result, they remained dark and cavernous until called into action. Then, the heavily tasseled, dark plum velvet draperies would be drawn away from tall windows at the front of the parlor, light penetrating into the still room, framing the activities on the street outside.

Jews in Baltimore did not own slaves. One reason was economic: a slave cost at least $600 and slaves were not a part of the urban economy. As members of the Oheb Shalom Congregation, the Adlers agreed with their opinion on the subject and were generally "neutral" on the issue of slavery, as were the great majority of American Jews. "If a Baltimore Jew owned a slave, he would not have known what to do with him."[6]

Right, top: Postcard of Eutaw Place. Adler home 3 buildings in from the right.
Right, lower: Postcard of Eutaw Place Fountain, c. 1903. Both collection of the author.

However, the Adlers employed a housekeeper, cook and butler to maintain their large house, with four bedrooms on the second floor and three small bedrooms on the third floor. The cook slept in one of these rooms. Early in the morning before the family rose, she would quietly descend the three flights of back stairs into the basement kitchen. The family's breakfast was ready and waiting for them when they entered the dining room each morning.[7]

The housekeeper and butler lived a few blocks away on Madison Street, in a neighborhood consisting of African-American families who worked for the wealthy families of Bolton Hill.[8] Every morning, they would walk from their small rowhouses up to Eutaw Place, where the grand homes sat amidst wide, tree-lined boulevards with elaborately planted gardens and fountains in the center of each block. This layout was a smaller-scale copy of the luxurious streets of the brownstone mansion district in Manhattan. The Adlers, like most of their neighbors on Eutaw Place, had a family carriage with horses, driven by a chauffeur. Every morning, he would take Charles downtown to his office at the Frank Building, 315 West Lexington Street.

Caroline Frank Adler spent her time performing her duties as mother, head of a large household, and devoted wife to her husband. Though her father had started the shoe company, he and her mother were less ostentatious, leading a more reserved, middle-class lifestyle. She was one of the middle children in a group of 12 siblings, and her loyalty to her family was very important to her. As a respectable lady of her time, her focus was to see to it that her children's needs were met and to spend time with her siblings, parents and cousins. She took care of staffing her large townhouse with the appropriate help and made sure that it was properly decorated and kept suitable for the many family and social functions that were held there.

Caroline always thought of herself as middle-class. She was thrust into the German social elite through her husband. Plain-looking, she continued to maintain a low profile, participating in social events as Mrs. Charles Adler, but preferring to concentrate on her family. Her eldest son, Simon, was a member of the Phoenix Cotillion Club, listed in the 1899 "Elite Hebrew Directory" of financially successful German Jews.[9] Family members would visit and receive other members on the German Society Visiting Lists in their parlors for refreshments at their homes on Wednesday afternoons.[10] Each visitor would present a calling card when arriving at the home of a member on the list. The parlors were always decorated with vases of fresh flowers for that occasion, and tea, small sandwiches and petit fours were served. Caroline would receive social guests and go visiting on Wednesdays, as was the custom, but she would not participate in planning or organizing social functions. Nor did she serve on any charitable committees—those duties were left to her husband.

The German-Jewish community living in Bolton Hill was unique in that they remained rather insular as a group, forming their own organizations and clubs, and attending the synagogues they built in their own neighborhood. Unlike most other immigrant groups in America, these German-origin Jews spoke only German in private gatherings and while worshiping.[11]

The Adler children were the first generation in the family to be instructed in the new reformed Jewish program at Oheb Shalom Congregation, the oldest reformed synagogue in Baltimore. Located a couple of blocks away, it was easy for the children to walk to Hebrew school on Sunday. During the Jewish holidays, the family walked together to temple for services along with their other Jewish friends and relatives. Following Blanche's confirmation in 1892, Charles became active at Baltimore Hebrew Congregation when it moved to its more convenient location on Madison Avenue. Saidie was confirmed there in 1894.

Jews have always felt a special kinship with their fellow Jews. The German Jewish population, as their financial status grew, became increasingly concerned for the new waves of Jewish immigrants pouring into the port cities. There were organizations to help the sick and homeless, provide help for children, jobs, and a Jewish burial at the time of one's death. Those who had lived in the United States for at least a generation kept their distance socially from the Eastern European immigrants. However, they were eager to employ the newcomers and organized programs to help them with all aspects of their new lives.

Charles Adler soon became active in organizing and overseeing the Baltimore chapters of some of these Jewish organizations. He served on the board of directors of the Hebrew Orphan Asylum, and as vice president of the Hebrew Free Burial Society.[12] He gave funds to Baltimore's Hebrew Hospital and Jewish Home for Consumptives. He was impressed with his hard-earned wealth, but wanted to give back to the community which had helped him. He modeled these ideals to his children, all of whom would become philanthropic during their lives.

He was a member of the Harmony Circle, the prominent Jewish social club, which for over 50 years held fashionable social events for those important Jewish charitable causes. These affairs were held at the Concordia Opera House, the center of Jewish social activities in Baltimore for twenty years until 1891, when the building was destroyed by fire.[13] "The greatest affair of its kind was the magnificent bazaar held in 1878 for the benefit of the Hebrew Orphan Asylum, which filled the halls of the Concordia Opera House on Eutaw and German streets for 10 days."[14] Charles and Caroline were annual attendees at the "most notable of all the year's gatherings," the banquet of the Hebrew Benevolent Society. "When the many hundreds of guests had finished the sumptuous dinner, they were addressed by men active in the work of charity, the Mayor of Baltimore and Governor of Maryland, and other men prominent in public life."[15]

Charles, and subsequently his son Simon, belonged to the Phoenix Club, the elite men's only Jewish social card club, incorporated in 1886. The group met in a magnificent home down the street from the Adlers' on Eutaw Place. It housed an elaborate dining room and card room on the first floor with a ballroom on the second floor, where many memorable sorority dances were held, including the popular Christmas "Snowball." During the week, German Jewish men would meet at the Phoenix Club for lunch to have a relaxing afternoon of card playing and socializing.[16] The

Adler men also belonged to the Suburban Country Club, where similar activities were held, along with tennis and golf.

Many of these families, having emigrated from Germany in the mid-nineteenth century, came from an environment where generations of Jews became accustomed to living in segregated ghettos, having very few rights as citizens of their country and few job opportunities. They were persecuted by German Protestants who did not understand their religion and culture and would not willingly accept them as equals. Many of them abandoned their orthodox ways by not practicing, or becoming "reformed" Jews. They changed the language of their prayers and hymns to German and added a choir and organ to the music of their services. A few were relatively successful in their attempt to assimilate into the Protestant community and German society, but most were not. However, in America, once they became financially established, they could own property, invest in their own businesses and live in whatever manner they pleased.

The Adlers were listed in the Hebrew Jewish Social Register and on the Society visiting lists. Simon, the eldest son, became an escort for the Jewish "Coming Out" parties for young "Hebrew" ladies of nineteen years, introducing them to the German Jewish society, the "Right families." All of this was modeled after those traditions of the Baltimore Anglo-Saxon Protestant community, although Jews were banned from living in their communities. Around 1882, Simon joined the business and worked in the administrative department until his death in 1923. His younger brother Abraham worked the floor.

Notes

1 Frank R. Shivers Jr., *Bolton Hill* (Baltimore: n.p., 1978), 13.

2 *Ibid.*, 19.

3 *Ibid.*, 21.

4 *Ibid.*, 12.

5 *Ibid.*, 13.

6 Louis F. Cahn, *History of Oheb Shalom 1853–1953* (Baltimore: Oheb Shalom Congregation, 1953), 31.

7 Interview with Ms. Audrey May, Madison Street, Baltimore Md., 2002.

8 *Ibid.*

9 Rose Sommerfeld, *The Elite Hebrew Directory or Visiting Register for the year 1899–1900* (Baltimore: Pierre E. Crowell & Co., 1899), 109. (Jewish Museum of Maryland, 1991.61.1), 9.

10 Philip Kahn Jr., *Uncommon Threads: Threads that Wove the Fabric of Baltimore Jewish Life* (Baltimore: Pecan Publications, 1996), 68.

11 Louis F. Cahn; *History of Oheb Shalom 1853–1953* (Baltimore: Oheb Shalom Congregation, 1953), 5.

12 Isidor Blum, *The Jews of Baltimore* (Baltimore: Washington Historical Review Publishing Company, 1910), 99, 129.

13 Philip Kahn Jr., *Uncommon Threads: Threads that Wove the Fabric of Baltimore Jewish Life* (Baltimore: Pecan Publications, 1996), 43.

14 *Ibid.*

15 *Ibid.*

16 Mrs. Barbara Katz, Interview with the author about the Phoenix Club, Pikesville, Md., February, 2001.

The Formative Years, 1884–1894

S aidie was born February 18, 1879. She was the baby of the family, the youngest of three girls and three boys, her mother's favorite. The three girls couldn't have been more different, even though they shared a room together. Blanche was two years older than Saidie, tall and thin, with long, straight brown hair and deep, chocolate eyes under lustrous velvet lashes. She was nearsighted and wore thin, gold-rimmed glasses, making her look all the more studious. Her manner was quiet and subdued and she was an excellent student with a voracious appetite for reading.

Saidie, on the other hand, was short and plump with full, rosy cheeks. Her head was full of wavy hair the color of golden wheat in the heat of summer. She favored the Frank side and was a vivacious, gregarious child. The third and oldest daughter, Helen, was self-absorbed and preoccupied with girly things. Being the oldest of the girls, she was the most independent of the daughters.

When the Adlers moved into the large house on Eutaw Place, Saidie was five, Blanche, seven, and Helen, ten. The three boys were considerably older than the girls; Simon was already seventeen. The boys had attended Baltimore's public schools, but now that the Adlers could afford private schooling, the girls were sent to the Sarah Randolph Academy—across the street from their house at 1214 Eutaw Place.

The three girls occupied one bedroom. Blanche and Helen shared a high-back walnut bed. Its soft coverlet was Blanche's magic carpet, transporting her to foreign lands as she lay reading her most treasured books. Saidie slept in a small trundle bed next to the older girls. Underneath was a colorful soft rug. Framed prints on the walls told of distant lands with rolling hills, where plump, happy cows grazed in large green pastures while puffy clouds floated in a robin's egg-blue sky. A small wood table with three matching chairs sat off to the side of the fireplace, across from the older girls' bed. The table was set with a miniature china tea service, complete with tiny spoons for stirring. Two porcelain rosy-cheeked miniature children sat on the chairs facing the table, their conversations frozen in time while their hostesses attended to other daily routines.

Left: Saidie Adler, around age 4, circa 1883. Saidie A. May Papers, Archives and Manuscripts Collections, The Baltimore Museum of Art. SM5.10.1A

Each morning, Caroline entered the girls' room, kissing each one to gently wake them. Brushing past the fireplace where a few coral-colored embers glowed silently among the dark ashes, she opened the louvered wooden blinds. As she pulled them back from the lower windows, light turned the quiet, dark room into a colorful menagerie of toys, books and child's paraphernalia. Daisy, the housekeeper, then entered the room with a large pitcher filled with fresh warm water and poured part of it into a wide bowl sitting on the drysink in the back corner of the room. Daisy placed soft, clean towels next to the washbowl.

The two older girls started their morning ritual first while Saidie stayed in her bed. Hiding under the cover, she teased her mother into tickling her, while she wiggled underneath. Muffled shrieks of laughter emanated from this tiny imp while Caroline squeezed the bundle, laughing and cooing all the time. Finally, she pulled the covers back. From the tousled head, an impish grin covered Saidie's face. "Allright, enough play, it's time to get ready for school". The older girls were already washed and starting to change out of their nightclothes. Each one slipped into a camisole and simple bloomers, stockings and high-buttoned shoes. The button hook clicked as each button was attached in place. A petticoat was hooked at the waist. A billowy, white, starched blouse buttoned down the back with tiny, luminescent mother-of-pearl buttons. Finally a long full skirt was smoothed over the petticoat. When the dressing ritual was complete, the girls peered into a tall mirror, admiring their reflections. Caroline helped little Saidie get cleaned up and into her garments. The four then proceeded down to the breakfast room, chattering like a gaggle of geese as they clomped down the steps. After breakfast, the girls walked across the street to school with their neighborhood friends, also walking from nearby houses.[1]

The renowned Sarah Randolph School fostered free and independent thinking. It was considered a first-rate finishing school for young women. Miss Sarah Randolph, a tall austere woman from Virginia, the great-niece of Thomas Jefferson, oversaw the school from 1885 through 1891.[2] Born in 1839, she was educationally advanced for her time. She was already an elderly woman by the time she started this school, having previously headed another successful school, Patapsco Heights, in nearby Ellicott City. In addition to teaching, she authored two books, *The Domestic Life of Thomas Jefferson* and *The Lord Will Provide*, the life of Thomas "Stonewall" Jackson.

This unusual program accommodated 75 students, many from as far as Colorado and Texas, which gave the local students an opportunity to meet girls from all over the country. During the fifteen years the school operated, the students never received diplomas for graduation. Ms. Randolph did not feel that a girl of 18 really knew enough to qualify for such an honor.

The school was an extension of the affluent community in which the Adler girls lived. Students were exposed to culture, the arts, and higher levels of critical and abstract thinking, subjects

Left: Adler home, 1214 Eutaw Place, Baltimore, Md. Photograph by the author.

1898 Confirmation Class, Blanche Adler far left, top. Collection of Congregation Oheb Shalom, Baltimore, Md.

unavailable to young women of lesser means. The family spoke German at home, while the girls learned English, French and Latin at school. Once a week, after school, a French tutor would spend the afternoon working with the girls and then have dinner with the entire family. During dinner, she would converse with the children in French, increasing their exposure to the language.[3] Charles and Caroline did not speak French, and sat listening to this beautiful language being spoken by their children.

Friends and Family

A cousin of Caroline's, Helen Guggenheimer Cone, moved to Baltimore in 1871 from Jonesboro, Tennessee, with her husband, Herman Cone, and their eight children. They quickly joined the neighborhood synagogue where Helen attended weekly services. Wanting to participate in the German Jewish social life in Baltimore, they visited the Adlers regularly as part of that social ritual.[4]

Having come to America from Bavaria in 1846, Herman Cone's first job was as a dry-goods peddler in the South. He had settled in Jonesboro in 1855 to assume co-ownership of a grocery store with an Adler cousin.[5] The family moved to Bolton Hill, where Cone and his sons opened their own grocery store below their residence on Lanvale Street.[6] The business prospered, and by 1880, they were able to purchase a spacious, elegant brownstone at 1607 Eutaw Place, several blocks north of the Adlers'. Two of their daughters, Claribel and Etta, were the same age as the Adler boys, their youngest son, Frederick, was close to Saidie's age.

In nearby Reservoir Hill, the Bacharachs (also German Jews) lived at 2408 Linden Avenue. Their recently orphaned niece, Gertrude (age 19), and nephew, Leo (17), came from California to live with them.[7] To help them become at ease in their new home, the Bacharachs introduced Gertrude and Leo Stein to other young Jewish teens, including the Cones and Adlers. Gertrude and Leo impressed their new Baltimore friends "with their hot arguments about art and the uninhibited way they flung themselves on top of stiff Victorian couches."[8] When Etta Cone met Leo Stein, they instantly took a liking to each other and spent much time together. In the evenings, they would join Gertrude and Frederick at "The Sociables" club, in which members discussed ideas and participated in a wide range of cultural activities.[9]

Return to Germany

As did many others in the community, Charles still felt a strong connection with his homeland and the family he had left behind. Beginning in 1892 and returning as often as he could, Charles traveled to Germany to visit his relatives, sailing back across the Atlantic as a prosperous, wealthy businessman with his well-mannered daughters. First they traveled by train from Baltimore to New York City, then boarded a boat for Paris, London or other European ports. Among the ocean liners they boarded were those of the Cunard line; their ships were luxurious, with lavish food, music and dancing, and the voyages across the Atlantic were floating parties on luxury ocean liners such as the *Aquitania* (1913) and the *France*. Many times, other Baltimoreans with whom they were friendly would be traveling as well. Since both Charles and Saidie had outgoing personalities, they made new friends on the cruise, keeping in touch with them and meeting them during their trips abroad. The visits to Germany included one to Charles' sister Berta, who lived in Fritzlar with her husband, Nathan Speier. The couple had six children before Nathan died at the age of 40 (1888). The family was poor, and their eldest son, Sussman, and younger son, Moritz, dropped out of school and worked to support the family.[10]

Left: Speier family, 1876–1877. Berta Adler Speier, center left. Collection of Clare Speier Baer.

Saidie and especially Blanche were interested in their cousins, and corresponded with them on a regular basis. Blanche sent colorful, exotic postcards from her destinations which her cousins always looked forward to. But Saidie observed that Charles always put on "airs" when he came home to Fritzlar. He seemed very impressed with his status in America, and the grand lifestyle that he led. He would flaunt his new wealth, which made Berta's situation all the more demoralizing for her. She did not look forward to his visits, except for the small amounts of money he would bring her to help out.

R.M.S. MAURETANIA R.M.S. MAURETANIA

CUNARD LINE

On these trips, the girls would spend time visiting museums and shopping. Germany was a vibrant new country, where universities, technology, business and German "Kultur" were markedly superior to their American counterparts.[11] Gradually, as the sisters matured, they became interested in collecting antiquities: artifacts from Egypt, Rome and Greece. Some of the items they bought had been robbed from graves or excavation sites, others were fakes, or poorly repaired damaged originals. Back at home, they would show off their "finds" to their friends when they entertained, describing their interesting trips.

Compared to most families of their financial stature in America, the Adler sisters were very sophisticated. They were well traveled, fluent in three languages, and attended a progressive school that gave them a strong traditional academic background, encouraging them to "enable" themselves. These were invaluable tools that would allow them as adults to embrace the new ideas of the twentieth century and have a clear vision of their tastes when collecting art.

Above: Brochure for Cunard Line, *RMS Mauretania*.
Collection of the author.

Notes

1   "Miss Randolph's School," Society Page, *Baltimore Evening Sun*, March 15, 1954, 12, A, B.

2   George W. Englehardt, *Baltimore City, Maryland: The Book of it's Board of Trade* (Baltimore: Balto. Board of Trade, 1865), 22.

3   Philip Kahn Jr., *Uncommon Threads: Threads that Wove the Fabric of Baltimore Jewish Life* (Baltimore: Pecan Publications, 1996), 69.

4   Brenda Richardson, *Dr. Claribel & Miss Etta, the Cone Collection of the Baltimore Museum of Art* (Baltimore: Schneidereith & Sons, September, 1985), 47.

5   *Ibid.*

6   *Ibid.*, 48.

7   Frank R. Shivers Jr., *Bolton Hill* (Baltimore: n.p., 1978), 29.

8   *Ibid.*

9   *Ibid.*, 53.

10 Clare Speier Baer Interview with author, Pikesville, Md., July 4, 1999.

11 Frank Toker, *Fallingwater Rising; Frank Lloyd Wright, E. J. Kaufmann and America's Most Extraordinary House* (New York: Alfred A. Knopf, 2003), 74.

The Young Women, 1894–1921

After graduating from the Sarah Randolph School in the mid-1890s, the sisters stayed in Baltimore and lived with the rest of their family on Eutaw Place. Charles' bachelor brother Michael had also lived with the family since Charles and Caroline's marriage. The family's home was a busy scene of social and domestic life.

Cultural Life

This period in time was the beginning of the loss of Jewish self-identity in these affluent families with the first American-born generation. The girls continued to go "visiting" on Wednesdays and followed the rituals surrounding their synagogue on Saturdays. They became more and more active outside the home in social, cultural and art-related activities in Baltimore. Saidie joined the Charcoal Club School of Art, then Blanche, pursuing interests in painting and drawing.

At Home
Mondays in July.
1722 Druid Hill Ave.

The club, which had more than sixty active members, was located within walking distance of their home at the northwest corner of Howard and Franklin streets. The school had been organized in 1885 and emphasized drawing from life. The well-known French illustrator, André Castaigne, was brought to Baltimore from France to head the school and teach still-life and live sketching classes there.[1]

The school operated under the atelier system, with both beginning and advanced students working side by side in any medium they chose. The upper floor comprised two

Left: Lehman Brothers & Kingsbaker Men's Boys & Children's Clothing Store, c. 1890.
Above: "At Home, Mondays in July, 1722 Druid Hill Avenue," calling card c. 1900. Collection of the author.

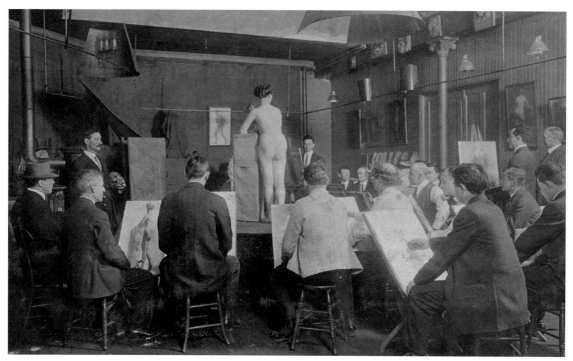

Charcoal Club School of Fine Arts, Life Drawing Class, 1911. Collection of the Maryland Historical Society, Baltimore, Md.

large studios with a fine north light for the day and good artificial lighting for evening classes. One studio was for men and the other for women, an innovative idea for that time.[2] The club featured frequent lectures on art as well as an annual exhibition of members' work.

S. Edwin Whiteman, the eminent landscape painter of the time, succeeded André Castaigne in 1894, overseeing classes. The school worked to advance interest in art in the Baltimore community and became well known on the East Coast, drawing many students of both sexes. An 1890 brochure offered free models for life drawing as well as classes beginning with drawing in charcoal from the "simplest forms of the round, and proceeding through the study of the antique, to drawing and painting from life." Classes ran Monday through Saturday mornings from 9:30 to 1:30, and again on weekday evenings from 8 to 10 p.m.[3]

The club's members were involved in the management of every art institution in Baltimore. Aside from serious art studies and some progressive exhibits, it was known for its "smokers," poker nights, masquerade balls, beer parties and "irreverent high jinks."[4] A spin-off of the Charcoal Club was The Art Club of Baltimore, formed in 1892. Women were admitted to The Art Club of Baltimore as club members in January of 1893 and could attend monthly meetings of the board of managers. They also served on committees for exhibitions and art instruction in 1893, but never played significant roles. Afternoon teas were introduced and later special "lady's nights" to preview exhibitions. Smokers were closed to women. Starting in 1894, summer sessions were added, featuring sketching excursions to the town of St. Michaels on the Eastern Shore, as well as other picturesque spots in Maryland.[5]

By 1895, there was discussion among the city leaders about opening an "academy of the fine arts" to display and house paintings for the study of art. To promote the idea, an arts commission was formed that fall by the Baltimore City Council.[6] The Charcoal Club initiated and sustained that effort, culminating in the creation of the Baltimore Museum of Art, incorporated in November of 1914. Blanche was one of its founding members.

Once a year, the Charcoal Club gave a Bal des Arts: a beautiful costumed masquerade ball staged at one of the large auditoriums of the city. This annual ball was a night of wild abandon, fervent merrymaking and drinking. Everyone dressed in elaborate costumes following the theme of the party. Fancy dress rules were strictly enforced, but despite the suggested themes, guests wore everything from buffalo robes to butterfly wings.[7] Each year the themes were different, and each year the ball presented a glittering reality as artist-members decorated the dance hall with breathtakingly elaborate settings. One such ball was entitled "A Night in a Burmese Temple," with decorations including a fourteen-foot tall golden Buddha flanked by coconut palms, thousands of giant artificial orchids and live parrots in gilded cages. This bohemian group partied late into the night.

All three of the sisters were dating at this time, participating in dances and parties at the Phoenix Club, attending performances at the Concordia Opera House and helping with German Jewish charities at venues familiar to the circle of aristocratic German Jews. Blanche, her brother Simon, and their parents were active in the Hebrew Society visiting schedule.[8]

The family was not without misfortune. Caroline had suffered for many years with complications from diabetes. During the winter of 1896, she slipped into a diabetic coma and passed away on December 29. It had been a long illness that left the family devastated. However, the sisters pulled together to continue the domestic duties involved in running the large household. Everyone in the family, with the exception of Harry, still lived in the Eutaw Place home.

Cousin Apprentice

In the fall of 1896, Caroline's cousin, Fanny Frank Lehman, sent her son, Albert Carl Lehman from Pittsburgh to Baltimore to begin an apprenticeship in the Adlers' family business. Fanny Frank had been born in Baltimore in 1856. Her family moved to Pittsburgh in 1863. Subsequently, she met Moses Lehman, an émigré from Frankfort, Bavaria, who had settled there in 1867. They were married on June 11, 1876, and later had three sons: Irvin Frank, born March 10, 1877, Albert Carl, October 14, 1878,[9] Chester H. Lehman, 1887, and a daughter, Lillian, in 1880. Coincidentally, Gertrude Stein had been born in 1874 on the north side of Pittsburgh in the town of Allegheny, on Beech Avenue, to a family of the same social stratum as the Lehmans.

In Pittsburgh, Albert attended public school and then went away to the Stone School, a preparatory boarding school in Boston, Massachusetts.[10] After graduating, he went to work in Baltimore from the fall of 1896 until the summer of 1898, when he returned to Pittsburgh. During his stay in Baltimore, he met Saidie at a family social function and started to spend a lot of time with her. He subsequently fell in love with this vivacious, gregarious, bright, witty and cultured young woman. At 4 feet 11 inches tall, she was dynamite in a small package.

The Frank and Lehman families were considered part of the Jewish dynasties of Pittsburgh and sent their sons to the finest colleges, such as the Sheffield Scientific School at Yale.[11] Moses Lehman's brother, Isaac, had 5 daughters, two of whom married into the Kingsbacher family of Pittsburgh. The Lehman brothers and Isaac's son-in-law, Louis Kingsbacher (married to Hannah Lehman), started a successful business manufacturing clothing for men, boys and children.

The Kingsbachers spent the summer of 1898 vacationing at Bedford Springs, Pa. They invited the Lehmans to spend a couple of weeks with them.[12] Albert joined them and then headed for Boston, where he was enrolled in the undergraduate program at Harvard University. By the spring of 1901, he had completed four years' worth of work in three and had his bachelor's degree in arts and sciences.[13] He then returned to Pittsburgh to help his father start a new venture with Mr. Jacob B. Blaw of Philadelphia.

Moses Lehman used the money he had made in the clothing business to finance the Blaw Collapsible-Steel Centering Company with Jacob Blaw, a construction contractor. While working in Philadelphia, Blaw acquired a background in the molding of metal statues of musical composers (a popular item around the turn of the century).[14] Just before he decided to start the company, Blaw signed a contract for construction of concrete sewers in Pittsburgh. Based on his background with making metal molds for casting art metal, he designed new "collapsible steel" molds for casting the concrete needed for the sewers. These new molds worked more efficiently and could be reused, unlike the former molds made of wood. He obtained patents for this idea, and with the financial help of the Lehmans, a new company was born.[15]

Nuptials

In August of 1901, the Lehmans announced the engagement of their son Albert to Saidie Adler of Baltimore.[16] Shortly thereafter, the Lehman family went to Baltimore to visit the Adlers to celebrate this occasion.[17] They stayed a full week and then brought Saidie and Blanche back to Pittsburgh with them. Albert's sister, Lillian, entertained them during the following week, introducing them to all of her friends and other family members, including the Pittsburgh Franks and the Kingsbachers. The night before they left for Baltimore, Lillian threw a large theater party to see the play, *San Toy* in their honor.[18]

Albert and Saidie's wedding was planned for January 9, 1902, with the reception to be held "in the parlors" at the Hotel Rennert in Baltimore. The Rennert was a famous Baltimore landmark from 1885 through the first quarter of the twentieth century, referred to as "The Palace of the South, a red-brick pile of high-Victorian exuberance topped with a pair of gilt-roofed cupolas."[19] It was well known for its Maryland seafood, prepared by an all-black staff of cooks, making such local delicacies as diamondback terrapin, canvasback duck, and oysters. The German-born owner, Robert Rennert, kept hundreds of the terrapin turtles penned up in the hotel's basement to use in their trademark dish. Pheasant, grouse and reed birds as well as hominy croquets and Maryland beaten biscuits were also on the menu. The raw bar offered thirteen oysters to the dozen, and the hotel's several restaurants featured deep-dish oyster pie and toasted soft-shell crabs.[20] The hotel's lobby, which featured overstuffed leather chairs, became a popular hangout for the city's Democratic bosses and other local celebrities, including editor and satirist H.L. Mencken, who ate there every day.[21]

So, the Lehman family of Pittsburgh came to Baltimore for their son's wedding to twenty-one-year-old Saidie Adler. The Jewish wedding ceremony began at 6 p.m. on January 9 at the Madison Avenue temple Baltimore Hebrew Congregation, officiated by Rabbi Guttmacher. Saidie's wedding gown was white organza over silk, trimmed with chiffon and white lace.[22] She wore a white veil and "diamond ornaments" and held a bouquet of bride roses. The parlors were decorated with palms, ferns and potted plants. Albert's brother Irvin was the best man. Three fraternity brothers of Al's (from Harvard) came into town for the wedding: Arthur Friend of Milwaukee, Milton Hirsch of Atlanta, and Max A. Ralshesky of Boston. They were fulfilling an oath taken at Harvard to be present at each others' weddings.[23] Afterwards, all the attendees enjoyed a lavish dinner at the Hotel Rennert to toast the bride and groom. The families and friends enjoyed themselves and danced into the night.

The newlyweds honeymooned in New England and then settled in Pittsburgh, purchasing a house in the fashionable Squirrel Hill area, where many affluent Jews resided. Squirrel Hill sat on a cliff overlooking the

Right: Postcard of Hotel Rennert, Baltimore, Md. Collection of the author.

city, taking advantage of the higher elevation to cool the houses in summer, with tree-lined streets and lush foliage landscaping the stately homes. The Lehmans' home at 1506 Beechwood Boulevard was an early Arts-and-Crafts-style "four square" with three stories. Typical of German-styled homes, the exterior detailing was painted a contrasting color. A wide porch ran the length of the front to take advantage of the summer breezes and the shade provided by the sycamore trees lining the street. The entrance foyer had long, leaded glass windows flanking the front door.

In those days, no one in Pittsburgh ever pulled their living or dining room blinds down in the evening. Pedestrians walking along the street could look into each house, where one could see lights burning brightly and the families reading newspapers, having dinner and talking, unlike today. These residents seemed to be mortally afraid of privacy.[24]

Albert became more and more involved in his new business, Blaw Collapsible-Steel Centering Company. With nine stockholders, Moses Lehman was president, Jacob Blaw consultant, and Albert was the general manager. Meanwhile, Saidie involved herself in the local arts activities and events and with philanthropic women's clubs.[25] She continued to travel with her family from Baltimore whenever she could. Periodically, Blanche would come out to stay with Saidie and Al, and visit with other members of the family. In January 1905, Blanche came to Pittsburgh to see Saidie, then pregnant with her first child. During her visit, Blanche attended a large midnight supper at Pittsburgh's Concordia Club, held to honor Bessie K. Frank.[26]

Saidie gave birth to Murray Charles Lehman on August 5, 1905. He was an adorable baby and the first of his generation in both the Adler and Lehman families. Saidie had it all: a handsome, intelligent husband, a beautiful house in which to raise her family, and a gorgeous new baby boy to dote on. She had lots of friends and the devoted Lehman family in Pittsburgh, the thriving cultural center of western Pennsylvania. She enjoyed her role as mother and her involvement in the "ladies'

Above: First home of Mr. and Mrs. Albert C. Lehman, 1506 Beechwood Blvd., Squirrel Hill, Pittsburgh, Pa. Photo by the author.
Right: Saidie Adler Lehman and Murray Charles Lehman at home c.1914, Pittsburgh, Pa.
Courtesy of Amalie Adler Ascher, Jewish Museum of Maryland, JMM 1989.167.009d.

Murray Charles Lehman and Charles Adler, Jr., c. 1907–08.

groups" playing cards and helping to plan and decorate parties with her friends.

Blaw's business boomed. They had four steel plants in the United States, as well as one each in France and Great Britain. That meant that Albert had to travel frequently. Saidie and Murray would occasionally accompany him on his overseas trips, but for the most part, Saidie was comfortable running her household, tending to Murray's needs and keeping up with her social activities.

In the meantime, Saidie played in a weekly bridge game and continued her involvement with the local social organizations. In February 1908, she and eight other women organized the entertainment for a "Leap Year Valentine's Party" for 125 people at the Concordia Club. This was the most successful affair given that season! The ballroom was creatively decorated with "Southern Similax which hung from the ceiling in feathery festoons. The walls were draped with red hearts of all sizes and the electric lights were veiled in blood-red shades." Solid silver valentines were given as party favors after the cotillion.[27]

Around this time, illness was to strike the family. When he was six years old, Murray contracted an illness which left him mentally disabled. His brain ceased to develop. With Albert's business involvement demanding more of his time, it became harder for Saidie to care for Murray on her own and she hired a nurse/companion to care for him. She started to research possible programs to get the finest help she could for her son. Saidie finally found the Bancroft School for Special Education in Haddonfield, New Jersey. It was already a well-established boarding school program for disabled children. Founded in 1883 by a Philadelphian, Margaret Bancroft, it was one of the first schools for children with developmental disabilities.[28] The program was very progressive, as prior to this time, handicapped children were rarely given decent housing or physical care within public institutional settings.[29] Murray was enrolled there sometime between 1914 and 1915.

Saidie visited Murray periodically but she found it very upsetting to see her son in this diminished capacity and not to be able to do anything for him. But she believed that Haddonfield was the best place for her son. The school even had a retreat in Maine where Murray and his classmates would go every summer to get away from the heat. He remained at this school until his death. Saidie never had any more children, focusing the rest of her life on philanthropic and social activities, and collecting art.

In 1909, Albert's younger brother, Chester, joined the business after also graduating from Harvard. When their father, Moses, died in 1914, Albert succeeded him as president of the Blaw Collapsible-Steel Centering Company. Meanwhile, older brother Irvin had become associated with another inventive genius, Luther Knox. Together they established the Knox Pressed and Welded Steel Company, where Knox pioneered the use of pressed and welded steel for the manufacture of water-cooled equipment for furnaces and other types of heating apparatus.[30] He and Saidie had a close relationship, and he acquainted her with the United Hebrew Relief Association of Pittsburgh (UHRA), which he had joined in 1910. This local philanthropic agency dealt with the poverty issues facing Jewish immigrants who had moved to Pittsburgh. It had been formed around the time of the Civil War and became especially important since World War I had started in Europe. Irvin became active in the Young Men's Hebrew Association (YMHA), serving as its vice president for years. Now that Murray was successfully placed, Saidie threw herself into helping this organization.

By 1915, Saidie was voted chairman of the executive board of the Jewish Children's Bureau, an offshoot of the UHRA devoted to addressing poor Jewish children's needs. Under her leadership, the Jewish Children's Bureau grew to coordinate the work of all of the agencies dealing with poor children's needs in the Pittsburgh area. There were eight committees: Education, Religious Training, Health, Mental

Mrs. Albert Lehman, May 31, 1918.
Jewish Criterion, p. 39, Pittsburgh, Pa.

Albert C. Lehman, October 13, 1922. *Jewish Criterion*, p. 9, Pittsburgh, Pa.

Hygiene, Vocational Guidance, Child Guidance, Standard of Living in Large Families and Recreation. In 1916, Saidie took on the added responsibility of chairman of the committee on Health. This group facilitated preventive health care for children through physical examinations administered by trained volunteers conducted at the Children's Clinic of the Tuberculosis League of Pittsburgh. During this time, Saidie also joined the sisterhood of Rodef Shalom Congregation, the oldest and largest reformed congregation in western Pennsylvania. The Lehman family had always belonged there. Its new synagogue was located in Squirrel Hill near the Lehmans' home. Saidie was actively involved on the board and with social functions. In January of 1917, she and nine other board members were selected to be sent to Baltimore to take part in the annual national convention of the UHRA.[31]

At this time, World War I was creating a major impact on the poor in terms of general welfare, health and housing. By June 4, 1917, the United States declared war on Germany. With America's official entrance to the war, Saidie felt compelled to become more involved in philanthropy and ran for the highest office in Rodef Shalom's Sisterhood. Over that summer, Saidie was made the unofficial president of this sophisticated, admired and well-educated group of women active in the community. At an open board meeting in October, Saidie was officially made president. At the age of 40, it was quite an honor to be chosen president of this organization.[32] She worked tirelessly for two years while the Sisterhood collected monies for the war effort as well as volunteering for the Red Cross. Sisterhood members worked on food conservation education and tended War Gardens to feed the local poor. They made clothes for their less fortunate neighbors and sent gift boxes to soldiers overseas for the holidays. Another important member of the sisterhood was Mrs. Edgar Kaufman, whose husband would eventually build one of the most famous homes in America, Frank Lloyd Wright's "Falling Water."

The Blaw Collapsible-Steel Centering Company and the Knox Pressed and Welded Steel

Company merged on July 6, 1917, bringing the three
Lehman brothers into one business. Albert took over
as president of the new corporation and continued in
this capacity until his death in 1935. By this time, the
Blaw-Knox Company became the largest producer of
water-cooled furnace equipment in the world, and one
of the largest fabricators of specialty steel items for heavy
industry. These included oil-refinery equipment, rolling-
mill machinery, steel forms for concrete and towers for
high-transmission lines. At its peak, Blaw-Knox was the
largest industrial organization of its kind in the United
States and it held several hundred company-owned patents
for new inventions and products.[33]

Pittsburgh, like Baltimore, was a town of remarkable
social backwardness, very cliquish and segregated. It was frowned upon for a man to appear
in public with a married woman. In America, bigotry, particularly against Jews, was unusually
vicious between the First and Second World Wars. Quotas were used by universities to restrict

Top: Lillian Lehman Wedding, October, 1917. Archives of the Senator John Heinz History Center, Pittsburgh, Pa.
Above: Irvin Frank Lehman, May 31, 1918. *Jewish Criterion*, p.48, Pittsburgh, Pa.

the admission of Jewish students. In 1922, Harvard president A. Lawrence Lowell defended the practice in the *New York Times*.[34] Similarly, newly arrived Jewish refugees commonly said that prejudice in the United States exceeded anything they had experienced in pre-Nazi Germany.[35] Jews were excluded from many social events, hotels and local clubs.[36] In spite of this, they worked hard at retaining their dignity, despite the smoldering resentment inside of them. Some Jews responded by becoming more "Jewish" in religious practice, while others hid their religious background or converted to Christianity.[37]

In Pittsburgh, as in other urban centers, prosperous Jews formed their own social clubs and organizations. Pittsburgh's Concordia Club, similar to the Concordia Opera House in Baltimore, was one of the most opulent. This exclusively Jewish club had a lavish dining room and ballroom, and a bowling alley in the basement. Many Jewish family functions and events were held in this building with the plain brick facade in the heart of the city. Both Albert and Irvin Lehman would serve as presidents of the Concordia and Westmoreland clubs during their lifetimes.

Around this time, Saidie became interested in Pittsburgh's Carnegie Institute of Art. Other patrons of the museum were conservative, quiet Protestants who collected mostly nineteenth- and early-twentieth-century landscapes and portraits.[38] In 1917, Saidie's first gifts to that museum were two Chinese boxes. The first was a small, round cloisonné and gilt bronze container from the Ch'ien Lung Period (1736–1795) and the second was another small painted enamel box.

That same year, Albert's sister, Lillian Lehman, got engaged, with her wedding set for October. Saidie was asked to be her sister-in-law's matron of honor. Family and friends came in from out of town for this large, prominent wedding. Several days of festivities were planned. A bridal party dinner was held the previous Saturday night at the Farmer's Building restaurant downtown. On Monday, Saidie had a bridge party for the women and in the evening hosted a dinner at the Nixon Restaurant, followed by a box seat party at the Nixon Theatre. Tuesday evening, Irvin and Albert held a dinner-dance at the Westmoreland Country Club. Wednesday afternoon before the wedding, Miss Gertrude Frank gave a luncheon for the bride.[39]

The Blaw-Knox company was growing internationally and Albert needed a more convenient "home base." He set up a New York office for the company and also rented an apartment nearby. When Albert went abroad for business, if it was convenient Saidie would accompany him. She would spend her time visiting museums and collecting things for the apartment, just as she had done on her childhood trips with her father. She and Blanche had displayed their "finds" in their home on Eutaw Place, and now she was purchasing antiquities and other oddities to furnish the grand Pittsburgh house and the new apartment. Records show her purchasing early Chinese pottery for one of their homes from New York's Roland C. Moore Gallery. While Albert worked, Saidie availed herself of all of the cultural activities in the cities they visited.

Postcard of Carnegie Library, Museum and Music Hall, c. 1930. Collection of the author.

Each year the Concordia Club held an extravagant and lavish New Year's Eve dance and dinner. If they were in town, the Lehman families and their friends would usher in the New Year together. The invitations to the "brilliant affair of 1918" were extended to members of the Westmoreland Club as well. Four hundred people attended the dinner-dance, decorated with palms, various types of ferns and flowers. An elaborate supper was served at 11 p.m. At midnight, "Happy New Year" flashed from electric lights hung on one of the walls.[41]

In May, 1918, Irvin Lehman became vice president of the UHRA, now performing constructive social services, rehabilitating families, and working to eradicate poverty.[42] Saidie presided over the Jewish Children's Bureau, which teamed up with the University of Pittsburgh to conduct a "mental hygiene" clinic. Each week, she met with a group of interested Jewish women to review case studies of impoverished families in the community and determine how best to help them.[43]

Meanwhile, at Albert's alma mater, Harvard, a group of young talented art historians (including Alfred Barr) were busy forming a small art gallery on campus called the "Coop." Their inaugural exhibit—their first attempt at forming and hanging an art exhibition—opened February 19, 1919, consisting of American Modern works borrowed from the Carnegie Institute of Art in Pittsburgh.[44]

In May, 1920, Saidie purchased a painting through the Carnegie Museum entitled *Tell us a Story,* by Robert James Enraght–Moony, a well-known Irish illustrator who had studied in Paris in the 1890s with Jean-Paul Laurens. Later, traveling through Italy, he came under the influence of the Italian Symbolist painter Giovanni Segantini. Enraght-Moony was best known for his illustrations of Kenneth Grahame's 1986 book of reminiscences, *The Golden Age*. Saidie purchased the painting for fifty-nine English pounds.[45]

The next month, the museum asked Saidie if it could include the painting in an International Painting Exhibition held at the Art Institute of Chicago. The Carnegie Museum shipped it with other privately held works and paintings for sale. The show ran from July 15 through September 15.[46] Afterwards, Saidie suggested to Carnegie's director, John W. Beatty, that they might benefit from her donation of the painting. Beatty was unsure, since its theme centered around children and might not be well accepted by the public. He discussed the matter with his wife, Helen, who was director of education and head of the Carnegie's Children's Museum. She wrote to Saidie[47] indicating that she would very much like to have the painting for the Children's Museum and would recommend its acceptance to their board. Thus, Saidie donated her first painting.

On a trip to London in 1921, Saidie purchased a sixteenth-century Flemish glass panel.[48] She had an excellent eye, haunting small shops in Rome and Paris and finding exciting paintings and objects by anonymous or unknown artists. Other wealthy Jewish New Yorkers (grand members of "Our Crowd" such as the Strausses and Lehmans) were filling their dim apartments with religious antiquities such as Renaissance Madonnas and altarpieces from Europe. Ironically, they lived with paintings of Christian subject matter painted by El Greco, Titian and Botticelli, even though they were Jewish.[49] Such traditional works seemed to be all the rage in the early 1920s.

While married to Albert Lehman, Saidie donated two more paintings to the Carnegie Museum, *Nocturne* by Arthur Davies and *The Sleigh Ride* by Julius Lankes.

Albert was also philanthropic in the Pittsburgh Jewish community. His gifts on behalf of social welfare and education were frequent. He was involved with the synagogue and well liked in the community. But after almost twenty years he and Saidie were drifting apart. They divorced in 1921.

Albert sold the house on Beechwood Boulevard and moved into the Hotel Schenley. Saidie's passion for collecting had had a great influence on him. He amassed an excellent collection of paintings containing both Old Masters and Moderna from the 1920s, as well as antique Italian furniture, art glass and silver. He became a trustee of the Pittsburgh-based Carnegie Foundation and became internationally known in art circles. In 1929, he established the Albert C. Lehman Prize.[50] This award of $2,000 was given for the best purchasable painting in the "International", an annual art exhibition held by the Department of Fine Arts at the Carnegie Institute. Albert further agreed to purchase the winning painting if it were for sale, for its list price up to a cost of $10,000. These awards continued until 1933. Albert eventually remarried in 1930 to another cousin on the Frank side, Adele Guckenheimer. They were married until 1935, when he suddenly died at the age of 58.

Right, top: Container with cover, 17.8.5 a-b, donated 1919–1920. Collection of the Carnegie Museum of Art .
Right, lower: Chinese box with cover, 17.8.6 a-b, donated 1919–1920. Collection of the Carnegie Museum of Art.

Notes

1   "Baltimore in Pictures, the Charcoal Club," *Baltimore News*, Vol. CXII, no. 119 (Baltimore, March 20, 1928), 4.

2   Henry H. Weigand, "The Charcoal Club of Baltimore," *Art & Archaeology* Vol. XIX, nos. 5–6 (May–June 1925), 227.

3   "The Charcoal Club School of Art, 1890–1891," Vertical File, Enoch Pratt Free Library, Baltimore, MD.

4   *Ibid.*

5   Liza Kirwin, "Back to Bohemia with the Charcoal Club of Baltimore," *Archives of American Art Journal*, 25, #1&2 (Washington, D.C., Smithsonian Institution, 1985), 41–46.

6   "The Charcoal Club," *The Women's Edition, Baltimore News*, February 29, 1896.

7   *Ibid.*

8   Rose Sommerfeld, *The Elite Hebrew Directory or Visiting Register for the Year 1899* (Baltimore: Pierre E. Crowell & Co., 1899), 109 (Jewish Museum of Maryland, 1991.61.1), 9

9   "The Albert C. Lehman Prize & Purchase Fund", *The Carnegie Magazine* II, no. 8 (January, 1929): 227–228.

10 Frank Toker, *Fallingwater Rising; Frank Lloyd Wright, E. J. Kaufmann and America's Most Extraordinary House* (New York: Alfred A. Knopf, 2003), 42.

11 *Ibid.*

12 "Items Personal," *Jewish Criterion*, July 15, 1898. http://js.library.cmu.edu.

13 A. H. Fromenson, "A Just Cause Cannot Fail—An Interview with Albert C. Lehman," *Jewish Criterion*, October 13, 1922, 9.

14 W. Cordes Snyder Jr., *Blaw-Knox: Growth Through Invention and Enterprise* (New York: Newcomen Society of North America, 1957), 11.

15 *Ibid.*

16 "Local Happenings," *Jewish Criterion*, August 30, 1901, 8. http://js.library.cmu.edu.

17 *Ibid.*, October 11, 1901, 8.

18 *Ibid.*, October 25, 1901, 8.

19 Brennen Jensen, "Groaning Boards," *Baltimore City Paper*, September 5, 2001, 13.

20 Joe Sugarman and Laura Wexler, "Baltimore Dines Out," *Style Magazine*, November 2004, 154–163.

21 Brennen Jensen, "Groaning Boards," *Baltimore City Paper*, September 5, 2001, 13.

22 "Weddings," *Baltimore Sun*, January 10, 1902, 5.

23 "Weddings," *Baltimore American*, Friday, January 10, 1902, 4.

24 Frank Toker, *Fallingwater Rising; Frank Lloyd Wright, E. J. Kaufmann and America's Most Extraordinary House* (New York: Alfred A. Knopf, 2003), 58.

25 "Columbian Council," *Jewish Criterion*, May 6, 1904, 9. http://js.library.cmu.edu.

26 "Dance at the Club," *Jewish Criterion*, January 27, 1905, 9. http://js.library.cmu.edu.

27 "Local News; Leap Year and Valentines," *Jewish Criterion*, February 14, 1908, 10. http://js.library.cmu.edu.

28 Bancroft NeuroHealth, www.bnh.org/Corporate/aboutus.html.

29 W. L. (Polly) Cuthbertson, *Unforgettable Margaret Bancroft, A Personal Recollection* (Pottstown, PA: privately published). www.bnh.org/about/mb_unforgettable.html.

30 W. Cordes Snyder Jr., *Blaw-Knox: Growth Through Invention and Enterprise* (New York: Newcomen Society of North America, 1957), 13.

31 "Rodef Shalom Sisterhood Board Minutes," January 2, 1917, Archives of Rodef Shalom Congregation, Pittsburgh, PA.

32 "Rodef Shalom Sisterhood Board Minutes," December 4, 1917, Archives of Rodef Shalom Congregation, Pittsburgh, PA.

33 "Lehman, Irvin Frank," *The National Cyclopedia of American Biography*, vol. 30 (New York: James T. White & Co., 1943), 575.

34 Frank Toker, *Fallingwater Rising; Frank Lloyd Wright, E. J. Kaufmann and America's Most Extraordinary House* (New York: Alfred A. Knopf, 2003), 56.

35 *Ibid.*, 57.

36 *Ibid.*, 58.

37 *Ibid.*, 57.

38 Richard Armstrong, Interview by the author at the Carnegie Museum of Pittsburgh, April 2005.

39 "Local News: Lehman-Strassburger," *Jewish Criterion*, October 11, 1907, 10. http://js.library.cmu.edu.

40 Roland C. Moore to Mrs. A.C. Lehman, January and November 4, 1919. Saidie A. May Papers, Archives and Manuscript Collection, Baltimore Museum of Art.

41 "Social Page," *Jewish Criterion*, 50:19, January 3, 1919, 12. http://js.library.cmu.edu.

42 Charles I. Cooper, "The Story of the Jews of Pittsburgh," *Jewish Criterion*, 49:41, May 31, 1918, 19–42. http://js.library.cmu.edu.

43 *Ibid.*, 39.

44 Russell Lynes, *Good Old Modern, an Intimate Portrait of the Museum of Modern Art* (Kingsport, TN: Kingsport Press, 1973), 24.

45 Carnegie Museum to Albert C. Lehman, Correspondence #3500, May 7, 1920, Carnegie Institute, Museum of Art Records, 1896–1940, Archives of American Art, Smithsonian Institution, Washington, DC.

46 Mrs. Albert C. Lehman to The Art Institute of Chicago, June 21, 1920, Carnegie Institute, Museum of Art Records, 1896–1940, Archives of American Art, SI.

47 Carnegie Museum to Mrs. Albert C. Lehman, Correspondence #777, December 14, 1920, Carnegie Institute, Museum of Art Records, 1896–1940, Archives of American Art, SI.

48 St. Anne's to Mrs. Albert C. Lehman, September 3, 1921, Saidie A. May Papers, BMA.

49 Frank Toker, *Fallingwater Rising; Frank Lloyd Wright, E. J. Kaufmann and America's Most Extraordinary House* (New York: Alfred A. Knopf, 2003), 54.

50 Carnegie Museum to Albert C. Lehman, Correspondence #5887, December 26, 1928, Carnegie Institute, Museum of Art Records, 1896–1940, Archives of American Art, SI.

The Seasoned Traveler, 1922–1929

Blanche dated as a young woman and was engaged once, but a few months after her engagement, her fiancé was killed in a car accident. She never married. Her older sister, Helen, eventually married and moved out of the house, leaving Blanche to manage the domestic affairs of the household and care for her father, her bachelor brother Simon and "Uncle Mike," until the two elders' death. After the turn of the century, Blanche was traveling to Europe almost every year with her father until his death. He would only travel on the large, exclusive ocean liners, always with first-class accommodations. In addition to the *France* and the *Aquitania,* they sailed on the *Kaiser Wilhelm II*, the *Kronprinzessin*, *La Provence*, *Kaiserin Augusta Victoria*, and the *George Washington*. Their last trip together was on the SS *Ryndam*, when on September 1, 1914, they came back to the U.S. from the Netherlands.

Blanche collected all kinds of artworks and antiquities on these trips and displayed her treasures at home. She also loved textiles, and bought antique remnants of everything from velvets to laces. In addition, she became interested in drawings and the printing process during visits to Germany, where she frequented the art galleries and museums. During one such visit, she purchased a few paintings and the more affordable prints done by the Old Masters.

On October 6, 1922, Saidie, now 43, married a widower, Herbert Louis May (also from Pittsburgh).[1] Herbert had known Albert Lehman through membership in the Concordia Social Club and the Rodef Shalom Congregation. Pittsburgh, like Baltimore, had a relatively close-knit German Jewish population. Most of this community, especially the more affluent residents, lived in Squirrel Hill, where they all belonged to the same synagogue, social clubs and philanthropic organizations.

The Mays were well-known, affluent members of the community, and though we don't know the exact circumstances of their meeting, it would not be beyond reason

Left: Saidie A. May, 1922. Collection of Regina Bogat Jensen, Glen Ridge, New Jersey.

Above: Display of art objects on a table in rooms at Park Lane, c. 1923–1933, Saidie A. May Papers, Archives and Manuscripts Collections, The Baltimore Museum of Art. SM5.2.2. Right: Rooms at Park Lane with art objects surrounding fireplace, from the right, c. 1923–1933, Saidie A. May Papers, Archives and Manuscripts Collections, The Baltimore Museum of Art. SM5.6.2A.

to speculate that the Lehmans and Mays were socially friendly and may have gone out together as couples. Herbert's wife, Lillian, died in 1921, the same year that Saidie and Al divorced. An interesting article was published in the *Jewish Criterion*, a local paper, the week after their marriage. The *Criterion* lauded Albert C. Lehman for his philanthropy within the Pittsburgh community, but no mention was made about the marriage of Saidie and Herbert May.[2]

Saidie's marriage to Herbert was the second marriage for both of them. Afterwards, Herbert retired from the family drug business at age 45, and they rented an apartment in New York City.

Saidie spent her time furnishing the apartment with heavy Gothic oak furnishings, and antique oriental art and rugs, similar to the furnishings in the Cone sisters' apartment in Baltimore. She even went as far as to purchase an entire period "wormy oak" paneled room from a New York auction of objects from the Hearst estate.

Herbert Louis May had been born in Philadelphia to Barney May and Pauline Fleishman in 1877. The Mays were a moderately well-to-do family. Herbert's father had made money by following the gold rush to British Columbia, Canada, and was the first postmaster of the town of Caribou Diggings (later called Mayville).[3] Later he moved to Philadelphia, where he met Pauline.

Herbert grew up as a healthy, well-adjusted boy in the rough atmosphere of Philadelphia at

the turn of the century—more interested in baseball than in his studies. But the family was to experience misfortune. When he was 16, his father lost his savings in the stock market on "Black Friday"—the Panic of 1893. Herbert then won a scholarship to Cornell University, majoring in Law, and completed his degree at New York Law School at the age of 20.[4]

In 1901, after marrying his first wife, Herbert was stricken with typhoid pneumonia, which ruined his health. As a means of recovery, he set out on a grand tour of Europe and two years of reading, observing and meditation. During this time, Herbert learned the art of living, and acquired a speaking knowledge of German, French, Italian and Spanish. He spent much of his time visiting most of the world's great art galleries, becoming particularly interested in the Realistic painting of the late nineteenth century.[5] He then started to paint and continued to pursue landscape painting for the rest of his life.

Returning from Europe in 1904, Herbert entered his family's business in the sale of pharmaceuticals with his father and two brothers. By 1928, the May building at 111 Fifth Avenue in Pittsburgh was the executive center for a number of drugstores owned by the family in the Midwest. Herbert oversaw the legal and public relations aspects of this business. He lived in Pittsburgh with his wife, Lillian C. Brilles, at 5725 Aylesboro Ave, until her death in 1921. They had two daughters, Katherine and Dorothy. He loved traveling, and went abroad for business any chance that he could. But the family business affairs did not satisfy him totally, so he became involved in local civic activities.

Saidie and Herbert made an interesting-looking couple, he was six feet tall and she was under five feet. After their move to New York, Herbert worked with the Opium Research Committee of the American Foreign Policy Association. Specifically, he helped to formulate basic principles for the international control of narcotic drugs. He was asked to study the problem of opium-smoking in the Far East.[6] To research the subject, Herbert read extensively on the subject, traveling to Washington, London, Paris and Geneva. During this time, Saidie traveled back and forth to Europe to spend time with him and to visit museums and collect antiquities for their New York apartment.[7]

In August, 1924, Saidie invited Blanche and Herbert's two daughters to accompany them on a three-week tour of Europe. Blanche had not been out of the country since her father had died nine years previously. The five had a good time traveling from one famous city to the other. While in Berlin, the group spent time visiting the Berlin Museum of Art, where Blanche purchased a portfolio of 54 impressions from the original woodblocks carved by the German Masters. This portfolio, printed in 1922, came from the collection amassed in the second half of the eighteenth century by Hans Albrecht, Freiherr von Derschau. In 1844, this collection was sold to the King of Prussia, who allowed the museum to clean and re-use them. Most of the blocks were in good condition, having been little used.[8] Blanche was thrilled with her purchase, being fond of the Old Masters, especially Albrecht Dürer.

Postcard of Geneva, Switzerland, sent by Blanche Adler to Moritz Speier, September 12, 1926. Collection of Evelyn Held, Baltimore, Md.

Blanche begins a Relationship with the BMA

Suddenly Herbert had to cut his trip short, and left for home eleven days early on the *Leviathan*. The others continued on their trip and came back to New York on the *France* August 23.[9] After arriving back in Baltimore, Blanche moved in with her sister Helen, and her husband, Bob. Blanche started volunteering her time with the Baltimore Museum of Art. The museum had been founded in 1914, and was still relatively young. Blanche gave her recently acquired portfolio of German woodblock prints to them as a gift, the first of many. She continued to become more and more involved as this institution quickly grew.

In 1925, Herbert was chosen by the Foreign Policy Association of the United States delegation to the Geneva Convention to study the problem of limiting the production of opium to medical and scientific needs, and reducing the illicit smoking of opium. This survey took him nearly a year to complete, but it would be a major contribution to the development of an international control policy. He started the survey in England, proceeding to Geneva, Switzerland. There he rented an apartment, which he used as his base of operations in Europe.

Postcard of Cairo, Egypt, sent by Blanche Adler to Moritz and Bertel Speier, 1926. Collection of Evelyn Held, Baltimore, Md.

In September, Saidie and Blanche came to Europe to spend time with Herbert. He was personally researching the effects and problems associated with opium smoking and eating. As such, he was always busy with meetings and work, and he was not available to spend much time with Saidie. So as soon as they arrived, the sisters toured Norway and then came back to Germany to visit with their family and take in the local museums. By the end of November, both Saidie and Blanche returned by boat to New York, where Saidie spent the winter, while Blanche headed down to Baltimore, eager to get back to work at the new Baltimore Museum of Art.

Saidie Becomes a Collector and Donor

At the beginning of June, 1926, Saidie traveled back to Europe alone. While she was away, she lent the Carnegie Museum three important etchings for them to exhibit in her absence.[10] She spent time in London visiting museums and haunting small antique shops, where she picked up many treasures, including an old oriental rug, a bronze sculpture and paintings by Derain and Renoir.[11]

At the beginning of September, Blanche again sailed to Europe to join Saidie. This time, the two women would accompany Herbert on his journey to the Middle East and Central Asia. Saidie met Blanche at the boat terminal in Northampton, and the two took the train to Geneva, arriving on September 12, 1926, to find the city overrun by politicians attending that year's Geneva Convention meeting. Blanche did not want to stay with Saidie and Herbert, but there were no rooms available in town. Once Herbert finished at the meeting, the three flew to Cairo, Egypt. For two days, the sisters visited archaeological digs, saw the pyramids and rode camels, while Herbert pursued his work. Saidie had a wonderful time haunting the small, dusty antiquities shops, purchasing small statuettes (most probably looted from Egyptian grave sites). They included the *Head of a Pharaoh*, a *Rearing Horse*, a *Walking Courtesan*, *Head of a Man*, a *Fauness* and a *Figure of a Man*. (All were eventually given to the Baltimore Museum of Art.)

The three then hopped on a train bound for Jaipur, India, where the sisters spent two more weeks sightseeing and drinking in the culture. Finally, Blanche had to leave to return home and she bid her sister goodbye, heading home alone.

Top: 6th century Byzantine Cast Gold "Fede" Ring, symbolizing faith, love, marriage, 57.1715. Collection of the Walters Art Museum, Baltimore, Md.
Lower: 4th cent. red carnelian intaglio ring, found in 1888 in Catania, formerly belonging to the great archeologist, Sir Arthur Evans. 42.1343. Collection of the Walters Art Museum, Baltimore, Md.

She had collected hundreds of postcards from this exotic trip which she gave to the Baltimore Museum of Art upon her arrival. Saidie and Herbert spent three more months traveling through the Middle East and Far East, visiting Java, Sumatra, Singapore, Malaya, the Philippines, China and Japan. (They were prevented by floods from visiting Siam.)

Returning to the United States in 1927, Herbert wrote a report published by the American Foreign Policy Association which had an important impact on the League of Nations' decision on dealing with foreign narcotics problems.[12]

A Momentous Decision

Saidie came with him and accompanied Blanche in April to the American West, on a trip to visit American Indian tribes. Both Saidie and Herbert knew that each was immersed in their own interests, living what were essentially independent lives, so they decided to divorce.

Saidie kept their furnished apartment in New York, but moved to Paris. Herbert married a year later and, until the beginning of World War II, resided at 12 Grand Mezel, in Geneva, Switzerland. His home was a kind of informal international center, especially for visiting American diplomats, journalists and writers.[13] From 1930, he was on the board of directors of the American Foreign Policy Association and served as councilor to the Nansen International Office for Refugees from 1933–1935. He was a poet, painter and avid art collector until his death in February 1966.

Notes

1   "May, Herbert Louis," *Who is Who in America, 1940–1941* (Chicago: A.N. Marquis Co., 1940), 623.

2   A. H. Fromenson, "A Just Call Cannot Fail—An Interview with Albert C. Lehman," *The Jewish Criterion*, October 13, 1922), http://js.library.cmu.edu.

3   "Herbert May, 88, Drug Expert, Dies," *New York Times*, Wednesday, February 2, 1966, 35.

4   "Herbert L. May," *Bulletin on Narcotics*, January 1, 1957, Issue 2-001, United Nations Office for Drug Control and Crime Prevention, 2.

5   *Ibid.*

6   Harry J. Anslinger, "Herbert L. May," *Bulletin on Narcotics*, January 1, 1963 Issue 2-001, 3.

7   Carnegie Museum to Mrs. Albert C. Lehman, Correspondence #3500, Carnegie Institute, Museum of Art Records, 1896–1940, Archives of American Art, SI.

8   Blanche Adler, *Prints in the Museum's Collection.* (Baltimore, Md: Baltimore Museum of Art, 1926).

9   Correspondence, "Saidie and Company" to Mrs. Herbert L. May, August 11, 1924. Saidie A. May Papers, BMA.

10 Carnegie Museum to Mrs. Herbert May, June, 1926, Correspondence #2500, Carnegie Institute, Museum of Art Records, 1896–1940, Archives of American Art, SI.

11 Purchase receipts to Mrs. Herbert L. May, July 19, 1926, October 23, 1926 & April 9, 1927, Saidie A. May Papers, BMA.

12 Harry J. Anslinger, "Herbert L. May," *Bulletin on Narcotics*, January 1, 1963 Issue 2-001, 3.

13 *Ibid.*, 6.

The Most Modest, Retiring Little Spinster, 1923–1933

After Charles Adler died on May 19, 1915, Simon and Blanche continued to live in the Adler family home, remaining active with the social activities that they had become accustomed to. But when Simon unexpectedly died in 1923, Blanche sold the house, as it was too large for one person to manage.

In September, 1924, after returning from the European trip with Saidie and Herbert's children, Blanche moved into the enormous apartment that her older sister, Helen, and her husband, Robert Lauchheimer, rented at the Riviera Apartments. Designed by the Baltimore architect John Freund, Jr., and opened in 1914, the Riviera was hailed for its beauty and luxury, combining Beaux Arts and Renaissance Revival architectural details. The building was located in Reservoir Hill, on fashionable Lake Drive, one mile north of where the girls had grown up in Bolton Hill. There were four lush apartments per floor, each with a large kitchen and four bathrooms. The Adlers' apartment was located on the top floor, with a view of Baltimore city on one side and the picturesque reservoir in Druid Hill Park on the other. This community would remain predominantly Jewish until the 1940s.[1]

Blanche had a separate suite decorated with French furnishings. It contained a bedroom, private bath and large sitting room where she displayed her favorite works of art. Meals were served in the elegant dining room with her sister and brother-in-law. The apartment had a formal circular foyer with cove ceilings and elaborate moldings, a bright and cheery sunroom, a parlor and separate suites for Helen and Bob. Each of the three had plenty of individual space, enabling them to live together harmoniously.[2]

This luxurious apartment needed to be maintained, and it had a staff of three daily workers: George the butler, Kate the cook, and George's younger sister, Katie (called "Little Kate"), who was the housekeeper. They lived in the same Madison Street neighborhood occupied by the earlier staff at the Adlers' Eutaw Place house. Close to them was Whitelock

Blanche Adler, age 30.

Street, the retail section for the Reservoir Hill neighborhood. Here one could find delicatessens, butcher shops and general stores that supplied basic necessities.[3] In addition to the house staff, Helen and Blanche had chauffeurs who drove their large, dark cars, a Pierce-Arrow and a Packard.

Fashion and Antiquities

Saidie and Blanche had a love for and an affinity for art. Helen also loved beautiful things and all three lived an affluent lifestyle. Of the three sisters, Blanche was conservative and studious, dressing smartly, but plain. Helen was flamboyant, wearing lots of heavy makeup and tight, long skirts. Everything she wore had to be the same color; if she wore red, her dress, coat, hat, gloves, shoes and handbag all had to be the same shade of red. Her skirts were so tight, except for a small slit at the bottom, she walked like an oriental Geisha girl, one short step at a time. She was small in stature, but made an impression wherever she went. Her husband, Bob, was a dandy who worked as a salesman for one of the local men's clothing haberdashers, traveling often. He was never seen without his top hat and white spats, wearing expensive jewelry. Whenever he and Helen traveled together, they stayed at only the poshest hotels, and would turn heads whenever they "stepped out."[4]

Museum Donations

All throughout the decade of the 1920s, both Blanche and Saidie actively collected art and amassed a large number of European antiquities. Blanche had continued her deep involvement with the Baltimore Museum of Art and became an indispensable contributor. The museum was founded and incorporated in 1914 with a thirteen-member executive committee headed by Mr. Blanchard Randall, a well-respected businessman in Baltimore. Another member of the committee was Dr. Alfred Robert Louis Dohme, a successful pharmacist and owner of the Sharp & Dohme Pharmaceutical Company, and a devotee of the arts. Mary Garrett-Jacobs donated her home, which was situated on the west side of Mount Vernon Square, overlooking the city.

The Friends of Art and the Handicraft Club established their headquarters in the building, while the Watercolor Club and the School Art League became affiliated members.[5] (The Watercolor Club and the Handicraft Club were spin-offs of the Charcoal Club.) Upon Mary Garrett's death, the home would be willed to Miss M. Carey Thomas, former president of Bryn Mawr College. She turned the property over to the BMA, rent free, as a home for local art societies, exhibitions and meetings.[6]

The Garrett-Jacobs Mansion

When it was built in the 1850s, it was one of the grandest homes of its day, with an imposing portico and two flights of steps to the front door, ten to twelve feet above the sidewalk. In the center of the building was a thirty-by-eighteen-foot entrance hall, embellished with tall teak wood carvings from India and a fine marble floor. It was flanked by a reception room on the left and

Repeat border with the Adoration of the Christ Child, colored and metal thread, Florence(?), 1450–1500, 11 x 18-1/2 in. Walters Art Museum, inv. 83.649, gift of Mrs. Saidie A. May, 1945.

two large mahogany-paneled drawing rooms with sliding doors on the right. Behind the reception room was a spacious dining room with a twenty foot square glass-domed palm garden off of it. The palm garden led to a vestibule with a twenty-three-by-sixty-foot picture gallery at the back of the house. The second floor had two bright, large rooms with bookcases and storage for prints (Miss Mary Garrett had collected prints.) On the third floor, libraries opened into each other and ran the full length of the house.[7]

By the end of 1924, the house had been adapted for its new purpose, and shows were held at the newly formed Baltimore Museum of Art. Opening on January 9, 1925, was an exhibition of Modern French art composed of sculpture, works on paper, prints, etchings, charcoal drawings, watercolors and gouache paintings. All of these items were lent to the exhibit by local art collectors, most of whom (including Blanche) were members of the museum's Friends of Art. This exhibition attempted to show the transformation of art from Romanticism and Materialism in the nineteenth century to the decorative motifs of the twentieth century.[8] The museum proved to be popular and, by June of 1925, it was mentioned in a national art magazine. Baltimore was described as being a "print" city, with many avid collectors of prints.[9]

The Baltimore Museum of Art continued to use the building for exhibitions, hiring Miss Florence Nightingale Levy from the staff of New York's Metropolitan Museum of Art to be its first director.

Blanche continued to volunteer, even writing a brochure for the museum in 1926. Called, "Prints in the Museum's Collection," it sold for 5 cents in the museum's lobby. In the brochure, Blanche talked about the museum's various collections, including her reprint collection of early German woodcuts, and how they were made. She also pointed out that some items were available on loan: photos of early prints in the British Museum and twenty-seven photo-mezzotints after noted painters. Such photos could be loaned to schools and neighborhood centers to promote the study of art history and to familiarize the public with the masterpieces of the great painters. Educating the public was certainly one of the important missions of the new museum. Also included in the collection were mezzotints by S. Arlent Edwards, as well as the Conrad Collection of etchings (given by Mrs. Conrad Lehr), and some modern original prints by Benson, Hayley Lever (which Blanche had recently given) and Frederick Reynolds.

Blanche especially loved Albrecht Dürer's work, and collected many fine

Virgin and Child, c. 1330–1350, France, limestone, 69-1/2 in. H, The Baltimore Museum of Art: Gift of Saidie A. May, BMA 1942.46.

etchings produced by his studio in Germany. She was instrumental in forming a new exhibition of his better works at the BMA and persuaded General Lawrason Riggs to add to his Durer collection to the show in April of 1928.

Whenever Blanche was in town, she would be found at the museum, working on special projects and helping out wherever needed while encouraging others in the community to donate and participate.[10] Late in April of 1928, Blanche was named a member of the museum's board of trustees.[11] Several months later she went to Germany and stayed at the Hotel Kaiserhof in Berlin.[12] During her visit she purchased a Renoir oil, *Cabanes à Cagnes,* for $700.

Throughout 1928 and 1929, Blanche was donating large numbers of prints to the museum. In December, 1928, she donated a collection of eighty-eight contemporary English and American woodcut engravings by artists Rockwell Kent, David Jones, Claire Leighton and others.[13]

The museum's collections expanded and would soon outgrow the Garrett mansion. The executive committee began an extensive and innovative plan for the construction of a new building, designed by John Russell Pope. For example, two former presidents of the board of trustees who were print collectors, suggested the addition of extra lighting, extensive exhibit areas and adequate storage space for the print department offices. These and other suggestions came to fruition in April, 1929, when the Baltimore Museum of Art finally moved into its present location on Wyman Park Drive, next to the Johns Hopkins University campus.

In June 1929, Etta Cone purchased a large lot of artwork for herself from the Edmond Sagot Gallery in Paris. She had the items sent to her apartment in Baltimore. Included in the purchases were works by Dufresne, Picasso, Pissarro and Vlaminck. A Marie Laurencin painting, *Les Espannoles,* was also part of the lot, purchased by Etta for Blanche to hang in her sitting room. When the paintings arrived at Etta's apartment, Blanche called on her to see them and pick up her piece.[14]

In the spring of 1930, the museum decided to start an active print department and hire an official curator to care for the prints. Blanche offered to help the board look for a curator and interview prospects. The board wanted to lure the Garrett print collection back to Baltimore from its storage at the Library of Congress in Washington. It had been sent there in 1903 because "there was no suitable fire-proof institution to house them in Baltimore" at that time.

Adelyn Breeskin

The final choice for curator was the daughter of Dr. Dohme, Adelyn Breeskin. Mrs. Breeskin worked on the staff of the Metropolitan Museum of Art in New York and was especially interested in prints and drawings. She grew up in a home in Baltimore with lots of art on the walls, and manifested an early interest in painting during her years attending Roland Park Country School and Bryn Mawr School, from which she graduated in 1914. Before she left for college, she entered

a painting in an exhibition at the Charcoal Club, where it was stolen. She then moved to Boston and attended the School of Fine Arts, Crafts and Decorative Design.[15] She took supplementary courses at Harvard and Boston universities. Her first training in the field of prints was from Mr. Fitz Roy Carrington while he was still at the Boston Museum of Fine Arts. Then it was on to the Metropolitan Museum of Art.

When Breeskin was hired for the curatorial position in Baltimore, she was married, with three daughters. She returned to her home town, hired a full-time nanny and set to work at the museum. The first order of business (now that a state-of-the-art print space was available) was to bring the Garrett collection back to Baltimore.

Top: Postcard of the Baltimore Museum of Art building. Collection of the author. Above: Postcard of the 1929 Exhibition of the Jacob Epstein Collection at the Baltimore Museum of Art. Collection of the author.

Blanche offered to help and immediately the two formed a bond. They spent hours combing through the collections and talking about prints: styles, artists, schools, techniques, and methods. Adelyn needed help transporting the Garrett prints back to Baltimore. For three weeks, during the worst heat of that summer, they commuted back and forth to Washington to transport and catalogue the 120,000 prints in that collection.[16] Once the prints were safely stored in their new facility, the two women set about curating a showing of the best the collection had to offer. The official opening of the Baltimore Museum's Print and Drawings Department was held on October 15, 1930, featuring the long-awaited Garrett Print Collection.

After that official opening, Blanche was named an honorary curator of the Print and Drawings

Department of the Museum.[17] For the next few years, every few months Adelyn and Blanche, "the most modest, retiring little spinster," would go to New York to the galleries, look over what was available and purchase additional prints.[18] They worked very hard to collect a comprehensive grouping of the best examples of artwork which spanned all stages of the printing process. Their goal was to expose Baltimoreans to the exciting artwork being produced in this particular medium, drawn or printed works on paper, in black and white or color. The two women worked to strengthen the museum's collection where it was weak and to expand into important but previously unexplored areas.

Blanche had an uniquely close relationship with Adelyn Breeskin, who used to refer to her as the "perfect patron." They worked together on planning and executing showings, and talked "art" continuously. Blanche would ask Adelyn what the museum needed, whether new acquisitions, books on art, or other services that she could provide. Then when she traveled to New York or abroad, she would shop for specific items to round out the print collection, and add new finds which she felt would be important to keep the collection on the cutting edge. On occasion, she would come for an informal visit to the museum with several prints under her arm. Casually, she would hand them to Mrs. Breeskin, and then proceed to discuss other matters.[18] Throughout the decade of the 1930s, when times were tough in America, the BMA was her baby, and she continually fed and nurtured her "special child."

The Lucas Collection

In the spring of 1933, the Maryland Institute College of Art Library contacted Adelyn Breeskin about the George A. Lucas collection. The collection comprised 14,000 prints and had been left by Lucas to Henry Walters, the important Baltimore collector who started his own museum in the city. Walters had not been in a position to care for the collection and had it stored (temporarily) at the school's library in 1909. The Institute had insufficient resources to exhibit or care for the prints, hence they called on the Baltimore Museum for help.

The Print Department, that is, Adelyn and Blanche, volunteered to catalogue the collection for the school. Each day, for three months, Blanche would summon her chauffeur to the front door of the Riviera Apartments and step into her Packard and head for the Baltimore Museum of Art, five miles away. There, she would fetch Adelyn Breeskin, and the two would be escorted to the library at the Maryland Institute College of Art. By July, 1933, the two women persuaded the Institute's board of trustees that the prints should be moved to the Baltimore Museum of Art where they would be well cared for. The prints would continue to be available to the college for study purposes.

Amazingly, the entire Lucas collection of 14,000 prints, plus 550 fine reference catalogues, sales catalogues, and books relating to nineteenth-century art were transported from the college to the museum in one day. Soon after, the French nineteenth-century drawings, also part of the Lucas Collection, were transferred to the BMA for safekeeping. Among this collection were three of the finest Daumier watercolor drawings, two fine Millets, Barye's watercolors and pen sketches by Delacroix, Gavarni and others. By the beginning of 1934, the Print and Drawings Department had the task of caring for 40,000 prints containing works from the fifteenth through the nineteenth century.

Blanche volunteered hundreds of hours helping to catalogue and organize the prints. They were arranged alphabetically under the engraver's name with a corresponding catalogue card for reference. Blanche helped prepare a brochure explaining the various print processes, with a history of the various media. She also included a list of the artists whose work illustrated those media to the best advantage and emphasized those whose work might be seen and studied in the Print Department at the museum.[19] Along with all of the time she devoted to the museum, Blanche also spent time at the Sinai Hospital, where her brother, Harry, was president. Once a week she would spend an afternoon rolling bandages. The gauze material came in large rolls, and had to be cut down into usable sizes. This became a social activity for the hospital's auxiliary members, and Blanche participated in this volunteer project for many years.[20]

In May of 1941, after Blanche's death, the museum opened an exhibition of contemporary American printmaking. The display was arranged to show a cross-section of the work of the most outstanding printmakers of the 1930s. When the exhibition was planned, they thought it would have to be supplemented with other pieces from outside the museum. But Blanche's collection had been so carefully compiled, that there was an abundance to draw from right there. Most of the printmakers were painters who also worked in graphic arts. Included among the artists were Thomas Hart Benton, Yasuo Kuniyoshi, José Clemente Orozco, Diego Rivera and John Sloane.[21]

Notes

1   Thomas Verande, "123 Years of Change—The History of the Upper Eutaw/Madison Neighborhood" (Baltimore, MD: self-published), 5.

2   Clare Speier Baer, Interview by author, July 4, 1999, Baltimore, MD.

3   Audrey May, Telephone interview by the author, 2216 Madison Ave., Baltimore, MD., 2001.

4   Clare Speier Baer, Interview by the author, July 4, 1999, Baltimore, MD.

5   E.L.L., "Loan Exhibit Marks Opening of Museum," Blanchard Randall Papers, Archives and Manuscripts Collection, Baltimore Museum of Art.

6   "Gives Garrett Home for Art Museum Use," Friday June 30, 1923, Blanchard Randall Papers, BMA.

7   Blanchard Randall to Henry W. Kent, August 15, 1922, Blanchard Randall Papers, BMA.

8   *An Exhibition of Modern French Art*, January 9–February 1, 1925 (Baltimore, MD: H.E. Houck & Co., Baltimore Museum of Art), 3.

9   Warren Wilmer Brown, "The Baltimore Museum of Art: Its Evolution and Future," *Art & Archaeology: The Arts Throughout the Ages* 19:5–6, May–June, 1925, 247–251.

10 "Recent Museum Exhibitions," *News-Record of the Baltimore Museum of Art*, 1:4, April 1928, 1.

11 "Museum Acquisitions," *News-Record of the Baltimore Museum of Art*, 1:5, May 1928, 2.

12 Purchase Bill, July 18, 1928, Saidie A. May Papers, BMA.

13 "Woodcuts in the Museum Collection," *News-Record of the Baltimore Museum of Art*, 2:1, January 1929, 1.

14 Purchase Bill, June 6, 1929, Saidie A. May Papers, BMA.

15 Adelyn Breeskin, Interview by Paul Cummings, June 27, 1974. Archives of American Art, SI.

16 Adelyn Breeskin, "1930 Report of the Print Department," Adelyn Breeskin Papers, Archives and Manuscript Collection, BMA.

17 "Print Department to Open," *News-Record of the Baltimore Museum of Art*, 3:3, October 1930, 2.

18 Adelyn Breeskin, "1930 Report of the Print Department," Adelyn Breeskin Papers, BMA.

19 "Two Bequests," *Baltimore Museum of Art News*, 3:5, May 1941, 36.

20 Dr. Samuel Abrams, Interview by author, September 20, 2006, Baltimore, MD.

21 "Contemporary American Printmaking," *Baltimore Museum of Art News*, 3:5, May 1941, 35.

Wings of Her Own, 1928–1931

In 1928, Saidie started taking regular painting courses in Paris at the Académie Scandinave, founded by a Scandinavian-born sculptress, Lena Börjesson, located at the Maison Watteau, 6 Rue Brea in Montparnasse.[1] This particular school had one of the most highly regarded art programs in Paris at the time. Their art classes were popular both with European artists as well as expatriate Americans. All of the teachers were working artists who freelanced as teachers at the school. France had become the focus of artistic expression in Europe after WWI. During the 1920s, one dollar bought 20 French francs and stabilized at 14 francs. One could live easily and well on five dollars a day, including hotels and traveling expenses. The cost of living was half of what it was in the United States.[2]

One beautiful spring morning in Paris, Saidie woke, sat out on her balcony in the soft breeze, had a leisurely breakfast, then took care of a few bills and correspondence. Afterwards she dressed in her ordinary "painting clothes," stockings and comfortable shoes, a simple dress covered by a cream-colored muslin smock smudged with dried oil paint. Today she had her painting class at the Académie Scandinave with one of her favorite teachers, Othon Friesz. She so looked forward to working with him, and sharing ideas and painting philosophies with the other students in the class. She was almost 50, but she appeared to be in her late thirties, with a short, slightly stocky build, short, bobbed hair, bright, sparkling brown eyes, and a great inviting smile. She was finally on her own, able to do what she really wanted to do, after having been in two marriages to high-energy businessmen. They were wonderful people, both very interested in art, culture and collecting, but immersed in a world that demanded a lot of their time and was constraining for free-spirited Saidie. She managed to get by in that environment for quite a few years, but during her forties, she realized that she no longer wanted all of that responsibility, the societal demands and all of the duties and obligations involved in being the wife of a rich American businessman. She wanted to live a more "bohemian" existence, and be with people who were interested in the philosophy of life rather than in its trappings.

Saidie headed off to the atelier (studio) in her old painting clothes. She walked through the narrow cobblestone streets, feeling at home, the warm spring breeze carrying sweet scents of lilacs and hyacinths planted among the houses along the block. There was also the irresistible scent of fresh baked bread in the air. She carried a wooden box filled with her oil paint tubes, brushes, painting palette and turpentine. The Académie Scandinave was in a large home. Once inside, Saidie had to climb two sets of steep steps to get to her destination. As she entered the large classroom, the creaky, paint-splattered wooden floor greeted her with its whines. Tall wooden easels were arranged around a center square platform, where a model would stand, or a table could be arranged with a still life on it. Saidie was in the middle of working on a painting, and when she arrived, she conversed with a couple of other students, and then she set to work.

As students came and went during the classes, Saidie continued to work with Othon Friesz from the start of one class right into the next one. She liked his manner and teaching style and felt very comfortable painting in this environment. On this particular day, a few new faces appeared in the class, creating a buzz in the room. Three young men, all around the age of 30, had transferred from Munich, Germany, where they had been working under Hans Hofmann. Al Jensen, Carl Holty and Vaclav Vytlacil (the latter two Americans) had arrived, and their presence intrigued Saidie, especially Al Jensen. He was a rather short man: a couple of inches taller than Saidie, stocky but muscular (he had worked on the German ship that brought him to Europe). A little rough around the edges, "savage" as Saidie put it, but possessing a kind face with intense eyes and a warm smile. There was an instant chemistry between them. Al's painting and ideas were fresh and original, and Saidie was drawn to his looks, his manners and his mind. Immediately, she realized that he and his friends, all artists, were living a hand-to-mouth existence, working odd jobs to survive and continue following their passion for painting.

Alfred Julio Jensen was born December 11, 1903, in Guatemala City to a Danish father and a German-Polish mother. In 1910, Alfred's mother died, and he and his three siblings went to live with his uncle in Denmark. After graduating from day school in 1917, he got a job as a cabin-boy on a ship and sailed around the Pacific until he finally got off in San Francisco, California. Alfred moved to San Diego and continued his education at the San Diego High School, where he eventually received a scholarship and enrolled at the San Diego Fine Arts School at Balboa Park. While attending the school, he heard about the Hans Hofmann School in Munich, and decided to go to Germany to enroll there. He was hired onto a German ship to work for his passage.

By the time he got to Munich, he had forgotten the name of the school that he was supposed to attend, except that the last name started, with an "H," so he ended up at Moritz Heymann's school for a short time. There he met two American students of Hofmann's, Carl Holty and Vaclav Vytlacil. Then he joined the Hofmann school, where he and Vytlacil concentrated on drawing after the Old Masters, in particular Bruegel and Dürer. The two friends frequented museums where they could find the works they admired so much.

Between 1927 and 1928, the three young art students broke with Hofmann, feeling that he was restricting their growth as artists, and they traveled together to Paris to further their artistic education. They took an apartment together and attended the Académie Scandinave to work with the newer generation Fauvists. Vytlacil was quite a bit older than Al and had already been teaching art for a number of years in the United States before saving enough money to live in Europe to study.

Alfred Julio Jensen. Collection of Regina Bogat Jensen, Glen Ridge, New Jersey.

He had worked with Hofmann throughout the mid-1920s, first as a student and subsequently as a teaching assistant. In 1924, he organized Hofmann's summer school on the island of Capri off the coast of North Africa. Saidie attended that session. In 1929, after a year in the United States, Vytlacil moved back to Paris and set up a studio, interacting with many of the leading artists of the day. Over the next six years, he painted in France and Capri. Saidie encouraged his work.

Saidie found herself thinking about Al a lot after the initial encounter in the painting class, and she looked forward to spending time with him again at the next class. Within a couple of weeks, she felt comfortable enough to offer to help Al with some financial assistance, and they started spending time outside of class. Saidie met Al at a time where she was reassessing her life. She had grown up in a family of affluence, become accustomed to having the best, staying in the finest hotels and eating in good restaurants. She was fluent in three languages and had traveled the world with her family and two husbands. She was well educated, self-confident, outgoing and funny. Everybody liked her, she was witty and fun-loving. She loved creating art and collecting it—all types—and media. She was open and willing to try anything. She had always been interested in painting and took advantage of classes with different artists since she had been a child. She was tiny and appealingly cute, and she charmed everyone that she met. However, some people did find her a bit eccentric, especially since she was so self-assured and knowledgeable.

In July of 1928, Blanche and Helen sailed for Germany, where they vacationed and visited their cousins. Saidie left Paris and took the train up to Berlin to meet them, and for two weeks they shopped, ate at fine restaurants and toured the German museums. Then on to Italy for two more weeks where they visited Florence, Rome and Naples. Blanche was overwhelmed by the beauty of this country, and described her feelings in postcards which she sent to her cousin's children in Germany.[3] Finally, just before her two sisters were ready to leave, Saidie confided to Blanche about the new, exciting man that she had met.

Al was very philosophical and artistic, but never had the opportunity to live without worrying where his next meal was coming from. He had spent so much time surviving on his own, that in his own way he was also very worldly and street-smart. At 33, when he met Saidie, he had a very sharp mind and strong background in painting. He was friendly and outgoing, and in art class he became interested in the philosophical aspects of the Old Masters' works. Saidie's experience in collecting Old Masters' etchings with Blanche, particularly Dürer's work, created a close bond between the two. They were both enamored of the same artists. Saidie availed him of a world of cultural awareness, and invited him to share in her pursuit of artistic knowledge and collecting. Al started to accompany her to museums, galleries and artists' ateliers. They met art dealers and the foremost artists of the 1930s, from whom Saidie bought directly.

The two continued to patronize the Académie Scandinave, where they took painting classes with Othon Friesz and Charles Dufresne as well as Modern sculpture with Charles Despiau. After working with Charles Dufresne for a time, Al referred to him as his "spiritual and painter father" and was encouraged by Dufresne to change his style to paint with thick impasto, a style that he employed the rest of his career. During the summer of 1929, Saidie and Al traveled and painted together in Italy, on the Isle of Capri in North Africa and Spain. At the same time, Blanche, Helen and Bob rented a villa for the summer in a fishing village in Gloucester, Massachusetts.[4]

In the fall, Saidie and Al were back in Paris, spending their mornings painting, and in the afternoons having leisurely lunches at the famous Café Le Dôme in Montparnasse. This was the hangout for Americans interested in the arts, and the two spent the "art season" discussing art and philosophy with Leo Stein, brother of the famous Gertrude Stein.[5] Both he and Al were intensely interested in mysticism and the insights of Freud, and even though Stein was having a difficult time with his hearing, he was happy to spend hours conversing on his favorite subjects.[6]

Meanwhile, across the Atlantic in New York City, on November 8, a preview reception was being held for the first show at the new Museum of Modern Art.[7] According to Paul Sachs, one of the original trustees, its vision was a kind of "halfway house" for art on its way from obscurity to immortality. But of course, at its inception it was a venue to show off the collections of the original seven members of its forming committee.[8] Saidie was excited with the prospect and planned to see the director of this exciting new project when she headed back to the States. She felt that this would be a perfect venue to show off her collection of up-and-coming new modern artists.

That same year, Saidie and Herbert finally divorced and she kept their furnished apartment in New York, continuously adding items to it from her travels. But now she also wanted to purchase artwork to donate directly to American art museums to expose the American public to the exciting and meaningful Modern art being produced in Europe. Saidie arranged a meeting with Alfred Barr at the end of April, 1930, to see the museum and to talk about making donations.[9]

Once Saidie's divorce came through, she and Al became an "item." They saw each other every day. He was living in a tiny flat at 16 Bis Rue Bardinet. They were inseparable, and according to at least one source they had a "hot love relationship with dramatic explosions." Their tempestuous relationship was not surprising, Al Jensen may have had a wretched temper, but Saidie certainly was not one to reckon with either! Saidie was the only person at that time to recognize the strange but very original talent of this rather uncouth, neglected young man from a poor family. She paid to have his teeth fixed and began teaching him social graces: how to use a knife and fork like a gentleman and how to behave in a fine restaurant. In later years, after Saidie's death, he would become recognized as an artist of the New York elite.

Throughout this period of time, Saidie continued to collect, donating many of the items she bought directly to museums. By June of 1930, she had donated the first work by Pablo Picasso to any museum collection in the United States,[10] a strong and historically important gouache from his "Negro Period." This was also the first foreign painting to belong to the Museum of Modern Art, especially important since it was given by a non-trustee.[11] Along with the Picasso, Saidie gave them a sculpture of a small standing female figure by Swiss artist Hermann Haller.[12] Between its opening and the time Saidie made this donation, the Museum of Modern Art held six exhibitions in their small space on the twelfth floor of the Heckscher Building (with no air-conditioning and poor ventilation). They were already bursting at the seams at this location and needed better space.[13]

It was more prestigious to donate art to the Museum of Modern Art than the Baltimore Museum of Art; however, that prestige came with a cost. Every item that Saidie offered MOMA had to go through a "juried" acceptance by museum trustees. Quite a few items she offered were declined, because they were not considered the best examples of that artist's work, or they were artists that the museum did not deem important enough to own.[14] Alfred Barr commented in a memo to a trustee that he felt Saidie was a bit eccentric, but they would accept her donations which met their criteria.[15]

84 Saidie May

An Unexpected Treat

Helen was always playing the stock market, and made a fortune from a shrewd stock purchase. She invited Blanche to travel to South America to escape the summer heat. They left Baltimore for an ambitious three-week trip to South America on June 27. It would be cool and relaxing, being wintertime there, and a welcome change from the stifling heat of the city.

They took a train to New York and then a Pan Am flight directly to picturesque Rio de Janeiro, Brazil, where they spent a week, then on to São Paulo for three days. Pan Am had just started direct flights to South America. From Brazil, they took a boat trip down the coast of the Atlantic Ocean to Montevideo, Uruguay, for a day, and then on to Buenos Aires, Argentina, where they disembarked. They spent a week in Buenos Aires and took a train across the Andes Mountains towards Chile, but the weather kept getting worse. Snow was piling up, and eventually the train got stuck in Mendoza, on the west coast of Argentina, not too far from Santiago, their destination. They were scheduled to board another cruise ship the day after next, and were afraid that if they waited for the train to get through, they would miss it. So they caught a small commuter plane. It was frighening, flying over the snow-capped peaks of the western mountain region; the plane was old and creaky, and if they looked down through the crack in the side door, they could see the ground below.

After a two-day visit, they boarded a cruise ship in Santiago and cruised up the Pacific Ocean, stopping

Left: Picasso, *Head*, gouache drawing, 12.1930. Collection Museum of Modern Art. ©2011 Estate of Pablo Picasso/Artists Rights Society (ARS), New York. Right: Hermann Haller, *Standing Girl*, bronze, 1926, 13.1930. Collection Museum of Modern Art.

Woman with Sun Hat, Greek, 3rd. century B.C., 30.117,
Gift of Mrs. Saidie Adler May, 1930, Metropolitan Museum of Art.

at one port of call after another. Eventually, the ship made its way to Lima, Peru, where they visited for a couple of days and then finished the cruise up the coast to the Panama Canal. After returning to Miami, Blanche and Helen stayed for an additional two weeks before returning home.[16]

Blanche was hard at work as a board member of the small Baltimore Museum of Art. Saidie decided to offer the artwork declined by MOMA to the Baltimore Museum of Art, which was more than happy to accept it. These included Giorgio de Chirico and Alexander Archipenko. MOMA accepted Saidie's gifts on the condition that if later they no longer wanted to include these works in their collection, they could be sold off or disposed of to add new items.[17] Other smaller institutions in the United States did not have this luxury, and were more than thrilled to receive Saidie's gifts on a more permanent basis.

While in New York in October 1930, Saidie donated a very important painted terracotta figurine excavated from Tanagra, Greece, in the third quarter of the 19th century. This statuette had been part of the collection of Vicomte du Dresnay and was published in the catalogue of that collection, but unfortunately, it had been broken into a number of pieces and put back together. She purchased the female figure from the Brummer Gallery and had it sent directly to the Metropolitan Museum of Art.[18] It was a very important addition to their collection of classical Greek sculpture. The twelve-inch young woman with a fan, dressed in a tunic and rose-colored mantle had a pointed red hat on her head and red shoes. It had originally been brightly glazed, but faded over time. The figure's rendering of drapery was one of the finest examples in Greek art.[19]

The next month, Saidie and Al left New York and went back to Paris with Blanche, who had been busy helping the Baltimore Museum of Art with their new print department, as well as purchasing and donating all kinds of interesting works of art. She purchased a portrait of an Egyptian pharaoh incised in rose granite, of the 18th–19th Dynasty, from a sale of the collection of Maurice Nahman, which she donated in February, 1931.[20] By April she donated another sculpture,

Left: *Relief Fragment of Ramesses II*, c. 1279–1213 B.C., Dynasty XIX, Reign of Ramesses II, Pi-Ramesses ("The House of Ramesses"), Eastern Delta Region, Egypt, rose granite, 73.7 cm H, The Baltimore Museum of Art: Gift of Blanche Adler, BMA 1931.4.1.

this time a Greek parian marble head of the goddess Aphrodite (4th century, B.C.), a fine example, beautifully preserved, from the island of Lemnos, which she also purchased from the Brummer Gallery who acquired it from a Parisian collector of antiquities.[21]

Blanche extended her stay at the Hotel Royal from January through September. She and Saidie had a wonderful time shopping, attending art classes and visiting with vacationing friends and expatriates such as the Cone sisters. Blanche purchased artwork from two of Saidie's favorite teachers at the Académie Scandinave: E. Othon Friesz and Charles Dufresne. She also bought a gilt bronze standing nude female statue, *Coralie,* directly from A. Cornet.[22] In February, 1931, Blanche, Saidie and Al visited Barcelona and Saidie purchased antique sculptures and a painting on ivory from the J. Moragas Gallery. Then they went to Majorca in March.

In the 1930s, Saidie was purchasing a lot of foreign artworks to donate to American museums; she was concerned not to donate more items than she was entitled to deduct from her income tax. She even wrote to the various museums asking them to hold works until January of the next year before accepting them, so as to take advantage of the income tax situation (the global depression had an effect even on her seemingly limitless finances). On June 29, 1931, she made her first purchase from her companion, Alfred Jensen. She bought three paintings from him for 4,000 francs, *Still Life*, *Blue Interior* and *Interior* (see page 277).[23] All three of these works were sent to the United States in the containers she shipped in September with Blanche. *Still Life*, a simple vase of flowers, painted in the impasto style, is still owned privately by the Adler family.

On July 1, 1931, Saidie paid $232 to Galerie Georges Petit for artwork. She also purchased a painting by Vuillard as well as Bonnard's *Breakfast in the Garden* (1924) from Galerie Paquereau in Paris (19-1/2 x 16-1/2). She was aware, that of Bonnard's work (he was already well established by this point), this painting had one of the strongest resemblances to Impressionism. Bonnard used brush strokes with vague touches of color, which had no satisfactory shape in themselves. These strokes established a local tone, but still maintained the fluid, iridescent hues characteristic of his mature style.

The two sisters made so many purchases that they had to ship them in large wooden crates to the United States. They sent a total of four crates. The crates were shipped on the SS *Vincent*, sailing from Le Havre, France on September 12, 1931. When the curators opened the crates in Baltimore, it must have been like opening a virtual treasure chest: paintings, prints, catalogues, art books, textiles and sculptures (bronze, terracotta, stone, wood and ivory). Some items were new, some antique. Most of Saidie's purchases from the School of Paris were bound for the Museum of Modern Art on loan. The curators at the Baltimore Museum of Art were disappointed at not being able to keep everything that was sent.

Blanche and Saidie collected voraciously—every style and medium, from textiles to jewelry, to examples of sculpture from Greece to Asia, giving the majority of it to waiting museums. Saidie was also financially philanthropic, giving to Jewish charities and local "helping hands" organizations in New York City. After their whirlwind shopping spree, Blanche left France for home, and Saidie and Al headed to Majorca, Spain, in October to paint.

Notes

1   "A Sculptor in Paris," Gudmar Olovson, *History*, 31, www.warne.se/docs/Gudmar_S.pdf.

2   *Anton Gill, Art Lover, a Biography of Peggy Guggenheim* (New York: Harper Collins, 2001), 67.

3   Blanche Adler to Bertel Speier, August 10, 1928. Collection of Evelyn Held, Baltimore, MD.

4   Blanche Adler to Bertel Speier, June 18, 1929. Collection of Evelyn Held, Baltimore, MD.

5   Alfred Jensen to Jane Cone, May 27, 1972. Saidie A. May Papers, BMA.

6   Brenda Wineapple, *Sister and Brother, Gertrude and Leo Stein* (Baltimore: Johns Hopkins University Press, 1996), 400–401.

7   Alice Goldfarb Marquis, *Alfred H. Barr, Jr., Missionary for the Modern* (Chicago: Contemporary Books, 1989), 67.

8   Russell Lynes, *Good Old Modern, an Intimate Portrait of the Museum of Modern Art* (Kingsport, TN: Kingsport Press, 1973), 13–14.

9   Alfred Barr to Saidie A. May, April 22, 1930. Alfred Hamilton Barr Papers, Archives of American Art, SI.

10 Alfred Barr to A. C. Goodyear, June 17, 1930. Alfred Hamilton Barr Papers, Archives of American Art, SI.

11 Russell Lynes, *Good Old Modern, an Intimate Portrait of the Museum of Modern Art* (Kingsport, TN: Kingsport Press, 1973), 82.

12 Saidie A. May to A. Conger Goodyear, June 4, 1930. Saidie A. May Papers, BMA.

13 Russell Lynes, *Good Old Modern, an Intimate Portrait of the Museum of Modern Art* (Kingsport, TN: Kingsport Press, 1973), 67.

14 Alfred H. Barr to Saidie A. May, October 20, 1930. Saidie A. May Papers, BMA.

15 Alfred Barr to A. C. Goodyear, June 17, 1930. Alfred Hamilton Barr Papers, Archives of American Art, SI.

16 Blanche Adler to Bertel Speier, postcards from July, August, September, 1930. Collection of Evelyn Held, Baltimore, MD.

17 Alfred H. Barr to Saidie A. May, October 20, 1930. Saidie A. May Papers, BMA.

18 Bill of Sale from the Brummer Gallery, October 30, 1930. Saidie A. May Papers, BMA.

19 "Tanagra Figurine Given to Museum," January 31, 1931, Saidie A. May Papers, BMA.

20 "Portrait of a Pharaoh," *News-Record of the Baltimore Museum of Art* 3:8, March 1931, Cover.

21 "A Valuable Acquisition," *News-Record of the Baltimore Museum of Art* 3:10, May 1931, 2.

22 Bill of Sale from A. Cornet, August 24, 1931, Saidie A. May Papers, BMA.

23 Bill of Sale from Alfred Jensen to Saidie A. May, June 29, 1931. Saidie A. May Papers, BMA.

Championing the Fauvists, 1931–1934

During the 1920s and 1930s, both Saidie and Blanche were collecting drawings, prints and paintings, as well as amassing an important collection of antique textiles from Asia and the Middle Eastern countries. These early textiles spanned the time period from the Middle Ages through the nineteenth century and would influence later decorative arts and textile designs.

The sisters' tastes were quite diverse and they were each receptive to new images and ideas. Once Saidie was free to attend art school as frequently as she wanted, she concentrated her efforts on the latest works by the contemporary artists with whom she worked or studied. Unlike most art patrons, she was fortunate to have daily, firsthand knowledge and insight into those artists' works.

Many of the paintings Saidie donated during this period were produced by the circle of early-twentieth-century French painters known as the "Fauvists." The Fauvists included followers of Henri Matisse, one of the important Impressionist artists at the turn of the last century.[1] Aware that Etta and Claribel Cone had actively collected his work and planned to leave their collection to the Baltimore Museum of Art, Saidie sought instead to collect the "next generation" of French painters. The Fauvists were among that generation.

Artists such as Raoul Dufy, Maurice de Vlaminck, Paul Vuillard, Georges Braque, André Derain and Achille-Émile Othon Friesz had been acquainted with and worked with Matisse, sharing their ideas about "non-naturalistic colors." They experimented with the techniques they admired in the paintings of Vincent van Gogh, Paul Gauguin and Paul Cézanne which they saw exhibited between 1901 and 1906 in Paris. Othon Friesz and Raoul Dufy had been school friends and studied the works of Boudin in the Le Havre Museum. Along with Georges Braque, the three painted together in Le Havre and then joined the Chatou group after they saw Matisse's work.[2]

André Derain, French, *Head of a Girl*, 1928, 1936:44. Collection of the San Diego Museum of Art. ©2011 Artists Rights Society (ARS), New York/ADAGP, Paris.

Breaking with the Past

The Fauves represented the first break with the painting traditions of the past. They believed in color as an emotional force and many of their paintings had a "primitive wildness" to them, hence the name Fauvism, French for "wild beasts." The Fauves used pure, brilliant color, applying it straight from the paint tubes in an aggressive and direct manner, creating the sense of an explosion on the canvas. They painted directly from nature with a strong, expressive reaction to their subjects and sought to create a new picture space, defined by movement of color, applied with short, forceful brush strokes. During the height of the Fauvist movement in Paris, their works were primarily exhibited at the Salon des Indépendants and the Salon d'Automne.

Fauvism was a transitional learning stage for most of these artists. By 1907, their styles were beginning to evolve in other directions, many moving toward Cubism or other Modern art movements. Andre Derain and Maurice de Vlaminck had met in 1900 and painted together at the school of Chateau.[3] In 1908, they renewed their interest in Paul Cézanne's work related to the vision of the order and structure of nature, which led them to reject the turbulent emotionalism of Fauvism in favor of the logic of Cubism.

Expatriates

Like many other expatriate Americans, Saidie took advantage of the low exchange rate and was able to live in France very inexpensively. The decades after the First World War also witnessed a time of artistic progressivism in Paris. Seemingly, the French accepted all cultures and were quite permissive, allowing avant-garde ideologies to flourish. As a result, it was a unique time of heightened creativity. Artists, writers, musicians, dancers and actors shared their ideas freely and without prejudice or fear of reprisal. Gertrude Stein coined the term, "the Lost Generation," for this unique gathering of creative individuals, including such writers as Ernest Hemingway and F. Scott Fitzgerald. "Paris represented a life unrestrained by routine, duty or ritual obligation."[4] People lived for immediate gratification.

From 1932 to 1933, Saidie and Al studied at the Académie Scandinave, where many of the Fauvists taught as a means of supplementing their incomes. Saidie was enamored with the artists from whom she learned new painting techniques and discussed art philosophy. She bought many works from her instructors and others in her classes, directly off their easels. Their work would someday form the core of her substantial collection and she felt strongly about supporting their efforts.

Many of Saidie's young artistic friends had very little money, trying to establish themselves and sell their work, surviving by working odd jobs. Saidie helped support quite a few of them with a monthly stipend, and purchased works that she liked and felt were important examples of their style. She had faith in the potential of these young artists and believed in the ability of the American public to eventually appreciate this new art. She attempted to contact Alfred Barr with the goal of placing these works in the Museum of Modern Art's collection.

Saidie and Al befriended another young artist, Theodore Schempp, who accompanied their painting group to North Africa between 1930 and 1933, and afterwards became an art dealer in Paris. He and Saidie ran into each other only once after that, when they were both passengers on the same boat traveling from France to New York between 1937 and 1938. After they landed in New York, she went to see paintings that he had brought with him, and purchased Derain's *Head of a Girl*. According to Schempp, Saidie was a rather spontaneous buyer who made up her own mind, even though many people thought that Al Jensen had a strong influence on her purchases.

Daniel Kahnweiler and Galerie Simon

One day, Saidie's instructor Othon Friesz suggested that she go see his work displayed at Galerie Simon, a local gallery at Rue Vignon[5] in Paris. The gallery's owner, Daniel-Henry Kahnweiler, would be her single biggest influence and help shape her collecting career. Henry Kahnweiler and his wife became good friends with Saidie.

She purchased her first work by André Masson, *Little Tragedy*, from Galerie Simon in 1933 and became a loyal patron of the shop. Kahnweiler gave her invaluable advice on what to buy and how the worldwide art market was faring. In conversation with Saidie, he claimed, "the worldwide depression from 1929–1936 saw a total collapse of all prices, including old paintings as well as modern. In every town in the United States, there was a museum you never heard of. These museums were supplied not only by their own purchases, but by gifts. In America, a collector could deduct gifts to charities or museums from their income tax. Consequently, a collector who bought a painting cheaply could leave it to a museum but keep it in his home during his lifetime. He could deduct from his income not only its purchase price, but the value of the work as assessed by experts, usually many times the original value."[6] European governments did not adopt that policy, and as a result they lost many of their most important artworks to American museums. They also lost the revenue that would have been generated by tourists visiting the European museums to see those works.[7]

Saidie heeded Kahnweiler's advice and started to think about what artworks she would donate to American museums, and how that would benefit her financial situation each year. Up to this point, she had limited experience with donations, only with the Carnegie Museum in Pittsburgh more than a decade earlier. Now she was giving items to the Baltimore Museum of Art, and wanted to be more involved in the newly formed Museum of Modern Art, where she felt that her friends' work belonged. At that time, there were no museums in France dedicated exclusively to Modern Art.

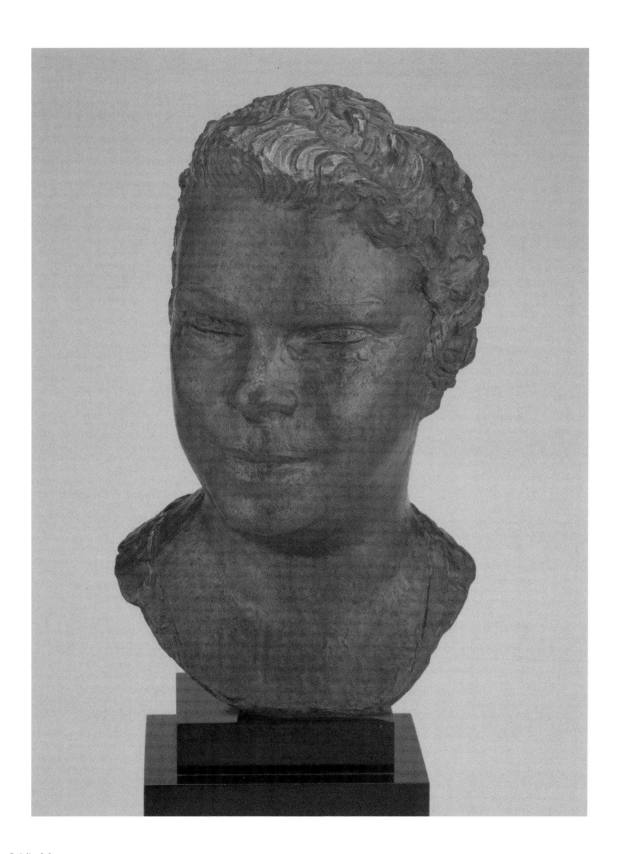

Charles Despiau

In February 1931, Saidie commissioned her teacher, Charles Despiau, to sculpt a bust of her wearing a simple strand of pearls. Initially, the cost was to be $1,000.[8] It took him quite a while, and many sittings, as he would become immersed in his work, losing track of time. Anatole de Monzie described him as the "French Donatello," having worked in his younger days with Rodin. Saidie went to his studio on Rue Brillat-Savarin in Paris for the sittings, which took forty-eight sessions to complete. Al Jensen would occasionally accompany Saidie to the sittings, as well as Theodore Schempp. Both artists were interested in watching Despiau's artistic process.

Saidie's bust would be modeled in the traditional way: first out of clay, then plaster, and then cast in bronze. Twenty-two sittings were done working with wet clay, after which time Despiau took a three-month rest. Then fifteen sittings were done using a plaster mold and a sculptor's knife to mold the plaster paste. After that, two more plaster heads were done with a sable-hair brush, using little dots of plaster in the style of pointillism, creating the realization of light form. This took eight more sittings. Three final sittings in wax were done by touch, with Despiau pressing the wax down with his fingers here and there to finish it off.[9]

Back in his studio, the final casting was done in bronze, and under Despiau's direction two young apprenticing sculptors hammered the bronze into the final finish. Six copies, including Saidie's original, were to be made. Saidie knew that Despiau was an important artist, and she was anxious for her portrait to be included in museum collections in the United States. Her original bust was left to the Baltimore Museum of Art (there is no edition stamped on the base), and the first copy was offered to the Museum of Modern Art. They vacillated about accepting it since they already had two other heads by Despiau.[10] Despiau eventually gave the Musee de l'Art in Paris three plaster casts (working models), and sold a bronze corresponding to the third plaster cast to a private Parisian collector. By the time it was finally finished, the entire undertaking cost Saidie around three thousand dollars.

Despiau would never sculpt without a model, and he had a hard time bringing an end to his quest for perfection and the inner beauty of the sitter. His approach was classic: a continuation of Greek and Roman art, and of flamboyant Italian sculpture, with its lively, expressive finesse. He was a student of Rodin, and in turn taught his own students, whom he welcomed with "delight, patience, kindness and benevolence." Treating the artists who came to see him to talk "shop" as equals, he willingly gave them the advice they sought.

Saidie and Al went with their painting group to Majorca from October, 1931, until the spring of 1932. Then Blanche took a boat over from Baltimore to visit her sister and then continue on to Moscow. During her trip, Blanche purchased some Russian icons to send back to the BMA.[11]

After returning to Paris, Saidie exhibited one of her paintings, a simply framed landscape, *Trees*

Charles Despiau, French, 1874–1946, *Saidie A. May*, 1934, bronze, 14-1/4 in. H, The Baltimore Museum of Art: Bequest of Saidie A. May, BMA 1951.375. ©2011 Artists Rights Society (ARS), New York/ADAGP, Paris.

and Walls of France, at the Salon des Tuileries. Charles Despiau had suggested that she show this work there; he was one of the founders of the gallery and showed there all the time.

Saidie wrote to Alfred Barr to offer forty items to the Museum of Modern Art, including drawings, paintings, sculptures, lithographs and watercolors from the School of Paris. Some of the works she offered were by well-known artists of the time: Pablo Picasso, Henri Matisse, Aristide Maillol, while others were from unknown artists.[12]

Negotiations with Alfred Barr

During the winter of 1932, Saidie and Al went to Madrid to the Hotel Victoria, a mammoth, old Victorian-style hotel. They enjoyed themselves so much that they extended their stay through the middle of 1933.[13] At the beginning of June, Saidie sailed back to the U.S. Her first stop was in New York to pick up the artworks that MOMA had declined. While at the museum, Saidie talked to Alfred Barr about her donations and what she would offer them in her next shipment of artworks.

Barr was interested in owning a piece by Achille-Émile Othon Friesz, her teacher. Over tea they discussed what she had learned in his class and where Friesz's work was headed. Barr was enamored with Friesz's *Figure Composition* (1908), purchased in 1929 by the city of Detroit for the Detroit Art Institute from A. C. von Frey.[14] Barr wanted to acquire a similar piece for his museum, where Friesz's work showed brutality, using bright colors and hints of Cubism. Saidie agreed to visit Friesz's studio when she went back to Paris to identify his best works for donation. She then took the train to Baltimore to visit with her family, and to offer MOMA's rejects to the Baltimore Museum of Art.

At the end of the month, Saidie accompanied Blanche on a three-day, four-night train trip to California, where they stayed for a month before venturing north to Canada to spend a week at the Chateau Frontenac in Quebec, where it was "nice and cool."[15] Then it was off to Chicago for the 1933 World's Fair, where they exhausted themselves seeing all of the new and interesting exhibits. Compared to Canada, Chicago in August was beastly hot, but they still had a great time together. Deciding to spend another two weeks in Canada, they took a train back up north, heading west to breathtaking Lake Louise in Alberta. Finally the summer was over and it was time for Saidie to sail back to meet Al and spend the winter months of 1933 painting in Spain.

Saidie's teacher, Achille-Émile Othon Friesz had been closely associated with Matisse from 1905 to 1908 and adopted the bright, anti-naturalistic palette of the Fauves. Paul Gardner, director of the William Rockhill Nelson Gallery of Art in Kansas City, wrote Saidie, "The story is told that in 1900, Friesz met the aged Pissarro on the Pont Neuf in Paris, and the great Impressionist told the young beginner that there were only two artists worthy of his notice, Cézanne and Seurat. Since 1906, Friesz abandoned his early enthusiasm for the violent and the astonishing, and developed his technique and style in the more conservative school."[16]

"In the summer of 1907, painting with Braque in La Ciotat, in the Midi, he began to follow

Cézanne's example, seeking to emphasize a strong sense of pictorial construction which he felt had been sacrificed to Fauvism's coloristic excesses… Like Cézanne, Friesz was anxious to re-establish connection between contemporary avant-garde painting and the classical tradition, which he studied frequently at the Louvre."[17]

In 1933, Friesz offered a large painting of a nude to the Luxembourg Museum. They stalled for a while before rejecting it. Saidie tried to get Barr to take it for MOMA, but he would not accept it without seeing a picture of it first. By May of 1934, it was sent to Venice, Italy, for a big international exposition.[18] Finally Saidie sent the photo of it to Barr, to which he replied, "This is not brutal enough, would you please continue to look for me?"

In the spring of 1934, Saidie and Al headed north to Paris for the summer. A few years earlier, Al had become friendly with the sculptor Aristide Maillol, and he was anxious for Saidie to visit his studio and see his work for herself. Al made arrangements to visit the studio on the Seine et Oise on June 20. Saidie immediately fell in love with Maillol's work, and was particularly taken with a small terracotta statue of a nude girl that was sitting around in the studio, having been damaged. She bargained for a lower price based on its condition. The two negotiated 13,000 francs, with Maillol repairing the damage.[19]

Saidie spent a considerable amount of time corresponding with Alfred Barr about the works that she was amassing for MOMA. She felt that she was educating him on what was "state of the art," and what new trends she observed in Paris. In June, she wrote to him concerning what she was going to send. She went to Friesz's studio at 73 Rue Notre-Dame-des-Champs "to send him up the step-ladder to pull down this-n-that canvas,"[20] to find something from the 1910 to 1915 period that would satisfy Barr. "He had one, *Spring*, but I didn't take it because there were two female nudes dancing together towards the middle, and I was afraid they might be considered Lesbians, and so too suggestive"[21] for provincial American tastes.

Saidie finally settled on a "characteristic one from 1909": four nudes near a lake with mountains in the distance, which had been shown at the Salon des Galeries in 1932, "brutal, tormented nudes." The painting was *Landscape with Figures (Baigneuses)*,[22] which had been designed to be made into a tapestry.[23] Friesz felt that it showed the carrying of the rhythm of the figures in the background. She also purchased *Landscape with Quarry*, 1928, and a small nude, purchased from Kahnweiler's gallery at the beginning of June 1934 in exchange for the big nude, which Friesz kept. A few years previously, Saidie had donated Friesz's *Youth in the Garden* and two of his watercolors. *Youth in the Garden* happened to be painted on weak canvas (when he painted it in 1930, Friesz had little money), which made the painting very fragile and difficult for the museum to show.

In 1932, Saidie and Al had become friendly with the young artists Pierre Brune and Paul Cornet and their spouses. During the summer of 1934, Brune wrote to Saidie concerning his interest in creating a museum of Modern art for French people in the town of Céret, the "mecca" of Cubism,[24] close to

Othon Friesz, *Landscape with Figures, Baigneuses*, 1909, 5.1935. Collection of the Museum of Modern Art.

the Spanish border.[25] After World War II, Pablo Picasso and Henri Matisse aided him with his endeavor and each donated work to the museum. With additional support from other artists and collectors, Brune realized his dream. He assembled a fine collection of works and inaugurated the museum June 18, 1950.[26]

At the beginning of July 1934, Saidie busily filled two more large trunks with art to be shipped to the United States: one to her New York apartment and one to the Baltimore Museum of Art. This time, most of what she sent had been made by her Fauvist teachers and the younger artists she befriended. In the New York shipment, she sent the two paintings by Friesz and his small nude, a Derain landscape, Vuillard's *Mother and Sister of the Artist*, Saidie's *Trees and Walls of France*, the Cornet *Materuit (Mother and Child)* bronze sculpture, Despiau's bronze head of Saidie and André Masson's *The Little Tragedy 1933*. She was very excited about bringing this new work to the United States, and anxiously awaited the museum directors' reactions.

A Visit to San Diego

By the middle of July 1934, Saidie and Al were back at sea, headed for New York. When they arrived, Blanche met them and the three took the three day train to California to spend the summer together.[27] Al had attended high school and art school in San Diego ten years previously, and fell in love with the area. There they took two apartments at the "Miles Cottage" in the Barcelona Hotel in Grossmont, a suburb of San Diego.

The lifestyle in California was much more "open" than anywhere else in this country, and closer to what Saidie and Al had been used to in Paris. It was also more progressive: Jews were able to join the social scene in the West, even though there was still discrimination in certain clubs and hotels.[28] Saidie and Al enrolled in workshops painting from live nude models.[29] Blanche read, did some drawing and corresponded with her family and Adelyn Breeskin at the BMA.

Grossmont was transformed at the turn of the century from a desert-like mesa into a thriving, intellectual artist colony. Fabulous homes were built on the gentle hills of La Mesa, overlooking the valley of El Cajon, twelve miles from San Diego. The design of each home reflected the artist's particular needs and tastes, as well as complementing the environment in which it was placed.[30]

Architects for the community worked with the landscape, creating the homes on or around boulders and beautiful trees.

Top: André Masson, French (1896–1987), *The Little Tragedy*, 1933. Oil on canvas, 10-3/4 x 18 in. (27.3 x 45.7 cm). The Nelson-Atkins Museum of Art, Kansas City, Missouri. Gift of Saidie A. May, 36-20/2. ©2011 Artists Rights Society (ARS), New York/ADAGP, Paris. Photo by Jamison Miller. Above: Edouard Vuillard, *Mother and Sister of the Artist*, 1893, 141.1934. Collection of the Museum of Modern Art. ©2011 Artists Rights Society (ARS), New York/ADAGP, Paris.

Many famous writers, musicians, actors and directors of the day visited or had residences in the Grossmont art colony. This is where they relaxed and got away from the rigors of their demanding careers. Even in this relaxed atmosphere, they were so enamored with their surroundings, they felt committed to give back to the community. "Always ready to help a cause with a personal

Above: Grossmont Inn near La Mesa, California. Courtesy of San Diego Histoty Center, San Diego, California. Right: 1948 postcard of Lily Pond Lagoon, Balboa Park, San Diego, California, 1948 postcard. Collection of the Author.

appearance, money or their work, they took an active role in the life of San Diego."

Eventually, Blanche, Saidie and Al rented a house next door to the legendary diva, Madame Schumann-Heink. This famed Wagnerian soprano hoped to surround herself with many of the rich and famous celebrities living in California, and she encouraged the ones she knew to settle there. Such figures as Zane Grey and Carrie Jacobs-Bond spent some time there.

Saidie also wished to support the community. The La Jolla Art Center had just been formed and she was excited about the prospect of helping them get established, especially in the area of French Modern Art. She fell in love with a superb Rubens painting in the small collection, commenting about the joy it brought her to view it, and how she felt strongly about repaying the gallery by adding her own touch to its collection.[31] Along with Baltimore Museum of Art, Saidie adopted the Fine Arts Gallery of San Diego in Balboa Park (it later shortened its name to the San Diego Art Museum).

The Fine Arts Gallery of San Diego

At the end of September, Blanche headed back to Baltimore. Saidie and Al stayed on in San Diego to paint. When the trunk of art from Paris arrived at the New York apartment in September, the artworks were picked up by curators from MOMA. A month went by before Alfred Barr wrote to Saidie in Baltimore concerning the donation. He declined Saidie's bust. (Sometime later he changed his mind and requested to have another casting done to add to their collection of Despiau

sculptural heads, but Saidie declined). In her letter on November 13, 1934, she asked Alfred Barr to ship her rejected donations from MOMA directly to the Fine Arts Gallery of San Diego for their collection. Included among those were her bust by Despiau and the landscape that she had painted.[32]

Now Saidie had a completely different venue for the latest works she had purchased. She had spent quite a lot of time corresponding with Alfred Barr in order to place her collections in the appropriate places. It was important to her, knowing how the artists worked, to have their paintings in the right settings. Depending on where in Europe the paintings were painted, what kind of feeling they had and what type of light they represented, she wanted them to "fit in." Things that had an "East Coast appeal" would not be placed in San Diego. Works which she felt had a "desert feel or light" she offered to San Diego to complement their collection of local work. She wrote to Alfred Barr about her strong feelings towards this aim.

Barr was still dissatisfied with the Friesz paintings which Saidie had sent, and asked her to help in exchanging what she purchased for another painting from the period between 1910–1915. There were quite a few letters back and forth between them. Barr hammered Saidie about getting the "finest example" of Friesz's work that was available. He was not happy with any of the works which she sent to him, and finally, out of frustration, she offered them to the San Diego Museum. She asked for *Three Figures near a Lake (Bathers)*, the small nude and *Landscape with Quarry* (1928) to be sent from MOMA to San Diego.

By December 1934, Barr wrote to Saidie again, this time asking her to try and procure Friesz's large 1910 nude for the museum. Saidie conceded and sent a note to Friesz, indicating that MOMA was interested in the painting, *Spring*, for which he was willing to exchange the big nude for 12,000 francs (at that time this would approximate $800.00). Saidie asked Barr to send back Friesz's *Landscape with Figures* (1909) in exchange for *Spring*, since she wouldn't invest in any more of Friesz's work at that time. This deal was never accomplished. MOMA kept the *Landscape with Figures* (1909) as part of its permanent collection.

Notes

1 "Fauvism," WebMuseum, Paris http://www.ibiblio.org/wm/paint/tl/20th/fauvism/html.

2 "Art Periods-Fauvism," http:/www.discoverfrance.net/France/Art/fauvism/shtml.

3 Jean Louis Ferrier, *The Fauves, the Reign of Color* (Paris: Terrail, 1995) 59.

4 Lee Hall, *Betty Parsons, Artist, Dealer, Collector* (New York: Harry N. Abrams, 1991), 33.

5 Alfred Jensen to Jane Cone, May 27, 1972. Saidie A. May Papers, BMA.

6 *The Documents of Twentieth Century Art*, "My Galleries and Painters" by Daniel Henry Kahnweiler with Francis Cremieux, 1971, Thames & Hudson, 61.

7 *Ibid.,* 62

8 Canceled check to Charles Despiau, February 2, 1931, Saidie A. May Papers, BMA.

9 Alfred Jensen to Jane Cone, May 27, 1972. Saidie A. May Papers, BMA.

10 M. Despiau to Saidie A. May, Paris, March, 1934. Saidie A. May Papers, BMA.

11 Bill of Sale for Russian Icons, November 17, 1932. Saidie A. May Papers, BMA.

12 A. Conger Goodyear to Saidie A. May, January 18, 1933. Alfred Hamilton Barr Papers, Archives of American Art, SI.

13 Saidie A. May to Mr. Alan Blackburn, Jr., January 25, 1933. Saidie A. May Papers, BMA.

14 Regina Schreck, Assoc. Registrar, Detroit Art Institute, Interview by the author, 2008, (*Figure Composition*, 1908, by Othon Friesz, was deacessioned in 2005).

15 Blanche Adler to Bertel Speier, July 30, 1933, Collection Evelyn Held, Baltimore, MD.

16 Paul Gardner to Saidie A. May, August 27, 1936, Saidie A. May Papers, BMA.

17 Jean Louis Ferrier, *The Fauves, the Reign of Color* (Paris: Terrail, 1995), 162.

18 Saidie A. May to Alfred Barr, May 19, 1934. Saidie A. May Papers, BMA.

19 Aristide Maillol to Saidie A. May, June 23 & 24, 1934. Saidie A. May Papers, BMA.

20 Saidie A. May to Alfred Barr, June 18, 1934. Saidie A. May Papers, BMA.

21 *Ibid.*

22 *Ibid.*

23 Informal list of Modern Paintings in the Saidie A. May Collection, Saidie A. May Papers, BMA.

24 Art & Artists, "Martin O'Brien", http://travelintelligence.net/wsd/articles/art_185.html-63k.

25 Pierre Brune to Saidie A. May, France, 1934. Saidie A. May Papers, BMA.

26 "Musee d'art moderne de Ceret—Historique," http://www.musee-ceret.com/mam/historique.php?page=3.

27 Blanche Adler to Bertel Speier, August 3, 1934. Collection of Evelyn Held, Baltimore, MD.

28 Franklin Toker, *Fallingwater Rising: Frank Lloyd Wright, E.J. Kaufman and America's Most Extraordinary House*, (New York: Alfred A. Knopf, 2003), 60–61.

29 Saidie A. May to Alfred Barr, November 4, 1934. Saidie A. May Papers, BMA.

30 Kathleen Crawford, "God's Garden: The Grossmont Art Colony," *The Journal of San Diego History*, 31:4 (Fall 1985), http:/sandiegohistory.org/journal/85fall/gardenimages.htm.

31 Saidie A. May to Alfred Barr, December 20, 1934. Saidie A. May Papers, BMA.

32 Saidie A. May to Alfred Barr, November 13, 1934. Saidie A. May Papers, BMA.

A Daring Rescue, 1934–1938

During her trips to Europe, Blanche made sure to visit the Adler relatives in Frankfurt. She became close to her cousins, and frequently sent the families postcards from her travels. She had a particular fondness for the wife of her first cousin, Jeanette Speier.

During the mid-1930's, Saidie started buying art specifically for the purpose of donating to museum collections. She continued to favor the Museum of Modern Art in New York, but she also started to give things to the Baltimore Museum of Art, a pattern that would continue for over twenty years. Saidie donated well over one thousand items to the Baltimore Museum alone, from Egyptian antiquities to jewelry, textiles, sculpture, paintings, drawings and many fine art books.

While in Paris, Saidie commissioned three different portraits of herself, one sculpture by Despiau in 1933, an oil by Giorgio de Chirico, painted between 1932 and 1933, and another oil by Émile Othon Friesz, started after 1934. Saidie offered the de Chirico to MOMA in 1934, referring to it in a letter to Alfred Barr as it "being neither fish nor fowl." She added: "I don't think much of it, and was considering painting over it myself, to put the canvas to better use."[1]

Acquisition Philosophy

Blanche and Saidie were aware that the Cone sisters were thinking about leaving their entire collection of Impressionist work to the Baltimore Museum, and were careful to not purchase items that would compete with the Cones' collection. Their strategy was to focus on works from the first half of the twentieth century, to continue the museum's collection from the Cones' Impressionist work through Cubism, Surrealism, and the beginnings of the Modern Art movement in America.

Bertel and Clare Speier in Germany, c. 1934. Collection of Evelyn Held.

A Portrait of the Artist

When Saidie wasn't collecting or donating, she was painting. She adored painting, and she and Al worked in any nearby studio they could find. In terms of collecting, she was always adamant that "a work of art, though bought by a person or institution, actually belongs to the public for study and enjoyment through the years."[2]

In 1935, Blanche ventured 3,000 miles to California to spend another summer with her favorite sister. This time, she and Saidie headed east on a motor trip through Yosemite Park, deep into the mountains. As they traveled, Saidie and Blanche continued to send postcards from their colorful trips to the young children of their German cousins.[3] The two sisters visited some Native American reservations, where they found the crafts very interesting. They purchased antique Native American jewelry and beadwork to add to their collections.

The La Jolla Art Center

During the winter of 1934, Saidie had loaned paintings from her collection to the La Jolla Art Center for two exhibits. Some of these works had been rejected from the group she had sent to the Museum of Modern Art. A few other paintings, prints, drawings, sculptures and books related to art were donated to the La Jolla Art Center directly in 1935. The local San Diego newspaper reported on her philanthropy and described a room in the small museum as "Mrs. May's room." It was filled with the colorful works she lent them.[4] Saidie worked closely with curator Freda Klapp, who introduced her to a fellow artist, Elise Donaldson. From this meeting, Saidie began to mentor this younger woman.[5] Elise Donaldson was the adopted daughter of Rachelle Slobodinsky Yarros and Victor S. Yarros. Dr. Rachelle was a well-known physician and medical reformer around the turn of the century, and her husband, Victor, a journalist and anarchistic writer, was a critic of the judicial system in the United States.[6] Elise had been born in Elkridge, Maryland, and over the years made her way to California via Chicago, where her mother went to teach at the University of Illinois. Elise studied at Bryn Mawr College and the Art Institute of Chicago before moving to the San Diego area. Saidie, Al and Elise became very close as friends and as artists. Elise even painted a watercolor portrait of Saidie which she subsequently gave to the La Jolla Art Center.[7]

Reginald Poland, the director of the La Jolla Art Center, was actively courting potential donors, but Saidie and Al were not among them. Instead, he sought the financial support of two sisters, the Putnams', for their money and interest in the museum. Every time a new painting was acquired or an authority on art visited, Poland would personally invite them to participate in the activities surrounding those events. He did not take the same interest in Saidie and Al, and this annoyed Saidie.

A newly hired curator, Julia Gethman Andrews, was assigned to work with the artworks in "Mrs. May's room." Andrews was interested in modern works of art and took it upon herself to learn all she could about Saidie's collection. The museum took part in the California Pacific

Elise Donaldson, Saidie A. May and Alfred Jensen, La Jolla, California, Winter, 1936–1937, Collection of Regina Bogat Jensen, Glen Ridge, New Jersey.

International Exposition, held in Balboa Park from February 12 to September 19, 1936. Their large exhibition of artworks and local crafts was held in the Palace of Fine Arts building at the center of the Exposition. Five works from Saidie's collection were chosen to add to the museum's display, including Raoul Dufy's *Promenade*, 1913, Georges Rouault's 1928 collotype *The Dictator*, *The Favorite*, Maurice de Vlaminck's *Factory*, and Othon Friesz's *The Creek*. Another work she lent the museum in 1935, André Derain's *Head of a Girl*, 1928 was also requested for display in the show. Julia Gethman Andrews hung the works in that particular gallery devoted to the School of France.

One day while in La Jolla, Saidie came into the gallery and saw Julia working. As Julia was contemplating where to hang things, Saidie addressed her "I have stopped donating to this museum because I feel completely neglected." Julia stopped what she was doing and walked over to Saidie. "In what way?" she asked. "I have not been shown the courtesies that I feel my position in the art world demands. I am a rich woman, and since I have been involved with this museum, the director has not made me aware of new acquisitions, nor has he included me in any programs where art authorities came to look at the collections." Julia countered, "But Walter Pach, the great American art historian raved about the Derain *Tête de Fille (Head of a Girl)*, which you so generously gave us at the beginning of this year. He said that it was one of the finest Derains in this country." "I never heard that," Saidie replied.[8] Even though Mrs. Andrews tried to pacify her, Saidie was not convinced of the museum's sincerity.

The Exposition

At the beginning of June 1936, Blanche took the train from Baltimore to visit and Saidie invited her to attend the Exposition with her to see the works she had donated. Together they toured the park, filled with flowering shrubs and trees, offering up a palette of exquisite sights and smells. Most of the buildings were light-colored stucco, with a Moorish accent. Each was embellished with different columns, pedestals, lintels and decorative architectural elements. The sisters felt like they were in a dreamworld.

The Palace of Fine Arts

Through a maze of color, Saidie directed her sister to the Palace of Fine Arts. The aim of this exhibit was to encourage everyone to see the La Jolla Art Center as a friendly, fun and interesting place to visit. It was mainly concerned with the display of painting, sculpture and crafts. As the two walked into the foyer, they were greeted with sixteenth- and seventeenth-century panel paintings, tapestries and wood sculpture. Along with these was an ancient chest of Cordova leather and *varguenos*, (Spanish decorative desks, heavily carved and inlaid with ivory). Two separate galleries to the right were devoted to the art of Mexico, with prints and paintings by the well-known Mexican artists of the day. There were also superb examples of Mexican folk art to study and compare with the art by the European-trained Mexican masters such as Diego Rivera and José-Clemente Orozco.

Across the rotunda was the gallery of Far Eastern art, with many antiquities and religious artifacts, transitioning to the adjacent gallery showing works from the School of France. Many of these Impressionist and Fauvist works reflected themes and shapes seen in the previous galleries, but possessing a more human, communicative quality.[9] Blanche was impressed with the display of Saidie's collection in that gallery. After studying the pieces for a while, the two meandered upstairs to the large gallery devoted to American work. Early, important work by painters such as Winslow Homer and James Whistler were followed by contemporary works by Mary Cassatt and Arthur B. Davies. The room beyond contained the Old Masters' works from Europe, such as Rembrandts and El Grecos. Walking down from these galleries to the rotunda, the two were met with American sculpture: Gaston Lachaise and the younger Harold Cash. The two had a relaxing day together, and Blanche found it very pleasant and informative to look at works from a new museum. Quite

Saidie A. May (left) and Blanche Adler (right) leaving the Palace of Fine Arts, San Diego Exposition, 1936. Collection of Evelyn Held.

innocently, a street photographer recorded this excursion as the two were leaving the building, and sold the picture to the sisters as a souvenir. Blanche was happy to have this memento of a wonderful day spent with her sister. She then returned to Baltimore.

Depression, Europe and the War

The effects of the severe economic crisis of the 1930s, the Great Depression, were far reaching and would eventually spread to Europe. In addition to economic downturn in Europe, there was also political upheaval. Thus far the Adlers' family wealth had insulated them from these problems and Saidie and Blanche remained committed to the museums with which they formed relationships. But travel in Europe was becoming more frightening, in France and especially in Germany, where their cousins lived. Each sister dealt with the problem in their own unique way, Blanche worked with family matters, and Saidie helped a close friend and important French Surrealist artist, André Masson.

Cousins Jeanette and Moritz Speier: A Plan of Escape

Blanche and Saidie had two first cousins in Germany with whom Blanche had become particularly close. She regularly corresponded with Jeanette and Moritz Speier and always sent postcards from her travels to their girls, starting as early as 1923. Blanche became concerned for their family's safety when she learned that the situation in Germany was becoming more and more threatening for the Jewish population there. She wanted to try to get her German relatives out while there was still time. She wrote to Moritz and Jeanette, offering to sponsor their two daughters to come to America by boat, and live in Baltimore until it was safer in Germany.[10] Blanche was taking an enormous risk because she really did not know the girls, having met them only briefly. In spite of that, she was determined to do anything to help her German relatives and convinced Helen and Harry to help support the girls once they came to America.

In 1930, in the face of steadily rising unemployment, President Herbert Hoover requested that the State Department curb immigration. This was not the first time the laws were enforced to restrict immigration, but it would make it difficult for Europeans fleeing Nazi Germany to come to America. In this most recent legislation, the U.S. government reinterpreted a provision of the Immigration Act of 1917, which excluded persons likely to become public charges. Under this new interpretation, the government assumed that immigrants would be unable to find employment. Thus, immigrants either had to have enough money to support themselves without employment, or produce affidavits that relatives or friends in the United States would provide for them if they could not find work. By 1935, restrictions would be eased under the Roosevelt administration, facilitating the entry of German Jews fleeing persecution in Germany.[11]

Postcard of 14th-century house in Fritzlar, Germany, at Markt Platz (now Zwischen den Kramen) where Moritz Speier rented a second floor apartment. Collection of the author.

Most of the refugees were younger people who believed there was no future for them in Germany. Older people did not want to start over in a new country (learn new customs and languages) and had friends and family whom they did not want to leave. It was difficult to leave with the uncertainty of the Nazi government as well as getting a sponsor, waiting for clearance and frequently having plans postponed.[12] Most faced emotional anxiety about the voyage, of meeting their sponsors and the uncertainty of determining where and how they would live. Once they arrived in Baltimore, most completed their education in public schools, and when they were not studying, they worked in businesses owned by their sponsors or their sponsors' friends.[13]

Blanche as Sponsor

Blanche also sent word to another German cousin, offering to sponsor her daughter. That cousin thanked her for her generosity, but refused to part with her child. Eventually she, her daughter and husband were sent to a concentration camp and killed. Blanche was taking a huge risk herself, sponsoring German refugees. The German and the United States governments knew who the American Jewish sponsors were, and those people who helped Jews in Europe were watched and suspected.

The American public felt that the European immigrants were "wretched refuse" and they rejected most of the skilled and educated Jews of Germany.[14] They used the unemployment problem as their excuse to cover up the true reason for rejection: anti-Semitism.[15] Even so, between 1933 and 1940, 140,000 German and Austrian Jews came to the United States through American sponsorship.[16] Baltimoreans did not consider the German refugees to be inferior like the other European Jewish immigrants. Culturally, they were refined, well educated and many had been wealthy.

Blanche made the arrangements for her cousin's children through applications made to the Jewish Welfare Agency in Baltimore. The Nazi government strictly limited them to only what they could carry on their person when they left the country. As a result, most of their personal belongings stayed with their family left behind or were confiscated.[17] Each of the girls highly valued their albums full of postcards from Blanche and Saidie. As a result, these were brought with them to America.

Clare and Bertel

Moritz and Jeanette's two daughters, Clare and Bertel, left Germany on June 5, 1936, and sailed for New York on the Cunard Line's SS *Manhattan*. Blanche acquired tourist class tickets for their voyage. They arrived in New York harbor on the afternoon of June 11, and were greeted by the famous Statue of Liberty. Clare was 16 and Bertel was 23. As was the case with millions

Blanche Adler and Clare Speier, c. 1938. Collection of Evelyn Held.

of immigrants, the two were processed at the immigration center at Ellis Island. Here, Blanche met them and took them on the evening train from New York's famous Pennsylvania station to Baltimore. The girls had their first meal in America on the train. This was the first time that they had been away from their family, and this trip took them thousands of miles from home to a new land and a new, unknown family.

The girls missed home, but they were also excited about their trip to America. Blanche embraced them as if they were her own children. To her credit, Blanche's involvement extended far beyond mere sponsorship. She made all of the day-to-day arrangements for the girls, while her siblings helped pay for the children's "upkeep." Blanche generously rented an efficiency apartment for them in the basement of the Riviera Building, furnished it and bought their food and clothes.

The young girls from Germany knew a little English when they arrived, and Blanche, speaking German fluently, worked to teach them the language and customs so that they would become acclimated to their new home. The girls were well-behaved and made a good impression on the family. After three weeks, Blanche took the girls to Canada on a three-week cruise on the Saint Lawrence River, visiting Quebec, Toronto and the Chateau Frontenac, and getting to know her charges. She shared a berth with them on the boat, and taught them not to eat with a knife and fork at the same time (as they had done in the "Old Country"). On the boat, Clare celebrated her sixteenth birthday quietly, without her parents for the first time. Outwardly, Blanche seemed somewhat cold and reserved, but she was the warmest and most caring member of her family.

Six months after Clare and Bertel arrived, their brother, Norbert, was invited to come over as well. He was a few years older than Bertel, and since he and Bertel had already completed their schooling, Blanche found them jobs. Bertel worked as a secretary, and Norbert got a job in the receiving department at Gutman's, a local department store on Saratoga Street in downtown Baltimore. Blanche's good friend, Estelle Gutman, got Norbert the job through her husband, Edwin. Blanche enrolled the youngest sister, Clare, at Western High School.

Early Sunday evenings, the children were expected to go upstairs to join Helen, Bob and Blanche for a formal family dinner. Dressed in their best clothes, they boarded the elevator exactly at 4:30 p.m. Riding to the top floor of the building, they stood quietly, staring at the ornately inlaid floor. They then walked down a long, carpeted hallway to the last door on the left. Hesitantly, Norbert lifted the thick, brass knocker on the heavy oak door. It hit the door with a thud. The three waited quietly. A minute went by before they heard shuffling from behind the door. As the right side of the door slowly pulled back, a soft triangle of light expanded from around the edge of the door, growing larger as the door receded. A slight, uniformed black female figure appeared from behind the door. This was Little Kate. She let the three pass through the doorway, and as they entered the hexagonal foyer, they were enveloped in the mouth-watering aroma of roast turkey and gravy.

An Introduction to Elegance

As the three newcomers cautiously made their way from the foyer to the parlor on the right, they saw two adults, already planted in their stiff, tall gothic chairs. "Hello children," the adults spoke in German, "Come in and have a seat." Helen was on her throne. The chair was so large that she had to perch her tiny body onto the seat by stepping onto a stool placed in front. Helen presided as if she were "holding court," with husband Bob on one side and sister Blanche on the sofa opposite Bob. The three were sharing hors d'oeuvres and drinks before the Sunday meal.

The family sat and talked while waiting for dinner to be served. A sterling silver plate of dainty finger sandwiches sat on a small table in the middle of the group. Each adult held a cut-crystal highball glass with a clear, chestnut-colored liquid inside of it. The young adults were motioned to sit on the sofa near Blanche. They sat quietly as the adults continued to talk. Blanche picked up the plate and offered the small sandwiches to each of them. Within a few minutes, George the butler, a tall, thin black man, came into the room and announced, "Dinner is served." The group adjourned to the dining room.

Dinner was elegant and formal. The large, heavy furniture in the parlor and dining room were imposing, especially for tiny Clare, who appeared much younger than her age. Kate the cook had prepared an elaborate meal. The massive dining table was set with a crisp white linen tablecloth covered with sparkling silver and fine china. It was as if the family was entertaining royalty. Bob sat at the head of the table, with Blanche at his left. Helen sat at the foot, and the children were in between. Wearing a tuxedo and white gloves, the butler carried large sterling silver trays from the kitchen, full of hot, aromatic food. He offered the platter of food to each person, and served their portion with a large, bright sterling spoon that reflected light from the crystal chandelier overhead. Tonight Kate fixed a fresh turkey for dinner, and George sliced the meat and laid the skin back over it before bringing it out. When he presented it, no one even knew that the turkey had been cut, its crisp, brown skin glistening from hours of basting. Kate also baked a fruit pie for dessert, with a sweet flaky crust, the perfect complement to the tangy fruit inside. These Sunday night dinners were routine, the most family-oriented affair that the stiff Germanic Adlers' would conduct. On occasion, Harry and other members of the family would come over to visit for the afternoon and stay for dinner.[18] After dinner was finished, the three were free to leave.

In the evenings after dinner, Blanche and Helen would sit together in the sun parlor and listen to their favorite radio program, "Information Please: the Great Radio Program for the Intellectual Set," broadcast from May 1938 on and off through 1951.[19] Its producer, Dan Golenpaul, envisioned an intellectual program to educate the public on current events, science, politics and any other interesting topics of the day. This idea was his response to his dissatisfaction with the mediocre, "rigged" quiz programs currently on the airwaves. His panel of four contestants consisted of authorities on many different subjects, with one celebrity. This program helped to bond Blanche's relationship with Helen, and gave them food for thought for conversations during the daily dinners together. This was the only public radio program that Blanche would listen to.

Blanche once took Clare and Bertel to visit her cousin, Etta Cone, who had amassed a fabulous collection of paintings and sculpture by Pierre Matisse and other Impressionists with her sister, Claribel. She lived at the Marlborough Apartments, about a block from Blanche and Helen's building. Blanche, Saidie and Helen would visit Etta Cone when they were in town, and were familiar with the fact that they had collected this "new" modern form of art, and with their own interest in collecting, they enjoyed discussing the collection with Etta. On this particular afternoon, Blanche wanted Etta to meet the children she had sponsored. They were greeted cordially and visited together for a few hours. The Cones' apartment was furnished in a similar style to the Adlers', except that Clare vividly remembered the bathroom being filled with unusually bright paintings hung all over the walls from floor to ceiling.[20]

All during the period when Blanche was involved with her cousin's family's escape to the United States, she continued to work diligently with Adelyn Breeskin in the Prints and Drawings department. She kept in contact with the art dealers in New York whom she had patronized for years, and had them send newly acquired works to the museum for donation. Blanche was also instrumental in courting other members of the BMA, recommending that they leave their collections to the museum. As a result, the Print Department received the Lucas collection in 1933 and the Riggs collection (after Blanche's death) in 1943.

Eventually, the Speier children were able to sponsor their parents, Moritz and Jeanette to leave Germany and join their family in Baltimore. None of them ever returned to Germany. Even though she never married nor had any children of her own, Blanche was the most family-oriented of the siblings. She was caring and generous to other members of the Frank and Adler families. In 1938, she gave her niece a gift of $5,000 to pay for her first home for her new family in Mt. Washington, an affluent area in northwest Baltimore. Blanche's personality was quite different from her other siblings, more like the Frank side of the family: quiet, reserved, studious and intelligent.

Blanche had a much closer relationship with Saidie than she did with Helen, even though Saidie lived out of town. They liked each other, and loved learning about and collecting art. Blanche was about five feet tall, a few inches taller than Saidie, but Saidie made up for her stature by laughing a lot. She was bubbly, vivacious and lots of fun to be with.

Notes

1 Saidie A. May to Alfred Barr, December 20, 1934, Saidie A. May Archives, BMA.

2 Reginald Poland to Saidie A. May, January 13, 1935, San Diego Fine Arts Museum Archives, San Diego, Calif.

3 Blanche Adler to Bertel Speier, July 2, 1935, Collection of Evelyn Held, Baltimore, MD.

4 Messenger, Ivan, *San Diego Art and Artists*, 1935.

5 Lasch, Christopher, *Notable American Women Vol. III, Rachelle Slobodinsky Yarros 1869–1946*, Radcliffe College, 1971.

6 Peterson, Martin E., Telephone Conversation with Elise Donaldson, May 18, 1979, San Diego Museum of Art Library.

7 Donaldson, Elise, *Portrait of Mrs. Saidie A. May*, 1948, watercolor, 1982:84. Bequest of the Artist, San Diego Museum of Art.

8 Oral Interview with Julia Gethman Andrews, May 15, 1979, San Diego Historical Society Oral History Program, San Diego, Calif.

9 "San Diego's Second Year," Andrews, Julia Gethman, *The American Magazine of Art*, Vol. 29, #6, June, 1936, The American Federation of Arts, Washington, D.C., 386–422.

10 Blanche Adler to Bertel Speier, November 30, 1934, Collection Evelyn Held, Baltimore, MD.

11 Wyman, Davis S., *Paper Walls—America and the Refugee Crisis*, 1968, University of Massachusetts Press, 4.

12 Kahn, Philip Jr., *Uncommon Threads—Threads that Wove the Fabric of Baltimore Jewish Life*, 1996, Pecan Publications, Baltimore, MD, 207.

13 *Ibid.*

14 O'Neill, William L., *A Democracy at War, America's Fight at Home and Abroad in World War II*, 1993, Harvard University Press, U.S.A.

15 Wyman, Davis S., *Paper Walls—America and the Refugee Crisis,* 1968, University of Massachusetts Press, 3.

16 Kahn, Philip Jr., *Uncommon Threads—Threads that Wove the Fabric of Baltimore Jewish Life*, 1996, Pecan Publications, Baltimore, MD, 205.

17 Interview with Clare Spier Baer, July 4, 1999, Baltimore, MD.

18 *Ibid.*

19 Kahn, Philip Jr., *Uncommon Threads—Threads that Wove the Fabric of Baltimore Jewish Life*, 1996, Pecan Publications, Baltimore, MD, 207.

20 Dunning, John, *On the Air, the Encyclopedia of Old-Time Radio*, 1998, Oxford University Press, New York.

Moving On, 1935–1938

A few days after Blanche left, Saidie came back to the Palace of Fine Arts, entering the room where her paintings were hanging. Julia was giving a lecture about the works to a local women's group. She turned around, and when she saw Saidie she stopped and introduced her as the benefactor of these works. Saidie announced: "Take a good look at these paintings, girls, because I'm taking them all back, every one of them." The women's mouths dropped. She continued: "I have been shown no courtesy by this museum of any kind, and this is, in a way, the first recognition of my interest in art. And it'll be your last chance." The group was shocked at this frank outburst. "They haven't even published any of my works in the articles written by the staff."

Julia then rushed out of the room, leaving the group hanging, and grabbed the latest issue of the *American Magazine of Art*. Returning, Julia exclaimed, "This is the leading magazine on art, and here is the first article that I have had published concerning this fine painting by Derain that you have given this museum." Saidie beamed with pleasure and said, "I will give this painting to the gallery." Then Julia continued, "We have announced the opinion of one of our best critics in the United States that this is the best Derain in our country, and we were very proud to be able to show it." Saidie turned to Julia, "I want you to present this painting as a gift from me to the Fine Arts Gallery board at their next meeting." Julia was happy that she had appeased Saidie, and that she would also finally get some recognition for all of her hard work. Later that day, she went to Reginald Poland with the great news.

Of course, Reginald Poland had no interest in crediting Julia's work, and announced the acquisition himself to the board. The board members were pleased by the news. Afterwards, Saidie had the rest of the paintings loaned to the art center shipped back to the Baltimore Museum of Art, and she discontinued her involvement with the San Diego Fine Arts Gallery.

Portrait of Blanche Adler by Saidie Adler May, 1937, 21 x 25 in. Collection of Phyllis Cahn Meyerhoff.

Eastward Bound

Saidie decided to leave the West for home and invited her new friend, Elise Donaldson, to accompany her and Al to the East. On September 29, 1936, the three boarded a train for Los Angeles and on to Baltimore for a month where they visited Saidie's family and friends and tied up loose ends at the BMA. By this time, Blanche had become indispensable at the museum and was elected vice president of the BMA's board of trustees.

Afterwards, Saidie, Al and Elise ventured to New York for a while, attending a retrospective exhibition of Joan Miró's work at the Pierre Matisse Gallery. In this exhibit, Pierre Matisse had a collection of Miró's paintings spanning his career from 1918 through 1936. Saidie purchased *Figures Attracted by the Shape of a Mountain* (1936),[1] which she eventually gave to the BMA.

Art Class

In Paris, many artists were supplementing their income by opening small art schools and teaching what they practiced. Such was the case with André Lhote, a Cubist painter who taught painting and sculpture in his atelier. In the spring of 1937, Saidie, Elise and Al traveled to Paris to study art at Lhote's school in Montparnasse. Lhote spoke limited English, so Elise attempted to be his interpreter for the group, even though her French was limited.[2] Lhote held a morning and afternoon class, and quite a few American artists attended, including Conrad Fulke O'Brien-ffrench, Arthur Secunda, Christian Title of California and others. Artist John O'Leary was from Ireland. Since Lhote was a better teacher than artist and stimulated his students to push beyond their limits, both of his classes were always full of students.

One entered Lhote's two-story studio through an alleyway. Everyone enjoyed the "Parisian bohemian" environment in these classes, although Lhote's wife hated the fact that he and his mistress were cavorting with his students.

Montreux

At the beginning of the summer, Blanche accompanied the trio to Switzerland to a seaside resort in Montreux on Lake Geneva. While there, Saidie painted a watercolor portrait of Blanche which she later used as the basis for an oil portrait of her sister. By July, the party was off to Lucerne for a month and then back to France for six weeks before heading to New York by boat. Blanche then took the train back to Baltimore and resumed her duties as the BMA's vice president of the board of trustees, (the only woman on the board), with Philip Perlman (a close family friend) presiding as the museum's executive vice president. A print committee was formed to consult on policies and procedures for the department and Blanche participated with that as well.[3] She had a very full schedule as a volunteer at the museum.

Alfred Jensen, Saidie A. May, Blanche Adler and unknown others, Montreaux, Switzerland, June, 1937. Collection of Regina Bogat Jensen, Glen Ridge, New Jersey.

A Return to Europe

In October, Saidie, Al and Elise returned to Europe. They spent some time in Amsterdam before heading south to Paris for the winter months to study painting with Lhote again. Saidie worked on converting her watercolor portrait of Blanche into a full oil painting in the Impressionistic style as a gift for Blanche. This painting was then packed in a large box of artworks and gifts for the BMA, including a pastel of Mary Cassatt in a fine, genuine Louis XIII frame, valued at $450.[4] Saidie's attention was drawn to another young artist whom she admired, Tal-Coat, a painter from Brittany. She described him as looking "like a sailor, tall, blue-eyed and blond, but shy, sensitive and very serious." Born in 1905 as Pierre Louis Corentin Jacob, he later took the pseudonym "Tal-Coat," a Breton term meaning "wooden forehead." A self-taught artist, he devoted himself to painting, drawing and sculpture.[5] In 1924, he worked as a porcelain painter in the Faïence factory at Quimper, but a year later he was called to Paris for military service.

In Paris, Tal-Coat was drawn into the artistic circles that Saidie and Al frequented. When they first met him, his paintings were experiments with whites, browns, grays and blacks. One day, Al told him about Matisse and his use of color, and the next year Tal-Coat began incorporating more vivid colors into his work. Saidie purchased a sculpture of a head from him.[6] Tal-Coat joined the artist's group, Forces Nouvelles, and in 1935 he took part in their first exhibition at the Galerie Billiet-Vormes.

Pierre Jacob Tal-Coat, French, 1905–1985, *Gertrude Stein*, 1937, oil on canvas, 29 x 23-1/8 in. (73.7 x 58.8 cm), The Baltimore Museum of Art: Bequest of Saidie A. May, BMA 1951.360. ©2011 Artists Rights Society (ARS), New York/ADAGP, Paris.

According to Saidie, he wanted to make a name for himself in the art world, so he used photographs of well-known individuals in Paris to paint from, including Gertrude Stein. He had not met Stein when he executed her portrait, and Saidie doubted whether he ever did meet her, although he painted a series of portraits of her.[7] Some paintings were large, using the vivid colors he was experimenting with. Saidie purchased one of these portraits from him in 1937 for $90. Another portrait of Gertrude Stein won him the Prix Paul Guillaume.

After that prestigious event, Tal-Coat became friendly with Francis Gruber, who worked in Miserabliste painting, a French style characterized as intimate and melancholy. Gruber had been more imaginative with his work in his early years, but then began painting models and still lifes after 1933, incorporating his sadness and anti-war feelings into the subject matter. Tal-Coat also met Alberto Giacometti, whose portrait he later painted. One day Al stopped in to Tal-Coat's studio while he was working on that portrait, and was so impressed with it that he told Saidie about it later that afternoon.

Between 1936 and 1937, Tal-Coat assimilated the influence of Picasso in a series of paintings concerning the Spanish Civil War, entitled *Massacres*. In 1938, Saidie purchased his *Woman with Disheveled Hair* and *Birds*, oil painted on a wooden panel. She gave both of these paintings and the Gertrude Stein portrait to the Baltimore Museum of Art.

By the 1940s, Tal-Coat became a revivalist of landscape painting. He worked with André Masson at Aix-en-Provence. In his painting *Sur la Table,* he worked with broad brushwork and fluid outline drawing in the style of Matisse. During his regular extended visits to Aix-en-Provence between the 1940s and 1950s, Tal-Coat began to adopt a more vigorously geometric framework for his compositions, reminiscent of Paul Cézanne's painting. An example of that style was *Rooster and Hen in the Studio* (1946).

The Surrealist Exposition

During one of Lhote's classes, there was a discussion of a new controversial exhibit that had recently opened on January 17. The 1938 Exposition Internationale de Surrealism had been installed by the famous artist, Marcel Duchamp, and the show was creating quite a stir![8] Saidie had to see it, so the next day she took Al and Elise to get a firsthand look at this unique art exhibition, where visitors had to view many of the works by flashlight! They had never seen anything like the art in this quirky show and were excited and intrigued by the modern ideas they observed.

In the summer months, Lhote and many of his students would hop a boat to the Isle of Capri, Italy, to paint the unique landscape there. This tradition continued for a few years during the late 1930s. After the spring 1938 session ended, Elise Donaldson parted company with Saidie and headed back to the States because of the war. Saidie and Al accompanied Lhote's group to Capri to paint.

As students, Saidie and Al studied traditional painting but also sought to learn modern techniques. The nineteenth-century painter Eugène Delacroix once wrote of his own struggle to be modern. The problem as he saw it, was how to keep the freshness of a first sketch when making a final, finished painting. Pablo Picasso had learned an old weaver's trick from his father: pinning a paper pattern to a half-finished canvas. This was an old, formal means for academic painters to build a painting. According to Picasso: "Cut-and-pasted paper was a way for a painter to conceptualize his work."[9]

André Masson

In the beginning of April, 1938, Saidie and Al became interested in the work of André Masson and went to visit him at his studio. At this time, Masson was being represented and supported by Daniel-Henry Kahnweiler, a pioneering German Jewish dealer in Modern art, working in Paris. His business, Galerie Simon, dealt exclusively in Modern European works, especially those of Pablo Picasso.

Kahnweiler had started his shop in Paris a couple of years before World War I. At that time, Picasso had suggested to him that he become a French citizen, since he was married to a French woman and his business was in France. Kahnweiler decided against this advice. He had already performed his national service in his native Germany and didn't want to serve again, especially with World War I looming.

At the outbreak of the war, Kahnweiler's possessions were sequestered, and all of the pictures in his gallery and personal collection were auctioned off. The most important works he lost were Picasso's Cubist work painted between 1911 and 1914. Kahnweiler then fled Paris and hid during the war. When he returned, most of his stable of Cubist artists had abandoned him for other galleries.[10]

Daniel-Henry Kahnweiler met André Masson in 1921, when Masson was living in a furnished room in the Hotel Becquerel on the Rue Vieuville in Montmartre, before he moved to 45 Rue

Blomet. The artist Joan Miró lived next door to Masson.[11] Masson knew almost all of the painters in Montmartre and was, along with philosopher André Breton, an intimate part of the Surrealist circle.[12] Kahnweiler's brother-in law, Elie Lascaux, also lived near the Massons. Through a "coincidence" arranged by Max Jacob and Lascaux, Kahnweiler came to visit Lascaux's studio, where he saw two paintings by Masson hanging on the wall. Kahnweiler, impressed with these works, approached Masson about representing him.[13] Caught in financial difficulty himself at this time, Kahnweiler couldn't offer a lot, but his meager offer gave Masson the means to devote himself to painting.

Masson was born January 4, 1896, in the village of Balagny in the region of Senlisis, in the heart of the old royal domain of France, home to generations of his family. Masson and his two other siblings lived there for seven years. Surrounding them were abundant ponds, fresh rivers, fertile fields and rich forests of the Ile-de-France, scenes that would be painted by Corot, Monet and other Barbizon and Impressionist painters. Having experienced this lush environment as a child, Masson was inspired to a lifelong, passionate love of nature.[14]

As an adult, Masson moved his young family to Rue Blomet, and he found their residence to be an absolutely miserable studio. Next door was a factory that ran all day and shook the studio. Everything moved until evening, when the machines finally stopped running. Masson's first wife and daughter spent more time with the Kahnweilers because the sanitary conditions in the studio were so poor.[15]

The artist Max Jacob was also part of this artistic group. He held court at the Café Savoyard in Montmartre, a bohemian quarter of Paris that drew many of the French Surrealist painters and writers: "not at all a group, but a melting pot of friendships."[16] Ernest Hemingway frequently stopped by. Hemingway, Gertrude Stein and Armand Salacrou were among the first patrons of Masson's work. The young painters and poets who gathered in the Rue Blomet made the studio a place of impassioned intellectual discussion.[17]

Saidie and Al started dealing with Galerie Simon early in 1938, and she made her first purchase of Masson's work from there. Kahnweiler gave her Masson's address and sent them to see him. Saidie and Al stayed with the Massons at his studio in the rural town of Lyons-la-Forêt for three days. They found him working vigorously on paintings which had been started, but were unfinished, since he had gone to London for a while to exhibit some of his work in a show there.[18] One of these paintings was entitled *In the Tower of Sleep*, a painting that he claimed "resumed all my experience in the dream and metamorphic sense." The painting was so paroxysmal that he put it aside for three weeks before going back to "dominate it and bring it to good conclusion." He felt the painting embodied both "invention and technique," and that may have been the reason that he was afraid of it, something that summed up a past experience and which exploded that experience.[19]

In the early months of 1938, Al and André Masson both had an avid interest in the theories of Goethe on color and nature.[20] They spent many hours during their visit conversing on the subject.

André Masson, French, 1896–1987, *In The Tower of Sleep*, 1938, oil on canvas, 32 x 39-1/2 in. (81.3 x 100.3 cm), The Baltimore Museum of Art: Bequest of Saidie A. May, BMA 1951.329. ©2011 Artists Rights Society (ARS), New York/ADAGP, Paris.

Another interest between the two men and Saidie concerned artist Juan Gris' conception of the primordial function of life. Masson had been a pupil of Juan Gris.[21] According to Al, the subject was one which they would not stop from pushing further and further.

Masson was extraordinarily perceptive and widely read.[22] Saidie and Al also spent a lot of their time reading aloud to each other. Masson told them that his greatest influences were the writings of Nietzsche and Heraclitus. He had discovered Nietzsche at the age of seventeen, and said that he fell from the sky to give him birth, that before encountering the thought of Nietzsche, his own thought did not exist.[23] Saidie and Al had also found his writings inspiring. Heraclitus believed that metamorphosis was the reconciliation of the opposites and hidden realities. He taught that: "The knowledge of Logos is not given to all men, but only to those with the ability to look inside themselves to read the signs delivered by the senses and also to look within themselves to fathom the secrets of the soul." The obvious Surrealist equivalent for Logos was desire or love.[24]

Between 1924 and 1928, Masson was intimately linked with Surrealism through his friendship with André Breton. In his automatic drawings and sand paintings from that period, he combined opposing elements with a psychological unity, filling his work with semi-abstract imagery.[25]

Saidie and Al were excited over the painting *In the Tower of Sleep*, and bought it immediately, donating it to the BMA. According to Masson, it was during this visit that Saidie first suggested he travel to America.[26] Masson's work was considered to be "degenerate art" by the Nazis and, as a result, he was on their list of "subversive intellectuals." She strongly urged him and his second wife who was Jewish, and their two young sons, to leave as soon as possible, pledging her financial support for their trip. Masson would not hear of it. Soon after that Masson was contacted by his longtime friend, Ernest Hemingway, to join him in Key West, Florida, an offer which he also declined.[27]

After this visit, Saidie and Al sailed back to the U.S. Meanwhile, on a weekend trip to New York, Blanche purchased three Walt Disney original colored drawings, "cels," for the BMA. They were animated characters from his movie, *Snow White*: *Dopey*, *Snow White Baking a Pie* and *Snow White Dancing with the Seven Dwarves*.

The Renaissance Room

On April 21, 1938, Saidie and Al arrived in Baltimore to start a new project at the BMA. Ever since Saidie and Herbert May had split, Saidie had kept her apartment in New York. She decided the time had come to give it up, since she was spending so much time elsewhere. She gave many of the furnishings to the Baltimore Museum of Art, where she planned to set up a "Renaissance Room" to display the collection of Gothic and early European furnishings and decorative items. She approached Mr. Henry Treide, director of the Baltimore Museum of Art, with the idea and he welcomed it and encouraged her to move ahead with the project. He recommended that she avoid creating a "gallery" setting for her collection, and instead look into the possibility of purchasing a "period room" to complement the pieces.

Randolph Hearst had a warehouse in New York filled with approximately forty million dollars worth of ancient art and period rooms. The Chase National bank took charge of the sale of these items. Saidie, with the help of the Baltimore Museum of Art found a reasonably priced seventeenth century "Jacobean" room consisting of "wormy oak" wall paneling, a stone mantelpiece and fireplace. They would be perfect as a complement to her collection. Perfect timing![28]

After working on arrangements for the Renaissance Room objects, Saidie and Al then sailed to Holland, where they went museum-hopping in Rotterdam for a couple of cold weeks, reveling in the collections of Rembrandts and van Goghs. Van Gogh particularly appealed to Al, with his directness, purity of color and thick paint application.[29] By the middle of May, they were back in Paris for the summer at the Hotel Lutetia.

Notes

1 Jennifer Tonkovick, *Pierre Matisse and His Artists*, (New York: Pierpont Morgan Library, 2002).

2 Martin E. Peterson, Telephone Conversation with Elise Donaldson, May 18, 1979, San Diego Museum of Art Library.

3 Blanche Adler to Adelyn Breeskin, October 7, 1937, Adelyn Breeskin Papers, BMA.

4 Saidie A. May to Henry Treide, April 12, 1938, Saidie A. May Papers, BMA.

5 http://www.spaightwoodgalleries.com/Pages/Tal_Coat.html.

6 Martin E. Peterson, Telephone Conversation with Elise Donaldson, May 18, 1979, San Diego Museum of Art Library.

7 http://www.spaightwoodgalleries.com/Pages/Tal_Coat.html.

8 Exposition Internationale du Surrealisme, January 17–February 24, 1938, Galerie Beaux-Arts, 140 Rue du Faubourg, Saint Honore, Paris.

9 Paul Tratchtman, "Matisse & Picasso," *Smithsonian Magazine*, 33:11 (February, 2003), 70.

10 Anton Gill, Art Lover, *A Biography of Peggy Guggenheim* (New York: Harper Collins, 2001), 96.

11 William Rubin, *André Masson* (New York, Museum of Modern Art, 1976), 86.

12 Doris Birmingham, *André Masson in America—The Artist's Achievements in Exile 1941–45* (Ann Arbor, Michigan, UMI Dissertation Services, 1978) Ch. 11, 1.

13 Daniel-Henry Kahnweiler, *My Galleries and Painters* (New York, Viking Press, 1971).

14 William Rubin, *André Masson* (New York: Museum of Modern Art, 1976), 81.

15 Anton Gill, *Art Lover, a Biography of Peggy Gugenheim*, (New York: Harper Collins, 2001), 96–97.

16 William Rubin, *André Masson* (New York, Museum of Modern Art, 1976), 86.

17 *Ibid.*

18 Francoise Levaillant, *André Masson, Les Annees Surrealistes, Correspondence 1916–1942* (Paris, France: 1990), 382.

19 *Ibid.*

20 Linda L. Cathcart, *Alfred Jensen, Paintings and Diagrams from the Years 1957–1977*, catalogue, Albright Knox Art Gallery, January 15–February 26, 1978.

21 Doris Birmingham, *André Masson in America—The Artist's Achievements in Exile 1941–45* (Ann Arbor, Michigan: UMI Dissertation Services, 1978), Ch. 1, 19.

22 William Rubin, *André Masson* (New York: Museum of Modern Art, 1976), 81.

23 Doris Birmingham, *André Masson in America—The Artist's Achievements in Exile 1941–45* (Ann Arbor, Michigan, UMI Dissertation Services, 1978), Ch.1, 9.

24 *Ibid.*, 97.

25 *Ibid.*, Ch. 1, 11.

26 *Ibid.*, 29.

27 *Ibid.*, 29.

28 Saidie A. May to Mr. Scarff, June 17, 1938 Saidie A. May Papers, BMA.

29 Linda L. Cathcart, *Alfred Jensen, Paintings and Diagrams from the Years 1957–1977*, catalogue, Albright Knox Art Gallery, January 15 - February 26, 1978.

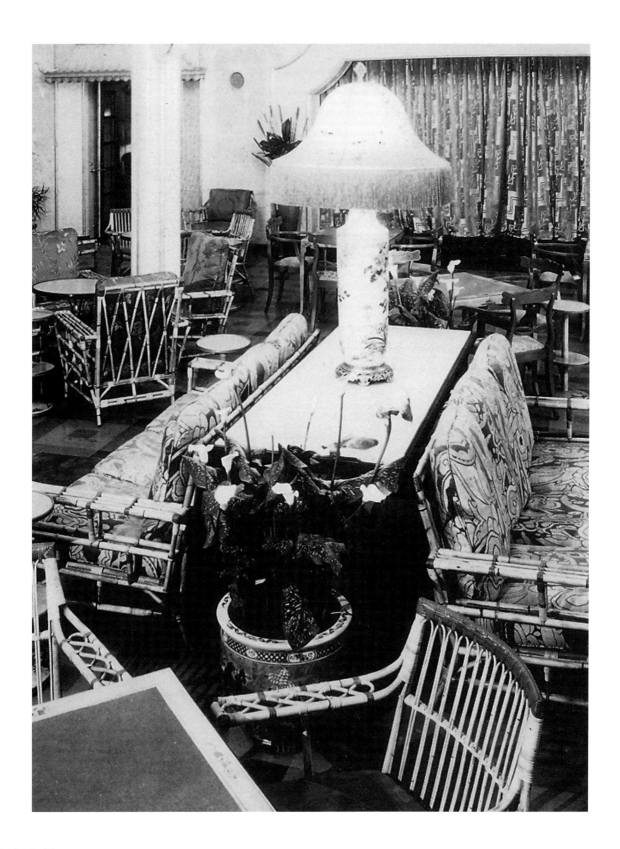

Travel and Correspondences, 1938–1939

12

In June 1938, Blanche and Helen took the train from Baltimore to New York. There they picked up a "Boat Train" bound for San Francisco to coordinate with the sailing of the SS *Luriline* to Hawaii.[1] The two spent a week enjoying the city of San Francisco before boarding the luxury liner bound for Honolulu for a five-day cruise.[2] Boarding from the Embarcadero began at one o'clock, and sailing was at four.[3] This trip was one large, floating party. The two dined like royalty, pampered and indulged the entire trip. Each day at 10:30, they had hot tea, followed by luncheon at noon. Dinner was a lavish affair, formal attire with twelve seated at a large table, to get to know other travelers on the trip. Each night there was a different form of entertainment available after dinner.

Hawaii

Finally, as the ship arrived within sight of Oahu, the air changed. Soft breezes with a hint of a floral fragrance wafted across the deck. Islanders came out to greet the ship with brightly colored fragrant leis for everyone.

Their next destination was Waikiki and the Royal Hawaiian Hotel, the "Pink Palace," with swaying palms and sparkling blue water. Blanche and Helen had reserved a lavishly appointed room with a private bath. Everything about the island was warm and relaxing, from the air to the lush tropical gardens to the white sandy beaches. Each afternoon, tea was served on the Coconut Grove Lanai at 3:30, complete with hula dancing and singing. Helen and Blanche lunched at this time.

This trip was a memorable experience for both sisters, and they made the most of it. They spent a quiet week relaxing at the hotel before boarding the ship again for the return voyage to San Francisco.

Postcard of First Class Main Lounge, Matson Liner, *Luriline*, 1938. Collection of the author.

Saidie in Paris

Meanwhile, shopping in Paris, Saidie picked up an oil painting, *Portrait #1,* and several mixed-media gouache works by Joan Miró at Kahnweiler's Galerie Simon. These and other recently purchased works were crated and sent to the Baltimore Museum of Art on the SS *Shodack,* sailing out of Le Havre. In July, Saidie and Al took the train west to picturesque Granville (on the English Channel) to paint for three weeks.

Alaska

A continent and a half away, Saidie's sisters were again leaving San Francisco, this time for a rugged ten-day journey up the Inland Passage by boat to the Alaskan interior and McKinley Park.[4] They hopped on a train from San Francisco to Seattle, Washington. As the train wound its way through

Above: Joan Miró, Spanish, 1893–1983, *Portrait No. 1,* 1938, oil on canvas, 64-1/4 x 51-1/4 in. (163.2 x 130.2 cm), The Baltimore Museum of Art: Bequest of Saidie A. May, BMA 1951.339. ©2011 Successió Miró/Artists Rights Society (ARS), New York/ADAGP, Paris. Lower: Postcard of Alaskan Indian chief, Ketchikan, Alaska, 1938. Collection of the author.

the mountains and scenic valleys, the two were mesmerized by the pristine scenery. The snow-topped peak of Mount Rainier was especially impressive. They spent the evening in Seattle, and the next day boarded the Alaska Steamship Company's *Columbia* bound for Ketchikan, Alaska.[5] This trip would be anything but luxurious.

The sisters spent a day in Ketchikan, a scenic fishing village where salmon swam along in the river running through town. Locals made traditional Alaskan crafts that were for sale. The sisters indulged themselves on the spectacular seafood and then were back at sea for two days, bound for Seward, where they boarded the

Postcard of Mt. Eielson Camp, Mile 66, McKinley Park, Alaska, 1938. Collection of the author.

train for the interior part of the trip. Their group took the Alaska Railroad train from Seward to Denali, and then on to Mt. Eielson Camp, Mile 66 in McKinley Park, where they spent two days reveling in the untamed scenery. They observed wild bears, elk and eagles in the enormous region surrounding the majestic Mt. McKinley. The days were pleasantly warm and long, lasting from 5 a.m. until 10 p.m. Nights were chilly, but the air was refreshingly clean. This was a different kind of paradise from Hawaii, but equally breathtaking. Here they feasted on the exotic meats the area had to offer, quite different from the sweet fruits of the Hawaiian Islands. Waiting for dinner, they were tempted by the aroma of roasted elk as they sat in mammoth log chairs at the lodge, taking in the splendors of Mt. McKinley. Dinner couldn't come soon enough, as the mountain air gave one quite an appetite.

Coming home, the trip was the reverse, a relaxing train ride through the park to Denali, and down towards the sea to Seward. This was the last cruise that Blanche would take. As pleasant as it was, her stomach bothered her the entire time.

France

In August, Saidie and Al headed back to Paris and on to Juan-les-Pins, where they planned to spend several months. Because of the mounting fears about war, they went back to Paris in September.[6]

There had been some controversy surrounding Saidie's purchase of the Miró works in June from Henry Kahnweiler's gallery. When she got back to Paris, Saidie received a letter from Kahnweiler, relating a discussion he had had with Christian Zervos and Pablo Picasso, questioning the merit of the Miró works and *Portrait #1*. Both Picasso and Kahnweiler were very interested in and admiring of Miró's work. In his letter, Kahnweiler reassured Saidie that Picasso felt that they were very good representations of Miró's work, and certainly worth owning.[7] It is not clear whether Saidie had ever met Picasso, even though his work is represented in her collections.

During September, Saidie bought a Marie Laurencin watercolor, *Young Girl,* directly from the artist's studio through the Galerie le Nivea for 2500 francs.[8] By the middle of October, aware that the Germans were going to invade France, Saidie and Al left that country for the last time and headed to Holland. There they boarded one of the last ships bound for America, the *Rotterdam,* heading for New York. It was their last trip from Europe before the war broke out. Had she stayed, Saidie's life would also have been in danger, and she still had much to tend to at home.

The Renaissance Room

Back in New York, Saidie started working on the Renaissance Room in earnest. Othon Friesz and his wife were visiting the city for a few weeks while he tried to sell some of his canvases to several museums, including the Barnes Collection. He wanted to encourage interest in his work in the United States by promoting it himself. The Museum of Modern Art had contacted him about the large nude painting that Saidie had offered to them in 1934. Now they were ready to purchase it. In the end, it cost the museum $1,200.[9] While the Frieszes were in town, Saidie tried telephoning them at the Barbizon Plaza Hotel to make a date. Unfortunately, they were not easily reached by phone, and therefore the couples were not able to spend much time together before the painter and his wife returned to France. Saidie was able to purchase a small painting from him for $100, though.[10]

Soon Saidie and Al headed for the Oak Hall Hotel near the arts colony in Tryon, North Carolina, for a few weeks. There Saidie received a letter from Henry Kahnweiler with a photograph of a painting by Masson, from the same group that he had been working on during their visit. Masson had finished this piece. On the back of the photo, Kahnweiler wrote, "Oil on canvas, 100 x 50 cm, the last of the pictures like the *Tower of Sleep*. You didn't see it at Lyons, I believe that is why I send you the photo."[11] The title of this painting was *Erotic Transmutation*, and Kahnweiler was so sure that Saidie would buy it, he wrote the word "sold" under the title on the photograph.

Al had become fascinated with Masson's painting of the metaphysical; he adored this painting and was ready to purchase it for himself. Saidie put him in his place with the comment, "One collector in the family is enough."[12] Though Saidie never acquired that painting, she continued to buy other works directly from André Masson and Galerie Simon, where Henry Kahnweiler gave her advice on other artists and purchases outside of his gallery to add to her collection.

Any time Saidie became aware of write-ups concerning the artists which Kahnweiler represented, she sent him copies of the articles or catalogues so that he could see for himself how Americans felt about this new art. Many times even the curators did not truly get what the works were all about.

At the beginning of November, Saidie took the train to Baltimore to work on the Renaissance Room project. Then on to New York to purchase the Jacobean oak room (originally from Shrewsbury, England, c. 1617) from the Hearst collection to use for her Renaissance Room. Her lawyer, Philip B. Perlman, oversaw the legal aspects of the room's installation. Perlman was a Baltimore native who

Philip B. Perlman, *Baltimore Muncipal Journal*, October 13, 1925, Vol. 13, #4. Collection Maryalnd Department of Enoch Pratt Free Library, Baltimore, Maryland.

graduated from Baltimore City College in 1908. He worked as a reporter while studying political economy and law in college. In 1910 he began working for the *Evening Sun*, first as a court reporter and then as city editor from 1913 to 1917, when he got to know H.L. Mencken.

Perlman then moved into public service, maintaining a private law practice. While working on private cases, he moved up the Democratic political ladder, eventually becoming U.S. Solicitor General under President Harry Truman in 1947. Perlman was an avid print collector and was involved with both the Walters Art Gallery and the Baltimore Museum of Art. Besides tending to the legal needs of the Adlers, he was friendly with Blanche and Saidie due to his interest in art. He was active with Blanche in the BMA's print department, working to make it one of the finest collections in the country. He also worked hard to help Saidie bring her Renaissance Room to reality. The Renaissance Room installation was supposed to start at the end of 1938 and scheduled to open in the early spring of 1939. They hired the architect J.H. Scarff to design and oversee the installation.

By the middle of November, Saidie and Al had settled into the Pine Needles resort at Southern

The Pine Needles, Knollwood, Southern Pines, NC, c. 1915–1939. Saidie A. May Papers, Archives and Manuscripts Collection, The Baltimore Museum of Art. SM3.4.32.B.

Pines, North Carolina. This was a restricted resort. Jews were not allowed, but Saidie managed to sneak in by registering with the last name of May, which did not necessarily sound Jewish. Her nieces, Clare and Bertel wanted to send her a Jewish New Year greeting, and decided to send it by way of a telegram (a special correspondence). When Saidie received the telegram at the Hotel, she was furious, concerned that her secret was out.

Events at the BMA

Blanche's pet project, the Prints and Drawings Department, was being utilized by several different colleges for the study of the museum's collection. During the academic year between 1938 and 1939, Dr. Jacob Rosenberg conducted an art seminar in the print room, through Goucher College's Fine Arts Department. Rosenberg used the exhibition space as a laboratory for his classes.[13]

The secretary of the BMA's board, Dr. George Boas organized a small showing of Saidie's collection of Modern art to open November 8, 1938. It included works by Gris, Masson, Lascaux, Braque, Roger and two terracottas she had recently purchased from Henry Kahnweiler at the Galerie Simon. It was appropriately titled, "Modern French Art from the Saidie A. May Collection."[14]

Saidie sent programs from the show to both André Masson and D.H. Kahnweiler. They each wrote back thanking her for her thoughtfulness.[15] Kahnweiler sent a letter back with corrections to the program, while expounding on the greatness of French art, and the up-and-coming young artists as yet "undiscovered."[16] In the meantime, installation of the Renaissance Room stalled. Saidie continued to advocate for having the room installed, but the contractor quit at the beginning of the project, and the museum was having a difficult time finding a replacement.

In January, 1939, Saidie sent a letter to Kahnweiler describing the BMA exhibit, along with a couple of newspaper reviews that she didn't care for. Kahnweiler wrote back, describing Paris as being quiet. He was still trying to live normally by continuing to show new artworks and going about his daily business, trying not to worry about the impending war. He described a new exhibit of Picasso's works at the Rosenberg Gallery as "nearly all still-lifes from 1936–1938, all painted in the country during weekends, and very coloured."[17] These works were very different from Picasso's paintings of Guernica and other works depicting Spain's war.

The Museum of Modern Art

At the end of April, Saidie and Al headed north to Baltimore for two weeks, and then on to New York for the month of May. Saidie frequented the Museum of Modern Art in order to focus on how they ran a successful museum.[18] It kept re-inventing itself to attract new visitors with lectures and performances keyed to their current exhibitions. They had a sculpture garden, a museum store, and a restaurant. They even sold "subscriptions" to its corporation, with the fee deductible on one's individual income tax.[19] It became a lively, cultural center and a place to meet friends. Most amazing was the fact that at that time, it was the only museum in midtown Manhattan.[20]

A California Retreat

In June, Saidie and Al met up with Blanche, and the three took a cross-country train to Santa Barbara for the summer. They stayed at the El Encanto Hotel, a premier California retreat, catering to "plen air" or "open-air" painters who often favored landscapes. The hotel also drew celebrities and the rich from the East Coast as well as Hollywood. Some of the notables associated with the hotel were Hedy Lamarr, Clark Gable and Carole Lombard. Built in 1915, the hotel featured Craftsman-Cottage style architecture, as well as Spanish Colonial revival accents, typical of the Santa Barbara area. Saidie and Al rented one of the original buildings set up as an individual home overlooking Santa Barbara, the Pacific Ocean and the Channel Islands. Blanche rented a smaller cottage in the same complex, amidst gardens of flowers, banana palms and lemon, orange and grapefruit trees.[21] They spent that summer creating sculptural constructions and in the evenings sketching live nude models in the San Diego Fine Arts atelier libre. They frequented a couple of local art galleries in La Jolla. One day Saidie and Al went into town to the small canteen near the Fine Arts Museum. There they met the Cubist painter Lyonel Feininger who was on his way to Mills College in Oakland to teach art for the summer. He had stopped in San Diego to take a look at its new museum.

The three had a long conversation about art in Europe.[22] "I had been fully established as a teacher at the Bauhaus, but soon realized that the War was coming. As an American married to a

Postcard from the El Encanto Hotel, c. 1940. Collection of the author.

Jew, we had to leave." "I know," said Al, "when we left Holland in 1938, it was full of refugees from Hitler's War." Feininger continued, "I was shocked by the Munich arrangement with Chamberlain, and as a result I accepted a professorship with Mills College. I had taught one course there last summer, when my wife and I visited America, but then we returned to Germany, only to be forced to having to leave again." Al turned towards Feininger, "Tell us about your experience at the Bauhaus." "Well, I had been a very good friend of Paul Klee, and we were part of the musical hours that were held in the late afternoons after school. We played quartets, and my favorite pieces were by Bach." Al replied, "Being a romantic, I prefer Beethoven."

After the three finished their coffee, they headed over to the museum to look at a new exhibit of local talents from New York City, featuring sculpture by Gaston Lachaise and paintings by Guy Pène du Bois. They walked around for quite a long time and discussed every work in the show.

Kahnweiler and Masson

While André Masson was in Paris for a few days with his family, he told Kahnweiler about a very large canvas that he had started. Kahnweiler tried to entice Saidie with the prospect of a new purchase, *Tour de Sommeil*, which, when it was finished, he offered to her for his "especially low price of $340."[23] Saidie cabled him immediately to make the purchase. Kahnweiler felt that it was one of the best paintings of Masson's career, commenting that Saidie's collection "shows the development of Masson's art in his most important works."

In a subsequent letter to Saidie dated July 20, Kahnweiler commented that Paris was "rather quiet, few Americans, mostly dealers."[24] Michel Leiris, Kahnweiler's brother-in-law, was a writer. Kahnweiler published his books through his "Editions de la Galerie Simon."[25] Leiris had come from a Parisian bourgeois background and his poetry was heavily influenced by Max Jacob. Kahnweiler had published *Glossaire j'y serre mes gloses*, illustrated with lithographs by André Masson. This work was a poetic anthology of terms that had lost their common usage or original meaning. Leiris destroyed that vocabulary in current usage, and showed its meaninglessness, reconstituting it in his Surrealistic poetic fashion.[26]

Saidie and Al were interested in his books and they had discussed them with Kahnweiler. Al had not liked Leiris' book, *L'Afrique Fantôme*, but on Kahnweiler's recommendation he and Saidie read *L'Age d'Homme (Manhood)*, published later in 1939, with artwork by Gaston Gallimard. Even though Kahnweiler distrusted psychoanalysis, he lost himself in this autobiography and was profoundly affected by its words.[27]

In his letter of July 7, Kahnweiler wrote that he and his wife spent four days in the resort of Lucerne, Switzerland, attending the Entartete Kunst: the sale of paintings (many degenerate) sponsored for the Nazi party. The auction was held at the elegant Grand Hotel National on June 30, organized by Theodore Fischer.[28] One hundred and twenty six paintings and sculptures were offered that day, including works by Braque, van Gogh, Picasso, Klee, Gauguin, Chagall, Mondrian, Modigliani, Matisse and 34 others, including a group of German painters of the "Brüke." The auctioneer had been worried about the public's perception that the auction proceeds were to go directly to finance the Nazi party, since those artworks in the sale had been specifically "purged" from German museums under the orders of the Nazi leaders. He sent a personal letter to the leading art dealers who were interested in the works, to assure them that all the profits from the sale would be used for German museums.[29] D.H. Kahnweiler, along with most of the other recipients of those letters was not convinced, and many prominent people in the art field did not attend. Kahnweiler had initially declined the invitation, but at the last minute, curiosity got the best of him, and he took his wife up to Lucerne to see what would happen to his beloved Picasso works. The artworks had been exhibited in Zurich and Lucerne for a few weeks, so the auction attracted a large group of international buyers. Included in the audience were the well-known German dealer Walter Feilchenfeldt, the famous producer of the film *The Blue Angel*, and his wife, Marianne; Josef von Sternberg; American publisher and art collector Joseph Pulitzer, Jr.; Belgian museum officials; and the art dealers Pierre Matisse and Curt Valentin.[30]

What made this auction unusual was the provenance of the artworks, many of which came from public museums throughout Germany, including those in Munich, Hamburg, Mannheim,

Frankfurt, Dresden, Bremen, the Wallraf-Richartz in Cologne, the Folkwang in Essen and Berlin's National Galerie. The assembled works were considered major masterpieces of each artist's career, including Picasso's *Absinthe Drinker* from his Blue Period (now at the Hermitage Museum in Leningrad), Matisse's *Bathers with a Turtle* (presently at the St. Louis Art Museum, gift of Mr. & Mrs. Joseph Pulitzer, Jr.) and van Gogh's great *Self Portrait* from the museum in Munich. Kahnweiler had been interested in another of Picasso's works, the *Deux Harlequins*, which fetched 750,000 francs and was bought by an American. His *Famille Solier* was purchased by the Museum of Liege in Belgium. According to Kahnweiler, "The Germans won't buy many airplanes for what these pictures fetched. The whole sale did not bring more than $100,000, as lots of pictures of the poor German painters of the Brücke, etc. have not been sold, there being no buyers."[31]

Joseph Pulitzer was quoted as saying that "the joy and excitement usually at such a sale was missing. To safeguard the art for posterity, I bought—defiantly! The real motive in buying was to preserve the art."[32]

Alfred Barr was in Paris that weekend, arranging MOMA's blockbuster Picasso show, and declined the invitation, since it had unpopular connotations.[33] He also instructed his staff to assure the public that recent acquisitions from Germany had been bought from the new Buchholz Gallery in New York, for whom Curt Valentin worked, and not obtained through illicit means.[34] However, Barr instructed Valentin to use money that had been donated to MOMA to purchase new artworks. Barr wanted him to bid on certain items at the auction which he felt needed to be saved. He did not want the public to know that MOMA was involved in the purchase of stolen items and insisted that any press releases concerning the new works would state that they were purchased from the Buchholz Gallery in New York. Perhaps to return the favor, when Valentin applied for American citizenship in 1943, Barr vouched for his good character.[35] In 1938 the "Commission for the Exploitation of Degenerate Art" was formed by the Nazi party. Karl Buchholz, Curt Valentin's mentor, was named to that commission. This had given Valentin an "in" to that auction. At this time, he was still a German citizen and he was able to obtain much of the inventory that would later establish him as a major New York art dealer. He continued to make risky trips to Germany in order to purchase more purged art through his friend Karl Buchholz, for whom he named his New York gallery.[36]

Notes

1   Blanche Adler to Bertel Speier, June 27, 1938, Collection of the author, Baltimore, MD.

2   Blanche Adler to Bertel Speier, June 29, 1938, Collection of the author, Baltimore, MD.

3   Lynn Blocker Krantz, *To Honolulu in Five Days, Cruising Aboard Matson's* S.S. Lurline (California: The Speed Press, 2001), 20.

4   Blanche Adler to Bertel Speier, July, 1938, Collection of the author.

5   "Serving Alaska the Year 'Round," *Ketchikan Alaska Chronicle*, July 28, 1938, Alaska Steamship Company Sailing Schedule.

6   Saidie A. May to Henry Treide, July 10, 1938, Saidie A. May Papers, BMA.

7   Daniel-Henry Kahnweiler to Saidie A. May, September 27, 1938, Saidie A. May Papers, BMA.

8   Bill from Galerie le Niveau, September 14, 1938, Saidie A. May Papers, BMA.

9   Othon Friesz to Saidie A. May, November 9, 1938, Saidie A, May Papers, BMA.

10 Othon Friesz to Saidie A. May, October 24, 1938, Saidie A, May Papers, BMA.

11 Alfred Jensen, Interview by Doris Birmingham, Glen Ridge, N.J. July 25, 1974.

12 Levaillant, Francoise; *André Masson, Les Annees Surrealistes, Correspondence 1916–1942*, 1990, (Paris, France), 551.

13 Adelyn Breeskin, "Report of the Department of Prints and Drawings, 1939," 1, Adelyn Breeskin Records, BMA.

14 Saidie A. May to Robert M. Levi, November 5, 1938, Jacques Seligman and Co. General Correspondence 1913–1978, Box 064, 1.3, Archives of American Art, Smithsonian Institution.

15 André Masson to Saidie A. May, December 28, 1938 Saidie A. May Papers, BMA.

16 Daniel-Henry Kahnweiler to Saidie A. May, December 13, 1938, Saidie A. May Papers, BMA.

17 Daniel-Henry Kahnweiler to Saidie A. May, February 7, 1939, Saidie A. May Papers, BMA.

18 Alice Goldfarb Marquis, *Alfred H. Barr Jr., Missionary for the Modern* (Chicago, Illinois: Contemporary Books, 1989), 175.

19 Russell Lynes, *Good Old Modern, an Intimate Portrait of the Museum of Modern Art* (Kingsport,Tenn.: Kingsport Press, 1973), 15.

20 *Ibid.*

21 Blanche Adler to Bertel Speier, July 6, 1939, Collection of the author.

22 Alfred Jensen, Interview about his life in San Diego, California, 1919–1938 by Regina Bogat, May 8, 1979, Glen Ridge, New Jersey.

23 Daniel-Henry Kahnweiler to Saidie A. May, July 7, 1939, Saidie A. May Papers, BMA.

24 Daniel-Henry Kahnweiler to Saidie A. May, July 20, 1939, Saidie A, May Papers, BMA.

25 Pierre Assouline, *An Artful Life, A Biography of D.H. Kahnweiler 1884–1979* (New York: Fromm Int'l Publishing Corp., 1991), 264.

26 *Ibid.*, 264.

27 *Ibid.*, 265.

28 *Ibid.*, 257.

29 *Ibid.*, 4.

30 Lynn H. Nicholas, *The Rape of Europa, The Fate of Europe's Treasures in the Third Reich and the Second World War* (New York: Vintage Books, 1995), 4.

31 *Ibid.*, 4.

32 *Ibid.*, 4.

33 Barr to McKay, July 1, 1939, Alfred Hamilton Barr Papers, Archives of American Art, SI.

34 *Ibid.*, 4.

35 Alice Goldfarb Marquis, *Alfred H. Barr, Jr., Missionary for the Modern* (Chicago, Illinois: Contemporary Books, 1989), 178.

36 Lynn H. Nicholas, *The Rape of Europa, The Fate of Europe's Treasures in the Third Reich and the Second World War* (New York: Random House, 1994).

Impending War, 1939–1940

On September 1, 1939, Germany invaded Poland, and by the third of the month, both England and France declared war on Germany. Saidie and Al were staying at the El Encanto Hotel in Santa Barbara from August through October 2, 1939. Saidie, through correspondence with Henry Kahnweiler, purchased *Tour de Sommeil* by André Masson from the Galerie Simon in Paris. Kahnweiler, still in France, was forced by the German censors to write in French only.[1]

Saidie and Al then came to Baltimore for about a month, working with the Baltimore Museum of Art in trying to get the Renaissance Room installation started. At the same time, Yves Tanguy, Kaye Sage and Roberto Sebastian Matta Echaurren slipped out of France and sailed for New York together. They arrived at Ellis Island with no money. Tanguy immediately went to his former schoolmate from the Lycee Montaigne in Paris,[2] Pierre Matisse, for help. Matisse agreed to show Tanguy's work informally in his gallery, and supported him until he was able to earn money on his own. Sage and Tanguy began a liaison which eventually resulted in their marriage in the United States on April 17, 1943.

Saidie and Al again wintered at the Pine Needles, since the war prevented them from returning to Europe. The Nazis were slowly moving through France, penetrating the northern part of the country. Many French citizens were becoming concerned for their lives, especially those who were Jewish or opposed the Vichy government. They fled south to Marseilles to try to acquire passage on a boat to America.

D. H. Kahnweiler packed his truck with his possessions on September 20. He and his wife headed for St.-Léonard-de-Noblat in the area of Limoges. He lived on hope. The war for him was a source of endless sorrow; he suffered from insomnia and was on the verge of a breakdown. At night he read, wrote and reflected.[3] He subsequently went back to Paris and reopened the gallery in December, closing every day at 5:00 when it became dark.

Alfred Jensen, Saidie A. May and unknown man, summer 1939, San Diego, California. Collection of Regina Bogat Jensen, Glen Ridge, New Jersey.

Kahnweiler

Kahnweiler barely sold any work to Europeans. His customers were in Scandinavia and the United States. He sent letters to his American patrons, enticing them with his artists' new work. As soon as they replied back to make the purchase, he would rush to send those shipments to New York, lest he miss the last American boats leaving the port of Le Havre. The works were sent on commission, with previous letters indicating that if the patron did not receive the painting, Kahnweiler would refund their money. Luckily most works got to their buyers.[4] Due to the war, American ships started avoiding the French ports. Ships of other nationalities that did dock, demanded such exorbitantly high insurance rates that shipping became prohibitively expensive.

Masson Considers a Departure

Kahnweiler continued to keep in close contact with Masson and found some new patrons who were very interested in his work. This helped the Masson family survive during those tough times. Kahnweiler spent time with his brother-in-law, Michel Leiris, helping lift his spirits.[5]

On October 6, 1939, André Masson sent a letter to D.H. Kahnweiler indicating that the oppression of the Nazi movement was troubling him, though he was moving forward with his painting. His focus was more distinctly metaphysical, with the Pythagorean theory and the law of numbers interspersed throughout his work. He commented, "The activity of my spirit is not concerned with the present time." His work saved his sanity and he immersed himself in his dreams, thoughts and intellectual pursuits, translating these motivations onto the canvas, creating his unique art as an independent statement of who he was. Many of his friends had gone away, including Saidie and Al, but they still kept in touch, which meant a great deal to him.[6] He mentioned his concern about the absence of boats to America for those who were anxious to leave. Now he was concerned for his family's safety, since they were Jewish and he was a target due to his outspoken political views and his unusual artwork.

The next day, Kahnweiler wrote to Saidie. The gallery was still open in Paris, and he had been in touch with Masson, still living in Lyons-la-Forêt. Masson was cheerful and only concerned with his paintings.[7] Many of the shops and galleries in Paris had been closed, but Galerie Simon remained open several hours every day. Kahnweiler was sufficiently concerned about his collection being confiscated by the Nazis, so he had made arrangements at the end of August to send many of the more controversial paintings to another brother-in-law, Elie Lascaux, who was in the rural town of Limoges, where they had been living since the war,[8] and where the paintings would be hidden more successfully. He told Saidie that he felt that it was of the utmost importance that the gallery stay open, so they could help support the painters who were not soldiers, but continued working despite the war.

While Masson had been living in hiding in Lyons-la-Forêt, his paints and colors had run out. Not able to acquire additional materials, he could only draw. Most of his work from those months consisted of sketches for future paintings. Once he and his family left for Marseilles, they stopped for a couple of days to visit the Kahnweilers. Kahnweiler gave him some paints he had acquired in Paris. Once the Massons arrived in Marseilles safely, he worked with the few canvases and paint that he had.

Kahnweiler, a German Jew residing in Boulogne, France, continued living in his home with his wife; a dangerous decision, given his background. In his letter to Saidie, he updated the condition and whereabouts of her friends and some of the artists whom he represented: Suzanne Roger (whose husband was serving as a soldier) was staying with friends in a chateau near Amboise; Picasso was working near Paris; Léger was at his farm in Normandy; and Braque was at Varengeville. He lamented that he saw only old people at his gallery, as his younger friends were all fighting in the war. He was adamant about his hatred of the Nazis, wanting the oppression and the terrible war to end as soon as possible.[9]

Around November, 1939, André Masson was approached by the American painter Kaye Sage, who had returned to France after the declaration of war. Sage was actively organizing assistance for artists by arranging exhibitions in the United States for them. The only other time Masson's work had been shown in the United States was at the Pierre Matisse Gallery, where he had two solo exhibits in 1933 and 1935. He also contributed a few works to thematic shows related to French art and the Surrealists, held in New York.[10] Sage worked to prepare for Masson's departure by the beginning of March, 1940, for an exhibition and conference in New York.[11]

Increasing Worries

Masson's second wife, Rose, was born a Jew, and their two sons, Diego and Luis, were also Jewish. Masson knew from the news reports and the political situation in Europe that it was just a matter of time until he and his family would be summoned to the authorities. There was the real possibility that they would be deported or killed. He and many of his friends—artists, musicians, poets and intellectuals—had been "blacklisted" as known dissidents and troublemakers. Some had been interviewed by the authorities and others had fled the northern countries to southern France to be with their friends and relatives, or they left the continent fearing for their lives. André Masson had those same fears as well. His friends were urging him to make arrangements to flee the country, but he loved France dearly and hated the thought of leaving his home and family. He didn't speak English, and his lifeline—the sophisticated intellectual circles that had given him a sense of belonging and purpose—was fraying in front of him. Life as he had known it in his beloved France was slipping away forever.

Kahnweiler Planning with Curt Valentin

Curt Valentin, a German who fled his country after 1933, was a friend and protégé of Kahnweiler. In 1937, he moved to the United States and established the New York showroom of the Buchholz Gallery, first located at W. 46th St.; then in 1939 they moved to a larger space with two rooms and an office at 32 E. 37th St.

In 1939, Kahnweiler started sending French paintings to Valentin to sell for him, since he was having a harder time selling them in Paris.[12] Kahnweiler asked Valentin to organize an exhibit and conference for the same reason: to get Masson out of France. Kahnweiler sabotaged Kaye Sage's attempts to get Masson's show organized, offering Valentin the exclusive representation of Masson for the duration of the war while Masson was exiled in the United States.[13] Kahnweiler had contracted Masson's work exclusively in France since 1922, and Saidie was the major private collector of his work through him.[14]

When Masson was planning for the exhibit, he was under the impression that he would stay in the U.S only for the show and conference, returning to France afterwards. He worked diligently to get organized, writing commentaries for a catalogue and requesting his works from Kahnweiler's gallery to be packed and ready to be shipped with him on the boat. When Kaye Sage asked Kahnweiler to loan her the Masson paintings in his possession, his excuse was, "the absolute condition of the trip, preventing the realization of the project." In other words, the passage of these important works on a small boat full of refugees could create a perilous journey. Unable to acquire the works she needed, Kaye Sage gave up.

Preparations

Masson titled his talk, "What is the profound motive which pushes a man to give himself to artistic expression? To what degree can men bring to other people entangled like them in the confusion of life, a representation which resists a little against chaos, against change?"[15] He was disappointed at the cancellation of Kaye Sage's plans, and apprehensive about working with Curt Valentin, but he continued to plan for the exhibit nonetheless.

Masson requested that the *Labyrinth*, a painting in Kahnweiler's possession, be the focal point of the exhibit, since it was "the key to a whole series of paintings undertaken since the spring of 1938." He also wanted to borrow Saidie's *In the Tower of Sleep* to complement the exhibit.[16] As it turned out, the *Labyrinth* was not to leave France as Masson had hoped. In a letter dated November 4, 1939, Kahnweiler specified that nearly all of the paintings of the Galerie Simon, notably the *Labyrinth,* were hidden in the town of Limousin, France, and that it would be difficult to get them returned in order to ship them on the same boat with Masson.

During that same month, Saidie and Al ventured north to New York where she couldn't resist making some new purchases for the BMA. The first was *Flowers in a Dream*, an oil and gouache on heavy paper by Marc Chagall, purchased from the personal collection of Israel Ber Neuman, owner of the Neuman Gallery down the street from the Weylin Hotel where they stayed. She also bought two works from the Pierre Matisse Gallery, *Amoureaux* by Masson and *Deux Personages* (a watercolor) by Miró. Pierre Matisse had been mobilized, and worked as a porter in the heavy artillery in France, so his wife ran the gallery in his absence.[17] All three works were sent directly to the BMA to be displayed along with her other recent purchase by Masson, *La Tour de Sommeil*.

The beginning of 1940 was bitterly cold both in France and on the East Coast of the United States. The biting winds and heavy snow in France penetrated the old stone buildings which had no central heating and little firewood. Kahnweiler and his wife, Lucie, no longer left their home in the evenings or on weekends. They spent much of their time sitting in their library with their windows shut, curtains drawn and shutters closed. They read to each other, mostly English novels, which Kahnweiler borrowed from the local library. The rest of the time Kahnweiler was glued to the radio, often turning the dials to find new sources of the bitter news of the depressing war, keeping ties to the rest of the world through the spoken word.[18]

Assistance by Peggy Guggenheim

The gloomy weather and food restrictions (whatever good food was available was saved for the German soldiers in town) wreaked havoc on the emotions of the already stressed families waiting to leave. Again Kaye Sage tried to help those artists caught in France. She implored her friend Peggy Guggenheim to pay for the U.S. passage for the Breton family and Max Ernst, a well-known former German artist living in France who had just moved into "Air-Bel" with the Bretons. Peggy agreed and decided to pay a visit to Marseilles to meet with Varian Fry to see for herself what was being done to get the artists out of the country.[19] At "Air-Bel," Peggy was welcomed warmly by the artists, some of whom had sought her financial support. In the end she did make a generous contribution to the American Rescue Committee and paid for the passages of the Bretons and Max Ernst. While visiting at "Air-Bel," she purchased some paintings and then promptly left Marseilles to find safe storage for her new acquisitions.

Saidie and Al left New York to visit her son, Murray, in Philadelphia and then on to Baltimore for the holidays. By the beginning of January, the two were headed south again to the Pine Needles for the rest of the winter, corresponding with the BMA, San Diego Museum and other dealers and friends. Later in the month, the BMA opened a show of Modern painting in which Saidie's collection played an important role. The show included works by Masson, Friesz, Vlaminck, Utrillo and Klee. The premise of the show was to look at the progression of Modern art from the nineteenth century to the present. Her comments to the director, Leslie Cheek, in her letter of January 15, 1940, were, "Before we know it, the Baltimore public will be awakened from its long sleep, and will begin to see what's what."[20] She sent the catalogue from that show to D.H. Kahnweiler.

That same month, Blanche purchased a painting by J.C. Georgi, *Tropical Fish*, an abstraction which she planned to add to Saidie's collection at the BMA.[21] Simultaneously, the Pierre Matisse Gallery put on a show for Yves Tanguy, for which James Johnson Sweeney wrote the preface to the catalogue. The show ran from January through August.[22]

The Installation of the Renaissance Room

By February of 1940 the installation of the Renaissance Room had begun. On February 13, Kahnweiler wrote to Saidie thanking her for sending the catalogue, adding that he found the show rather "funny" and pedestrian in its comments. He told her that the Masson show that was supposed to have been put on by Curt Valentin was postponed, due to difficulties (in acquiring the works which were in hiding), as well as the expensive shipping cost.[23] He sent pictures of new works by Masson, Eugène de Kermadec and Beaudin. Saidie was mostly interested in larger, "more important" works by Masson, many of which were at his studio in Lyons–la–Forêt, unfinished. Kahnweiler asked her to cable her decision on the works he offered, and then he would send the paintings, "insured against any risk, even war risk, if you receive it, you pay it, and you pay what I paid for packing, freight and insurance."[24]

In his correspondence, Kahnweiler mentioned that Pablo Picasso was in Paris. Masson had also come to Paris on February 12 to see Madeleine Milhaud's one-act opera-ballet, *Médée*, based on the Greek goddess Medea. Earlier in 1939, Masson was commissioned by Jewish composer Darius Milhaud to design the costumes and sets for his wife's one-act libretto. Even though Masson had fled to Marseilles, he felt compelled to see this work performed before he left for the United States, and risked his life going back to Paris for this purpose.[25]

He had become interested in the theater around 1924 when he drew his first model for a theatre set design. In the 1930s, while working on his painting series *Massacres*, he was commissioned by Léonide Massine to design sets and costumes for the ballet *Les Presages* set to the music of Tchaikovsky. Masson was fascinated with how his drawings would translate into three dimensions on the stage. He believed that "the painter can express movement and color into the animated world of the theatre."

After spending two years in Spain, Masson met the French actor and director Jean-Louis Barrault in 1936. He started to design sets and costumes for Barrault's avant-garde productions, including Miguel de Cervantes' tragic play, *La Numancia*, performed in 1937. In 1938, Masson again designed for Barrault. This time, he recreated the unusual pieces of furniture which he had represented in his Surrealist paintings[26] for *Faim*, based on the novel *The Hunger*, by Knut Hamsun.

Saidie and Al spent the winter at the Pine Needles painting voraciously. By the middle of March, the bad weather had cleared out and they had warm days and cool nights. Saidie was anxious to donate a couple of works to the San Diego Art Museum to help modernize their

Spanish collection. She chose the paintings *Quelque Part dans le Sud* by Francisco Bores and *Deux Personages* by Juan Miró. These two works had been at the Baltimore Museum of Art, and the former director, Mr. McKinney, had not shown any interest in them. Saidie felt that they would be better utilized in San Diego, as there was more interest in Latino artists in that area.[27] When Leslie Cheek received her request, he quickly replied, assuring her that he was very interested in anything she had to give them. Reluctantly, he agreed to send the works, asking that she not take any more out of the Baltimore Museum's collection, as she was their only benefactor of Modern art.[28]

On March 9, Saidie cabled the Galerie Simon to purchase four works from Kahnweiler's offerings, including Masson's *Ville Crânienne (Town in a Skull)*, 1938, for $140. This work was derived from a lithograph he had done for Kahnweiler's brother-in-law, Michel Leiris for his literary work, *Glossaire*, published by Kahnweiler.[29] She also bought another work by Francisco Borès. All of these were to be sent directly to the Baltimore Museum of Art. By the end of March, Kahnweiler requested all payments from his patrons in the U.S. to go through the Chase National Bank in New York.[30] His last shipment to Saidie, including Masson's *Ville Crânienne* and two Miró paintings, *Men and Fish* and *Personages Attracted by the Form of a Mountain*, was supposed to have gone out March 11 on an American export ship, but it didn't make the ship in time, and was stuck in France. Kahnweiler tried again on March 24 and successfully got them out.[31] By April, his communications to the States had been cut off. Even if he could sell paintings, there was no way he could receive money from New York, as the U.S. government had frozen all French assets.[32]

All of the museums in Paris were closed that spring, as were most of the museums and galleries in Europe, due to the war.[33] Saidie wrote to Leslie Cheek on April 9, "I saw in the newspapers two days ago that the American export lines, after April 4 are no longer allowed to go to Marseilles (a belligerent port)."[34] The Kahnweilers spent a quiet Whitsuntide and Easter with the Massons at Lyons-la-Forêt. Masson was happy, working well and full of ideas. One would never know that there was a war going on around that area.[35]

On April 2, 1940, Peggy Guggenheim was invited to a fiftieth birthday dinner party for Max Ernst in Marseilles. Varian Fry commented on her earrings and her social manner, "Long crescents, which at the bottom hung tiny framed pictures by Max Ernst. Her conversations were a series of rapid, nervous questions."[36] She and Ernst spent the evening flirting with each other, and afterwards Peggy arranged to spend some time at "Air-Bel" to be close to him. By April 7, MOMA cabled that Ernst's passage had been purchased. On May 1, the majority of his papers were ready and Ernst escaped by train to Madrid, and then on to Lisbon where he rendezvoused with Peggy and her entourage.[37] The Guggenheim family in the United States sent a Pan American Clipper to collect "Peggy & Company."[38] They all escaped and flew back to New York on July 13.[39] The Bretons and the Massons were still left in Marseilles.

Work on the Renaissance Room continued. At the end of April, Saidie came north, taking

Above: Joan Miró, Spanish, 1893–1983, *Personages Attracted by the Forms of a Mountain*, 1936, tempera over graphite on masonite, 13 x 19-3/4 in., The Baltimore Museum of Art: Bequest of Saidie A. May, BMA 1951.338. ©2011 Successió Miró/Artists Rights Society (ARS), New York/ADAGP, Paris. Left: Juan Gris, Spanish, 1887–1927, *The Painter's Window*, 1925, oil on canvas, 39-1/4 x 31-3/4 in. (99.7 x 80.6 cm), The Baltimore Museum of Art: Bequest of Saidie A. May, BMA 1951.306.

a short trip to Boston to visit the Boston Museum of Fine Arts' medieval and Modern collections, Harvard's Fogg art collection and the Garden Collection. Prior to the trip, Saidie had written to Leslie Cheek at the BMA to ask him to alert those museum directors to her arrival. Saidie hoped she might obtain a personal tour of some of those collections, as she had previously done in Chicago.[40] In a letter that he sent to Mr. George Harold Edgell, director of the Boston Museum of Fine Arts, Mr. Cheek wrote, "Mrs. May is a rather strange character…she has given quite a number of Modern paintings for our collections. She appears hard and cold at first meeting, but her interest in art is warm, and I know she will appreciate any attentions you will be able to show her."[41]

After four days in New England, Saidie left for New York. She would meet Al there and remain for ten days. They visited the Valentin Gallery, where she purchased Juan Gris' *The Painter's Window* and *Composition* by Fernand Léger, a patterned abstraction

Postcard of Boston Museum of Fine Arts building, c. 1906. Collection of the author.

against a yellow ground.[42] She had these works shipped directly to the Baltimore Museum of Art to add to her Modern collection. By the middle of May, the two went to Baltimore for another ten days to visit family and to see the progress being made on the Renaissance Room.

On May 10, 1940, the French lines were suddenly broken by the German blitzkrieg divisions. Kahnweiler canceled his visit to Masson at Lyons-la-Forêt—he was afraid to be out on the roads.

Santa Barbara

By the end of the month, Saidie and Al left for Santa Barbara again, staying at the El Encanto Hotel for the summer. By May 27, Kahnweiler was again able to ship more paintings to Saidie, this time through Bordeaux.[43] Blanche left Baltimore to join them on July 1, and the three spent the rest of their summer enjoying the beautiful weather together, painting, reading and drawing. "Dear Bertel, We are now at Santa Barbara in a lovely cottage in a charming garden with all sorts of flowers, lemon, orange and grapefruit trees and banana palms. The weather is delightful. Hope to see you all. Love, Aunt Blanche."[44] On July 9, Saidie and Blanche had a lovely day together attending the 1939 Exposition in San Diego.[45]

Exile

In Paris on June 12, at six in the morning, word came over the radio that the French army was in full retreat on all fronts. The Kahnweilers literally fled Boulogne for Limousin, taking the back roads to avoid troops and refugees. The very next day, the Germans marched into Paris, and Kahnweiler became exiled in the French countryside for the next four years. He had to keep a very low profile. He was Jewish, a draft-dodger during WW1, openly anti-Nazi, no longer of

German nationality and a promoter of "degenerate" art.[46] He and his wife, Lucie, moved in with his brother-in-law, Elie Lascaux, and his wife and daughter. On June 15, in a handwritten letter to Saidie (all of his other letters to this point were typed on Galerie Simon stationery) Kahnweiler wrote, "We are here a bit bewildered by the absolute quietness of this place which is 3km, even from the small town of Saint Léonard. In Paris you had every night the gunshots against airplanes, and one got rather accustomed to the noise and didn't waken entirely."[47]

Notes

1 Pierre Assouline, *An Artful Life, A Biography of D.H. Kahnweiler 1884-1979* (New York: Fromm Int'l. Publishing Corp. 1991), 260.

2 Stephanie Barron, *Exiles and Emigrees—The Flight of European Artists from Hitler* (New York: Los Angeles County Museum of Art, Harry N. Abrams, 1997), 170.

3 Pierre Assouline, *An Artful Life, A Biography of D.H. Kahnweiler 1884-1979* (New York: Fromm Int'l. Publishing Corp. 1991), 261.

4 *Ibid.*, 263.

5 *Ibid.*, 264–265.

6 André Masson to Daniel-Henry Kahnweiler, October 6, 1939, Paris Archives of the Louise Leiris Gallery.

7 Daniel-Henry Kahnweiler to Saidie A. May, October 7, 1939, Saidie A. May Papers, BMA.

8 Daniel-Henry Kahnweiler, *My Galleries and Painters* (New York: Viking Press, 1971), 112.

9 Daniel-Henry Kahnweiler to Saidie A. May, October 7, 1939, Saidie A. May Papers, BMA.

10 Stephanie Barron, *Exiles and Emigrees—The Flight of European Artists from Hitler* (New York: Los Angeles County Museum of Art, Harry N. Abrams, 1997), 166.

11 Martica Awin, *Surrealism in Exile and the Beginning of the New York School* (Cambridge, Mass.: MIT Press, 1995) 121.

12 *Ibid.*, 110.

13 Francoise Levaillant, *André Masson, Les Annees Surrealistes, Correspondence 1916–1942* (Paris, France: 1990), 552.

14 Stephanie Barron, *Exiles and Emigrees—The Flight of European Artists from Hitler* (New York: Los Angeles County Museum of Art, Harry N. Abrams, 1997), 166.

15 Francoise Levaillant, *André Masson, Les Annees Surrealistes, Correspondence 1916–1942* (Paris, France: 1990), 437.

16 *Ibid.*

17 Saidie A. May to Leslie Cheek, November, 1939, Saidie A. May Papers, BMA.

18 Pierre Assouline, *An Artful Life, A Biography of D.H. Kahnweiler 1884–1979* (Canada: Fromm International Publishing Corporation, 1991), 265.

19 Sheila Isenberg, *A Hero of our Own, the Story of Varian Fry* (New York: Random House, 2001), 136.

20 Saidie A. May to Leslie Cheek, 15 January, 1940, Saidie A. May Papers, BMA.

21 Leslie Cheek to Saidie A. May, January 17, 1940, Saidie A. May Papers, BMA.

22 William M. Griswold, *Pierre Matisse and his Artists* (New York: Pierpont Morgan Library, 2002), 86.

23 Daniel-Henry Kahnweiler to Saidie A. May, February 13, 1940, Saidie A. May Papers, BMA.

24 *Ibid.*

25 *Ibid.*

26 Exposition André Masson-Le Theatre Comme Necessite, October 5–December 16, 2000, Galerie Brimaud.com/fr/expo-theatre.htm&prev.

27 Saidie A. May to Leslie Cheek, March 1, 1940, Saidie A. May Papers, BMA.

28 Leslie Cheek to Saidie A. May, March 5, 1940, Saidie A. May Papers, BMA.

29 Daniel-Henry Kahnweiler to Saidie A. May, February 14, 1940, Saidie A. May Papers, BMA.

30 Daniel-Henry Kahnweiler to Saidie A. May, March 12, 1940, Saidie A. May Papers, BMA.

31 Saidie A. May to Leslie Cheek, April 9, 1940, Saidie A. May Papers, BMA.

32 Pierre Assouline, *An Artful Life, A Biography of D.H. Kahnweiler 1884–1979* (Canada: Fromm International Publishing Corporation, 1991), 267.

33 Daniel-Henry Kahnweiler to Saidie A. May, May 2, 1940, Saidie A. May Papers, BMA.

34 Saidie A. May to Leslie Cheek, April 9, 1940, Saidie A. May Papers, BMA.

35 Daniel-Henry Kahnweiler to Saidie A. May, April 3, 1940, Saidie A. May Papers, BMA.

36 Varian Fry, *Surrender on Demand* (Boulder, Colorado: Johnson Books, 1997), 185.

37 Sheila Isenberg, *A Hero of our Own, the Story of Varian Fry* (New York: Random House, 2001), 138.

38 Martica Awin, *Surrealism in Exile and the Beginning of the New York School* (Cambridge, Mass: MIT Press, 1995), 141.

39 Alice Goldfarb Marquis, *Alfred H. Barr, Jr., Missionary for the Modern* (Chicago, Ill.: Contemporary Books, Inc. 1989), 188.

40 Saidie A. May to Leslie Cheek, March 28, 1940, Saidie A. May Papers, BMA.

41 Leslie Cheek to George Harold Edgell, April 2, 1940, Saidie A. May Papers, BMA.

42 "Current Exhibitions, the Saidie A. May Collection," *Baltimore Museum of Art News*, 2:7 (September, 1940), 51.

43 Daniel-Henry Kahnweiler to Saidie A. May, May 28, 1940, Saidie A. May Papers, BMA.

44 Blanche Adler to Bertel Speier, July 6, 1939, collection of the author, Baltimore, MD.

45 Blanche Adler to Bertel Speier, July 9, 1939, collection of the author, Baltimore, MD.

46 Pierre Assouline, *An Artful Life, A Biography of D.H. Kahnweiler 1884–1979* (Canada: Fromm International Publishing Corporation, 1991), 273.

47 Daniel-Henry Kahnweiler to Saidie A. May, June 15, 1940, Saidie A. May Papers, BMA.

The Emergency Rescue Committee, 1940

W ith the fall of France in June, 1940, most of the Surrealist artists realized they were in danger and fled south to the area around Marseilles. They soon heard about the Emergency Rescue Committee and the American, Varian Fry, who was helping people escape. Kurt Seligman, a Surrealist artist who immigrated to New York in 1939, worked with the Emergency Rescue Committee along with MOMA's Alfred Barr and his wife, Margaret Scolari Barr. Varian Fry had studied Greek and Latin at Harvard at the same time Barr was there. Later, after the Depression had wiped out his fortune, he had been considered for a job as a MOMA librarian.[1]

On July 10, from Saint Léonard de Noblat, Kahnweiler wrote to Saidie, greatly upset that Paul Klee had died on June 29th. He was also distressed about the war and "the sad and terrible events which have taken place since I last wrote you. The Germans did not come here, and so we are in the non-occupied part of France. There have been bombardments by Italian airplanes on the towns, villages, hamlets and main roads, with quite a lot of dead in the country around."[2]

After receiving this grim letter, Saidie wrote to Kahnweiler, offering to pay for passage for himself and his wife to the U.S.[3] He would have no part of it. Through his sister-in-law, Louise Leiris, Kahnweiler wrote to Saidie to entice her to buy additional works by other artists in his stable. He tried to interest her in buying art by Juan Gris and Suzanne Roger by sending recent photographs of their latest work. However, unbeknownst to him, Saidie had just purchased Juan Gris' *Painter's Window* from Valentin Dudensing.

In August, the Pierre Matisse Gallery closed the show of Yves Tanguy's work. Matisse arranged with Tanguy to pay him $100 each month in return for a medium-sized painting. Tanguy was also free to sell his other work to private clients at gallery prices. Tanguy continued to have shows of his work in the gallery in 1943, 1945 to 1946 and in 1950.[4]

Refugees line up outside the American Consulate, 6 Place Felix Baret in Marseilles, September, 1941 (photograph #48842) by Hans Cahnmann. Collection of the United States Holocaust Memorial Museum. Courtesy of Hiram Bingham.

The American Rescue Committee

Alfred Barr made a list of the stranded artists whose work he admired and collected for the museum. Records of the Emergency Rescue Committee show that, during the fall of 1940, the Barrs also gave their support to other artists whose names were supplied by concerned individuals outside of the museum. Kurt Seligman had brought Masson's plight to the Barrs, as well as that of André Breton, Paul Éluard, Pierre Mabille and Benjamin Péret.[5] The Barrs and Seligman helped to obtain affidavits and guarantees of support from American sponsors attesting to the fact that the émigrés would be supported, or self-supporting, in order for them to obtain visas for travel outside of France.[6] Other artists in need of help were Max Ernst, Jacques Lipschitz and Marc Chagall. Each person with whom the American Rescue Committee agreed to work was assigned a number in order of the importance to get them out—Masson was #858 on this list.[7]

Along with the daunting paperwork, Margaret Barr lobbied her friends at parties, asking for contributions of money and affidavit signatures. She worked closely with Inez Warburg, who ran the New York office of the American Rescue Committee. They worked feverishly to assemble the biographical material, affidavits from individuals, and cultural institutions and invitations to teach and lecture. These were prerequisites to getting a visa from Washington as well as an exit permit form the Vichy government to leave. Additional funds were needed to help the exiles exist in Marseilles during their months of waiting, as well as for their passage.[8] Between 1933 and 1944, 717 artists and 360 architects arrived in the United States. Many settled in New York City within close proximity to the Museum of Modern Art.[9]

Blanche's Illness

Blanche continued her routine of traveling and volunteering at the Baltimore Museum of Art; however, she was plagued with increasingly severe stomach problems. Some Jews are genetically predisposed to stomach ulcers. Such was the case for the Adler family. As a result, after his formal medical training, Dr. Harry Adler concentrated his practice on the study of nutrition and digestive-related illnesses. His interest was clinical and personal. He had suffered with stomach ailments for years, as did Blanche.

During the summer of 1939, while visiting with Saidie and Al, Blanche had a lot of problems with her stomach. The summer before, her trip to Honolulu and Alaska with Helen had been enjoyable, but even then she was nagged with stomach pain and bleeding. She tried to be careful what she ate, but she started to lose weight. The last week of September, 1940, Blanche, accompanied by Saidie and Al, flew back to Baltimore so that she could see the stomach doctor.

Saidie and Al headed to New York for a couple of weeks and stayed at the Hotel Gotham before the opening of the Renaissance Room. While there, they attended at least one party given by

Right: A new period room for the Baltimore Museum of Art, *The Sunday Sun*, September 29, 1940, Metrogravure Section, p.1. Photo by A. Aubrey Bodine. Reprinted with permission of the *Baltimore Sun* Media Group. All Rights Reserved.

Margaret Scolari Barr to raise funds for the American Rescue Committee, and were eager to help their close friends. On October 4, Saidie went into the Buchholz Gallery to see Curt Valentin's new acquisitions. She fell in love with a large painting by Fernand Léger, *Étude pour les Saltimbanques* (1939), which she purchased for $700.

"By October, 1940 the Vichy government proclaimed its so-called humanist racial laws." These laws defined the status of Jewish citizens, barred from society and any jobs which would earn them a decent wage or prestige.[10] Saidie and Al took the train from New York to Baltimore on October 16, and stayed at the Belvedere Hotel for two weeks.

The Renaissance Room Reception

Friday night, October 18, 1940, was the official opening reception of the Renaissance Room at the BMA. The room's contents represented various cultures in Europe, some earlier, but none later than the Jacobean period. The furniture was mostly French, with three Italian primitives. Other objects included Mille Fleurs tapestries, a state chair (Henry II period), paintings from the school

Left: *Majolica Plate*, c. 1720–1740, Deruta, Italy, tin-glazed earthenware plate with polychrome and luster decoration, 16 in. diameter, The Baltimore Museum of Art: Gift of Saidie A. May, BMA 1935.34.1. Above: *Three Saints from an Orphrey*, 16th century, Netherlands, silk and metallic embroidery threads, linen, silk velvet, 34-1/2 x 26 in., The Baltimore Museum of Art: Bequest of Blanche Adler, BMA 1941.141.

of Simone Martini, including a "Crucifixion" and "Madonna and Child," a wood carving of St. Catherine, textiles, small bronzes, a book of hours with rich illuminations and, as Saidie described it, "everyday articles which a Jacobean gentleman might have had in the Great Hall of his manor house."

With the exception of the paneled room, all of these items had been collected by Saidie over the years and used to furnish her New York apartment before she disassembled it.[11] Saidie and Al attended the opening, where Mr. Alfred Frankfurter, editor of the *Art News*, gave his insights into the project. A dinner was held beforehand by the Cheeks to celebrate the opening, including the Frankfurters, Saidie and Al. In the temporary galleries near the Renaissance Room, an exhibit entitled, "Again, Arms and Armor" displayed dramatic weaponry from a collection lent specially for the occasion by the Metropolitan Museum of Art in New York.[12] Throughout the evening, an orchestra played in the Garden Court, during which coffee and refreshments were served.[13]

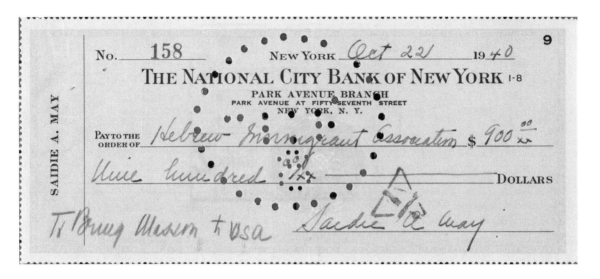

Arrangements are Made

During her stay in Baltimore, Saidie spent time with her sisters and visited other relatives. But on October 22, Saidie made a special visit to the Baltimore office of the Hebrew Immigrant Association to fund the Masson family's passage out of France to the U.S. The amount needed to accomplish this was $900. She was happy to finally help them. Blanche had been hospitalized for stomach cancer, and Saidie spent as much time as she could with her sister. By the end of the month, she and Al left for the Pine Needles for the winter.

In Marseilles, Varian Fry used the funds from the patrons in New York to support the artists who could not take care of themselves. He sought to reassure them that they would eventually be free. During the winter of 1940 into the spring of 1941, André Breton (poet and philosopher and the originator of Surrealism), his wife, Jacqueline Lambda, and their daughter, Aube, fled from northern France to live with Fry and other refugee intellectuals, artists, musicians and scientists— the top minds of the day. Once they were blacklisted, they could not work or live a normal life in their communities, and they were watched constantly by the Gestapo. More of them fled to Marseilles to request help from the American Rescue Committee to obtain visas and book passage on any type of vehicle they could obtain to get out of Europe. Many of them had previously been denied visas, either because of their importance or because their political views challenged Nazi policy. They hid at a chateau called villa "Air-Bel," hidden on a deserted farm about one half-hour train ride from Marseilles in the suburb of La Pomme, in Montredon.[14]

The Masson Family at La Pomme

Masson finally came to the realization that he would not leave France for an American showing of his work and became fearful for his family's safety. He was invited to leave Lyons-la-Forêt to stay with his family at Château La Pomme, the estate of Countess Lily Pastré. Pastré was heiress

Left: Cancelled check to Hebrew Immigrant Association for $900.00, October 22, 1940. Saidie A. May Papers, Archives and Manuscripts Collections, The Baltimore Museum of Art. SM2.13.33. Above: (l–r) Max Ernst, Jacqueline Breton, André Masson, André Breton, Varian Fry, Marseilles, France, 1941, Photographic Archive, The Museum of Modern Art Archives, New York, gift of Mrs. Varian Fry, YLLA (Camilla Koffler, 1911–1955).

to the Noilly Prat Vermouth fortune and an arts benefactor. She lent her home, Château Pastré, to approximately forty refugees, including Josephine Baker and the Russian harpist Lily Laskine.[15] Countess Pastré's great interest was in music. The mixed group of refugees would eat dinner in her formal dining room, followed by concerts performed by Jewish musicians who could no longer perform in public under the Vichy laws. Plays were even performed at the chateau during this time. Members of the refugee community kept themselves busy creating and performing to fill the void of the uncertainty while they waited to leave. Ironically, under the wary eye of Vichy, the city of Marseilles became an artistic and intellectual center.[16]

As soon as the family was settled at La Pomme, Masson went over to see the Bretons at the Villa "Air-Bel" and became a regular guest at the picnics they held on the grounds of the estate.[17]

He spent most of the rest of his time painting with oils and watercolors, creating a new series of works. He sent those pieces to the Galerie Simon in Paris for Henry Kahnweiler to sell for him. As he received the new work, Kahnweiler would write to Saidie May in America, and other patrons, offering the new canvases for sale.

The Masson family was housed in the hunting lodge on the grounds of the Pastre estate due to the fact that they had young children. It was not a very spacious building, and Masson was extremely restricted finding a place to paint. As a result, his production slowed and, in his frustration, Masson spent considerable time drinking in the local cafés. He made many antagonizing remarks concerning the Vichy government, prompting André Breton and Masson's wife, Rose, to conclude that they needed to get him out of the country as soon as they could, in order to keep his remarks from getting them all into trouble.[18] Rose convinced her husband to go and see Varian Fry to work on the possibility of emigration for all of them.

While they waited to escape, Breton and his Surrealist friends held "camp." This was an intimate, fun, carefree existence, where they felt free to experiment and create art, music and writing. From November through May, this wild, uncensored "party" lifestyle thrived, enticing other artists from Marseilles and nearby towns to rush over and join the fun. This Surrealist group rebelled against the social order, European politics and culture, and all of the traditional art forms in Europe. Their artwork and poetry were based on the idea that the true artist relies on his subconscious mind to guide the work, as well as occasional random chance. Many of these ideas were formulated based on the works of Sigmund Freud, Friedrich Nietzsche and other European philosophers, as well as current scientific ideas and new discoveries—which these artists interpreted in their work. They were even starting to experiment with new man-made materials in their artworks.

Masson was very close to André Breton. The two had been friendly for many years, and Breton considered him to be the quintessential Surrealistic artist. During the fall of 1940, the two men spent hours together discussing Surrealist ideology, and practicing their respective crafts.

Villa Air-Bel

Air-Bel was situated in a pastoral area of southern France with big trees, a fabulous garden and long expanses of pastureland. The autumn air that fall was unusually warm, and the group took advantage of the good weather by congregating at a long table on the lawn, singing, listening to poetry readings, playing games, creating art and sharing meals together.[19] Many other families, friends and followers of Surrealism would come and spend Sundays at Villa Air-Bel, where Breton would lecture on his philosophy of Surrealism, while everyone feasted on local food. It was a very special and productive bonding time for the families and their friends. They "basked and frolicked

Fernand Léger, French 1881–1955, drawing study for the *Saltimbanques*, 1939, gouache on paper, 40-1/2 x 55 in. Collection BMA, 1951.324. ©2011 Artists Rights Society (ARS), New York/ADAGP, Paris.

madly in each other's daily company."[20] Many of the games they played were the genesis of colorful and inventive works of art.

Even though they were technically in exile, they used their time together discussing life, Surrealist ideology and new ideas in all fields, as well as creating art. Families whose lives were in jeopardy would come and go as they were able, depending on whether they obtained visas, legally or illegally, to leave the country. Even though it was dangerous, Masson would occasionally travel to Paris himself, according to one letter that Kahnweiler wrote to Saidie May.[21] Masson was a true Frenchman, the country was in his blood, and he insisted on trying to lead as normal a life as possible, up until the day he left for America.

While residing at the chateau brought safety, it didn't necessarily bring comfort. The biggest problem the Massons faced was the cold weather during the winter months. There was no central heating in those large, drafty chateaus. They had been built as holiday retreats, perfect in the summer months, and usable for an occasional weekend other times of the year, but not equipped for extended stays during cold weather. The residents had to spend part of each day foraging in the nearby woods for anything that they could burn to try and keep warm. There were small, round

iron stoves in the bedrooms which were stuffed with paper and wood before they went to bed at night, to be ready for lighting in the morning. With a shortage of blankets for the residents, they slept under their overcoats in the cold. Wood was their only fuel, but they never cooked with it. Food was scarce; it was rationed, but not much was available in the local shops anyway.[22] Everyone suffered.

Marc Chagall Decides to Leave

Fry visited another reluctant refugee, artist Marc Chagall, #210 on the ARC list. Fry wrote that he "lived in an old stone cottage in Gordes, refusing to believe that he might be in danger. He was quite comfortable living in Gordes and working in his studio, containing a big kitchen table, a few wicker chairs, a cheap screen, a coal stove, two easels and his pictures."[23] Fry invited Mr. and Mrs. Chagall to meet him in town for a glass of wine and bouillabaisse one evening after visiting them at their studio. They were to try and discuss the possibility of their emigration to the United States. The Chagalls were reluctant until, during their meal, air-raid sirens went off outside. The restaurant owner quickly drew the black-out curtains, and they continued to dine by candlelight. When they finished eating, they left before the raid was officially over, walking quickly to the station at Noailles, where they waited out the raid. This incident frightened them sufficiently into making the decision to leave.[24]

Fernand Léger

Once in New York, after he opened the Buchholz Gallery, Curt Valentin started selling art to Saidie. He wrote to D.H. Kahnweiler and let him know that he was dealing with her. Kahnweiler's friend, Fernand Léger, managed to escape from France through Lisbon, Portugal, and came to New York on November 16, 1940. He arrived planning to paint a mural using Saidie's recent purchase from Valentin, *Étude pour les Saltimbanques*, as his study. Valentin wrote to Saidie, inquiring whether she would be willing to lend Léger the painting to work with, as it was already at the BMA.[25]

Saidie wrote to Leslie Cheek, suggesting that the BMA take the opportunity to highlight the work, and make it a "living interest matter" by displaying it prominently in the front of the museum. She further explained that the museum should permit the artist to use it towards his next work. Leslie Cheek offered to take this idea one step further, and have a large showing of Léger's work. Saidie suggested enlisting the help of Curt Valentin to invite Léger to speak about his work at the museum. This was tentatively scheduled for May 1941.[26] The only drawback to this idea was that Fernand Léger refused to learn English while he was temporarily in the United States for the duration of the war. BMA officials realized they would be forced to work with interpreters during the lecture. As a result, this project never came to fruition.

On November 10, Saidie wrote to Kahnweiler that she had paid for the Masson family's passage and requested that he pass on the information to Masson. She also wrote about her sister Blanche's illness, and how devastating it was for her. It wasn't until December 23 when he finally received that correspondence. Two weeks previously, he got a letter that Saidie had written July 31, which had ended up somewhere else in France, and had been opened and read by German censors.[27]

Blanche's Illness Worsens

All through the winter of 1940, while Saidie was vacationing in North Carolina, Blanche suffered with terminal stomach cancer. She and Saidie had lost their brother, Harry, a few years earlier on November 1, 1937, at the age of 65. Now Saidie was faced with losing the sibling she was closest to. Blanche had been admitted to Sinai Hospital soon after she was diagnosed, and remained there until her death. She had a private room and was hooked up to an intravenous drip, hardly able to eat. She became weaker and started sleeping more during the day. When friends and relatives came to visit, she tried to be gracious and attentive, but it was becoming increasingly difficult to maneuver each day, as she tired easily and experienced more pain. Eventually she was placed in an oxygen tent which covered her upper body. Having been previously used, the milky-colored plastic sheeting had been patched, having been torn or pierced by nurses administering to other patients. Atop this bubble was a sickly green rubberized tube extending over to a tall, dark-green oxygen tank, pumping vigilantly.[28]

As time dragged on, Blanche's sterile room with its pale yellow walls started to fill with colorful flowers arranged in vases of dark sea-green glass. The wall across from her bed had framed copies of her favorite Dürer prints, hung up high for her to see. An enormous window from the ceiling to the floor revealed the thriving, bustling activity outside on Monument Street—a world from which Blanche was now excluded. A small metal radiator ran the length of that wall, seeming to support the window, belching and clanging as it filled the room with warmth. Blanche's thin, weakened torso lay helplessly on the stark, colorless sheets atop the grey metal bed.

At the end of December, Saidie came back to Baltimore to see Blanche. She again stayed at the Belvedere Hotel and came to the hospital in the afternoons, spending the mornings taking care of her business and checking on the Renaissance Room. She had decided to hire Mr. Marvin Chauncey Ross, a friend and curator of Byzantine Art at The Walters Art Gallery to catalogue her entire collection at the BMA, with a separate catalogue for the Renaissance Room collection. This would be her next project with the BMA.

It was so disheartening to see her sister withering away, but Saidie tried to act positive and upbeat. Helen also spent afternoons with her sisters in the small hospital room. As Saidie left the hospital, rain and sleet fell, creating dark slush along the curbs, dreary, damp and cold. Saidie hated cold weather, and the short days and darkening skies made her sad. She felt hopeless: of all her siblings, Blanche was her favorite—they had shared so many interests.

On Wednesday, January 8, 1941, Blanche lost her battle with cancer. Her funeral service was held in the apartment, with the casket in the large dining room. Afterwards she was cremated.[29] She left her financial estate to the Sinai Hospital of Baltimore, where the money was to be used to subsidize the cost of care for those who could not afford it. Her entire art collection was left to the Baltimore Museum of Art.[30]

Saidie had lost her closest confidant and she was devastated. She related her grief in a letter to D. H. Kahnweiler. That same day, a continent away, André Masson wrote to Saidie, acknowledging her generosity in securing his family's passage to America, and indicating how much they looked forward to seeing her and Al again.

Notes

1   Alice Goldfarb Marquis, *Alfred H. Barr, Jr., Missionary for the Modern* (Chicago, Illinios: Contemporary Books, 1989), 186.

2   Daniel-Henry Kahnweiler to Saidie A. May, July 10, 1940, Saidie A. May Papers, BMA.

3   *Ibid.*

4   John Russell, *Matisse, Father and Son* (New York: Harry N. Abrams, 1999), 208.

5   Stephanie Barron, *Exiles and Emigres—The Flight of European Artists from Hitler* (New York: Harry N. Abrams, Los Angeles County Museum of Art, 1997), 105.

6   Sheila Eisenberg, *A Hero of Our Own, The Story of Varian Fry* (New York: Random House, 2001), 129.

7   *Ibid.*, 126.

8   Martica, Sawin, *Surrealism in Exile and the Beginning of the New York School* (Cambridge, Mass: MIT Press, 1995), 116.

9   Alice Goldfarb Marquis, *Alfred H. Barr, Jr., Missionary for the Modern* (Chicago, Illinios: Contemporary Books, 1989), 187.

10 Pierre Assouline, *An Artful Life, A Biography of D.H. Kahnweiler 1884–1979* (Canada: Fromm International Publishing Corporation, 1991), 279.

11 "The Opening of the Renaissance Room," *Baltimore Museum of Art News*, 2:8 (October, 1940), 61.

12 Leslie Cheek to Saidie A. May, October 10, 1940, Saidie A. May Papers, BMA.

13 "The Opening of the Renaissance Room," *Baltimore Museum of Art News*, 2:8 (October, 1940), 62.

14 Sheila Eisenberg, *A Hero of Our Own, The Story of Varian Fry* (New York: Random House, 2001), 129.

15 Martica Sawin, *Surrealism in Exile and the Beginning of the New York School* (Cambridge, Mass: MIT Press, 1995), 121.

16 *Ibid.*

17 Sheila Eisenberg, *A Hero of Our Own, The Story of Varian Fry* (New York: Random House, 2001), 130.

18 Martica Sawin, *Surrealism in Exile and the Beginning of the New York School* (Cambridge, Mass: MIT Press, 1995), 136.

19 Sheila Eisenberg, *A Hero of Our Own, The Story of Varian Fry* (New York: Random House, 2001), 131.

20 Varian Fry, *Surrender on Demand* (New York: Random House, 1945), 115.

21 Daniel-Henry Kahnweiler to Saidie A. May, February 12, 1941, Saidie A. May Papers, BMA.

22 Varian Fry, *Surrender on Demand* (New York: Random House, 1945), 121.

23 Sheila Eisenberg, *A Hero of Our Own, The Story of Varian Fry* (New York: Random House 2001), 122.

24 *Ibid.*

25 Saidie A. May to Leslie Cheek, November 17, 1940, Saidie A. May Papers, BMA.

26 Saidie A. May to Leslie Cheek, December 12, 1940, Saidie A. May Papers, BMA.

27 Daniel-Henry Kahnweiler to Saidie A. May, December 23, 1940, Saidie A. May Papers, BMA.

28 Dr. Sam Abrams, Telephone interview with author, Pikesville, MD, April 19, 2006.

29 Clare Speier Baer, Interview with author, May, 2006, Baltimore, MD.

30 "Hospital gets Bulk of Adler Estate," January 8, 1941, *The Baltimore Sun*.

Escape, 1940–1941

15

aidie received a letter from André Masson dated January 8, 1941, stating that he and his family had finally obtained an American exit visa,[1] so long awaited! They were very excited about the voyage and grateful to Saidie for making it possible. Wary of German censorship, Masson was careful to indicate the reason for the trip as exhibiting his work in America. The letter got through!

Saidie remained in Baltimore after the funeral to help Helen deal with Blanche's estate. One personal item that Blanche especially wanted the museum to have was a charm bracelet with antique coins that she had purchased in Paris.[2] She wanted the coins removed from the bracelet, since they were museum pieces themselves. Among them was a Louis XIV piece, one of Alexander the Great and an eighteenth-century-silver-gilt German mark which Saidie had given her. Another charm was a tiny enameled man, a historical copy of an Italian renaissance work.

The BMA Members' Room

Over the years, both Saidie and Blanche helped build the BMA library by donating many books on art and related subjects. Consequently, the BMA became the center in the area for books on contemporary art and artists and books on artistic printing.

At the beginning of February, Saidie met with the board of the BMA about opening a "Members' Room for Modern Art," modeled after the same design already in place at MOMA in New York.[3] This room would be a comfortable place for the staff to hold study and discussion groups related to Modern art, and where patrons could admire Saidie's modern art collection. Members would also have access to current books and magazines on the subject. At that time, the Baltimore Museum of Art had no place intended for the display of its growing Modern art collection, and Saidie suggested converting the print room for that purpose. She was very specific as to how the room was to be used: "only Modern art be shown, no work of local artists, the spirit of the room is to inspire the artist

Standing over a bridge, American Vice Consul Hiram Bingham looks out over the port of Marseilles. Collection United States Holocaust Memorial Museum #34475

Fernand Léger, French, 1881–1955, *Yellow Composition*, 1928, oil on canvas, 36 x 29 in. (91.4 x 73.7 cm), The Baltimore Museum of Art: Bequest of Saidie A. May, BMA 1951.322. ©2011 Artists Rights Society (ARS), New York/ADAGP, Paris.

in the expression, not to exhibit that expression. To exhibit modern paintings, prints, sculpture and drawings only. No craft, photographs or architectural plans or designs. To exhibit rotating shows displaying modern art in small amounts, agreeably placed in a handsome interior—of which a certain approximate percentage must come from my collection of modern art."[4]

Saidie wrote another letter to the BMA board suggesting that non-members be allowed to view the exhibit by receiving permission from the director's office and being accompanied by a museum employee.

The Members' Room was donated in Blanche's memory. Saidie and Adelyn Breeskin planned to have a separate catalogue of her Modern art collection compiled by James Johnson Sweeney, MOMA's nationally recognized curator of Modern art. After making all of these arrangements, Saidie then boarded a train for North Carolina to winter with Al at the Pine Needles.

Chagall's Departure is Arranged

On February 16, 1941, Saidie heard that Marc Chagall and his wife were waiting in Marseilles to acquire visas to leave, but they needed money to pay for them. She immediately wired the money to New York for that purpose.[5] At the end of the month, she and Al headed to New York. On February 25, Saidie gave an additional check to Curt Valentin at the Buchholz Gallery to help the Chagalls travel from Marseilles to the U.S. The money was funneled through the Fund for Jewish Refugee Writers to the American Rescue Committee for them.[6]

Furnishing the Renaissance Room

Saidie received a telegram from Marvin Chauncey Ross that the "antiquities" department of Gimbel's department store was having a sale. On his recommendation, she purchased at a bargain price six thirteenth- and fourteenth-century Gothic stained glass panels, one out of the Bourges Cathedral in France. These panels were of the early "pot metal" variety, that is, they had acquired their colors in a melting pot. Due to this process, the glass was uneven in its hue, creating a unique brilliance that could never again be attained in later windows.[7] She also purchased a group of Renaissance glass medallions and three groups of seventeenth-century Flemish Grisaille roundels. All of these objects would illustrate the development of European glass, and enhance her collections in the Renaissance Room.

At the beginning of March, she and Al headed back to the Pine Needles for the rest of the winter. While they relaxed in the warmth and safety of North Carolina, their artist friends were desperately trying to leave the horrors of war in Europe. The Breton family was able to escape sooner than the Massons, as Peggy Guggenheim had paid for their passage. The Bretons, the Lams and three hundred fifty others left Marseilles on March 23, 1941, in an old cargo ship, the *Capitaine Paul-Lemerle,* bound for Martinique. This group was lucky: ships leaving Marseilles for

Group portrait of European refugees assisted by the Emergency Rescue Committee on board the *Capitaine Paul-Lemerle*, a converted cargo ship sailing from Marseilles to Martinique, Tuesday, March 25, 1941. Courtesy of Dyno Lowenstein, collection United States Holocaust Memorial Museum, #34444.

Casablanca or Martinique were few. Often the ships were Portuguese, as it was believed Portugal's neutrality would give its ships immunity from German U-boat attack.[8] Remaining behind was painful for André Masson, as he wondered whether he would ever see his good friends again. It took the ship one month to get to Fort-de-France, Martinique, which was a compulsory "last stop" on French territory.

Meanwhile, in New York, Pierre Matisse sent a letter to Saidie on March 20 concerning a new artist represented by his gallery, Yves Tanguy. Matisse had acquired Tanguy's entire production of his latest work since emigrating from France. He was excited and anxious for Saidie to see these new pieces and add one to her collection.[9]

Eleven days later, nervous and scared, the four members of the Masson family were smuggled out of southern France in the middle of the night by the American Rescue Committee on another old, dilapidated Portuguese cargo ship, the *Carimaré*. Rose's mother had to be left behind, even though twelve other people crowded onto that small boat with them.

It was a very difficult voyage to America, the same trip that the *Capitaine Paul-Lemerle* had made, also at sea for thirty days, under orders from Vichy to steer a zig-zag course across the Atlantic to aggravate the refugees. The dark, unventilated hold inside the ship was turned into an improvised dormitory, with straw pallets on a makeshift scaffolding constructed by the ship's carpenter. On the deck were crudely improvised communal sanitary facilities, nauseatingly rank.[10]

The ship finally disembarked at Fort-de-France, Martinique, where Masson met up with André Breton and Wilfredo Lam, who had arrived a week earlier. Aimé Césaire, a Surrealist poet and native of the island, hooked up with the group and guided them around the entire island where they explored its exotic culture for three weeks.

The artists hiked on the bleached sand through tropical, feathered palms, gently winding through secret trails hidden by green, sun-soaked foliage. Camouflaged beasts peered between the leaves, mysteriously watching as the visitors passed through their serene world—eyes following every movement. Miniature blooms of periwinkle, canary and carrot, laced undergrowth like colorful bouquets tossed at will.

The men sat on the beach and watched silently as a formation of mushroom-brown pelicans rode on strong wind currents like contented kites, then swooped down low over the liquid crystal with mounting anticipation. One spied a school of long silver fish drinking in the bright sun's rays. Its torpedo-like beak rammed the glass, splintering shards in all directions, scooping the shiny prize, swallowing it whole. Content for the moment, it rejoined its brothers in their airforce-like formation, moving onto the next encounter.

Masson walked alone in the early morning when the beach woke as the sun rose, squinting as its rays gently washed the sand with color. The low mounds of creamy shells lay like seals napping on the shore. He looked out over the horizon where a flat, blue-brown line cut the sky away from the water, razor-sharp from one end of the milky white beach to the other. Endless blue-green, flat as a newly formed ice rink. As his eyes focused where the beach met the water, Masson watched small ripples curl on the sand. Tiny pink-coral and white shells spilled forth from the water—new to the day's light. The water's motion repeated endlessly, undulating in timeless rhythm as the gems rolled up and down the waters edge in an ancient dance.

As the wind awakened, it pulled strands of blue towards the beach in a quickened pace. The flat abyss gave way to gentle hills. As they approached the curls enlarged, and salt-foam began to surf along the mounds. As it rode along, it teased the water until finally lunging forward into a glassy spiral, spilling itself onto the glistening wet sand, spreading its fingers to reach as far up the beach as it possibly could, turning and pouring back from where it came, over and over.

That same breeze gently pushed the stately palms, swaying their long, slim trunks as the native dancer shook her grass skirt, the fronds waving to sailors far-off in the distance along the horizon.

This sojourn into nature profoundly affected Masson, influencing how he would look at the world and create art for the duration of his exile in America.

"The spectacle of lush tropical jungle vegetation, the aroma of baobabs, wild orchids and other flowers and ripe fruit, and the sight of Mount Pele, the still-active volcano which had given birth to the island, and had the capacity to destroy it, would enrich his mythology of nature and later emerge in painted dreams and fantasies."[11]

Masson Travels from Martinique to America

The classical beauty of the island's native inhabitants also had a powerful effect on him, inspiring his American painting, *The Antille of 1943*. He wrote of his experience, "The artist is seen as one with nature and his creations as one with nature's handiworks."[12] Because he found Martinique's folklore so fascinating, he later explored other cultures' mythologies during his stay in Connecticut, influencing more of his paintings. Masson, having been refreshed and now optimistic about the future, embarked on the last part of his journey to America with his friends, André Breton and Wilfredo Lam. En route to America, the boat stopped at one exotic island after another, until the Lams got off in Cuba—the place of Wilfredo Lam's birth.

Wilfredo Lam

As a young man, Wilfredo Lam immigrated to Barcelona, Spain where he became friendly with Pablo Picasso who introduced him to the art dealer, Pierre Loeb. Lam and his wife, Helena Benitez (a German chemist), then moved to France to be part of the vibrant arts community. But Loeb, who had purchased a lot of Lam's work, was compelled to close his gallery in response to the anti-Jewish laws that were in place. Lam and his wife decided to leave France and went to Marseilles, joining André Breton and his group. The Lams were frequent visitors at the Villa Air Bel salons, although they did not live there while waiting for their visas.

Group portrait of European refugees saved by the Emergency Rescue Committee on board the *Due d'Aumale*, a French passenger ship that transported them from Martinique to New York, #34443. Collection United States Holocaust Memorial Museum.

Wilfredo Lam, Cuban, 1902–1982, *The Jungle*, 1943, gouache on paper mounted on canvas, 94-1/4 x 90-1/2 in. The Museum of Modern Art, New York, 140.1945. ©2011 Artists Rights Society (ARS), New York/ADAGP, Paris.

Life in Cuba was not easy for the painter, as the couple had limited supplies and little money. They could not leave, and Lam could not afford oil paints and canvas. As a result he was resigned to work with less expensive gouache and pencils on paper.

The Massons Arrive in New York

At the beginning of May, Saidie and Al headed for the Hotel Gotham in New York for two weeks and then took the train back to Baltimore. Throughout the month, she anxiously awaited word of the Massons' arrival at Ellis Island.[13]

They finally arrived in the port of New York on May 29, 1941. Due to the unpredictable arrival time of their ship, the group scheduled to meet them was not there. André and his family were exhausted. Their interactions with customs officials was frustrating, as they spoke only French. The officials were suspicious at best. After reviewing Masson's drawings, the customs officials ultimately confiscated his portfolio, declaring the drawings obscene. They specifically objected to a drawing featuring a landscape with a cave that was the body of a woman with a small figure entering the cavity of her vagina.[14] It would take Masson four months to have the drawings returned, requiring the intercession of his friend, poet Archibald MacLeish, librarian of Congress.[15]

Saidie and Al arranged for the Massons to stay in an apartment in the Hotel Van Rensselaer in Greenwich Village.[16] Then she and Al moved out to New Mexico for the summer. New York's artistic community was vibrant and cohesive. The surrealist painters who had immigrated to New York remained close-knit. They lunched together frequently, wandered the streets as a group and edited surrealist magazines together. Their meeting places included those galleries sympathetic to them as well as the Free French Canteen.[17] André Breton and his family had settled up the street from the Massons. He approached Pierre Matisse and persuaded him to add Wilfredo Lam to his stable, even though Lam and his wife could not get out of Cuba.

Masson hated cities and mentioned this to Curt Valentin. Valentin wrote to Saidie, offering to help find the Massons a place in the country.[18] He contacted Alexander Calder who was procuring rental homes for his artistic friends in Connecticut, where he lived. Within a couple of weeks he had found a place and Saidie paid for the rental of their home. Thus like so many other exiled émigrés, the Massons moved to northwestern Connecticut, which became an enclave of refugee artists and their American friends. It was inexpensive, secure and isolated. Marie and Eugene Jolas and Naum and Miriam Gabo already lived there. This area became a "Surrealist outpost," visited frequently by André Breton and his family, as well as Marcel Duchamp and others."[19] For one full year, Masson and his family had been on the move, from Normandy to the Auvergne to Marseilles to Martinique to New York and then on to Connecticut. Masson had never stopped drawing but he could not paint on the move.[20] He and his family remained in Connecticut for the duration of the war.[21]

Masson was pleasantly surprised at the "ruralness" of Connecticut and wrote to Saidie praising the flora and fauna. He delighted in discovering flowers like the native "Indian Pipe" and the beautiful butterflies in the fields around his residence. Emigration seems hardly to have interrupted his artistic activity; a mere three weeks after his arrival in New York he wrote to Saidie that he was "slowly returning to work."[22] Once he started to paint again, it was as if a pent-up force was released, and he became richly productive with a newer, updated style.[23] In addition, he and André Breton had plans to publish, by the fall of 1941, the texts, drawings and collages on which they had collaborated during their stay on Martinique.

Further Planning for the Members' Room

On June 21, Marc Chagall and his wife, took the train from Marseilles to Spain and then on to Lisbon, Portugal, from where they left for the United States. That same day Leslie Cheek sent a letter to Saidie and Al at the Santa Fe Inn, discussing the approval of the planned BMA "Members' Room for Modern Art." Saidie suggested devoting the opening to a showing of Modern works from her collection, but Leslie Cheek thought that they might

André Masson in New Preston, Conn., courtesy of the Estate of André Masson, Paris, France.

showcase André Masson's work in her collection. He also suggested they invite him and his wife, Rose, to the opening to give the event at this local "small-town" art museum a national exposure. He wrote, "Of course, the mere opening of the room will make a big splash in Baltimore, but if the splash can be enlarged to national proportions, it would help our general local situation, since Baltimoreans never value anything particularly unless an out-of-town organization says it is good."[24] A few days later, Cheek sent Saidie a notice from MOMA announcing a lecture by J.B. Neumann about Paul Klee's work, and an announcement of a small exhibit by Léger in New York. He suggested that possibly Neumann could come to Baltimore with the Klee exhibit, or they could invite Léger to talk about Saidie's collection of his work for the opening of the Members' Room.

Saidie wrote to Leslie Cheek with concern about the Arts Club of Chicago planning a Masson show for three weeks in November. They had written asking her to loan them her collection of Masson's paintings for their show. She refused, basing her decision on the fact that it would "defeat the purpose of the collection—which is to aid and inspire Baltimore artists."[25] She told Leslie Cheek to contact André Masson in Connecticut to see if he could fit the Baltimore show into his schedule for October. She also suggested getting in touch with Curt Valentin, Masson's representative in America and MOMA, which had a large important work of Masson's in its collection. The Pierre Matisse Gallery also had some pieces. At this point, Saidie's letters reflected her concerns about her health: she had a tenacious cold and was reluctant to travel to attend openings.

After hearing from Masson, Saidie encouraged him to have the show he had prepared for before he left France. Upon her suggestion, and in gratitude for her kindness, Masson arranged to give his first show in America at the Baltimore Museum of Art. The basis for his lecture was material based on the development of the "imagination in Modern Art"—specifically in Cubism and Surrealism. He worked on formatting the experience of the painter "objectifying" the painting, using his imagination, no longer relying on imitating existing objects in reality. In his view, "the painter stays a tributary of nature in the universal forces, and his work will have lasting importance when it is nourished by his elementary powers."[26]

In the meantime, Marc Chagall had arrived safely in New York with the help of Curt Valentin, who had sold some of his drawings to pay for the passage. Chagall sent an etching to Saidie, dedicated to her in gratitude for her help.[27] Jacques Lipschitz had also arrived safely.

Notes

1 André Masson to Saidie A. May, January 8, 1941, Saidie A. May Papers, BMA.

2 Saidie A. May to Leslie Cheek, February 16, 1941, Saidie A. May Papers, BMA.

3 Saidie A. May to Adelyn Breeskin, February 10, 1941, Saidie A. May Papers, BMA.

4 Saidie A. May to Leslie Cheek, March, 1941, Saidie A. May Papers, BMA.

5 Saidie A. May to Leslie Cheek, February 16, 1941, Saidie A. May Papers, BMA.

6 Fund for Jewish Refugee Writers to Saidie A. May, February 25, 1941, Saidie A. May Papers, BMA.

7 "Rare Stained Glass New Gift to Museum," *Sunday Sun*, November 16, 1941, Section 1, Col. 2, P.9, Baltimore, MD.

8 Martica Awin, *Surrealism in Exile and the Beginning of the New York School*, (Cambridge, Mass: MIT Press, 1995), 116.

9 William M Griswold, *Pierre Matisse and his Artists* (New York: Pierpont Morgan Library, 2002), 86.

10 Sheila Isenberg, *A Hero of Our Own, the Story of Varian Fry* (New York: Random House, 2001), 181.

11 Doris Birmingham, *André Masson in America: the Artist's Achievements in Exile 1941–1945* (Ann Arbor, Mich: UMI Dissertation Services, 1978), 30.

12 *Ibid.*

13 Saidie A. May to Leslie Cheek, May 9, 1941 Saidie A. May Papers, BMA.

14 Martica Awin, *Surrealism in Exile and the Beginning of the New York School*, (Cambridge, Mass: MIT Press, 1995), 140.

15 *Ibid.*

16 Stephanie Barron, *Exiles and Emigrees—the Flight of European Artists from Hitler* (New York: Los Angeles County Museum of Art, Harry N. Abrams), 140.

17 Doris Birmingham, *André Masson in America: the Artist's Achievements in Exile 1941–1945*, (Ann Arbor, Mich: UMI Dissertation Services, 1978), 99.

18 Robert Motherwell interview by Paul Cummings, Greenwich, Conn. 11/24/71 Archives of American Art, SI.

19 Saidie A. May to Leslie Cheek, June 23, 1941, Saidie A. May Papers, BMA.

20 Martica Awin, *Surrealism in Exile and the Beginning of the New York School*, (Cambridge, Mass: MIT Press, 1995), 176.

21 *Ibid.*, 140

22 André Masson to Saidie A. May, June, 1941, Saidie A. May Papers, BMA.

23 André Masson to Saidie A. May, 22 and June, 1941, Saidie A. May Papers, BMA.

24 Leslie Cheek to Saidie A. May, June 21, 1941, Saidie A. May Papers, BMA.

25 Saidie A. May to Leslie Cheek, June 29, 1941, Saidie A. May Papers, BMA.

26 André Masson to Saidie A. May, August 28, 1941, Saidie A. May Papers, BMA.

27 Saidie A. May to Leslie Cheek, August 15, 1941, Saidie A. May Papers, BMA.

The Opening, 1941–1943

Saidie wrote to Leslie Cheek that she had received correspondence from the Massons, who seemed happy in their new home. Rose was distressed about the members of her family remaining in France, particularly her mother, whom they had to leave behind. She was having trouble getting any documentation to try to leave. The Massons had $205 left over from the money Saidie had sent for their passage and wanted to return it to Saidie, but she encouraged Masson to use those funds to purchase new paints and materials to work with. They were grateful for the additional help.[1]

At the beginning of August, Saidie wrote to André Masson asking him if he would lecture at the BMA for the opening of the Members' Room in October.[2] She suggested that J.B. Neumann translate the lecture, "Painting is a Wager." In the lecture, Masson states his position on artistic freedom: "The artist should have the freedom of expression, with his choice of subject left up to him." He had rewritten his previous lecture while waiting to leave Marseilles.[3] These ideas were complicated, and neither Saidie nor Al was capable of translating his words into simple language. Saidie also wanted Neumann to give an introductory talk on Masson, interpreting his ideas for the audience. Of course, Masson was to design the invitation. Curt Valentin got involved by supplying rare material about Masson, suggesting that the museum publish a catalogue of the show. Saidie provided all the funds for the endeavor.

The September issue of the BMA's monthly news magazine contained an enticing article about the new "Members' Room for Modern Art." The room was described as a spacious, pleasingly decorated and furnished venue with a warm neutral color scheme (so as to focus on the artwork hanging on the walls) for chatting with friends, for afternoon tea and for admiring and learning about Modern art.[4] From the Modern Museum of Art, James Johnson Sweeney wrote to Saidie, asking to borrow Miró's *Figures Attracted by the Form of the Mountains*. He wished to include it in their retrospective exhibition of Miró's work scheduled to run from the middle of November through January 20.[5] Saidie agreed to let MOMA borrow it from the BMA. On September 28, Saidie and Al left Santa Fe, New Mexico, where she had been collecting Navajo artwork and headed to New York for a month.

A New York Sojurn

Saidie had a grand time during the two weeks she and Al spent in New York. She went to visit Pierre Matisse's gallery to see the new acquisitions he had written to her about. She purchased three large paintings. *The Earth and Air* (1941) was painted by Tanguy two years after he had come to the U.S. from France. This work was one of his "hermetic" landscapes, defying a single rational interpretation, related to the Surrealist theme of the subconscious.[6] The other two works were *Germination* (1934) by Brignoni and *Rocks* by Matta, painted in France when he was 26 years of age.

When Saidie had visited Masson at his studio outside of Paris in 1938, she asked him to recommend a promising young artist whose work she could start to collect. That person was Roberto Sebastian Matta Echaurren, a native of Chile. André Breton had also discovered Matta's work and convinced Madame Jean Boncher to carry his paintings in her gallery in Paris. Saidie's first purchase of his work was from her gallery before she left Europe for the last time.[7] Now she had work painted by him after his emigration.

Saidie wanted to include them in the second showing of Modern works from her collection in the Members' Room. The show would be entitled "Painting of the Last Decade: Modern Works from 1931 through 1941." This show, to run for the month of November, would be comprised of sculpture and 25 paintings from Saidie's collection including Miró, Beaudin, Matta and Bores. She held off paying for this purchase until January, 1942, to take advantage of the tax benefits. Her

Yves Tanguy, American, born France, 1900–1955, *The Earth and the Air*, 1941, oil on canvas, 45 x 36 in. (114.3 x 91.4 cm), The Baltimore Museum of Art: Bequest of Saidie A. May, BMA 1951.363. ©2011 Estate of Yves Tanguy/Artists Rights Society (ARS), New York.

financial contribution (the bulk of the funds) for the Members' Room for the year 1941 totaled $7,500.00.[8]

Leslie Cheek suggested that Saidie purchase a work by Salvador Dali to complete her Modern collection.[9] But Saidie was of the same opinion as D.H. Kahnweiler on that topic: "His is an extremely fine craftsmanship and very clever, but his academic and his art and expression is not lived. He's not a real artist."

Saidie telephoned Eileen Fry, the wife of Varian Fry, coordinator of the American Rescue Committee, to report on the safe passage of the Masson and Breton families. She also suggested that the organization consider holding a fundraiser in the Baltimore area, since there was a large Jewish community living there.

Saidie received a letter from Rose Masson. While the Massons were waiting for their home to be renovated, they were staying with Eugene Jolas and his family. In the meantime, they wanted to come to New York to visit Saidie and Al.[10] On October 2, Masson came to Saidie's apartment at the Gotham Hotel at 10:30 a.m. Rose arrived a little later. Over lunch, they had a wonderful time visiting and reminiscing about the great times they had in Paris. Then they went to Curt Valentin's gallery to discuss Masson's lecture and the biography that Valentin was going to write. While she was there, Saidie couldn't resist purchasing a pastel by Masson, *Birds Fighting*. She also picked up a 1913 watercolor by Juan Gris for her collection at the BMA. The Massons then went back to their hotel room to be with their two sons. Saidie continued shopping, purchasing thirteenth-century stained-glass windows from Gimbel's (on sale) from the McRay Collection, then on to the Weylin's bookshop for bargains on art books which she donated. At 4:30, she met the Massons and their boys, along with André Breton's daughter, Aube, for tea at Henri's. Afterwards, they all piled into a taxi cab and drove to a movie theater to see a new Laurel and Hardy film. The next day, the Masson family left New York for New Preston, Connecticut, to move into their new home for the duration of the war.[11] In a letter to D.H. Kahnweiler, André Masson described his house in Connecticut as an old transformed barn. On the ground floor was a large living room with old rafters and a fireplace and chimney fashioned from large stones. It was, he wrote, "very Fennimore Cooper, fields all around with rocks here and there—all of that very wild."[12]

In the BMA's October newsletter, Masson was described as having started out as a "diluted Cubist" and ending up being "phantasmagorical," according to a *New York Times* art critic. "The subject matter of his paintings is descriptive of certain tendencies that psychologists attributed to the modern mind." Many of them had to do with struggle, combat and pursuit. The titles included *Animals Devouring Themselves*, *Murder*, *Lovers*, *Massacre in the Sun*, and *Grave Diggers*.[13]

Mr. Gilman Paul finally translated Masson's lecture for the BMA in Baltimore, and then sent it up to Curt Valentin in New York for additions and corrections. Saidie and Al came to Baltimore on October 14 for a short visit to oversee her museum projects. While there Saidie received a letter from Eileen Fry informing her that the American Rescue Committee had indeed planned a luncheon in Baltimore on October 27 at the Southern Hotel, for which they already had many reservations and positive responses.[14] She was grateful to Saidie for the suggestion and asked her to attend if she could. Meanwhile, the staff of the Baltimore Museum of Art made preparations for the Members' Room opening, sending pictures and information to many publications, hoping to obtain national publicity for the event. Reporters from *Time* and *Life* magazines and the *Baltimore Sun* covered the opening.[15]

Saidie did not attend Masson's visit. She had not been feeling well and had already gone back to the Pine Needles resort. On the afternoon of October 31, she sent a telegram to Baltimore congratulating Masson and the BMA on the upcoming exhibit. In the meantime, André and Rose Masson, accompanied by Curt Valentin, departed by train for Baltimore. They arrived at Penn Station at around 5:15. During the ride, Valentin was very encouraging to Masson.[16] The museum sent a car to get them from the station. When they arrived at the museum, Masson quickly arranged his slides, and the three took a short tour of the exhibit in the Members' Room, which included his works from the collections of James Thrall Soby, Paul Rosenberg and Yves Tanguy.

The Evening of the Opening

Leslie Cheek and his wife invited the group to stay in guest rooms in their fashionable apartment house, the Warrington, about a half-mile from the museum. After they got settled, they dressed for dinner.

In their twelfth-floor apartment, the Cheeks held an elegant dinner for fourteen guests before the lecture, in honor of Saidie and André. As Masson could not speak English, they invited a few people who could speak at least a little French to put the artist at ease. The party had an international flavor. Among the guests were Etta Cone and Paul Rosenberg, Masson's former dealer in the U.S. After dinner the guests traveled to the museum to attend Masson's lecture and show.[17]

Unfortunately, the night of the opening was rainy, diminishing the turnout by at least one third. First, Masson read his lecture in French in the auditorium with the lights on, so that people in the audience (each of which had been handed a written translation as they walked in) could easily follow along. Then they lowered the lights and he showed his slides, repeating and reinforcing the ideas expressed in the lecture. Masson instructed the guests: "Lay the canvas flat on the floor, seize your inspiration in that state of ecstasy and paroxysm in which mind and body coincide and regain their lost unity. Let execution be a lightning-swift and automatic act….Think of creation as a risk to be taken and of the picture as a commitment and an adventure."[18]

Afterwards, everyone jammed into the Members' Room for coffee. Masson was "interrogated by numerous people in peculiar French concerning his work."[19] He and his work were the subject of more attention than either had ever attracted in France.[20] Following the reception, when the

André Masson, French, 1896–1987, *Ophelia (detail),* oil on canvas, 44-3/4 x 57-3/4 in. (113.7 x 146.7 cm), The Baltimore Museum of Art: Bequest of Saidie A. May BMA 1951.328. ©2011 Artists Rights Society (ARS), New York/ADAGP, Paris.

Above: Adelyn Breeskin and André Masson at Exhibition of Paintings and Drawings by André Masson opening in the Members' Room for Modern Art, October 31, 1941. Saidie A. May Papers, Archives and Manuscripts Collection, The Baltimore Museum of Art. SM5.7.4A (left) and SM5.7.6A (right). Opposite: Leslie Cheek and Etta Cone at Exhibition of Paintings and Drawings by André Masson opening in the Members' Room for Modern Art, October 31, 1941. Saidie A. May Papers, Archives and Manuscripts Collection, The Baltimore Museum of Art. SM5.7.5A.

museum closed officially at 11 p.m., the Cheeks invited a group of "interesting" people to come back to their apartment to continue their conversations. These continued far into the night. Masson was extremely pleased with this lecture, and thought of it as one of the highlights of his stay in the United States.[21]

Etta Cone

On Saturday, the Massons visited Etta Cone at the Marlborough Apartments in Reservoir Hill. She had invited them over during dinner the night before. They were very excited to be able to see the famous collection firsthand. Masson subsequently wrote to D. H. Kahnweiler about how impressed he was with Etta and Claribel's collection of French paintings.[22] Etta revisited the Masson show in the Members' Room three days later to consider purchasing a painting or drawing of his that was for sale.[23] After deliberating, she finally purchased a drawing. Masson reported that he felt honored, since she had not purchased anything new since Picasso's Rose Period: "Such an important step for a person her age."[24] Etta's sister, Claribel, had set an example of independence for women by being one of the first women graduates of Johns Hopkins Medical School. But it was Etta who, after her sister's death, used that independence to purchase some remarkable paintings and objects to add to their collection.

André Masson in a crowd at Exhibition of Paintings and Drawings by André Masson opening in the Members' Room for Modern Art, October 31, 1941. Saidie A. May Papers, Archives and Manuscripts Collections, The Baltimore Museum of Art. SM5.7.8A.

Leslie Cheek sent catalogues of the exhibition to all of the important museum directors in America. W.G. Constable, curator of painting at the Boston Museum, came on Monday, November 3, and gave positive feedback regarding his experience with the show. The next day, MOMA's Alfred Barr stopped in Baltimore, his home as a child, to see the room and exhibition for himself. He wrote to Saidie to congratulate her, commenting "You own all the best Massons—except ours."[25]

Leslie Cheek wrote Saidie a long, detailed description of the opening's events and included snapshots of the Members' Room after the lecture.[26] Saidie was delighted with the positive feedback she was receiving for all of her efforts. In her response to Leslie Cheek concerning his gossip about Paul Rosenberg, Saidie wrote: "Do you think Paul was trying to get Masson away from [Curt Valentin's] Buchholtz [sic] gallery to his? I heard he would like to have him again. [From the photos] his face had just the right expression for it."[27] Saidie would have loved to have been there!

Notes

1   Saidie A. May to Leslie Cheek, July 5, 1941, Saidie A. May Papers, BMA.

2   André Masson to Saidie A. May, August 12, 1941, Saidie A. May Papers, BMA.

3   Stephanie Barron, *Exiles and Emigrees—The Flight of European Artists from Hitler*, (New York: Los Angeles County Museum of Art, Harry N. Abrams, 1997), 165.

4   "The Members' Room for Modern Art," *Baltimore Museum of Art News*, 3:7, (September 1941), 55.

5   Saidie A. May to Leslie Cheek, September 13, 1941, Saidie A. May Papers, Archives and Manuscripts Collections, BMA.

6   Stephanie Barron, *Exiles and Emigres—the Flight of European Artists from Hitler*, (New York: Los Angeles County Museum of Art, Harry N. Abrams, 1997), 171.

7   Saidie A. May to Mrs. Earle, November 30 ,1941, Saidie A. May Papers, BMA.

8   Leslie Cheek to Saidie A. May, November 25, 1941, Saidie A. May Papers, BMA.

9   Saidie A. May to Leslie Cheek, November 27, 1941, Saidie A. May Papers, BMA.

10 Rose Masson to Saidie A. May, September 23, 1941, Saidie A. May Papers, BMA.

11 Saidie A. May to Leslie Cheek, October 3, 1941, Saidie A. May Papers, BMA.

12 Francoise Levaillant, *André Masson, Les Annees Surrealistes, Correspondence 1916–1942*, (Paris, France: 1990), 471.

13 "André Masson," *Baltimore Museum of Art News*, 3:8, (October, 1941), 67.

14 Eileen Fry to Saidie A. May, October 15, 1941, Saidie A. May Papers, BMA.

15 Leslie Cheek to Saidie A. May, October 31, 1941, Saidie A. May Papers, BMA.

16 Martica Awin, *Surrealism in Exile and the Beginning of the New York School*, (Cambridge, Mass: MIT Press, 1995), 176.

17 Leslie Cheek to Saidie A. May, November 5, 1941, Saidie A. May Papers, BMA.

18 "Origins of Cubsim and Surrealism," typescript of lecture by André Masson, October 31, 1941, Saidie A. May Papers, Archives and Manuscripts Collections, BMA.

19 André Masson to Saidie A. May, November 8, 1941, Saidie A. May Papers, BMA.

20 Martica Awin, *Surrealism in Exile and the Beginning of the New York School*, (Cambridge, Mass: MIT Press, 1995), 176.

21 Doris Birmingham, *André Masson in America: The Artist's Achievement in Exile 1941–1945*, (Ann Arbor, Mich: UMI Dissertation Services, 1978), 38.

22 Francoise Levaillant, *André Masson, Les Annees Surrealistes, Correspondence 1916–1942*, (Paris, France: 1990), 447.

23 Leslie Cheek to Saidie A. May, November 5, 1941, Saidie A. May Papers, BMA.

24 André Masson to Saidie A. May, November 8, 1941, Saidie A. May Papers, BMA.

25 Alfred Barr to Saidie A. May, November 5, 1941, Alfred Hamilton Barr Papers, Archives of American Art, SI.

26 Leslie Cheek to Saidie A. May, 9 November, 1941, Saidie A. May Papers, BMA.

27 Saidie A. May to Leslie Cheek, November 9, 1941, Saidie A. May Papers, BMA.

The Members' Room, 1942–1943

17

During her recuperative stay at the Pine Needles, Saidie actively corresponded with Leslie Cheek to plan upcoming shows in the Members' Room after the Masson show came down. Later in the year, they would concentrate on "older Masters" such as Cézanne, Renoir, Delacroix, Picasso and Gris.[1] Leslie Cheek decided to hand over these activities to his second-in-command, Adelyn Breeskin. She started corresponding back and forth about the specifics of the shows and how the works were to be hung.

At this time, the bulk of the Cone sisters' collection of Impressionist paintings was still in Etta Cone's apartment. Since Saidie's Modern collection was so different from any other holdings in the museum, any time the BMA held an exhibit on Modern art, the majority of the items were drawn from Saidie or Blanche's collections. The only exceptions were those paintings loaned to the show by outside collectors.

Through her correspondence, Saidie expressed her feelings about Modern art: "It's so difficult to understand Modern art and one reason is that it is painful, as well. The best art expresses its epoch and most of us cannot pull ourselves out of the comfortable Nineteenth Century into the turbulent Twentieth, and there is little incentive or urge to do so where certain critics write that Surrealism is a thing of the past here—they actually think they can push aside a living, pulsating expression of the time, just because they don't understand it, and so dislike it. But it always has been like this, and it's one of the reasons Hitler has achieved so much."[2]

There seemed to be only one negative outcome to the Members' Room project. This was expressed by a small group of artists who fostered radical viewpoints when it came to the museum's rules. They were dissatisfied with the policies of the Members' Room, which admitted only members and their friends, especially since this was allowed within a building built for the public good. They planned to demonstrate through the press. Leslie Cheek asked Saidie to write a statement of intent to clear up the matter internally for the

Member's Room for Modern Art, from the northeast, undated. Saidie A. May Papers, Archives and Manuscripts Collection, The Baltimore Museum of Art. SM5.7.2.

museum board, so there would be no question as to what the restrictions were.[3] He wanted to head off any bad publicity over the matter. In later years, this controversy would lead to the demise of the room.

Helen continued to live in the large top-floor apartment at the fashionable Riviera Apartments which she and Bob had shared with Blanche. Helen's long-time butler, George was close to the family and was intrigued with Saidie's new room at the museum. A week after the opening, he arrived at the office of the director and introduced himself, asking to see the exhibit. Ms. Breeskin personally took him through and explained some of the works to him. She then showed him the "Art of Mary Cassatt" exhibit, which he also liked. Even though he had trouble with spelling and grammar, he was so moved by the room and the artwork that he wrote a very touching letter to Saidie. George praised her idea, and reflected that it "makes you forget all the terrible things going on in the world" (in reference to the war).[4] Saidie was very pleased, as her goal in collecting was to expose everyone in Baltimore to the new Modern art.

Native American Art and the Junior Room

Saidie had begun to move into a new endeavor. When she had visited the West and lived in Santa Fe, she became interested in Native American artifacts and jewelry. She started a collection of beaded clothing and Navajo silver jewelry, which she felt would be of special interest to children. She wanted the museum to create a children's area with showcases designed to hold this collection.[5] Saidie was aware that Baltimoreans visited museums rarely, and often seemed uneasy when there. To address this, she focused on making art appealing to young people. Saidie reasoned that young people should be taught to use and enjoy museums as freely "as they use movie houses." In her opinion, this could best be accomplished by starting them off with a museum of their own, keyed to their age and inclinations. Saidie's idea came to fruition the following year (in 1942), when the museum set up a separate area for children's viewing called the Junior Museum.

The Arts Club of Chicago

During their train ride back to New York after his show in Baltimore, Masson and Curt Valentin discussed the possibility of another show at the Buchholz gallery in March. Masson's work from the Baltimore show had been positively reviewed in the *New York Times*. As a result of this exposure, Masson was subsequently invited to numerous conferences and participated in the writing of articles showing photos of his work in several national magazines. Masson sent a letter to Henry Kahnweiler, asking him to loan the paintings he had for the Buchholz exhibit.[6] After acclimating to the new lifestyle in the United States, Masson relaxed and was quite content with his full schedule, even while living in the country.

The Arts Club of Chicago got a copy of the Masson catalogue from the Members' Room exhibit.

Again they asked Saidie to lend them the Masson paintings from her collection for their exhibit of his work, postponed until May, 1942. The postponement permitted the BMA Members' Room opening to be Masson's first exhibit in the U.S. Saidie wrote back to the exhibition chairman, William Eisendrath, agreeing to send the six paintings listed in the catalogue.[7] She also wrote about the new Masson piece she had recently purchased for the museum, *Ophelia*, and offered that as well. At times, depending on the circumstance, she was very amenable to lending pieces from her collection to other institutions. But Saidie had become wary after Etta Cone cautioned her about lending out works from her collection: "All you get from it is broken frames."[8]

The Arts Club of Chicago, like MOMA, was founded in 1916 by a group of women upset with the fact that no institution in Chicago was interested in Modern art or music. The Chicago Art Institute did not show any Modern art, nor was it being shown by any art dealers in the Chicago area. However, these women prevailed, and the Arts Club of Chicago was born. One of their early shows was of the work of Pablo Picasso.[9]

Until this time, Saidie's acquisitions reflected her artistic interests and tastes, spanning 4,000 years in the history of art. When she donated the Renaissance and Members' Rooms, she was in control of what was given and was consulted on all decisions surrounding their installation. By 1943, she had also collected 115 works by "avant-garde" artists. Now that Masson and his work were in demand, Saidie was receiving requests for the loan of his pieces in her collection.

During the difficult war years, she felt that the BMA constantly bombarded her with requests to purchases items to enhance the Members' Room. However, they would suggest the purchase of something without giving a dollar figure for that purchase. She was growing weary of the daily requests she got for money from this and other sources. She wasn't feeling well and had a more difficult time rejecting requests.

Sundays for Soldiers

The Members' Room continued to be used by the museum for group meetings, receptions after lectures and other informal get-togethers. At the end of 1941, for the holidays, members of the Junior Board held a series of Sunday afternoon open houses called "Sundays for Soldiers". At these events, light refreshments were provided for the servicemen who were interested in spending their free time in the museum. There were movies for them in the auditorium as well.[10] This room created an attractive, serene environment for members and servicemen to relax during the stressful times the war had created. Even with the threat of attack, the BMA remained open and accessible to the pubic and viewed itself as an important community asset for coping with those frightening times.[11]

Leslie Cheek was interested in expanding the use of the Members' Room to the courtyard outside by acquiring garden-style terrace furniture—tables and chairs—and setting up an outdoor

Masson Family, New Preston, Conn., 1943. Top: Rose; left to right: Luis, André, Diego. Courtesy Estate of André Masson, Paris, France.

French sculpture display. He even suggested a series of summer evening "affairs," with music by their WPA orchestra, refreshments from a gaily decorated little stand and film showings. Normally the museum was relatively inactive during the summer months, but Cheek felt this would be another way to reach out to the community.[12] Saidie paid for the outdoor furniture for the project. Even though there was gas rationing and blackouts and money was tight due to rationing, the museum was becoming popular and membership increased by 160. The Members' Room became so popular that visitors wanted a keepsake picture of it. As a result, the museum published a photographic postcard of it, which sold very well.

The next show to be held in the Members' Room was a one-man showing of Max Weber's work, with the artist in attendance for the opening. His paintings appeared very colorful against the blond background of the walls, and he felt that this was the best showing he had seen of his work.

Curt Valentin's Buchholz Gallery held a one-man showing of André Masson's drawings and etchings from February 17 through March 14, and Saidie purchased a portfolio of prints of Masson's work put together by Valentin specifically for that show. She also bought a new work, *The Germ of the Cosmos,* for $600.[13] Masson had a very difficult time producing this painting, and for a while was not happy with the finished product. It was hard for him to sell it, but eventually he came to terms with what he had accomplished and was more comfortable with the work. After this show ended, Curt Valentin sent the work to another show of Masson's at the Wadsworth Athenaeum in Connecticut. From there, it traveled to the BMA, its permanent home.[14] Masson also exhibited *The Seeded Earth* in the Artists in Exile show at the Pierre Matisse Gallery from

March 3 to 28 and had a showing of his paintings, pastels and collages at the Willard Gallery.[15] Then the Rosenberg Gallery asked to show his work, and the Dwight Art Memorial in Massachusetts carried his work in 1942, 1944 and 1945. Masson took part in all of the major group exhibitions of European artists in exile, Surrealists in the United States and artists against fascism.[16] In this way, Masson worked tirelessly to make contemporary French art and culture better known.[17]

Saidie and Al Travel During the Summer

At the beginning of April, the war effort touched the Pine Needles resort, as the military moved part of its operations there. So, on April 13, Saidie ventured north again for a two-week stay at the Hotel Gotham in New York.[18] Once settled, Saidie and Al immediately invited André Masson to their hotel. Rose Masson was ill and Saidie wanted to be supportive during this upsetting time for him. She took him to see the Gershwin opera, *Porgy and Bess,* on Broadway. Even though the story was depressing, she thought the music was beautiful.[19] Later, when Rose felt better, she wrote to Saidie inviting her and Al to visit them in the country, where André was working with their garden like a "true peasant"—growing the vegetables that they were eating.[20]

At the beginning of May, Saidie and Al headed for the Pocono Mountains in Pennsylvania and stayed at the quaint Inn at Buck Hill Falls. That same month Leslie Cheek resigned from the BMA and wrote to Saidie, praising all of the generosity which she had provided to the museum, "in an almost

SOUTH SIDE
THE INN
AT
BUCK HILL FALLS
PENNSYLVANIA

From an Etching
by
Ernest D. Roth

Postcard of south side view of the Inn at Buck Hill Falls, Pa. c. 1950. Collection of the author.

continuous stream."[21] He and Saidie had grown close during the three years that he was the BMA director. Leslie Cheek had to resign from the directorship of the BMA because he was drafted into the Army. He left the museum and reported to Washington, D.C., as a captain working in the War Department building.[22] His family relocated to Asheville, North Carolina.[23] In the end, his idea for the summer terrace outdoor program never materialized, as he was unable to raise the necessary funds from the board. The following month, Adelyn Breeskin, whom Blanche had hired so many years ago, was named acting director of the BMA.

During that summer Masson formed a strong relationship with Arshile Gorky, whom he considered his only friend among American artists. Masson's worked evolved as he immersed himself in the natural surroundings, attempting to reconcile what was happening simultaneously within the earth as well as above the ground. He also approached the surface of the canvas as a flat surface on which the artist makes marks that activate and utilize the entire field, the idea that he developed for "Painting is a Wager."[24] For a while he collaborated with Jacques Lipschitz, forming some small sculptural pieces that were cast in bronze. He sent Curt Valentin a few examples of a piece entitled *Two Children*.[25]

A Rug for the Renaissance Room

In June, Saidie donated an antique Ispahan rug, which she purchased for the floor of the Renaissance Room from Gimbel Brothers department store. It had come from the collection of Clarence H. MacKay, a communications magnate from Chicago. Known as the "Vase Carpet," and thought to have been made in Kerman, it was worn and missing its outer borders. Even so, this rug, outstanding in its size and quality, was woven with approximately 192 senna knots per square inch, wool knotted on a cotton ground. There were only two other known examples of this type, one in Berlin and one in Constantinople. This enormous rug had an overall design of palm leaves with flowering shrubs and urns, with panels in Persian blue, green, old rose and gold. This really brought the entire Renaissance Room together as a lived-in entity.[26] According to an article in the *Evening Sun* on Monday, May 11, the carpet at one time sold for $90,000, but Saidie was able to purchase it for $4,399.50, due to its poor condition.

That same month, Saidie received a letter from Pierre Matisse inviting her to subscribe to *VVV*, the magazine devoted to surrealism. The quarterly was full of imaginative work by painters and writers at the forefront of their fields. Each magazine would contain fifty reproductions of their artwork, as well as critical and creative work in other fields such as anthropology, comparative religion, the evolution of science and "experiment in the wonderful." The contributing artists were André Breton, Leonora Carrington, Marc Chagall, Joseph Cornell, Max Ernst, David Hare, Matta, André Masson, Kurt Seligman and Yves Tanguy. They put together a special limited edition portfolio, numbered in order of subscription to 50, inscribed on the flyleaf: "Prepared Especially for…." The founding memberships cost $100, which included the portfolio and the first four issues of the magazine similarly inscribed. It was referred to as the *American Minotaur*.[27] Saidie signed up immediately, and convinced Etta Cone to subscribe as well. As a result, the BMA was the only museum in the world to have two complete subscriptions in its collection, one left by Saidie and the other by Etta Cone. This enabled them to use one set of the magazines and portfolios to show to the public, while preserving the other set in perfect condition. *VVV* was published from 1942 to 1944.

Notes

1 Leslie Cheek to Saidie A. May, November 8, 1941 Saidie A. May Papers, BMA.

2 Saidie A. May to Mr. Scarff, November 6, 1941 Saidie A. May Papers, BMA.

3 Leslie Cheek to Saidie A. May, November 8, 1941 Saidie A. May Papers, BMA.

4 George Williams to Saidie A. May, December 1, 1941 Saidie A. May Papers, BMA.

5 Saidie A. May to Leslie Cheek, November 9, 1941 Saidie A. May Papers, BMA.

6 Francoise Levaillant, *André Masson, Les Annees Surrealistes, Correspondence 1916–1942* (Paris, France: 1990), 474.

7 Leslie Cheek to Saidie A. May, December 9, 1941 Saidie A. May Papers, BMA.

8 Saidie A. May to Leslie Cheek, December 27, 1941 Saidie A. May Papers, BMA.

9 Russell Lynes, *Good Old Modern, an Intimate Portrait of the Museum of Modern Art* (Kingsport, TN.: Kingsport Press, 1973), 51.

10 Leslie Cheek to Saidie A. May, December 17, 1941 Saidie A. May Papers, BMA.

11 "Art Museum Offer Soldiers' Welcome," *Baltimore News-Post*, December 19, 1941.

12 Leslie Cheek to Saidie A. May, January 30, 1942 Saidie A. May Papers, BMA.

13 Saidie A. May to Adelyn Breeskin, June 10, 1942, Saidie A. May Papers, BMA.

14 Saidie A. May to Adelyn Breeskin, May 11, 1942, Saidie A. May Papers, BMA

15 Martica Sawin, *André Masson in America, 1941–1945* (New York: Zabriskie Gallery, 1996), 13.

16 Stephanie Barron, *Exiles and Emigrees—The Flight of European Artists from Hitler* (New York: Harry N. Abrams, Los Angeles County Museum of Art, 1997), 166.

17 *Ibid.*, 64.

18 Saidie A. May to Leslie Cheek, March 15, 1942, Saidie A. May Papers, BMA.

19 Saidie A. May to Leslie Cheek, April 15, 1942, Saidie A. May Papers, BMA.

20 Rose Masson to Saidie A. May, April, 1942, Saidie A. May Papers, BMA.

21 Leslie Cheek to Saidie A. May, May 11, 1942, Saidie A. May Papers, BMA.

22 Saidie A. May to Mrs. Earle, April 27, 1943 Saidie A. May Papers, BMA.

23 Leslie Cheek to Saidie A. May, May 11, 1942, Saidie A. May Papers, BMA.

24 Martica Sawin, *Surrealism in Exile and the Beginning of the New York School* (Cambridge, Mass.: MIT Press, 1995) 329.

25 Saidie A. May to Adelyn Breeskin, June 16, 1942, Saidie A. May Papers, BMA.

26 "Ispahan Rug," *Baltimore Museum of Art News*, 4:6, (June 1942), 48.

27 Pierre Matisse to Saidie A. May, June 8, 1942, Saidie A. May Papers, BMA.

Back and Forth to New York

A fter much persuasion from André Breton, Pierre Matisse offered Wilfredo Lam a showing of his work in November of 1942. Lam sent him the gouache paintings which he had been working on since he arrived in Cuba. During the month of July, he created a 3 foot by 4 foot drawing on plain brown paper, using gray and white opaque gouache as an "over painting." This work was among several studies for a larger painting, *The Jungle*, 1943 (see page 173). Lam sent the drawing along with some smaller gouache paintings for the fall show. Matisse purchased everything, including the smaller works for $30 each.[1] He asked for exclusive rights to Lam's gouaches in the United States.[2]

The Maillol Sculpture

That same month, Saidie received a letter from Alfred Barr at the Museum of Modern Art concerning a terracotta seated nude sculpture by Maillol which she had loaned them in 1934. Saidie had not had any dealings with MOMA for almost ten years, but she had planned to give this piece to the BMA when it was "ready to accept it"—for display in a permanent, prominent place.[3]

Saidie had first seen this sculpture, along with three other similar works, in Paris at a 1934 showing of Maillol's work at Mrs. John Garrett's Gallery. Saidie immediately fell in love with it, but was unsure about the purchase as it was unlike most of Maillol's cast bronze pieces. She consulted Joseph Brummer (another gallery owner) to ask his opinion as to whether the sculpture was a good representation of Maillol's work. Brummer suggested she buy this uniquely personal piece by Maillol for her collection.[4]

Saidie waited until the show closed and asked Maillol's friend (the French artist) Pierre Brune, to take Saidie and Al to Maillol's home on the Seine. Maillol personally gave them a tour of his studio and his latest work. Saidie knew that the sculpture had not sold at the show and had been returned to Maillol. She offered the artist $900, much less than the

Aristide Maillol, French, 1861–1944, *Seated Figure*, c. 1930, terracotta, 9 x 4 x 6-3/4 in. (22.9 x 10.2 x 17.2 cm). Gift of Mrs. Saidie A. May, The Museum of Modern Art, New York. ©2011 Artists Rights Society (ARS), New York/ADAGP, Paris.

gallery price. Maillol said he would write to Saidie if he accepted her offer.

After a time, Saidie received a bill for 13,000 francs (approximately $896), with an invitation to fetch the work personally. When Saidie and Al arrived at the artist's house, the Maillols and their guests were just finishing their midday dinner. Maillol invited Saidie and Al to join the group for coffee. Afterwards, the three went out to his studio where he repaired the leg of the nude figure that had broken during firing. Maillol then applied a special finish to the piece and packed it in one of his wife's hat boxes for Saidie to take back to the U.S. On her next voyage home, Saidie brought it with her in her steamer trunk. She loaned it to MOMA, and at the time it was considered a very important addition to their collection.[5] While in Maillol's studio, Saidie also purchased one of his drawings and sent it to the BMA by post.

Bitterness Toward MOMA

Since 1934, Saidie had become somewhat bitter towards MOMA. She had done a great deal for them: supporting the museum at its inception and donating art when few others did. She felt MOMA had never acknowledged her involvement sufficiently, and she felt slighted. Saidie was also disappointed that her name had not been included among those of other early donors and patrons that had been inscribed on the museum's stone wall. Conversely, the Baltimore Museum of Art had been more appreciative of her efforts, but the museum-goers were unsophisticated. Saidie felt that the Maillol was not appreciated and had not been properly displayed. In fact, much of the modern sculpture she gave was misunderstood and "inexcusably neglected."[6]

In 1941, Alfred Barr had approached Saidie about giving the Maillol figure to MOMA outright as a gift. Since she had already discussed the pending transfer with Leslie Cheek (who was thrilled to get the work for the BMA), she suggested that MOMA give them something in exchange for it. She liked a large gouache by Rouault—one of two Mrs. Nelson Rockefeller had bought for the museum, each costing $1,700. At that time, Alfred Barr was not in any position to make that deal with Saidie.

By July of 1942, Barr was back to set up the trade, but in the meantime, Etta Cone and her brother, Fred Cone, had each purchased a painting by Rouault, both of which were to be left to the BMA in their estates. Now it no longer seemed important for Saidie to set up the trade.[7]

Alfred Barr had been able to secure another excellent gouache by Rouault, *The Dancer*, by exchanging several other drawings that had been given to MOMA by Mrs. Rockefeller. The gouache, priced at $900, came from the Kraushaar Gallery, which had acquired it from Peggy Guggenheim's Bernheim-Jeune Gallery in Europe in 1929. It had been displayed both at the Toronto Museum of Art and the Art Institute of Chicago. Barr expected that this work would be a fair exchange, since Saidie had paid $900 for the Maillol terracotta (eight years earlier). He even finished his letter to Saidie by saying; "I think both would cost considerably less in Paris."[8]

Saidie was outraged by Barr's modest offer, as the Maillol had increased in rarity and value. She wrote a long letter consulting Adelyn Breeskin about this situation and sent a postcard to Alfred Barr to stall him until they could get the matter settled.

She and Al left the Poconos on October 8 for a visit to New York for ten days. On the 16th they went to the Pierre Matisse gallery to preview Wilfredo Lam's work for his upcoming show. For $350, Saidie purchased a large drawing, *Nude*, reflecting Cuban and African cultures and Picasso's influence. It was sent directly to the BMA to display in the Members' Room.

Wilfredo Lam, Cuban, 1902–1982, *Deity*, 1942, opaque watercolor and charcoal 41-1/4 x 33-1/4 in., The Baltimore Museum of Art: Bequest of Saidie A. May, BMA 1951.318. ©2011 Artists Rights Society (ARS), New York/ADAGP, Paris.

Saidie had read about a new exhibition by Marcel Duchamp, similar to the Surrealist show she and Al had seen prior to leaving Paris.[9] Duchamp had escaped France and was living with Katherine Dreyer at her home in Connecticut. This show, "The First Papers of Surrealism," was installed at the Whitelaw Reid mansion on Madison Avenue. It was referred to as the "Miles of String" exhibition, since Duchamp used one mile of string to weave his own version of a spider web from floor to walls to ceiling. Visitors were forced to climb through the web to get to the

André Masson, French, 1896–1987, *Tauromachie*, 1937, oil on canvas, 32 x 39-7/16 in. (81.3 x 100.2 cm), The Baltimore Museum of Art: The Cone Collection, formed by Dr. Claribel Cone and Miss Etta Cone of Baltimore, Maryland, BMA 1950.349. ©2011 Artists Rights Society (ARS), New York/ADAGP, Paris.

exhibit of the art, which was hung on temporary display panels.[10] Saidie and Al were mesmerized by yet another outlandish show by the eccentric Marcel Duchamp.

At the same time, Peggy Guggenheim was opening her New York gallery, Art of This Century, where she would hold one-man shows for Jackson Pollock, Robert Motherwell, William Baziotes and Saidie's former teacher, Hans Hofmann. The inaugural exhibit included a 1941 sculpture that Masson had created (with Jacques Lipschitz) of his sons, *Two Children*, as well as several of his earlier paintings.[11] Saidie and Al were not aware of this new gallery before they headed south to visit Baltimore.

By the beginning of November, Saidie had made her way to the Pine Needles for the winter months. Meanwhile, Lam's show opened at the Pierre Matisse Gallery. Most of the people who saw the show couldn't afford to buy anything, and many of Pierre's clients were away on military

André Masson, French, 1896–1987, *There is No Completed World*, 1942, oil on canvas, 53 x 68 in., The Baltimore Museum of Art: Bequest of Saidie A. May, BMA 1951.333. ©2011 Artists Rights Society (ARS), New York/ADAGP, Paris.

service. Collecting during wartime was certainly not a priority and the art critics were not prepared to understand Lam's work; the show did not fare well.[12]

Alfred Barr continued to write to Saidie about holding onto the Maillol. In early November, he sent her a letter suggesting an exchange with a work by Georges Braque, *le Journal*.[13] Adelyn Breeskin was planning a showing of Braque's work in the Members' Room starting November 16, 1942, and encouraged Saidie to accept the exchange, since *le Journal* would make a wonderful addition to the show.[14] She succumbed, and MOMA accepted Saidie's "gift" of the Maillol terracotta female figure in exchange for Braque's *le Journal*. The Maillol was sent to MOMA, and the Braque sent to the BMA in time for its show. Formally, *le Journal* was a gift to the BMA from Saidie for her collection.[15]

From the Pine Needles, Saidie wrote to Adelyn Breeskin to tell her that she had sold André Masson's *Tauromachie* (the Bullfight) to Etta Cone, so that she could buy Masson's new larger painting, *There is No Completed World*, shown at the Surrealist show at Curt Valentin's gallery in

New York.[16] *Tauromachie* was the only example of Masson's work of that particular period in any collection in the United States. Saidie felt confident that Etta Cone would keep it in her collection and eventually give it to the BMA with the rest of her estate, and loan it if needed in the meantime.[17] Etta Cone wanted it taken out of the BMA and delivered to her apartment, so she could live with it for a while. On December 4, Adelyn Breeskin personally delivered the painting to her apartment, where she and the movers had to "denude" a space on her overcrowded wall, taking down her early Marie Laurencin painting to go to MOMA for their portrait show. The Masson was hung in its place. Etta Cone was pleased with the Surrealist painting, but wanted to have a more elaborate frame for it, preferably one that would match her older ornate French ones used on her impressionistic works.[18]

Saidie asked Masson to make a labeled diagram of the symbolic content of *There is No Completed World*.[19] He wrote his explanatory diagram in French. Rose translated it into English and sent it to Saidie at the Pine Needles. Saidie was pleased with the artist's own key to his complex symbolic work and forwarded it on to the BMA to be displayed with the painting.[20] *There is No Completed World* can be read as an allusion to the cruelties of the European dictators and of Hitler's regime in particular. It can be understood in the context of the Minotaur myth—the visual

evocation of Pasiphae, Theseus, Daedalus and the Labyrinth, and to that of violent, erotic imagery in general.[21] "The subject as a whole," he explained, " is the precariousness of human life and the fate of its enterprise, always threatened, destroyed and recommenced."[22]

The "Members Only" Controversy

Ever since the Members' Room had opened there was controversy among local artists concerning the privilege of a "members only" facility located in a public institution funded by public monies. Before the room came into existence, the local artists resented having their one-man shows hung in the basement of the museum and, before that, they were upset because the museum didn't sell their paintings for them. It seemed there was always some problem with their perception of how the museum was handling things.[23]

In 1942, a delegation from a group known as the Artist's Union called on Baltimore's mayor, asking that the room be open to all visitors, trying to get him to intervene with the museum. They were unsuccessful.[24] BMA president J.D.G. Paul wrote to Saidie apprising her of the situation and asking for her suggestions. How might the museum open access to the room without destroying the delicate furnishings and the original intent of the project?

Saidie's response included her opinion that artists "are children with all of the child's nasty faults and amazingly fine qualities, who can never be satisfied, as they are external egoists."[25] She felt that these so-called artists would be as destructive to the fragile furnishings as would classes of schoolchildren, and to replace the nice furnishings with functional ones would change the feel and intention of the room.

The Rationale

Saidie was firm in her opinion of the purpose of the room and suggested that, as a compromise, the shows presented in the room could run for two weeks and then be moved to the upper galleries so that the general public could have access to them without jeopardizing the furnishings. The reason for keeping the room "members' only" was to encourage membership in the museum, since many of the public activities at the museum were financed by membership dues. Saidie, Leslie Cheek and Adelyn Breeskin felt that limiting the room to members would be a means to increase those revenues. And, in fact, membership at the museum had increased after the room opened. Prior to that, Mr. Treide, a former director, had spent $15,000 for a membership drive, because at the time the museum was open to the public free of charge with the exception of entrance fees for certain activities. That already limited those activities to people who could afford the entrance fees. Saidie felt that a bit of controversy helped to keep the museum "alive." She would not back down.[26]

William Baziotes, American, 1912–1963, *The Drugged Balloonist*, 1943, collage of printed paper, ink, graphite on paperboard, 10-1/4 x 24 in , The Baltimore Museum of Art: Bequest of Saidie A. May, BMA 1951.266.

204   Saidie May

In February 1943, the Members' Room held an exhibition of the Surrealist paintings from Saidie's collection, including works by Miró, Lam, Masson and others. At least three paintings were being shown for the first time, including Lam's large drawing *The Deity* and Masson's *Germ of the Cosmos* and *There is No Completed World,* together with the artist's explanation of that work. BMA director of research, Sylvia C. Shipley, made her own translation of Masson's chart to hang with his explanation.[27] This particular painting caused quite a stir among museum-goers, with a Dr. J. Hall Pleasants commenting that he hoped "the young cannot recognize all of the pathological implications that shook me."[28] At the same time, MOMA's twentieth-century portrait show, in which the Marie Laurencin portrait from Etta Cone's collection was included, came to the BMA for a month, rented by the museum. It was also well attended.

Postcard of Mary Lyon Hall, Mt. Holyoke College, South Hadley, Mass. c. 1940. Collection of the author.

In March, the museum held its 11th annual local artists exhibition. Saidie contributed one of her paintings. J.B. Neumann, director of the New Art Circle (art gallery) in New York, was asked to be a juror and to give a lecture. The lecture's topic: "Why we hate Modern Art" was appropriate for the unsophisticated Baltimore crowd. His slide lecture was a great success; he kept the audience mesmerized with his clever anecdotes.

The April show in the Members' Room consisted of work by Paul Klee, donated for the show by the Buchholz Gallery (Curt Valentin), MOMA and other private collectors. The exhibit included a wide variety of items, including Saidie's *Traveling Circus* (p. 212), which was one of the best Klee paintings in the show. There were so many works donated that there was room for only one painting from her collection, so they were unable to use Klee's *Arabian Princess* or *The Graveyard* in that show.[29]

Robert Motherwell, American, 1915–1991, *The Joy of Living,*1943, collage of construction paper, mulberry paper, fabric and printed map with tempera, ink, crayon, oil and graphite, 43-1/2 x 33-5/8 in., The Baltimore Museum of Art: Bequest of Saidie A. May, BMA 1951.344.

Left to right: Marc Chagall, Diego and Rose Masson, Bella Chagall, André Masson at the Pontigny-en-Amérique at Mt. Holyoke, August 6, 1943. Courtesy of the Estate of André Masson, Paris, France.

The Concept of Art as Therapy

The Baltimore Museum of Art hired two new curators, Claire Leighton and Belle Boas. Belle Boas had been hired by Adelyn Breeskin in 1943 as director of education, a new position at the museum. Miss Boas was the sister of Dr. George Boas, a trustee of the BMA and a professor of the history of philosophy at Johns Hopkins University, and one of their first Jewish professors.[30] In the next few years, Belle would become an invaluable asset to Saidie.

The two curators were experimenting with concepts related to using art within a therapy setting to help those with mental illness. This idea originated with an art show put on by MOMA as a traveling exhibition. In the middle of April, the MOMA show opened at the BMA. The program opened with a meeting of local therapists and included lectures by Dean Schaffer of Johns Hopkins University and Dr. Jacob Harry Conn of Johns Hopkins Hospital.[31]

On May 4, 1943, Saidie and Al left the Pine Needles, taking the overnight train to New York where they stayed at the Surrey Hotel. In preparation for the move north for the summer, Saidie wrote, "I've been packing for days and it gets so I wish I were a San Franciscan monk, not even owning the clothes on my back. You know my generation was sort of permeated with the search and desire for security—and now we must change this attitude and take a change in almost everything—it's rather exciting, but it leaves one a bit dizzy or wobbly to say the least."[32]

Peggy Guggenheim's Spring Salon

During her brief stay in New York, Saidie purposely stayed away from the art galleries, intending not to buy any art, so as to use the money to buy war bonds.[33] However, she had not realized that Peggy Guggenheim had opened an art gallery, and she wanted to visit her at her Art of this Century Gallery on 57th Street. Peggy's "Spring Salon" featured three young painters: William Baziotes, Jackson Pollock and Robert Motherwell (who was just starting his career).[34] "These young American artists, very much inspired by the European abstract and surrealist artists who had taken refuge in New York, started an entirely new school of painting. Robert Coates, art critic for the *New Yorker*, named the style "Abstract Expressionism."[35] Saidie couldn't resist this new work and purchased a Max Ernst, a Baziotes and a recently finished collage by Motherwell, *The Joy of Living*. This work was one of his early collages in which he worked with torn and pasted papers, a cut-out from a map, black polyhedrons and linear constructions similar to those in Matta's most recent works. This large, irresolute work contained paint spatters, blurred edges and areas of gestured brush drawing atop a softly brushed diaphanous ground. It declared the freedom to mix media without being bound by any existing style, attempting an autonomist spontaneity essentially emphasizing the process itself and composition.[36] Because of this, it was difficult to know whether to hang it horizontally or vertically.

Saidie was now 65 and having problems with her metabolism; in addition, she was overactive and nervous. She consulted a doctor about the problem and he prescribed a medication which helped to calm her down. Before she left New York, she attended MOMA's show "Spanish American Art of the Southwest," which she found reminiscent of the work she had seen while vacationing in Santa Fe, New Mexico, a few years earlier.[37]

On May 12, she and Al left New York to once again spend a quiet summer in the Pocono Mountains at Buck Hill Falls, Pennsylvania, reading and painting. For the first time, Saidie became interested in gardening, and asked for a small area behind the inn which she could work herself. She became immersed in the entire process and found comfort in growing flowers. She found the war so "overpowering, it seems to reduce to triviality what we before thought as so significant."[38]

The Annual Summit Meeting

André Masson was busy getting ready for the artist group meeting at the annual summit, the Pontigny Symposia at Mt. Holyoke College in August. He was invited by the art historian Lionello Venturi to join the group and give a talk on painting. Venturi had given several talks with George Boas at Johns Hopkins University. The gatherings at Mt. Holyoke provided a haven for intellectuals and other prominent European thinkers fleeing Hitler, including artists, philosophers and anthropologists. It was started in 1942 by Helen Patch, a Mt. Holyoke French professor who wanted to start an advance summer program in French civilization for her graduate students.[39] Patch was aware that the war had ended the famous annual gatherings of intellectuals at the Abbey of Pontigny in the Burgundy region of France. She approached her former Sorbonne professor, the medievalist Gustave Cohen, about the idea, and he and a couple of his friends in New York started the Pontigny-en-Amérique at Mount Holyoke.[40] The groups discussed emerging trends and new forms of creativity in all of the arts and reflected on their past cultures and the future.[41]

On August 6, 1943, Masson was asked to chair a session on art and give a talk on painting. He chose the subject of "Unity and variety in French painting," a subject for which he had to reflect and study to prepare. He wrote to Saidie lamenting the fact that he and Rose had not seen them for a while and wouldn't get to see them over the summer because of this commitment.[42]

After the symposia, Masson again corresponded with Saidie, reporting that Dr. George Boas from Hopkins was the first speaker, followed by Marc Chagall, whose words were as moving as his paintings. The general theme of the summit for 1943 was "The permanence of values and the renewing of methods," a subject that Masson knew would have been of interest to both Saidie and Al.[43] Had they been able, they could have attended part of the four-week program, since students and local faculty were welcome to hear the discussions.[44]

The Massons were anxiously awaiting the opening of a showing of work by their friend Alexander Calder. The show was to open at MOMA on September 29th. They hoped that Saidie and Al would come to New York to see the show and get together with them. At the same time, they were waiting for news of the liberation of France.

Masson became interested in working with portraiture, especially of his friends and his family. He was fascinated that his young sons had so quickly become fluent in English, commenting that next to them he appeared as a small baby, "a baby, which I am afraid will never grow up" (he would never learn to speak English).[45]

Both André Masson and Saidie were engrossed in the gardening process that summer, writing to each other about their progress in their pursuits. In a commentary on the necessary garden which he tended lovingly, he wrote, "There are prosaic and very devoted vegetables. I only reproach them for not knowing how to rid themselves of morning-glories, nettles and other parasitical plants, but they are brave persons, and they let themselves be strangled by their enemies, rather than making the least attempt to rid themselves."[46]

For a week at the end of October, Saidie traveled south to visit Baltimore, cutting out her New York visit as "unnecessary" due to the hectic pace there. She had been invited to New Preston, Connecticut, to visit the Massons, but she was feeling tired and having difficulty getting around. She could not deal emotionally with the inconvenience of travel and felt "paralyzed" by the idea.

She was also finding the war "overpowering" and had difficulty reading about all of the suffering and problems in Europe. She looked forward to spending some time conversing with Belle Boas on her work with art and psychotherapy. Even though she admitted that the pace in Pinehurst, North Carolina, was dull, she planned to spend the winter there, leaving Baltimore after visiting for a week.[47]

In November, Peggy Guggenheim's Art of This Century Gallery opened the first one-man showing of Jackson Pollock's paintings, very much under the influence of the Surrealists and Picasso.[48] Matta, a friend of Peggy's had urged her to help the financially strapped Pollock, and although the show was well publicized, few paintings were sold except for the *She Wolf*, purchased by Alfred Barr for the Museum of Modern Art. Peggy tried to get everyone she knew to buy Pollock's work, including Saidie, but she would have nothing to do with it.

Adelyn Breeskin wrote to Saidie about a gallery opening she attended at the beginning of the month in Washington, D. C. It was the new G Place Gallery opened by Caresse Crosby and David Porter, a close friend of Peggy Guggenheim's.[49] Crosby, the first to hold a patent for the modern brassiere,[50] had the first floor of an old house which she used to display works by Max Ernst, Tanguy, Matta and Wilfredo Lam. Tanguy and Matta attended the opening. Adelyn Breeskin spent part of the evening talking to Matta about his work. He mentioned that André Breton was the first person ever to buy his work and Saidie was the second. Her purchase really meant a lot to him, encouraging him to continue working.[51]

Buckminster Fuller also attended the opening, and he and Matta found a lot in common with each other. Adelyn Breeskin was privy to their fascinating conversation about the movement of objects in space and Fuller's dymaxion theory. She invited Matta and his wife, Miss Crosby and David Porter to come to Baltimore to see Saidie's collection of Surrealist works.[52] They all took advantage of her offer to give them a personal tour and found the works stimulating. Matta told Adelyn that before the war there was only one other collection in France that could compare with Saidie's. This was the Grenoble Museum collection of paintings of the Modern French School.[53] Saidie was thrilled to hear that Matta was so favorable about her collection and hoped that she could talk to him the next time she went to New York.[54] She still had not been able to gather her strength and remained in the warmer climate for the winter. She sent money to the Masson boys for Christmas, since she wasn't in New York to take them out. She subsequently received a nice letter from the Massons thanking her for the gift.[55]

Notes

1 Jennifer Tonkovick, *Pierre Matisse and his Artists* (New York: Pierpont Morgan Library, 2002), 106.

2 John Russell, *Matisse, Father and Son* (New York: Harry N. Abrams, 1999), 214.

3 Alfred Barr to Saidie A. May, July 7, 1942, Alfred Hamilton Barr Papers, Archives of American Art, SI.

4 Saidie A. May to Adelyn Breeskin, July 14, 1942, Saidie A. May Papers, BMA.

5 Saidie A. May to Alfred Barr, November 9, 1942, Saidie A. May Papers, BMA.

6 Saidie A. May to Adelyn Breeskin, July 14, 1942, Saidie A. May Papers, BMA.

7 Saidie A. May to Alfred Barr, August 8, 1942, Alfred Hamilton Barr Papers, Archives of American Art, SI.

8 Alfred Barr to Saidie A. May, July 7, 1942, Alfred Hamilton Barr Papers, Archives of American Art, SI.

9 Alfred Jensen to Jane Cone, May 27, 1972 , Saidie A. May Papers, BMA.

10 Arthur C Danto, "Seeking 'Convulsive Beauty,'" *The Nation*, March 11, 2002, www.thenation.com.

11 Martica Sawin, *André Masson in America, 1941–1945* (New York: Zabriske Gallery,1996), 13.

12 John Russell, *Matisse, Father and Son* (New York: Harry N. Abrams, 1999), 214.

13 Alfred Barr to Saidie A. May, November 5, 1942, Saidie A. May Papers, BMA.

14 Saidie A. May to Alfred Barr, November 9, 1942,Saidie A. May Papers, BMA.

15 Saidie A. May to Adelyn Breeskin, November 28, 1942, Saidie A. May Papers, BMA.

16 *Ibid.*

17 Saidie A. May to Adelyn Breeskin, November 28, 1942, Saidie A. May Papers, BMA.

18 Adelyn D. Breeskin to Saidie A. May, December 5, 1942, Saidie A. May Papers, BMA.

19 Martica Sawin, *Surrealism in Exile and the Beginning of the New York School* (Cambridge, Mass: MIT Press, 1995), 229.

20 Saidie A. May to Adelyn Breeskin, January 1, 1943, Saidie A. May Papers, BMA.

21 Stephanie Barron, *Exiles and Emigrees—The Flight of European Artists from Hitler* (New York: Harry N. Abrams, Los Angeles County Museum of Art, 1997), 165.

22 Martica Sawin, *Surrealism in Exile and the Beginning of the New York School* (Cambridge, Mass: MIT Press, 1995), 229.

23 J.D.G. Paul to Saidie A. May, January 23, 1943, Saidie A. May Papers, BMA.

24 *Ibid.*

25 Saidie A. May to J.D.G. Paul, January 28, 1943, Saidie A. May Papers, BMA.

26 *Ibid.*

27 *Ibid.*

28 "Surrealist Paintings in the May Collection," *Baltimore Museum of Art News*, 5:5, (February, 1943), 8.

29 Adelyn Breeskin to Saidie A. May, March 13, 1943, Saidie A. May Papers, BMA.

30 Adelyn Breeskin to Saidie A. May, April 6, 1943, Saidie A. May Papers, BMA.

31 *Ibid.*

32 Saidie A. May to Mrs. Earle, April 27, 1943, Saidie A. May Papers, BMA.

33 Saidie A. May to Mrs. Earle, May 26, 1943, Saidie A. May Papers, BMA.

34 *Ibid.*

35 Marguerite Guggenheim, *Confessions of an Art Addict* (New York: Universe Books, 1987), 104.

36 *Ibid.*

37 Saidie A. May to Mrs. Earle, March 26, 1943, Saidie A. May Papers, BMA.

38 Saidie A. May to Adelyn Breeskin, October 3, 1943, Saidie A. May Papers, BMA.

39 "Mount Holyoke to Re-Create Historic Pontigny Symposia," Nancy Doherty FP, *College Street Journal*, April 11, 2003, South Hadley, Mass.

40 *Ibid.*

41 *Ibid.*

42 André Masson to Saidie A. May, June 26, 1943, Saidie A. May Papers, BMA.

43 André Masson to Saidie A. May, August 19, 1943, Saidie A. May Papers, BMA.

44 "Mount Holyoke to Re-Create Historic Pontigny Symposia," Nancy Doherty FP, *College Street Journal*, April 11, 2003, South Hadley, Mass.

45 André Masson to Saidie A. May, August 19, 1943, Saidie A. May Papers, BMA.

46 *Ibid.*

47 Saidie A. May to Adelyn Breeskin, October 3, 1943, Saidie A. May Papers, BMA.

48 Marguerite Guggenheim, *Out of This Century, Confessions of an Art Addict* (New York: Universe Books, 1987), 315.

49 Adelyn Breeskin to Saidie A. May, November 9, 1943, Amalie Adler Ascher Collection MS89, Jewish Museum of Maryland, Baltimore, MD.

50 Mary Phelps Jacob aka Caresse Crosby, http://www.csupomona.edu/~plin/inventors/phelps_jacob.html.

51 Adelyn Breeskin to Saidie A. May, November 9, 1943, Amalie Adler Ascher Collection MS89, Jewish Museum of Maryland, Baltimore, MD.

52 *Ibid.*

53 *Ibid.*

54 Saidie A. May to Adelyn Breeskin, November 25, 1943, Saidie A. May Papers, BMA.

55 André Masson to Saidie A. May, December 26, 1943, Saidie A. May Papers, BMA.

Masson Goes Home, 1944–1945

O n April 11, 1944, Masson had a one-man show at the Art of This Century Gallery in New York, entitled "First Exhibition in America of Twenty Paintings."[1] On the 27th, Saidie and Al left the Pine Needles, eventually heading westward to Colorado Springs for the summer. As well as recuperating, Saidie planned to concentrate her efforts more heavily on her own work.[2] At this point, her favorite artists were Despiau, Maillol and Laurent.[3]

The Massons Learn the Occupation Has Ended

During the summer of 1944, Saidie purchased *Women and Bird in Front of the Moon* by Miró from his show at the Pierre Matisse Gallery. André and Rose Masson were driving to Mt. Holyoke College whenever possible to take part in the Pontigny Colloquia. At those sessions, Masson spent a lot of time with the young artist, Robert Motherwell, another frequent attendee.[4] The Massons avidly followed the events in France. On August 25, 1944, Paris was freed by the Allies. Soon the awful war would end. They anxiously awaited news of Rose's family. Masson yearned to go home, even though his two young sons were fluent in English, had acclimated to American society and were happy living in Connecticut. Masson did not want to stay a moment longer.

The Children's Wing

Over the summer, Saidie and Belle Boas corresponded about the idea of creating a "Children's Wing" for the BMA. Miss Boas believed that within a museum, children should have "a museum of their own, equipped in scale and purpose for the child."[5] Saidie was all for it, but unsure about being saddled with the entire cost of building it. In order to accomplish this, she would have to be cautious and careful not to spend excessive amounts of money, as she depended on the income from her investments to live.[6]

Paul Klee, Swiss, 1879–1940, *Traveling Circus*, 1937, mixed media on canvas, 25-1/2 x 19-3/4 in., The Baltimore Museum of Art: Bequest of Saidie A. May, BMA 1951.317. ©2011 Artists Rights Society (ARS), New York/VG Bild-Kunst, Bonn.

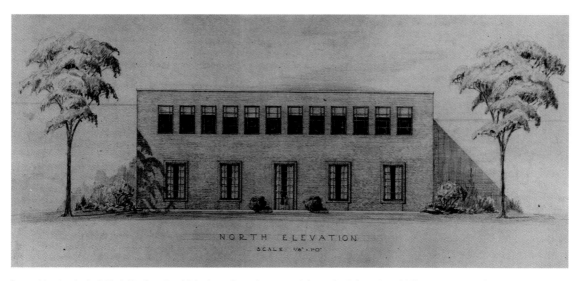

Proposal drawing for the Saidie A. May Young People's Art Center, September 6, 1947, *Baltimore Sun* Archives, Special Collections, University of Maryland Baltimore County Library. Reprinted with permission of the *Baltimore Sun* Media Group. All Rights Reserved.

Troubles at the Guggenheim Gallery

Peggy Guggenheim was having a difficult time with her gallery, and her assistant, Howard Putzel, quit. She quickly hired another man to assist her, but things did not run smoothly as before. Exhibits had to be rearranged for the 1944–1945 season, and on the advice of James Johnson Sweeney, she sent a request to Adelyn Breeskin to borrow two works that Saidie had recently purchased from the gallery to fill in the shows that she quickly put together.[7] The first exhibit, "Paintings and Drawings by William Baziotes," included only twenty-three works, so they asked for *The Drugged Balloonist* from the spring salon the previous May.[8] The show was the first of the season and was scheduled to open at the beginning of October.[9]

William Baziotes had been spending a considerable amount of time with the exiled Surrealist artists and learned a great deal from them. From this association, however, his own creative energies became crippled, which kept him from painting at all. His close friend, Robert Motherwell, was concerned and supported him emotionally through his difficulty, while encouraging him to break off his dependence and move on. Baziotes eventually got out of the city and spent the summer in his hometown, Reading, Pennsylvania, where within a month's time he produced twenty-eight oil paintings.[10]

On September 11, Saidie received a letter from André Masson, greatly encouraged by the liberation of Paris. In it he comments: "Here, we are living, 'like images, by heart.'"[11] On the 21st, Saidie sent a telegram to Adelyn Breeskin, granting her permission to lend paintings to Peggy Guggenheim and informing her that she would be in Baltimore on October 18. Saidie didn't make it to Baltimore that fall, however. It was getting colder in Colorado Springs, so she and Al left for Southern Pines to return to the Pine Needles, her winter home.

Guggenheim's Motherwell Exhibit

The second painting that Saidie lent was for the one-man show for Robert Motherwell, which went up after the Baziotes show came down. This exhibition was much larger: forty-eight works, including the collage Saidie had purchased at the spring salon, *The Joy of Living*. That summer, Motherwell had presented a talk at the Pontigny Colloquia on "the response of the abstract artists and the surrealist ones to a property-loving society." He met André Masson there and the two quickly became friends. Motherwell was very impressed with Masson, writing to Baziotes that "Masson is magnificent—simple, sincere, unpretentious, well-educated (and) very strong; in certain respects not unlike a French version of you."[12]

During the winter, Saidie corresponded with Belle Boas and Adelyn Breeskin about her new project, a separate wing for the museum which would have special rooms to house her collection as well as a small gallery for display. It would include studio spaces where children and art students could create new works based on the modern pieces from her collection hanging in the gallery.[13]

Early in 1945, the BMA decided to make a life-sized reproduction of Paul Klee's whimsical painting, *The Traveling Circus,* from Saidie's collection. Klee was a leader in the arts in Germany in the early 1900's and his work was chosen as part of the BMA's plan to make artwork accessible to the general public. The reproduction was framed in a copy of the original frame, just as a visitor would see it hanging in the gallery. This piece was the first in a series of selected paintings from the BMA to be reproduced by silkscreen in their original size by the New York Graphic Society. They were offered for sale as framed or unframed posters at the BMA.[14]

In January, Rose Masson wrote to Saidie to let her know that André was sad and depressed and not able to sleep well. They had finally received long-awaited letters from Henry Kahnweiler as well as their relatives who had weathered the war.[15] André was missing France and longed to go home.

In February the Members' Room opened a show by artist Jean Hélion featuring a stimulating talk on his work and his mental approach to painting. On March 11, the Members' Room opened an exhibit by Loren MacIver, an artist whom MOMA considered "the best woman painter of the day." Alfred Barr had purchased two of her paintings for MOMA's collection in 1935. Her paintings were dreamlike, with linear, symbolic and hieroglyphic forms reminiscent of Paul Klee's work.[16] Ms. MacIver arrived in Baltimore the evening before the opening and had dinner with Adelyn Breeskin.[17]

On April 30, Saidie and Al headed for the Belvedere Hotel in Baltimore for a week while Saidie met with Adelyn Breeskin, Belle Boas and Philip Perlman to make plans for the Children's Wing.[18] One day, Saidie breezed into the museum and asked to see the paintings which she had painted over the years. As she finished them, she would send them to the museum for storage, or enter them into the annual museum shows. In her opinion, most of those works had not stood the test of time, so she personally oversaw their destruction at the museum before she left for New York for 5 days.

67 Gallery

During this brief stay, she visited the new 67 Gallery, opened by Howard Putzel after Peggy closed Art of This Century.[19] There she purchased Dubuffet's *Orator at the Wall* (long before Dubuffet was generally known in the U.S.). Then she and Al moved on to the Hotel Hershey in Hershey, Pennsylvania, for a month.[20] As soon as they got settled, they started painting.

Saidie continued to donate textiles and pottery for the BMA's Children's Museum.[21] In June, she gave the Walters Art Gallery many textiles that she had been storing in a warehouse in New York. Most of these pieces were similar to ones given over the years to the BMA as gifts from both Blanche and Saidie. She invited Marvin Ross to accompany her to the storage facility to retrieve the items. Ross was to return to Baltimore and personally deliver the pieces to their respective collections at the BMA and the Walters.[22]

The French Connection

The BMA held an exhibition of French drawings over the summer. On June 22, the wife of the French Ambassador, Henri Bonnet, came to see it. A tea was held in her honor in the Members' Room and a nice article was written in the *Baltimore Sun* about the show. Saidie had met Madame Bonnet (of Greek descent) in 1938 in Paris at a tea at the home of Madame Cultolli, wife of the French Algerian senator. She had been impressed with her Greek charm, intelligence and style. Madame Bonnet spoke to Adelyn Breeskin of Saidie's acquaintance, Francis Gruber.

Saidie kept up correspondence with Paul Cornet's wife in Paris. She wrote to Saidie to say that her 23-year-old daughter was studying to be a painter and her son Jean Pierre would be a sculptor. In her next letter, Madame Cornet planned to write to Saidie about Charles Despiau and "Collaborating."[23]

Throughout the summer, Saidie worked with the BMA on plans for the new "Saidie A. May Children's Wing," which would have naturally lit studios with removable partitions, that when opened could function as an auditorium for groups up to 250 people. A children's library and a state-of-the-art storage facility for those parts of Saidie's collection that were not on view were planned. Saidie's youthful spirit kept her well attuned to the modern viewpoint and she embraced contemporary trends. She gathered splendid examples of all of the various schools of the day, from Masson to Miró to Motherwell and Dubuffet. In sculpture, she chose the finest works of both Giacometti and Naum Gabo.

Atelier 17

During the first few months of 1945, André Masson finished the illustrations for a book of poetry by George Duthuit entitled, *Le Serpent dans la Galere*. It was a limited edition of 65 printings, each including a signed lithograph by Masson. Masson also worked on another album of lithographs, *Bestiare*, which he planned to produce before returning to France.[24] Masson used the print studio of S.W. Hayter in New York City.

Hayter, a British Surrealist painter, had originally opened his printing studio, Atelier 17, in Paris in 1927, where his emphasis was on the creative aspects of printmaking.[25] He began to exhibit with the French Surrealists in 1929 and continued throughout the 1930s, becoming friendly with many of its members, some of whom including Masson made prints at his studio.[26] In 1933, Hayter moved his studio to 17 Rue Campagne-Premierè, near Montparnasse, where it remained until World War II. In September of 1939, the atelier was abandoned a day after war was declared in Europe.[27] The next year, Hayter made his way to New York where he re-opened his popular Atelier 17 studio, attracting numerous artists already working in New York including Ernst, Giacometti, Dali, Rothko and Pollock.

Hayter's studio was a place where the young American artists could work side by side with the masters of the European schools, most of whom had been brought to New York to escape being sent to concentration camps or killed. The young American artists fed on the energy of the elder statesmen of the craft, and many of the ideas that fostered European Surrealism were eventually transformed in New York to a new American abstract art movement in the 1950s. Sometime during 1945, Stanley Hayter introduced André Masson to the young American painter, Jackson Pollock, at the Greene Street Diner.[28] Masson's work was to have a profound influence on Pollock within the next few years.

Postcard of the Walters Art Gallery, Baltimore, Maryland, c. 1949. Collection of the author.

The New York artists were exposed to Masson's work through his numerous one-man shows and his influence reverberated through their work. Curt Valentin held one of these for him each year while he resided in the United States.[29] Masson also spent a considerable amount of his time lecturing on his ideas about automatism. "Painting is a Wager" and "A Crisis of the Imaginary" were two of the well-known lectures that he gave, both readily available to American artists. "Plastic Values in Painting" was a concept on which he lectured and discussed frequently when he was in New York City.[30] If one was to compare the early works and ideas of the future Abstract Expressionists with Masson's work and art theory during the war period, they would find many parallels of underlying principle.[31]

A Problem for Critics

Masson was the only European Surrealist linked with a group of artists whose work was shown in an exhibit organized by Howard Putzel. Putzel had become friendly with many young American artists through Art of this Century Gallery, and felt strongly about their work and wanted to exhibit it. He wrote a statement to accompany the exhibition in which he asked the New York critics to try to name the "New Metamorphism" that had been developing in America since 1940. This show, called "A Problem for Critics," ran from May 14 through July 16 of 1945. The exhibit included works by Mark Rothko, Hans Hofmamn, Arshile Gorky, Adolph Gottlieb, Lee Krasner, Richard Pousette-Dart, Rufino Tamayo, Jean Arp, Joan Miró, Pablo Picasso and André Masson.[32]

Masson Returns Home

As soon as the war ended, Henry Kahnweiler was anxious for Masson to return to France and exhibit his new work in Paris. Masson was restless and anxious to get back to his homeland.[33] At the end of July, 1945, he sent a letter to Saidie, looking to raise money for his family's passage back to France. In exchange for her support, he offered either a large gouache from one of his earlier periods or his handwritten manuscript, "Anatomy of my Universe," with some sketches in the text for $300.[34]

After receiving the letter, Saidie felt insulted and probably disappointed that Masson did not want to stay in America. She felt that he was lowering himself to "begging" for help instead of choosing to become a vital part of the American art scene and earning the money himself. Masson felt that his work as well as that of other exiled European artists "of talent" was discredited in America due to a "blindly nationalistic political attitude."[35] He wanted desperately to get back to his homeland to resume his work and shows with Henry Kahnweiler; in fact, the two were already planning his next show in Paris.

Saidie finally relented and sent Masson $300. He sent back a gouache, *The Metaphysical Wall*, painted in Marseilles in 1940 right before the family was smuggled out of France. Saidie donated this piece to the BMA as part of her collection.[36] The Massons left New York in October. While in America, between June 1941 and October 1945, Masson had executed well over one hundred paintings, fifty prints, twelve small sculptures and many drawings, watercolors and pastels.[37]

Notes

1   William Rubin & Carolyn Lanchner, *André Masson* (New York: Museum of Modern Art, 1976), 15.

2   Saidie A. May to Mrs. Earle, April, 1944, Saidie A. May Papers, BMA.

3   Alfred Jensen to Jane Cone Saidie A. May Papers, BMA.

4   André Masson to Saidie A. May, September 11, 1944 Saidie A. May Papers, BMA.

5   "Education: The Young People's Art Center," *Annual 1, The Museum: It's First Half Century*, (Baltimore, MD: Baltimore Museum of Art, 1966), 71–73.

6   Saidie A. May to Adelyn Breeskin, October 14, 1944 Saidie A. May Papers, BMA.

7   Saidie A. May to Adelyn Breeskin, September 21, 1944 Saidie A. May Papers, BMA.

8   Melvin Paul Lader, *Peggy Guggenheim's Art of this Century: The Surrealist Milieu and the American Avante-Garde, 1942–1947* (Ann Arbor, Michigan: UMI Dissertation Services, 1981), 259.

9   *Ibid.*

10 *Ibid.*, 261.

11 André Masson to Saidie A. May, September 11, 1944 Saidie A. May Papers, BMA.

12 Robert Motherwell to William Baziotes, September 4, 1944 The William Baziotes Papers, Archives of American Art, SI.

13 Belle Boas to Saidie A. May, October, 1944 Belle Boas Papers, BMA.

14 Adelyn Breeskin to Saidie A, May, March 10, 1945 Saidie A. May Papers, BMA.

15 Saidie A. May to Adelyn Breeskin, March 20, 1945 Saidie A. May Papers, BMA.

16 Jonathan Gilmore, "Loren MacIver at Alexandre," *Art in America*, September, 2002.

17 *Ibid.*

18 Saidie A. May to Adelyn Breeskin, March 20, 1945 Saidie A. May Papers, BMA.

19 Saidie A. May to Adelyn Breskin, October 14, 1944 Saidie A. May Papers, BMA.

20 Saidie A. May to Adelyn Breskin, April 13, 1945 Saidie A. May Papers, BMA.

21 "Education Department 1944–1945," *Baltimore Museum of Art News*, 7:9, (December, 1943), 8.

22 Saidie A. May to Adelyn Breskin, July 3, 1945 Saidie A. May Papers, BMA.

23 *Ibid.*

24 André Masson to Saidie A. May, first half of 1945, Saidie A. May Papers, BMA.

25 Atelier 17, http://www.ueclaa.org/ueclaaOnline/Definition.jsp?glossaryID=41&letter=A.

26 "Stanley William Hayter & Atelier 17, 1901–1939," http://www.ateliercontrepoint.com/a 172.html.

27 *Ibid.*

28 Doris Ann Miller Birmingham, "André Masson in America, the Artist's Achievement in Exile 1941–1945," dissertation, University of Michigan, 1978, 37-38.

29 *Ibid.*, 148.

30 *Ibid.*

31 *Ibid.*, 149.

32 *Ibid.*, 155.

33 André Masson to Saidie A. May, July 29, 1945 Saidie A. May Papers, BMA.

34 *Ibid.*

35 André Masson to Saidie A. May, August 10, 1945 Saidie A. May Papers, BMA.

36 Canceled check for $300.00 from Saidie A. May to André Masson, Saidie A. May Papers, BMA.

37 Doris Ann Miller Birmingham, "André Masson in America, the Artist's Achievement in Exile 1941–1945," dissertation, University of Michigan, 1978, 40.

Postwar, 1945–1948

20

André Masson resumed his painting and pastel work almost immediately after arriving in France. He and Rose moved in with Henry Kahnweiler, while Rose tried to find a new place for them to live closer to Paris. They left the boys with their uncle at his chateau near Poitiers. Then they found temporary housing at Aix-en-Provence, at the home of J.B. Piel, at "La Sablonnière" Vouneuil-sous-Biard.[1] Soon, Masson was back in the old groove, receiving a commission to make lithographs for Malraux's *L'Espoir*.[2]

Kahnweiler Returns to Paris

A long time had passed since Saidie had heard from Henry Kahnweiler. He moved back to Paris in the summer of 1945, having lost his wife right when the war ended. They had been extremely close but never had children, and he was lonely and missed her company. While they were hiding during the war, his sister-in-law, Louise Leiris, had purchased the gallery from him to prevent the Nazis from seizing it. She also stored all of their personal belongings.[3]

Arriving back in Paris, Kahnweiler returned to the Galerie Leiris. Each day he resumed his morning ritual of sitting at his desk in the gallery, writing letters to his friends and patrons. He also finished writing the book about his good friend, Juan Gris, and the Modern Art movement as he perceived it during his time in exile. Curt Valentin looked forward to publishing the book in English after it came out in French.[4]

The BMA Retrieves its Treasures

The Baltimore Museum of Art announced in October, 1945, that they would reassemble the most valuable and irreplaceable works of art in its collection. Those works had been hidden in the museum's vaults since the bombing of Pearl Harbor, to keep them safe. These masterpieces, all evidence of man's past cultural achievements, were being exhibited together for the first time in the museum's main gallery. From five different private

Jean Dubuffet, French, 1901–1985, *Snack for Two*, 1945, oil on canvas, 29-1/8 x 24-1/8 in. Gift of Saidie A. May, The Museum of Modern Art, New York, 280.49. ©2011 Artists Rights Society (ARS), New York/ADAGP, Paris.

collections (including some of Saidie's antiquities), this exhibit gave museum-goers a chance to study them as an entirety.[5] Saidie and Al headed south to Pinehurst, North Carolina for the winter.[6]

American Painting

London's Tate Gallery wanted to show the new art being done by American artists. They asked the National Gallery of Art to organize a retrospective exhibition of American painting to be displayed for two months over the summer of 1946. Alfred Barr and Duncan Phillips were on the selection committee and chose Robert Motherwell's early gouache and collage, *The Joy of Living,* to be a part of the show. Saidie was delighted that his work in her collection was finally becoming appreciated.[7]

Kahnweiler was busy in his gallery—by January of 1946 he had arranged a showing of André Masson's new work. It was a real sensation! André Gustave Beaudin and Eugène de Kermadec had each produced enough material for a show of their new work after Masson's show came down.[8] Kahnweiler was also awaiting the publishing of his new book on Juan Gris.

Saidie wrote to Madame Cornet. In her response, she informed Saidie that many of her friends in France were not aging well. Paul Cornet had gone to visit her former teachers. Charles Despiau and his wife were in an unhappy state. Charles hardly ate, taking only a little milk at his meals. Although he had lost a lot of weight, he continued to work steadily. Othon Friesz had an attack of diphtheria which had left his hands paralyzed, so he could no longer paint.[9] Saidie's past was slowly slipping away.

On May 1, 1946, Saidie and Al came up to Baltimore from Southern Pines for Saidie to meet with Belle Boas and Philip Perlman, to go over the first draft of the plans for the Junior Museum. Beforehand, she sent a box of dolls to Belle Boas to include for the exhibit. Adelyn Breeskin had taken part in a survey of the state of American museums through the Teachers College at Columbia University. The results found the BMA to have a "greater understanding of the problems and responsibilities of public education, and put this knowledge into action."[10] She was pleased and announced these results at the Junior Museum meeting.

The Mondrian

Afterwards, Saidie and Al headed to New York. They visited Pierre Chareau, a French architect and designer who had moved to the U.S. in 1940. He had worked in Paris for the British interior design firm of Waring and Gillow, where he designed Art Deco style functional furniture, mixing wood and metals in unique ways. While in New York he worked for the French cultural attaché, organizing exhibitions.[11] A number of his friends from Paris joined him in the U.S. during the war years.

Saidie started collecting the work of Robert Motherwell in 1942 and she may have made Chareau's acquaintance through Motherwell, since Chareau's only American architectural endeavor was designing a summer retreat for him in East Hampton, Long Island. Chareau's design

San Diego & Arizona Railway Short Line schedule, c. 1932. Collection of the author.

for the home/studio was made from surplus parts of Quonset hut hangars sold by the American Army. Motherwell ran out of money for its completion, so in exchange for the work, he gave Chareau an adjoining peace of beach property. Chareau started to build a home for himself there, but it was never completed before his death in August, 1950. Saidie convinced Chareau to sell her a small painting given to him in France by his good friend, Piet Mondrian, painted in 1927. He sold it to her for $650 under the condition that she donate it to the BMA and include him as a donor. The 15-1/8" X 14" oil painting, *Composition 5,* reminded Chareau of Greece.[12] When she purchased the painting, Saidie told Gertrude Rosenthal that she would give it to the BMA—on the condition that Rosenthal look at it every other week and learn from it. She finally gave it to the museum as a loan in 1949 and in 1951 it was donated to her collection with the rest of her estate.

Saidie and Al left for San Diego for the summer. In July, Saidie put together an exhibition of her work at the San Diego Fine Arts Gallery, which opened August 3, 1946. She gave a talk about her work at the opening.[13] In August, Philip Perlman drafted a letter to Saidie, laying out the procedure for the plans to erect the Junior Museum as a wing of the BMA. Saidie had pledged a total of $300,000 towards the project, even though the estimate at the time was $200,000–$250,000. She purchased securities, investing the money so that it would hopefully grow over the period during which the building was constructed. The construction could not be scheduled for one to two years, anyway. There was a shortage of building materials, contracts needed to be signed and the entire project and the workers needed to be scheduled before work could begin.

Philip Perlman suggested that Saidie make a gift of those securities (whose current value was sufficient to cover her pledge). As a gift, she might be able to take a deduction for what she paid as an educational contribution. In the event the securities increased in value over the waiting period, Saidie would not be penalized by the Federal Income Tax on long-term capital gains when they were finally sold to pay for the work.

Mrs. Wrenn, a BMA board member, recommended her brother, Mr. Francis Jencks of the firm of Wrenn, Lewis and Jencks to be the architect of the project. He submitted plans and designs for the project which had to be approved by the mayor and city officials, since they normally selected the architects for buildings located on city property. The plans and designs for the original Baltimore Museum of Art building, made by the firm of John Russell Pope, were studied so that the new wing would harmonize with it.[14]

Dubuffet

In September, Saidie received a letter from Pierre Matisse to introduce her to a new French artist joining his stable. Jean Dubuffet was a year younger than Matisse, and after the war ended his work was being shown in Paris at the Galerie René Drouin, adjacent to the Hotel Ritz in the Place Vendome. Drouin had a young associate working there, Leo Castelli, who was learning the art trade. Dubuffet's work created quite a scene in Paris. It was "something new", and though some responded favorably, many were violently against it![15]

Dubuffet felt that the only new art worth looking at was the work of mental patients and obsessive autodidacts, who knew nothing about museums and galleries and had never thought of

Jean Dubuffet, French, 1901–1985, *Orator at the Wall*, 1945, oil on canvas, 38-1/4 x 51-1/4 in., The Baltimore Museum of Art: Bequest of Saidie A. May, BMA 1951.293. ©2011 Artists Rights Society (ARS), New York/ADAGP, Paris.

selling their pictures.[16] At that time the contemporary art scene in New York was tiny, with a small group of serious collectors and museums who wanted to display these new works. Pierre Matisse was well aware of this, and through his quiet persuasion behind the scenes, he was able to quickly parlay the best new European works into major American collections, both public and private.[17] Saidie was among his three private collectors who liked Dubuffet's work. She had purchased *Orator at the Wall* from 67 Gallery the year before. The others were William McKim and Lee Ault. The Museum of Modern Art was also on the list.[18] He suggested two works by Dubuffet for Saidie to purchase, one she wanted for the Baltimore Museum of Art and the other she would give to San Diego. He also promised her a book about Dubuffet's work.[19]

Saidie stayed on in San Diego until October 14, when she and Al left to come back east to Baltimore. They took the train from San Diego to Union Station in Los Angeles and then caught a "sleeper" east through Chicago, which took two full days to reach New York. Then they took a four-hour train ride from New York to Baltimore's Belvedere Hotel. The next day, Saidie met Helen for lunch and afterwards headed to the BMA to meet with Adelyn Breeskin and Belle Boas, to go over the plans for the Children's Wing. She and Al stayed in Baltimore for a week, visiting family and friends and taking care of details at the museum, before heading back to San Diego for the winter months.

Almost as soon as she arrived back in San Diego and settled into the Park Manor Hotel, she received the BMA's November newsletter, inviting local Maryland artists to send in works for their annual juried show. Saidie wanted four of her new paintings submitted, "with no pull—a real test" of her own work. She sent a letter back to Adelyn Breeskin asking her to "take care" of the submissions, which included having each piece framed.[20]

At the beginning of December, Saidie received an airmail letter from Adelyn Breeskin, informing her that two books had been stolen from the Renaissance Room: a religious medieval manuscript of the "Book of the Hours" and a small book by Horace. Saidie had purchased the Book of Hours from Weyle in New York in 1924 for $800. Saidie's comment was, "They say that part of the education of our commandos was to be able to 'lift' things expertly, so perhaps that was the way the books disappeared."[21] Eventually a man appeared at a local antiques shop, offering them for sale. The owner became suspicious and did not purchase them. Unfortunately, he had not paid much attention to the man, so he was not apprehended. Breeskin heard about the affair from him and related the story in her letter to Saidie.[22]

In 1947, Saidie presented the BMA with a sum of money to officially start plans for a young people's museum and art center. That same year, Philip Perlman, longtime friend and lawyer for the Adler family, was appointed to the office of U.S. Solicitor General by President Harry S. Truman.[23] Although he was busy with political matters, he still tended to the Adlers' needs and helped Saidie see her museum project through to its completion.

Interested in art, Perlman had been a trustee of the Baltimore Museum of Art for 27 years and served on the Walters Art Gallery board for 28 years, holding the office of president of their board at his death. He had a special interest in rare books and medieval manuscripts and had amassed a good collection of prints. He eventually left his print collection to the BMA and the other objects which he collected were split between the two institutions.[24]

The Dubuffet Show

The Pierre Matisse Gallery in New York opened the show of Jean Dubuffet's paintings on January 7th, after a delay due to the late arrival of many of his works from Europe.[25] The paintings that Saidie had purchased through the mail, *Casse-croûte a Deux (Snack for Two)* (1944) and *Orator at the Wall* (1945), were included in this show. In one of the letters Matisse wrote to Dubuffet about the show, he ended with the words, "I hear gnashing of teeth in the Gallery, and I must go out and comfort the victims."[26] After the show finished, *Casse-croute a Deux* was sent to the Fine Arts Society of San Diego while *Orator at the Wall* went to Baltimore, where it was included in a French painting show in the Members' Room, which opened in March. The show featured works by Miró, Masson's *Metaphysical Wall* (recently purchased to help the Masson family return to France), and eight of the nine works recently done by Saidie. Her ninth piece was entered into the Maryland Arts show.[27] (These paintings were the ones she had shown at the San Diego Museum the year before.)

According to the write-up of the show, Saidie's paintings were "non-objective gouaches, which expressed what she had learned from her mentors at the School of Paris," including Joan Miró and André Masson. Saidie was mainly self-taught, and through observation and study she abandoned realistic content and tried to express herself spontaneously through arabesque and color. She especially ascribed to Kandinsky's statement, "The observer must learn to look at the pictures as form and color combinations as a representation of mood, and not as a representation of objects."[28]

The Fine Arts Society of San Diego declined Saidie's new gift by Dubuffet, *Casse crôute a Deux* citing that "As a municipal art gallery, we should represent varied arts with a certain balance, and we feel that Dubuffet's art does not add to our balanced collection at this time."[29] She subsequently offered it to MOMA, which formally accepted it on July 26, 1949.

Masson

In June, Saidie received a letter from Henry Kahnweiler, from whom she had not heard in six months. He sent her the catalogue for Masson's latest showing at his gallery. He planned to send some of his latest works to Pierre Matisse to be shown in his gallery in New York in 1948. According to his letter, the Massons were all well. André and Rose stayed with Louise Leiris during the show and the family was quietly living at la Sablonnière, near Poitiers. They had survived a rough winter there—after one blizzard they had no water, electricity or telephone for days. They liked it there, but felt that they might have to look for another place to live, which was not easy in France due to the destruction from the war.[30]

Saidie wrote to Kahnweiler, excited about her purchases of Dubuffet's work—with its child-like style which she found very appealing. Kahnweiler wrote back and made it clear that he, having known Dubuffet for twenty years, did not like him, and said, "Well, there is always the future to show who was right and who was wrong…Let us wait and see."[31]

Saidie had thought about visiting Paris over the summer, but that idea never came to fruition. Kahnweiler was disappointed—he wanted to catch up and spend time with old friends. Saidie and Al spent a routine summer in San Diego—both immersing themselves in painting. She was really producing a lot of work and was anxious to show it. Katherine Koo, of the Chicago Fine Arts Institute, was in San Diego and took a look at Saidie's work for their upcoming Surrealist show in October. She seemed interested in three of Saidie's paintings, which Saidie found gratifying.[32]

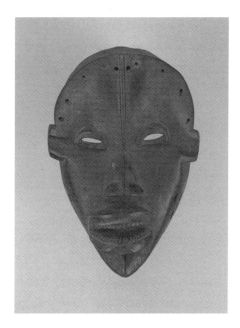

Dan peoples, Liberia, Mask *(Tankë Ge),* early 20th century, wood, 9.4 x 7.1 x 5.1 in. (24 x 18 x 13 D cm.), The Baltimore Museum of Art: Bequest of Saidie A. May, BMA 1951.388.

Betty Parsons' Gallery

During that summer, Saidie and Al read selections from the French novelist Marcel Proust.[33] She claimed that they stayed in San Diego all summer due to her having to take "treatments."[34] Then in October, they decided to head east by train to New York. The two arrived on October 20th and checked into the Ritz Carlton Hotel.[35] They spent nine days in New York, gallery-hopping and seeing friends. Saidie purchased a few new artworks from the Pierre Matisse Gallery[36] and the Babcock Galleries.[37] She also went to see the new Betty Parsons' Gallery at 15 E. 57th Street, opened in September of 1946.[38]

Parsons had been friendly with Peggy Guggenheim, who was having trouble keeping her gallery, Art of This Century. The people that she had employed to help run it were not keeping up with the demands, and she wanted to move to Europe. At the end of 1947, she closed the gallery with a retrospective show of Theo van Doesburg's work. Afterwards, she moved to Venice, Italy (where she would live for the next 12 years.) She left the contents of the gallery and promised her stable of artists to Betty Parsons, who promised to put on another show of Jackson Pollock's work.[39]

Television Comes to the BMA

Saidie and Al headed south to Baltimore for 5 days to check on the progress of the Children's Wing and to visit Helen. That same month, the *Baltimore Sun* purchased WMAR television (in order to keep television from supplanting the newspaper). With this totally new medium, they used any venue they could find for studio broadcast purposes. The BMA and its next-door neighbor, John Hopkins University, both had auditoriums, and the station would use these stages to broadcast live television shows when it could. They would literally "back the truck up to the backstage door and run the cables onto the stage." The owners of the *Baltimore Sun* were members of the board of directors of the BMA and were anxious to broadcast public affairs and arts programs as often as possible.[40]

At this period in time, seventy percent of all television sets were in bars and the viewing audience was not extremely well educated. Television only aired six days a week, Thursday through Tuesday, and anyone who had access to a television set would watch it—even a test pattern with music playing in the background. During the day, the station "played to the upper crust," airing public affairs programs, similar to those shown by the public television stations of today. In the evenings, after the news at 11:00 p.m. the stations would broadcast from live wrestling matches held downtown, or from local bars in the city, both of which would pay to advertise their businesses on the channel.

From the Members' Room

On January 25, 1948, an inaugural live broadcast "From the Members' Room" was aired. This program was WMAR's attempt to inform the general public about the new Modern Art collection at the BMA. It was produced and directed by Janet Baugher, a graduate of Western Maryland College. For 1 1/2 years on Sunday evenings from 8–9 p.m., Adelyn Breeskin, Belle Boas and other members of the museum's curatorial staff would lecture on subjects related to Modern Art—considered "weekly informal discussions."[41]

There were discussions on paintings and graphic works in the Museum's collections, children's art and local museum policies and plans. Gallery tours of current exhibitions or permanent installations were featured, as well as demonstrations of woodcraft, sculpture, drawing and painting, flower arranging, architecture and photography.[42] On February 8, 1949, Mrs. Robert Strauss, of Accokeek, MD, gave a lecture-demonstration on the basic elements of sculpture, showing the creative processes a sculptor goes through to make a piece. There was even an art quiz show—all intended to expose the general public to art and give them the opportunity to see artists at work.

In late January of 1948, Pierre Matisse opened a showing of Giacometti's sculpture. Matisse wrote enthusiastically to Saidie in San Diego, with the hope of persuading her to buy one of his works for the Members' Room at the BMA. Although Saidie did not purchase one of those pieces, she found his sculpture intriguing. She was hard at work painting again, anticipating the BMA's Maryland Artists' Show opening in March. This year, Max Weber was one of the judges of the show.

She had recently acquired the English version of Henry Kahnweiler's book on Juan Gris, and wrote to Belle Boas that she "was getting meat and drink" out of the book, "It's so rich and scholarly that it has given me a sort o' indigestion. His ideals are very high." Saidie felt herself to be more in the Romantic school, like Picasso, "not classical as Gris. Even if one flounders around some, there is a certain joy in the struggle, too."[43]

In April, Saidie and Al took the train back east so that Saidie could again meet with the director of the BMA and the architects about the Children's Wing. She arrived at the Sheraton Belvedere Hotel late Sunday evening, April 18, and met with them the next day.[44] The following week they went to New York to the Ritz Carlton. They visited the Pierre Matisse Gallery, where Saidie purchased Joan Miró's *Femmes et Oiseau devant la Lune*, painted in 1944 for $450[45] and had it sent to the BMA.

Later in the week, Saidie paid a visit to the American Museum of Natural History. She donated a pigeon-blood intaglio ruby ring she had purchased from the Sir William Cook collection in

Jackson Pollock, American, 1912–1956, *Water Birds*, 1943, oil on canvas, 26-1/8 x 21-3/16 in., The Baltimore Museum of Art: Bequest of Saidie A. May, BMA 1951.349. ©2011 The Pollock-Krasner Foundation/Artists Rights Society (ARS), New York.

London years before. It was a very early example of the use of that hard gem material, and had not been represented in their mineral collection previously. The museum was planning to further develop their section about the historical use of jewelry, and the gift was timely towards that end. Saidie met with the curator of geology and mineralogy, Frederick H. Pough, PhD., who accepted her gift.[46] Within a couple of days, Saidie and Al were headed back to San Diego to paint for the summer months, staying at the Imig Manor Hotel.

Harry Bertoia

One day in June, Saidie and Al went to Los Angeles to visit the studio of a young artist and sculptor, Harry Bertoia. There, Saidie purchased *Lines*, a colorful collage done on a panel with concentric circles, correlated lines and color tones (26"h X 40" w) as well as two prints, all for the grand sum of $25. Bertoia was preparing for a showing of his work later in the summer at the San Diego Fine Arts Gallery. She purchased the canvas, and Bertoia took it to be framed. Saidie donated the work to the San Diego Museum and it was used in Bertoia's show.[47] Bertoia also displayed silver jewelry for sale at the show.[48]

Saidie headed east alone on October 14 for Delaware, where she paid a visit to her son, Murray, at Haddonfield where he was institutionalized.[49] Then she came down to Baltimore late Monday afternoon, October 18, to stay at the Belvedere Hotel to work with the museum staff and the architects on bids for the work for the Children's Wing.[50] On the 23rd, she headed to New York to peruse the art galleries.

Dubuffet

On October 28, Saidie purchased a gouache by Jean Dubuffet for $180. This work was part of an upcoming show put on by the Pierre Matisse Gallery,[51] scheduled to open November 30 for a month, "Paintings, Gouaches 1946–1948." These paintings, some executed by Dubuffet while on vacation in Algeria during the winter of 1947–1948, were inspired by his fascination with the desert.

Unfortunately, Dubuffet felt hampered by the inferior quality of the materials he had brought with him on the vacation, and he considered the drawings he had done in El Golea, Algeria, to be mere studies for use in his studio back in Paris.[52] Once home, he wrote to Pierre Matisse about the new technique with which he was experimenting and would create the paintings for this exhibit, all in monochromatic tones. Nine gouaches from this series eventually made their way to the show. Saidie found the painting so interesting that she took it back to San Diego with her after leaving New York, to live with it for a while.[53]

Jackson Pollock

The following day, Saidie visited Betty Parsons' Gallery, where she "picked up" *Light* by the relatively new young artist, Jackson Pollock, for the sum of $212.50.[54] Back in 1945, Peggy Guggenheim had had a showing of Pollock's work at Art of This Century and Saidie attended the show. Peggy had begged Saidie to purchase a Pollock for her collection, but Saidie refused, because she didn't care for his work at that time. After making this purchase, she asked Betty Parsons to contact Peggy Guggenheim to let her know that Saidie had finally come around and purchased one of his works.[55]

Unfortunately for the BMA, it was not in pristine condition. There were a few small chips of paint missing in the

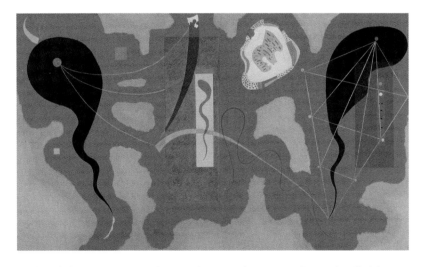

Wassily Kandinsky, Russian, 1866–1944, *Penetrating Green*, 1938, oil on canvas, 29-3/16 x 49-3/8 in., The Baltimore Museum of Art: Bequest of Saidie A. May, BMA 1951.310. ©2011 Artists Rights Society (ARS), New York/ADAGP, Paris.

center of the painting, showing the grain of the canvas, as well as a hole in the lower right side, previously punched half-out by a nail head. Aside from those "misadventures" which weren't crucial, the painting was very powerful and showed well.[56] Adelyn Breeskin found this piece rather puzzling, so she suggested that they take it over to the art history department at Hopkins University to have it studied by a graduate student under the supervision of the head of the department. Afterwards, the museum would use the findings to do a write-up on the painting.[57] Unfortunately, if this study was ever undertaken, there is no evidence of it in the archives of the BMA.

On November 4, Saidie visited the Sidney Janis Gallery to see the show of works by Wassily

Kandinsky and she purchased the painting *Penetrating Green* for $600.[58] That afternoon, she wrote a postcard to Adelyn Breeskin in Baltimore, excitedly sharing the news of her three new purchases—almost as if she were an archaeologist having just excavated a spectacular new find.[59] She had the Kandinsky piece sent to the BMA to display in the Members' Room. She asked Adelyn Breeskin to hold a reception for the local artists to come and study it.

By November 7, she was ready to go back to San Diego to join Al for the winter. Saidie "lent" most of her collection to the BMA—where they would house and care for it. Each year, she and the museum staff would select pieces that she would donate (at their current, increased value) for her to use as a tax deduction against the income she derived from the investments she lived off of.

Notes

1   Francoise Levaillant, *André Masson, Les Annees Surrealistes, Correspondence 1916-1942* (Paris, France: 1990).

2   Daniel-Henry Kahnweiler to Saidie A. May, March 30, 1946 Saidie A. May Papers, BMA.

3   Daniel-Henry Kahnweiler to Saidie A. May, August 19, 1945 Saidie A. May Papers, BMA.

4   Daniel-Henry Kahnweiler to Saidie A. May, March 30, 1946 Saidie A. May Papers, BMA.

5   "Liberated Treasures," *Baltimore Museum of Art News*, 8:1, (October, 1945), 1.

6   Saidie A. May to Adelyn Breeskin, December 18, 1945 Saidie A. May Papers, BMA.

7   Adelyn Breeskin to Saidie A. May, January 7, 1946 Adelyn Breeskin Papers, BMA.

8   Daniel-Henry Kahnweiler to Saidie A. May, March 30, 1946 Saidie A. May Archives, BMA.

9   Saidie A. May to Adelyn Breeskin, January 9, 1946 Saidie A. May Papers, BMA.

10 Kent Roberts Greenfield, "The Museum: Its First Half Century," *Annual I*, (BMA, Baltimore, MD, March, 1966), 71–73.

11 Pierre Chareau, http://www.artnet.com/Artists/ArtistHomePage.aspx?artist.

12 Alfred Jensen to Jane Cone, May 27, 1972 Saidie A. May Papers, BMA.

13 Adelyn Breeskin to Saidie A. May, August 28, 1946 Saidie A. May Papers, BMA.

14 Philip B. Perlman to Saidie A. May, August 2, 1946 Saidie A. May Papers, BMA.

15 John Russell, *Matisse, Father and Son* (New York: Harry N. Abrams, 1999), 273.

16 *Ibid.*, 274.

17 *Ibid.*, 277.

18 *Ibid.*, 278–279.

19 Pierre Matisse to Saidie A. May, January 8, 1947 Pierre Matisse Gallery Archives, Pierpont Morgan Library, New York Acc. # 5020.

20 Saidie A. May to Adelyn Breeskin, December 9, 1946 Saidie A. May Papers, BMA.

21 Saidie A. May to Adelyn Breeskin, December 13, 1946 Saidie A. May Papers, BMA.

22 Saidie A. May to Adelyn Breeskin, February 14, 1947 Saidie A. May Papers, BMA.

23 http://en.wikipedia.org./wiki/Philip_Perlman.

24 George M. Goodwin, *A New Jewish Elite: Curators, Directors and Benefactors of American Art Museums* 18.2 (Modern Judaism, 1998), 119–152.

25 Saidie A. May to Pierre Matisse, December 16, 1946 Pierre Matisse Archives, Pierpont Morgan Library, New York.

26 John Russell, *Matisse, Father and Son* (New York: Harry N. Abrams, 1999), 279.

27 Saidie A. May to Adelyn Breeskin, February 14, 1947, Saidie A. May Papers, BMA.

28 Breeskin, Adelyn, "Paintings from the Saidie A. May Collection," March, 1947, Saidie A. May Papers, BMA.

29 Fine Arts Society of San Diego to Saidie A. May, May 23, 1947 Saidie A. May Papers, BMA.

30 Daniel-Henry Kahnweiler to Saidie A. May, June 12, 1947 Saidie A. May Papers, BMA.

31 Saidie A. May to Adelyn Breeskin, August 23, 1947 Saidie A. May Papers, BMA.

32 *Ibid.*

33 Saidie A. May to Adelyn Breeskin, October 8, 1947 Saidie A. May Papers, BMA.

34 *Ibid.*

35 *Ibid.*

36 Canceled check from Saidie A. May to Pierre Matisse Gallery, October 23, 1947 Saidie A. May Papers, BMA.

37 Canceled check from Saidie A. May to Babcock Galleries Inc. October 27, 1947 Saidie A. May Papers, BMA.

38 Lee Hall, *Betty Parsons, Artist, Dealer, Collector* (New York: Harry N. Abrams, 1991), 77.

39 Marguerite Guggenheim, *Out of this Century, Confessions of an Art Addict* (New York: Universe Books, 1987), 320.

40 George Kronen, former employee of WMAR television. Interview by phone with author, 2004, Baltimore, MD.

41 "Television from the Members' Room," *Baltimore Museum of Art News*, 11:5 (February, 1948), 8.

42 "From Here to There: Television," *Baltimore Museum of Art News*, 12:2 (November, 1948), 7.

43 Saidie A. May to Gertrude Rosenthal, January 28, 1948 Saidie A. May Papers, BMA.

44 Saidie A. May to Adelyn Breeskin, April 7, 1948 Saidie A. May Papers, BMA.

45 Pierre Matisse Gallery bill of sale, April 27, 1948, Acc. #MA 5020 Pierre Matisse Gallery Archives, Pierpont Morgan Library, New York.

46 F. H. Pough to Saidie A. May, April 28, 1948 Saidie A. May Archives, BMA.

47 Reginald Poland to Saidie A. May, June 30, 1948 Saidie A. May Papers, BMA.

48 Harry Bertoia to Saidie A. May, June 19, 1948 Saidie A. May Papers, BMA.

49 Saidie A, May to Adelyn Breeskin, September 20, 1948 Saidie A. May Papers, BMA.

50 *Ibid.*

51 Pierre Matisse Gallery bill of sale, October 28, 1948, Acc# MA 5020, Pierre Matisse Gallery Archives Pierpont Morgan Library, New York.

52 Jennifer Tonkovick, *Pierre Matisse and his Artists* (New York: Pierpont Morgan Library, 2002), 217.

53 Saidie A. May to Adelyn Breeskin, November 15, 1948 Saidie A. May Papers, BMA.

54 Canceled check from Saidie A. May to Betty Parson's Gallery, October 29, 1948 Saidie A. May Papers, BMA.

55 Saidie A. May to Adelyn Breeskin, November 15, 1948 Saidie A. May Papers, BMA.

56 Adelyn Breeskin to Saidie A. May, November 23, 1948 Saidie A. May Papers, BMA.

57 *Ibid.*, (margin comments by Adelyn Breeskin)

58 Canceled check from Saidie A. May to the Sidney Janis Gallery, November 4, 1948 Saidie A. May Papers, BMA.

59 Saidie A. May to Adelyn Breeskin, November 4, 1948 Saidie A. May Papers, BMA.

The Children's Wing

21

Saidie's Show

On March 17, the Baltimore Museum of Art had its first comprehensive show of Saidie's collection of Modern paintings, sculpture and drawings, valued at $500,000. A newspaper article announcing the exhibit referred to the fact that Saidie knew the Cone sisters for years and purposely formed her collection to complement the Cones' without overlapping. Together, the collections represented a comprehensive survey of the entire background and development of twentieth-century European painting.[1] Articles started appearing all over the area announcing the show as well as Saidie's pledge of $300,000 towards a new Children's Wing for the museum.[2]

Construction Begins

The final bids for the Children's Wing were scheduled for March 1, 1949. Luckily, the stock market was heading upward, increasing Saidie's funds for that project. In the April BMA newsletter, Belle Boas authored an article announcing that construction of the Children's Wing had commenced. She describes the rationale for the wing: "It will be a special building, being equipped in purpose and scale for the child. To stimulate the imagination and develop creative ability, as well as increasing sensitivity and awareness of life in our environment."[3] Miss Boas, who had sight in only one eye, was a nationally recognized leader in the field of art education for children. She had written the book *Art in the School* in 1924, and it would be a standard text in the field of art education for many years.[4] Before and during the construction of the wing, she wrote many letters to other curators at many art museums in this country, comparing notes concerning costs, materials and concepts. One museum with which she had regular correspondence was the Hartford Children's Museum.[5]

Opening of Saidie A. May Wing at the Baltimore Museum of Art, Left to right: Miss Belle Boas, Saidie A. May, Mrs. Adelyn Breeskin, Mr. Philip Perlman, April 1, 1950, photo by Frank A. Miller, *Baltimore Sun* Archives, Special Collections, UMBC Library. Reprinted with permission of the *Baltimore Sun* Media Group. All Rights Reserved.

Site of the future Saidie A. May Wing on the campus of the Baltimore Museum of Art, April, 1949, *Baltimore Sun* Archives, Special Collections, UMBC Library. Reprinted with permission of the *Baltimore Sun* Media Group. All Rights Reserved.

Saidie planned to be in Baltimore by the middle of April for a week to oversee the ground-breaking for the wing.[6] She then proceeded to New York, where she met MOMA's print curator, Mr. Leberman, in the print room, where he showed her some new acquisitions: about forty etchings by a friend of Picasso's named "Adam." Saidie liked his work. In a postcard to Adelyn Breeskin, Saidie suggested that Belle Boas look him up and visit his studio the next time she was in Europe, and she could use funds from Blanche's bequest to purchase a few of his works for the BMA.[7]

A Painting is Destroyed

Later in the day, Saidie saw Alfred Barr. He had some bad news. A painting that she previously donated by Louis Vivin had recently been sent out to be reproduced for the museum. It had been placed in a fireproof room, but someone had removed it to a workroom to admire it, and forgot to put it back. This workroom caught fire and subsequently the picture was burned. It was insured for $600, and Alfred Barr planned to try to replace it with another Vivin on his next trip to Paris. Unfortunately for the museum, Vivin's work had increased in value so much that Barr would probably have to spend $2,000 for the replacement.[8]

Kahnweiler Arrives

Henry Kahnweiler was invited to the United States for a lecture tour of art institutes in New York and Chicago and at Harvard and Yale universities. It was his first visit to the United States, and his arrival made the front pages of the newspapers of each of the cities that he visited. Everywhere he became the ambassador of the avant-garde.[9] He loved public speaking, and the combination of his European culture and knowledge of three languages enabled him to travel easily.[10]

While Kahnweiler was in New York, he made arrangements for Saidie and Al to attend a lecture he gave on April 28. Afterwards, he spent a couple of hours with them, catching up on old times and bringing Saidie up to date on Masson's latest work.[11] He had some photographs of the paintings, and convinced Saidie that Masson's latest, *Cascatelle*, a landscape he painted while in Aix, was a "must have" for her collection. She agreed, paying $283 for it.[12] Saidie mentioned to Kahnweiler that she had questions as to the authenticity of a drawing done by Juan Gris, recently purchased from Curt Valentin. Kahnweiler wanted to take the frame off of the drawing to look at the back of the piece for Gris' mark.[13] Meanwhile, Curt Valentin sent a note to Douglas Cooper in London for a photo of his painting by Gris, which he claimed was the original. Within a couple of weeks, Valentin had his answer; Saidie's drawing was a fake. Saidie returned it and demanded her money be refunded.[14]

The next day, Kahnweiler took the train to Philadelphia to see the Barnes Collection. Then on April 30 he sailed back to France.[15] On the 29th, Saidie went to visit Rose Fried, owner of the Pinacotheca Gallery. She wanted to purchase a work by Theo van Doesburg, a Dutch painter of the De Stijl group, to add to her collection at the BMA. Van Doesburg's wife had sold off the rest of his works since his death in 1931.[16] The only large painting not sold, *Étude No. III—Interior*, was a work from 1917. Rose Fried told Saidie that Alfred Barr "approved of it, tho' it is a year before the one they have with the colored lines." Fried showed Saidie where Van Doesburg had scraped the canvas in one spot, which showed thin through the back, but that didn't harm it (it actually was painted over an old, previously scraped canvas.) In light of the damage, she sold her the painting for $700.[17] Then she sent it to the BMA.

A Visit to Connecticut

A couple of days later, Saidie and Al drove to Connecticut with the art dealer, Leo Castelli, to visit the studios of Naum Gabo and his neighbors, Alexander Calder and Yves Tanguy. Al had become interested in the work of Gabo, so he and Saidie approached the "Gentleman Dealer," Castelli, who represented Gabo and his brother, Antoine Pevsner.[18] Saidie enjoyed the ride, since she found Leo Castelli "most unusually cultured."[19]

Naum Gabo

Naum Gabo was born Naum Pevsner, August 5, 1890, in Briansk, Russia. He studied political philosophy, science and engineering in his homeland and in Munich, Germany, where he was a medical and engineering student. It was in Munich that he attended art history lectures by Heinrich Wolfflin and met members of the Blaue Reiter group, including Wassily Kandinsky, who along with Wolfflin was influential in Gabo's subsequent art career. Between 1913 and 1914, Naum joined his older brother, Antoine, a Cubist painter in Paris, and the two moved to Copenhagen and then to Oslo after the outbreak of WWI. At this time, Naum changed his name to avoid confusion with his older and then more famous brother. The two brilliant brothers carried the style known as "constructivism" to a high pitch of intellectual and formal elegance. Gabo was the more inventive of the two. In 1917, Gabo returned to Russia. As early as 1920, he made an electrically driven sculpture. He is also credited with rudimentary ventures into kinetic sculpture.

In the early 1920s, the Soviet government decided that only Realist art should be seen by the masses, so Gabo and Pevsner left their homeland. They went to Berlin, where Gabo stayed for ten years, teaching at the Bauhaus and painting. Pevsner went on to Paris and later became a French citizen, living there until his death in 1962. Gabo joined his brother in Paris in the early 1930s, but went on to England, where he remained for more than ten years. He had been friendly with Marcel Duchamp while they were living in Europe, and wrote to him to get help to leave for the U.S. and find work there. Duchamp had escaped with the help of Katherine Dreyer, and had asked her to also help Gabo, but she refused—believing that European artists would have a hard time finding work in America.[20] But Gabo came to the U.S. in 1946 to teach at Harvard as a professor in the Graduate School of Architecture.[21] Eventually, Katherine Dreyer saw his work and bought a miniature model for a large sculpture that was never built. In 1947, she asked him to be the president of the Société Anonyme for that year. He agreed.[22]

Saidie and Al's visit with Naum Gabo and his wife was very pleasant. The three spent much more time with the Gabos than they had anticipated and ran out of time to visit Alexander Calder. Saidie purchased one of Gabo's constructions made of alabaster and plastic. This piece from 1938 had been priced at $4,000 for the private collector, but since Saidie was having it installed at the BMA, Gabo gave her the museum courtesy discount price of $3,000. Leo Castelli would correspond with the BMA and make arrangements for Castelli and Gabo to go to Baltimore to install the work themselves. They planned to go by the end of May, so Saidie arranged for them to visit Etta Cone at her apartment and see her collection, and then to see Saidie's collection at the BMA.[23] Gabo's construction needed a four-foot tall pedestal to display it.[24] Saidie suggested that it be shown in the Members' Room. While they were there, Saidie and Gabo talked of the possibility of his designing an impressively large piece of sculpture to greet visitors to the new wing at the BMA. He agreed to work on the idea and come up with sketches for a proposal.[25] Saidie and

Al embraced the Gabos as they had the Massons, and Saidie continued to have a very close relationship with them until her death.

Saidie and Al found their meeting with Naum Gabo so inspiring that when they returned to San Diego the following week, they decided to switch media and start making constructions. Saidie worked on these cardboard constructions all summer, finding this work "strengthening." Towards the end of July, she invited Reginald Poland, director of the San Diego Fine Arts Museum, to see her new work. He was very impressed and took all of them, planning to show a couple at a time over the fall months. He encouraged her to also give a talk about her process.[26] In August, the museum showed two constructions and a watercolor by Saidie entitled, *Neon Lights*. Since the constructions were made of cardboard, Saidie felt that they were too fragile to ship to the BMA to show there.[27]

An Appreciation

In the article of September 11, 1949, Reginald Poland wrote in the *San Diego Union* describing the breadth of Saidie's gifts to the San Diego Fine Arts Gallery, which were on display that month. The objects ranged from an antique Tunisian bracelet to Masson's *Germ of the Cosmos*. He credits her as being a "Pioneer and creative producer in the field of the most modern art," and praises her study of the latest material on the subject, and vast knowledge of the arts and artists in Europe and in the U.S. One of the works mentioned in the article was *Flowers*, a colorful painting by a friend of Saidie's from Baltimore, Edward Rosenfeld, a local artist who painted many landmarks in Baltimore.[28]

At the beginning of September, Saidie was in Baltimore for about a week, checking on the progress of the new wing. By now, at the age of seventy, it was becoming difficult for her to walk steps,[29] and as there was no elevator, she did not go to the second floor, but she was pleased with what she was able to see. While she was there, she had the BMA send Dubuffet's *North African Wall* to the San Diego Fine Arts Gallery, as the BMA's board had declined to accept it. Along with it they sent Aaron Sopher's drawing of the *Archbishop Athenagoras*.[30] Then she headed to New York.

Saidie Returns to New York

On September 16, Saidie ran into Max Schnitzler, who had been a protégé of hers years ago in Paris; he invited her to see his studio and his latest work. She accepted and went to visit him. She admired his work and he begged her to accept one of his paintings to repay a loan she had given him in Paris. Saidie graciously accepted it and subsequently sent it to the BMA.

The next day, Saidie strolled into Knoedler's Gallery and picked up a small landscape by Max Ernst which she saw in the window. Even though she wanted to refrain from buying art to have enough money for the Children's Wing, Saidie felt she "had to have" the Ernst landscape for her collection at the museum. While she was there, she ran into Sam Kootz, Robert Motherwell and

Sidney Janis, who had recently returned from Paris. The four spent a while talking about "goings on" in Paris and the art world. Saidie enjoyed the encounter and described it as an adventure. Talking to the artists and dealers and seeing the latest art work gave Saidie a lift which made her feel as if she was back in the "main stream."[31] Even though San Diego was beautiful and relaxing, she occasionally felt isolated and missed the intellectual excitement of New York.

Saidie made another visit to her son, Murray, at the Bancroft School. She was there to help him and his aide, Mrs. King, with the transition from a large, comfortable apartment to a smaller one, also on the campus.[32] After getting Murray settled, Saidie returned to New York to meet Al. On September 28, they dropped in to see Pierre Matisse. She decided to purchase one of the last bronze statues from the Giacometti show held in January, 1948, *Man Pointing* for $1,900 and had it sent directly to the BMA for her collection.[33]

South Carolina

In November, Saidie and Al went to Charleston, South Carolina, and again spent the winter at the Francis Marion Hotel. She also leased a large, sunny studio near the waterfront, below the studio of William Melton Halsey, a local and well-known artist. At the studio, Saidie challenged herself making constructions with strips of aluminum, stainless steel and wood.[34] She and Al collaborated

on some of those constructions. In December, they commissioned a sculptor at the Sabel Ironworks to fashion a piece from a model they had made by welding iron pieces to form their sculpture. While they waited for the "ironman" to complete the welding, they went back to painting.[35] Saidie knew that her work could never be of the caliber of the art she collected, but she understood the processes and continued to work at the craft. "Of course, as Paul Valery said—enthusiasm is not sufficient to conceive a successful work—which I have found out thro' the actual doing."[36]

Florida

Towards the end of December, Saidie and Al decided to spend New Year's in Daytona Beach,

Postcard of clocktower on the boardwalk, Daytona Beach, Florida, c. 1941. Collection of the author.

Florida. They packed up their paints and canvases and took the train south from Charleston. They stayed at the Sheraton Plaza Hotel, and set up their studio to continue painting.[37] At the end of January, they headed back to Charleston, where they worked together in their studio, each making two three-dimensional reliefs on wood, using metal and worked paperboard. That used up all of their relief material, so, until more came, they would go back to painting (see page 4).[38] At the beginning of February, they picked up three of their finished constructions at the ironworks, and consequently sent them up to the BMA for display there (see page 264). The museum set them up outside in the little court adjacent to the Members' Room, planting some small yews to add color to the courtyard. Tarleton, the maintenance man, painted an extra coating of black paint on them to guard against snow and ice damage during the winter.

During the month of December, the Saidie A. May Children's Wing had been completed. Belle Boas was conducting art classes in the new facility.[39] Both classes, a daytime sculpture course and an evening painting class were filled, with the sculpture class having a waiting list of 75 people.

The First Show is Planned

Towards the end of January, the museum planned the first large comprehensive showing of the Saidie A. May collection. James Johnson Sweeney was hired to study the collection and write an introduction to the catalogue that would accompany the show.[40] Reginald Poland sent the small Miró painting from the San Diego Fine Arts Gallery to be included in the show.[41]

James Johnson Sweeney

On Friday evening, January 20, 1950, James Johnson Sweeney arrived at the BMA to see the opening of the Cone collection. The next morning, curator Gertrude Rosenthal took him for a personal tour of Saidie's collection. He seemed very impressed with it, especially with

Georges Seurat, French, 1859–1891, *Preparatory Sketch for the Painting "La Greve du Bas-Butin, Honfleur,"* 1886, oil on wood panel, 6-3/4 x 10-1/4 in., The Baltimore Museum of Art: Bequest of Saidie A. May, BMA 1951.357.

the Miró, Gris and Masson works. He found the small Seurat, the Renoir *Nude* and the Picasso still-life to be extremely fine examples of those artists' works. He understood why she bought her new acquisitions by Giacometti, Mondrian, and Ernst at the same time, and how they related to each other. He felt that the Giacometti was the best piece in the Museum's sculpture collection.

Of the Modern art in Saidie's collection, her paintings by Miró were the apex of the show, and he wanted to stress their importance in the catalogue.[42] He and "Trudy" Rosenthal together compiled a list of the works from which they would order a few photos for his article, which would discuss the pieces in more depth. Trudy gave the list to Adelyn Breeskin, who then sent Saidie a list of possible inclusions for the show, and solicited her input on additional works and suggestions.[43]

Saidie wrote to Adelyn, accepting the invitation to a dinner before the opening on the 31st of March. She was excited but a bit apprehensive, "The spirit is very willing, but the flesh is pretty weak, I am afraid."[44] Al wanted Freisz's portrait of Saidie in the show. Saidie was fond of Despiau's *Lady from Lyons* head, "the model for it was the wife of an important collector of Renoirs in Lyons, no doubt a banker or silk manufacturer."[45] She also wanted the pastel drawing *A Lady in a Black Hat* by Mary Cassatt to be included. Adelyn Breeskin didn't like the work, and didn't feel it merited showing. She claimed it was "rubbed," and came to the BMA in that condition. As such, she felt it would be detrimental to include it with the collection. When Saidie had purchased it for $350 from the Kraushaar Gallery in New York in 1936 or 1937, it was with the knowledge that this was an "unfinished sketch." Saidie and Al discussed the work with the gallery owner, and all three felt that it was "spontaneous," and well worth showing.[46]

Sketch of Mathilde in a Dark Hat, c. 1890 by Mary Cassat, pastel on gray paper, 18-1/2 x 14-1/2 in., unsigned, BMA, Saidie A. May collection, sold in 1958 to Miller Galleries then sold again in 1958 to Canajoharie Library and Art Gallery, now known as the Arkell Museum, New York.

The Catalogue

The March issue of the BMA's *News Magazine* would be the catalogue for the Saidie A. May collection. It featured an introduction by Adelyn Breeskin, admiring the breadth of Saidie's collection of French nineteenth- and early-twentieth century art. She also praised the importance of the "teachability" of the collection, and how Saidie built it around her interests as an artist and art student. The culmination of her giving was the Young People's Art Center Wing, which, when combined with her paintings, sculpture, drawings, antiquities, graphic arts and books, made for an impressive part of the entire museum. Her aim was to educate the public and give them an opportunity to appreciate Modern art.[47] Directly after the printing of the *News Magazine*, Adelyn Breeskin sent a copy of the May catalogue to Saidie in Charleston. She was delighted and touched by Adelyn's personal remarks and understanding in her introduction. Leslie Cheek sent a letter to Saidie regretting that he and his wife were unable to make the opening.[48]

James Johnson Sweeney, art critic and former director of the department of painting and sculpture for MOMA, raved about Saidie's collection as having her "unique signature" as a collection, formed by her selection of works to express a clear point of view. In his opinion, collecting is a "creative expression in its own right, with a selection of finished artistic expressions, rather than the raw materials of painting or sculpture." He indicated that the Cone collection, though representing nineteenth- and twentieth-century art, was "selectively focused, with a distinct period character." It was such an extensive representation of that period in French art, that Saidie took her collection as a continuation of these works and added the latest works in the mainstream, up to the twentieth century in Europe and the United States. "Within this time period, the May collection represents excellent examples of Renoir, Cézanne and Seurat, Bonnard, Friesz and Derain (Fauves—on the middle path), Dufy and Rouault, linking with Matisse in the Cone collection, Kandinsky and Marc, the Cubist Juan Gris then leading to Ernst and the De Stijl founders, Mondrian and Van Doesburg, Masson (the Cubist who turned to Surrealism), Miró (the Surrealist who left the movement), Lam (who brought his Caribbean memories to Paris), Tanguy (from Breton), and the sculptors, Giacometti (the ex-Surrealist) and Naum Gabo (the Constructivist)."[49]

After finishing his work at the BMA, Sweeney traveled to Charleston to visit William Melton Halsey. He arrived on February 4, and took a look at Halsey's work that afternoon in his studio above Saidie and Al's. Unfortunately, they were not there that day and missed seeing him.[50]

Halsey was very fond of Saidie and Al, and often invited them up to his studio to talk art. Saidie purchased one of his works and sent it to the BMA for their American collection. Halsey was pleased since he had met Adelyn Breeskin at Black Mountain College some years earlier.[51] He mentioned Saidie's work to a local bookstore and art gallery owner who sold his work. Along with operating the gallery, Mrs. Kyra Kuhar wrote art news for the local Sunday newspaper in Charleston.[52] She was interested in Saidie's work for an article for the paper, so Saidie made arrangements to take her to the Sabel Ironworks to see her finished constructions. This was the first time the foundry had ever produced work for modern artists, and Saidie was very pleased with the results and most anxious for them to receive recognition in an article by Mrs. Kuhar.[53]

Visitors at opening of Saidie A. May Young People's Art Center at the Baltimore Museum of Art, April 1, 1950, photo by Frank A. Miller, *Baltimore Sun* Archives, Special Collections, UMBC Library. Reprinted with permission of the *Baltimore Sun* Media Group. All Rights Reserved.

"Art of the Brain"

On the evening of March 17, 1950, a reception was held for the Saidie A. May collection of Surrealist and abstract art. In an article that day in the *Baltimore Sun*, Patrick Skene Catling called Saidie's collection "art of the brain," contrasting it with Cone's collection, "art of the heart." The art of the brain included Surrealist art, derived from the subconscious dream world, and Abstract art, analytic or synthetic. He referred to André Masson, "one of Mrs. May's favorites," as the "predominant engineer of catastrophe on canvas." Overall, the article strongly indicated the mood of the uninitiated: Modern art is tough to understand.[54]

Another article by Aline B. Louchheim in the *New York Times* Sunday Art Section told about the strong impact Saidie's artists made on their canvases with color. Having actually viewed the exhibit, Ms. Louchheim indicated that one could "know" the collector's personality through viewing the collection, an "exuberant, outgoing, energetic person who could have chosen paintings of such brilliant, intense, sometimes screeching color. Here is a collector who likes paint and texture, understands painting—there are so many painters' pictures here, interesting for the virtuoso painterly solutions of their problems."[55]

Officially, the Young People's Art Center opening was held two weeks later. The keynote speaker was Philip Perlman, Saidie's friend and lawyer. Perlman was now the appointed Solicitor General of the United States under President Truman, and his extensive scheduling commitments had prevented his speaking at the reception two weeks earlier. It was very important to Saidie that he speak at this event, the most important contribution of her collecting career. Perlman had been involved with Saidie's dealings with the museum from the beginning. He was also an avid print collector, and worked with Blanche at the museum in the early years. He was the perfect person to represent Saidie at the opening.

The formal opening of the Saidie May Young People's Art Center Wing began on the beautiful spring evening of March 31 with a dinner at the Hopkins Faculty Club. Hosted by Mr. and Mrs. Harold Wrenn, the dinner honored the now seventy-two-year-old Saidie and the collection she had been building for fifty years. The guests included Solicitor General Phil Perlman and Bartlett H. Hayes, Jr., director of the Addison Gallery of American Art, which was connected with the Phillips Academy in Andover, Massachusetts. Bartlett and Mrs. Hayes spent the night at the Wrenn's home, which was ten minutes from the BMA.

Saidie was the guest of honor at the gala opening of the Young People's Art Center Wing. Saidie had been advised by a friend to buy a suitable dress for the gala, and she finally did so, begrudgingly. During dinner her impatience with the purchase became evident. When one of the guests complimented Saidie on her beautiful gown, she remarked sharply, "The $100 would have been more wisely spent on a fine print for the museum."

After dinner, everyone convened in the auditorium. Tiny Saidie sat with a huge grin on her face in a chair in a corner of the auditorium stage, her feet not able to touch the floor. On her right were Robert Lewis and Francis Jencks, the Baltimore architects who had designed the new wing. Next to them was Belle Boas and Bartlett Hayes, who would give a forty-five minute lecture. On Saidie's left sat Philip Perlman, Adelyn Breeskin, Baltimore Mayor Thomas D'Alesandro, and Mrs. Breeskin's executive assistant, James W. Foster.[56]

Adelyn Breeskin served as mistress of ceremonies, and introduced the guest of honor, Saidie A. May. Everyone in the auditorium came to their feet, and there was a prolonged applause. Finally Adelyn spoke,

> "As all of you know who have watched the progress of this museum of ours, Mrs. May has added greatly to its growth. Her splendid collections are now on view throughout the upper galleries of the main building. In the Antioch Court there are many individual gifts from the classical period, The Renaissance Room is a magnificent gift from her, as is the Members' Room, which is a fine example of what such a room should be as can be found anywhere in the world. There is scarcely a single museum department, whether of textiles, prints or oriental objects to which she has not

contributed. Now we celebrate the most recent and greatest of her gifts—the Young People's Art Center Wing."[57]

Mayor D'Alesandro, who had broken ground for the new wing on a rainy day in the fall of 1948, spoke next. He declared Baltimore, "a rapidly growing art center," through the generosity of its public-spirited and civic-minded citizens.

Mrs. Breeskin then introduced Philip Perlman, who spoke of the impact of gifts and bequests in education by such notables as Johns Hopkins, George Peabody and Henry Walters. He added Saidie A. May to the end of this list. "These Baltimoreans influenced materially the equipment and training of men and women all over the nation, and even in distant parts of the world." He then summarized the history of his relationship with the museum, beginning before it existed, as an idea. As city solicitor of Baltimore, he had drafted the legislation for the General Assembly and the City Council under which the museum construction loan was authorized. As counsel to both Saidie and the museum, he had been asked to consider transactions between them from both points of view. "These matters," he remarked with a grin, "always ended to the benefit of the museum—and to Mrs. May's satisfaction—and I have escaped so far any public investigations or charges resulting from them…." He referred to the Young People's Art Center as a "Tribute of confidence and trust in Mrs. Breeskin and Miss Boas," in the integrity of that institution, and of her affection for it and the people of Baltimore.[58]

Years earlier, Phil explained, Saidie had told him that she wanted to provide a place in the museum where young people could learn about art directly. They would, in addition to seeing and learning about art and the society or culture in which it was produced, work with the art materials to create their own expressions. Her ambition was to help young people in developing whatever talents they might possess, to catch and retain in permanent form the beauties of nature and the works of man. Phil Perlman said,

"Usually she would come to Baltimore for a few days in the spring and fall. The winter finds her in the south or the far west, and the summer somewhere in the north, if she is not abroad. When she is away from Baltimore, she is usually hard at work on her painting (and sometimes on sculpture), to which she has devoted her spare time for the last twenty years. Until shortly before WWII, she made her headquarters in Paris, and it was there that she met and became associated with the outstanding artists of recent years. She also met many young artists struggling for recognition. For some of these artists she would provide scholarship money, so they could continue studying art. Her enormous curiosity and interest in what was being created impelled her to purchase from these painters, sculptors and graphic artists. Her purchases were shipped to the BMA to be added to her collection of modern paintings which give a rather complete view of what was done during that period. Her collection includes works from France, America, Spain, Russia, Hungary, Romania, Holland, Guatemala, Cuba, Germany, Chile, Italy and Denmark.

Saidie May continued to raise the standard of her collection, by not only adding, but looking at her collection with a critical eye, anything that she decided had not proven itself or stood the test of time, she eliminated, just as definitely as she made a purchase. Mrs. May, like the other members of the Adler family (who had contributed much and in many ways to the prosperity and welfare of the people of Baltimore) was modest and retiring, and prone to belittle her own efforts in behalf of the community whose interests she had at heart. She does things with charm and effortless grace, as to leave the impression that the beneficiary is doing her a favor by accepting. Her greatest pleasure comes from the gifts she makes."[59]

Art for Children

During the late 1940s, museums were starting to think about children's views of art, and as such were adding "children's museums"—collections that would interest children—to their institutions. Because of the impact of Belle Boas' work in art education, the BMA's Children's Art Center was unique in that the building was designed especially with an "education department." First, she would interest the children in art by letting them "try their own hands at creating it" in the studio. Then she would take them to the gallery to show them art as created by others, in a way that a child would understand. The third function would be to furnish loan exhibits to the public and private schools in the city, assisting teachers in illustrating the subjects taught, promoting art appreciation.[60]

Baltimore Mayor Thomas D'Alesandro models an Indian war bonnet from Ko-Ko-Mo Tribe No. 181, Improved Order of Redmen at the opening of the Saidie A. May Young People's Art Center at the Baltimore Museum of Art, April 1, 1950, *Sunday Sun*, April 2, 1950. Reprinted with permission of the *Baltimore Sun* Media Group. All Rights Reserved.

The Design

Plans for the new facility would include gallery space, a conference room, storage facilities for the loan materials, a workroom for the preparation of the exhibits and their packing, a lecture room and a theater. There was a separate children's garden off of the wing where summer classes would be held, weather permitting. The garden was decorated with the wrought-iron abstract constructions that Saidie and Al had made. There would be four

studios on the second floor, one equipped for clay. The studios would have lighting suitable for day or night use; even on dark days there would be adequate light of even intensity due to the window arrangements. Two walls of each studio had cork exhibition boards for display, another wall had a slate chalkboard over sinks, and shelving and cabinets for storage supplies. The wing was equipped with a sound system, enabling music to be played when the studios were in use.

J.G. Paul, president of the board of trustees, also spoke. He observed that Saidie, in common with most educators, felt that "a good museum must be something of a laboratory as well as a custodian of the great traditions of the past. She wanted it to be the abode of intellectual and artistic freedom."[61] Paul's dedication in the April, 1950 *News*, was devoted to the opening of the new wing. He wrote about the American museums' understanding of the importance of internationally recognized art treasures, which were brought to the U.S. and deposited in those public buildings. The museums also recognized the importance of educating the American public about those "legacies," as well as giving them and their children the opportunity to experience their own self-expression in the same media.[62]

The Saidie A. May Young People's Art Center was the model for children's art centers in museums in other parts of the country. As Francis W. Jencks observed: "Throughout the Wing the effort has been made to make the approach to art simple and easy, in contrast with the more usual arrangement of sumptuousness and majesty. Thus art can become something inviting and appealing, rather than an adjunct of the rich, formal and sophisticated life."

The *Baltimore Sun* ran an article about the new wing on Sunday, April 2, in which it stated, "The new Young People's Wing provides superb facilities for the development of aesthetic awareness among the young generations of present and future. Whether the facilities are well used now depends on the wisdom, learning and ingenuity of the museum staff itself."[63]

Notes

1   "$500,000 May Art Exhibit Opens March 17 At Museum," *Sunpaper*, March, 1949, Baltimore, MD.

2   "Museum Youth Center to Be Opened," March 31, 1949, Saidie A. May Papers, BMA.

3   "The Museum Grows," *Baltimore Museum of Art News*, 12:7 (April, 1949), 8.

4   "The New Program of Art Education," *Baltimore Museum of Art News*, 5:5 (February, 1943), 1.

5   "The Museum Grows," *Baltimore Museum of Art News*, 12:7 (April, 1949), 8.

6   Saidie A. May to Adelyn Breeskin, February 18, 1949, Saidie A. May Papers, BMA.

7   Saidie A. May to Adelyn Breeskin, April 29, 1949, Saidie A. May Papers, BMA.

8   Saidie A. May to Adelyn Breeskin, May 2, 1949, Saidie A. May Papers, BMA.

9   Pierre Assouline, *An Artful Life, A Biography of D.H. Kahnweiler, 1994–1979* (Canada: Fromm Int'l. Publishing Corp. 1991), 315.

Opposite, top: Staff dining room, Saidie A. May Young People's Art Center, The Baltimore Museum of Art, 1950, Sussman-Ochs. Saidie A. May Papers, Archives and Manuscripts Collections, The Baltimore Museum of Art. SM5.8.9. Lower: Third floor lobby, Saidie A. May Young People's Art Center, The Baltimore Museum of Art, 1950, Sussman-Ochs. Saidie A. May Papers, Archives and Manuscripts Collections, The Baltimore Museum of Art. SM5.8.2.

10 *Ibid.*, 314.

11 Saidie A. May to Belle Boas, April 29, 1949, Saidie A. May Papers, BMA.

12 Saidie A. May to Adelyn Breeskin, April 29, 1949, Saidie A. May Papers, BMA.

13 Saidie A. May to Adelyn Breeskin, May 2, 1949, Saidie A. May Papers, BMA.

14 Saidie A. May to Adelyn Breeskin, June 3, 1949, Saidie A. May Papers, BMA.

15 *Ibid.*

16 Saidie A. May to Adelyn Breeskin, April 29, 1949, Saidie A. May Papers, BMA.

17 *Ibid.*

18 Alfred Jensen to Jane Cone, May 27, 1972 Saidie A. May Papers, BMA.

19 Saidie A. May to Adelyn Breeskin, May 2, 1949 Saidie A. May Papers, BMA.

20 Societe Anonyme Inc., *Modernism for America, October 14, 2006–January 21*, 2007,The Phillips Collection, Washington, D.C.

21 "Naum Gabo, August 5, 1890–August 23, 1977," TheARTGallery, 21:1, Ivoryton, Conn., Hollycroft Press, (Oct–Nov. 1977), 3.

22 Societe Anonyme Inc., *Modernism for America, October 14, 2006–January 21, 2007*, The Phillips Collection, Washington, D.C.

23 Saidie A. May to Adelyn Breeskin, May 2, 1949, Saidie A. May Papers, BMA.

24 Adelyn Breeskin to Saidie A. May, August 2, 1949, Saidie A. May Papers, BMA.

25 Francis H. Jencks to William J. Casey, April 17, 1950, Saidie A. May Papers, BMA.

26 Saidie A. May to Adelyn Breeskin, July 30, 1949, Saidie A. May Papers, BMA.

27 Saidie A. May to Adelyn Breeskin, August 18, 1949, Saidie A. May Papers, BMA.

28 "Saidie May's Gifts Shown in La Jolla," by Reginald Poland, *The San Diego Union*, September 11, 1949, San Diego, Ca.

29 Saidie A. May to Adelyn Breeskin, September 17, 1949, Saidie A. May Papers, BMA.

30 Reginald Poland to Saidie A. May, September 30, 1949, Saidie A. May Papers, BMA.

31 Saidie A. May to Adelyn Breeskin, September 17, 1949, Saidie A. May Papers, BMA.

32 *Ibid.*

33 Pierre Matisse Gallery bill of sale, October 10, 1949, Acc# MA 5020, Pierre Matisse Gallery Archives, Pierpont Morgan Library, New York.

34 Saidie A. May to Adelyn Breeskin, November 29, 1949, Saidie A. May Papers, BMA.

35 Saidie A. May to Gertrude Rosenthal, December 21, 1949, Saidie A. May Papers, BMA.

36 *Ibid.*

37 Saidie A. May to Gertrude Rosenthal, December 24, 1949, Saidie A. May Papers, BMA.

38 Saidie A. May to Gertrude Rosenthal, January 28, 1950, Saidie A. May Papers, BMA.

39 Saidie A. May to Adelyn Breeskin, January 10, 1950, Saidie A. May Papers, BMA.

40 Adelyn Breeskin to Saidie A. May, January 21, 1950, Saidie A. May Papers, BMA.

41 Gertrude Rosenthal to Saidie A. May, January 22, 1950, Saidie A. May Papers, BMA.

42 *Ibid.*

43 *Ibid.*

44 Saidie A. May to Gertrude Rosenthal, January 28, 1950, Saidie A. May Papers, BMA.

45 Saidie A. May to Gertrude Rosenthal, February 5, 1950, Saidie A. May Papers, BMA.

46 *Ibid.*

47 "News," *The Baltimore Museum of Art—May Collection Catalogue*, March, 1950, 3–4, Baltimore Museum of Art Library.

48 Saidie A. May to Adelyn Breeskin, March 23, 1950, Saidie A. May Papers, BMA.

49 "News," *The Baltimore Museum of Art—May Collection Catalogue*, March, 1950, 5–7 Baltimore Museum of Art Library.

50 Saidie A. May to Gertrude Rosenthal, February 5, 1950, Saidie A. May Papers, BMA.

51 Saidie A. May to Gertrude Rosenthal, March 23, 1950, Saidie A. May Papers, BMA.

52 "Local Craftsmen Cast Iron For Baltimore Ornaments," by Kyra Kuhar, *Charleston Post and Courier*, March 26, 1950, Charleston, North Carolina.

53 *Ibid.*

54 "May Exhibition of Surrealist and Abstract Art Opens Tonight," by Patrick Skene Catling, *The Sun*, March 17, 1950, 24, 34.

55 "Baltimore Bonanza, The Saidie A. May Collection at Museum Extends Scope of Cone Bequest," by Aline B. Louchheim, *New York Times*, March 19, 1950, X9.

56 "Museum Youth Art Center to be Opened March 31,1950," Saidie A. May Papers, BMA.

57 Adelyn Breeskin, Speech for Opening of Saidie A. May Wing, March 31, 1950, BMA.

58 Address by Philip B. Perlman, Solicitor General of the Unites States, at the Dedication Ceremonies of the Saidie A. May Young People's Art Center, Baltimore Museum of Art, Baltimore, Maryland, Friday, March 31, 1950, BMA.

59 *Ibid.*

60 Bartlett Hayes, Speech for Opening of Saidie A. May Wing, March 31, 1950.

61 "News," April, 1950, Vol. 3, Issue #7, 1 Baltimore Museum of Art Library.

62 *Ibid.*

63 "Mrs. May's Handsome Gift to the Museum," *Baltimore Sun*, Sunday, April 2, 1950.

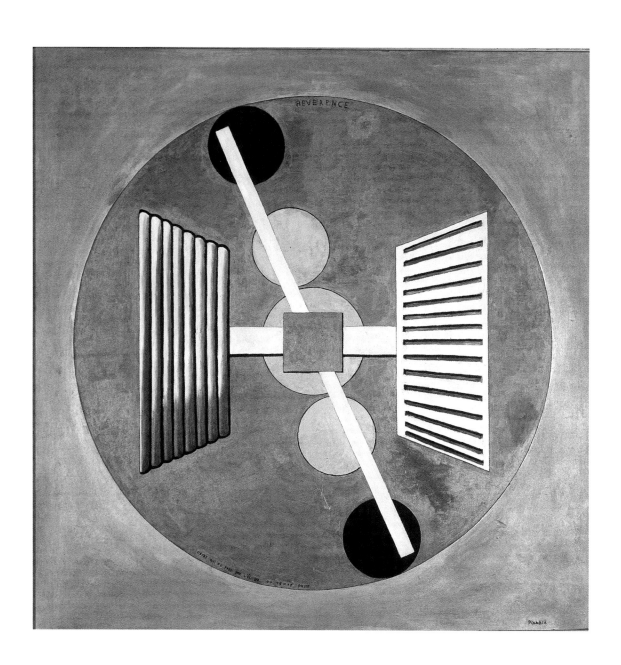

252 Saidie May

Back to Business, 1950

22

While in Baltimore for the opening of the Young People's Art Center, Saidie spent considerable time assessing her collection of Modern art. She identified the collection's strong and weak areas, recording gaps in the chronology of the works. Resolving to look for pieces to tighten up the collection, she took Al to New York. The two stayed at the Park Sheraton Hotel.[1] All of the excitement in Baltimore had raised her blood pressure twenty points. Since she had not done any creative work in a while, the temptation to collect was even stronger.

Cataracts are Confirmed

The day after arriving in New York, Saidie wrote to Belle Boas admitting to having gone on a "buying spree," since she had just been diagnosed with cataracts forming in both eyes. For years, Saidie had seen her ophthalmologist for annual checkups, unaware of any problem. This doctor had known since 1948 that Saidie had cataracts forming, but he didn't inform her until now. Instead he had prescribed the use of distance glasses, improving her sight by 20%. Now that the glasses were no longer effective, he told her about the cataracts. She became so distressed by this news that he had to reassure her that she would not experience any additional problems for at least another year.[2]

By 1950, New York City's 57th Street was the nerve center of the art scene. Contemporary American art, especially the avant-garde, would not command impressive prices. Because collectors of American art were scarce, they were able to bargain with the gallery owners, forcing their artists to struggle financially, living a hand-to-mouth existence.[3] While the mainstream press favored these works and artists, American museums remained indifferent to them.[4] It was commented that one could acquire a better understanding of what was going on in American art by attending gallery

Opposite: Francis Picabia, French, 1879–1953, *Reverence*, 1915, oil on cardboard, 39 x 39 in. (99.1 x 99.1 cm), The Baltimore Museum of Art: Bequest of Saidie A. May, BMA 1951.347. ©2011 Artists Rights Society (ARS), New York/ADAGP, Paris.

exhibitions than by going to museums. Clement Greenberg described Betty Parson's Gallery as more like a seminar in contemporary aesthetics than a commercial establishment. Openings at the 57th Street galleries were held on Tuesday nights, and one was likely to see the same twenty-five people there, mostly the artists and their friends, week after week.

Betty Parsons' Gallery

Artist and gallery owner Betty Parsons represented many first-generation Abstract Expressionist painters, including Jackson Pollock, Richard Pousette-Dart, Mark Rothko and Barnett Newman. Gallery owner Sam Kootz showed Robert Motherwell, Adolph Gottlieb and Hans Hofmann. It was commonly known that the allegedly "smart" money in the New York art world was buying mostly European art (and not always the best the Europeans were doing at the time). This preference for European art, and especially Parisian art, had more to do with cultural snobbery and financial investment than with any lack of galleries dealing in contemporary American art.[5]

Rose Fried's Gallery

Rose Fried's gallery had been open since the late 1930s. Previously known as the Pinacotheca Gallery, she changed the name to Rose Fried Gallery in the early 1940s. Fried introduced many important European abstract painters to the American market, and specialized in constructivism and geometrical abstraction. But she always represented a few American painters in her gallery as well.[6]

On this trip, Saidie stopped into Rose Fried's 5th Street gallery and bought three paintings to send to the BMA. One of the first paintings of the Dada period was from Francis Picabia's series, "Urachue Ironique," *Dedee d'Ameriqne*, 1915, oil painted on cardboard from the private collection of one of his wives, Madame Buffet-Picabia. (Later the name of this painting was changed to *Reverence*.) Saidie was happy to pay $1,500 for this work that would make an important addition to her collection. Both she and Al felt it was "spiritual as well as constructive."

Saidie's next purchase was a Sophie Täuber-Arp gouache, *Cercles et Demi-Cercles sur Fond Noir* for $150. Rose Fried, valuing Saidie's patronage, donated another Tauber-Arp gouache of the same value to Saidie's BMA collection. Additionally, Saidie purchased *Tonde #15*, a twenty-five inch round oil, recently painted by Swiss-born American, Fritz Glarner, for $350. Enamored of the work, Saidie likened it to "a personal something evolving out of Mondrian, and the best of his school of painting."[7]

Sidney Janis Gallery

At the Sidney Janis gallery, Saidie found a large painting by Robert Delaunay, painted in Portugal around 1915–1916. She found this work to be a powerful bridge between the Cone collection and her own. It filled in the gap from French impressionism to Delaunay's non-objective art to French surrealism. She knew it would be an invaluable tool in educating young artists about the origins of

Robert Delaunay, French, 1885–1941, *Portuguese Still Life*, 1915–1916, oil on muslin, 44-1/4 x 55-1/4 in. The Baltimore Museum of Art: Bequest of Saidie A. May, BMA 1951.286. ©L&M Services B.V., The Hague 20110310.

the Modern art movement.[8] Delaunay's wife was selling it out of her private collection, instructing Janis that it was to remain with a matte finish, never varnished. Saidie paid $2,500 in installments over seven months.[9]

Sidney Janis had been a financial success in the clothing business and, in 1948, opened a gallery with his wife, Harriet.[10] Knowledgeable about Modern art, he was invited to join the advisory board of the Museum of Modern Art. His gallery gained prominence in New York quickly; the exhibitions were scholarly and well curated, exhibiting well-known masters next to emerging artists.[11] Saidie was delighted to find a new gallery to work with.

The Janises invited Saidie and Al to see their art collection in their apartment, with their huge, impressive paintings by Henri Rousseau. Saidie was so impressed with their collection that she included a description of it in a letter to Adelyn Breeskin, along with her other experiences in New York. Adelyn replied that the museum staff was delighted with the new acquisitions, especially the Delaunay, which hung in a prominent place in the Members' Room along with the other new paintings.[12]

Saidie revisited Rose Fried's Gallery where she admired a construction by Antoine Pevsner which she had previously seen in a catalogue of his work. She knew Pevsner because he was Naum Gabo's brother. The work she was interested in, *Projection pour dans L'Espace*, 1927, had some damage, so Fried made arrangements for it to be repaired before sending it to the BMA.[13] While there, Saidie ordered a copy of Masson's *Mythologies*, with the drawing for the painting *There is No Completed World*.

Willard Gallery

Before she left New York, Saidie had time to visit the Willard Gallery, located on the East River. There she heard the latest gossip: Pierre Matisse had divorced his wife and in the winter of 1949 married one of Matta's ex-wives (the one with some money). Also Henri Matisse wanted to marry his nurse, but his family wouldn't let him.[14]

The new name in town was Midwestern sculptor Richard Lippold. Mrs. Willard had just signed a contract to represent him. Born in Milwaukee in 1915, he attended graduate school at the Art Institute of Chicago, where he started making precisely engineered and intricately arranged wire sculptures.[15] People were speaking highly of his work, and MOMA purchased one of his pieces for their collection. Unfortunately, Saidie didn't get to see his work before she left New York.

As she made her rounds of the galleries and museums, people complimented Saidie about how much they admired her new wing at the BMA. She was always thinking about it and how it functioned. Ecstatic over all her purchases, she suggested to Adelyn Breeskin that the museum put together a show of "non-objective" works based on Saidie's latest purchases instead of buying a traveling show for the winter of 1950. They could also add related objects from Saidie's collection to round out this show.[16]

One month after the wing opened, the architects sent Saidie a fine leather portfolio containing photos of the wing and all of the articles written about it. On the inside cover was their company label, and above it they had typed, "To the Most Perfect Client." Saidie reported that this gave her "No end of pleasure."[17]

Late in April, Saidie and Al attended a lecture given by Naum Gabo in New York. On May 1st, Saidie phoned Gabo to see how he was progressing with the construction piece for the May wing.[18] He asked that she and Al come up to his home in Connecticut later in the week to visit and see his work.[19]

That afternoon Saidie re-connected with the former wife of Julian Levy. She told Saidie that Levy and Joan Miró, along with Jean Arp were commissioned to do a mural for Harvard University in Pittsfield, Massachusetts, near where Saidie and Al were going to be summering.[20] They should go and visit.

Later in the week, Saidie and Al drove up to the Gabo's home. The four spent the day together and, according to Saidie, Gabo and Al had "some talkfest!"[21] Gabo showed them a painting he had been working on for three years, in which he sought to "unite the arts—to depart from specialization." Al found his painting to be a "sculptor's art" approach. He then showed them his stunning models for the Esso building (which were interesting but would prove to be too expensive to build).[22]

Saidie and Al left New York for the Sheraton Hotel in Pittsfield, Massachusetts on May 9 for the summer and, as Saidie described it, "to be out of mischief in New York."[23] Once settled in, they resumed their painting, with Al doing some color constructed painting. Saidie was approaching her painting as a sculptor, through the use of light.[24] During that summer, Pittsfield had a lot of rain. Saidie and Al worked in their large, airy rooms in the hotel, with a large window facing the square outside with big, old and impressive elm trees, a "mass of waving green."[25]

The two read voraciously, becoming interested in new scientific writings. They read *Einstein and the Universe* by John D. Barrow and Michael Barnett. Back in Baltimore, Gertrude Rosenthal was reading *Out of my Later Years* by Albert Einstein, and she corresponded with Saidie, comparing notes on their readings.[26] Saidie wrote that she found Einstein's credo in a 1932 issue of *The Forum* magazine continually inspirational. Saidie also read Siegfried Gideon's *Space, Time and Architecture,* 1949 edition, and told Gertrude that she was interested in getting her hands on Gideon's *Mechanization takes Command*, 1948.[27]

Saidie Hears from Murray's Nurse

Throughout May and June of 1950, Murray's private nurse, Mrs. King, was sending letters to Saidie, complaining about Murray and the challenges of caring for him. Mrs. King wanted to change the arrangement and return Murray to his former apartment at the Bancroft School, so that the staff could assist her in his care.

Alfred Barr Visits the BMA

On June 1, Alfred Barr came to Baltimore to pay a special visit to the Young People's Wing. He had a private tour with Adelyn Breeskin (mistaking her for Belle Boas). Afterwards he cabled Saidie in Boston about what a wonderful project she had created, and how it was an example for other museums to follow.[28]

At the end of July, Saidie wrote to Gabo, to see how the sculpture project was progressing. Writing back, he described certain problems he was encountering related to the suspension of the construction over the stairwell. He wanted the public to experience the work as "hovering" over them in the three-story space, as opposed to having it appear to be suspended. He continued to work on solving that problem.[29]

Saidie's financial advisor from New York, Mr. Turnbull, passed away in the beginning of June. He had been a close and trusted friend over the years, investing her money and helping her to finance the new museum wing. When she learned of his death, she took it very hard.[30]

Michael Loew and Henry Miller

Saidie had now become famous. She had reached the stature of nationally recognized Modern art collector and advocate for education in the arts, and was continually contacted by artists and advocates for the arts. One of many letters was from Michael Lowe, who had received a scholarship from Saidie in 1930. Saidie's sponsorship of the young man, then aged 17, permitted him to study painting in Paris. Afterwards, he had pursued his art career in New York, and later spent more time in Paris after marrying. Lowe had a one-man show in November, 1949, in New York, and the Whitney Museum took one of his paintings for their 1949 Annual.[31] Saidie was gratified to hear of his good fortune.

Another letter contained a solicitation from the author and artist, Henry Miller, from Big Sur, California. He had collaborated on a book *Into the Night Life*, 1947, with silkscreen artist Bezalel Schatz. His illustrations were abstract, and the text, in Miller's hand script, was also silkscreened. Miller was interested in having Saidie purchase a limited edition copy for the BMA.[32] She never did. It was time-consuming for her to keep up with all of the mail she was receiving.

An Update from Gabo

During the month of August, Saidie fell ill, and did not paint much. She had stomach problems and complications from diabetes. She received another letter from Naum Gabo about how much he enjoyed conversing with Al on the critical state of painting. He had a few friends visit from New York, among them a couple of art critics. Their conversations closely resembled those which he had with Al, and he wanted to update Saidie on the latest thinking on that subject.[33] The new emphasis was on artists' attempts to free themselves by breaking out of the two-dimensionality of the painted surface. Gabo had spent the entire summer working out the problems of the model for the BMA's construction. He was preparing to start building the actual piece by the fall.

Charles Green Shaw

In September, Saidie and Al headed south to New York. To lift her spirits they stopped in at Wittenborn & Co. and purchased art books for themselves and the BMA. On the recommendation of Naum Gabo, Saidie purchased a portfolio of ten El Lissitzky regional lithographs for the BMA's collection. According to Gabo, Lissitzky's contribution to typography and his influence on other artists in that field was immense.[34]

Afterwards, they stopped in to the Georgette Passedoit Gallery, where they picked up two paintings. The first, historically important and well-rendered, *Sur un Theme de Cirque,* 1917, by Albert Gleizes and *Figure in Space,* 1950, by Charles Green Shaw, a painting that Saidie wanted the BMA to add to their American Collection.[35] Shaw was multitalented; he had a successful career as a

freelance writer for *The New Yorker*, *Vanity Fair*, and *Smart Set*, chronicling the life of the affluent theater and café society of the 1920s. He was also a poet, novelist and journalist.

In 1927, Shaw became seriously interested in art, enrolling in Thomas Hart Benton's class in the Art Students' League in New York. He also studied privately and remained close friends with George Luks. Continuing his artistic education in Paris by visiting museums and galleries, his paintings evolved from a style imitative of Cubism to one inspired by it, though simplified and more purely geometric. Then in the 1940s, Shaw's work strayed from his strict geometrical format to one more whimsical, reminiscent of Paul Klee's work. He softened both his palette and edges in favor of lyrical balance and subtly modulated color.[36]

After a month in New York, Saidie came to Baltimore and donated two Modern sterling necklaces to the BMA, one made in Scandinavia and the other made by Betty Cooke, a young local jewelry designer.[37] While in town, she and Al stayed at the Sheraton-Belvedere Hotel. Cooke's tiny shop was a couple of blocks away on Tyson Street. Saidie found her work refreshing and she liked supporting a local female artist.

Slow Progress on the Construction

By November, Saidie and Al headed south to winter in Daytona Beach. Once there, Saidie followed her daily routine of painting, reading

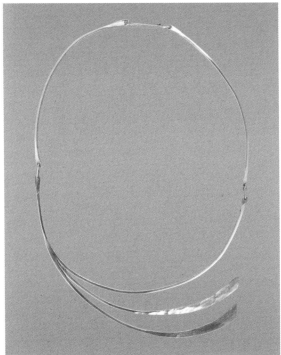

Top: Charles Green Shaw, American, 1892–1974, *Figure in Space*, 1950, oil on composition board, 35-7/8 x 24-7/8 in., The Baltimore Museum of Art: Bequest of Saidie A. May, BMA 1951.358. Lower: Betty Cooke, American, born Baltimore 1924, *Necklace*, c. 1948–1950, silver, 6-3/4 x 4-7/8 in., The Baltimore Museum of Art, Gift of Saidie A. May, BMA, 1950.91.

and walking on the beach.[38] Over the next two months, she regularly received letters from Miriam Gabo on Naum's progress with the construction. It was tedious! The piece required a particular thickness of bronze wire, and even though Connecticut and New York were the centers of the brass and bronze industry in the United States, it was nearly impossible for Gabo to acquire what he needed. Metals were scarce and sales were strictly controlled due to the military's need of those metals for the Korean War.[39] Gabo found this frustrating, aggravating a gastric illness from which he had suffered for years. Finally, he was able to acquire some of the materials from the metal factories in Connecticut and New York during December. Things were finally starting to progress on the project.

The artistic social circle around Saidie continued to grow. The English artist Claire Leighton had moved to Woodbury, Connecticut, in the fall, and when she met Miriam Gabo, they instantly struck up a friendship. Previous to that, Miriam had not met anyone in the area with whom she could relate.[40] During the unseasonably cold Florida winter, Saidie and Miriam kept up correspondence. Saidie had given Miriam a copy of Benjamin Franklin's autobiography to help her learn English. Miriam toiled over that during the cold, snowy days while her husband labored over the construction. Miriam also saw Claire Leighton whenever she could. She was her only female friend. The local paper, *Waterbury Republican,* interviewed Gabo about his work, and his current construction, and he gave them interesting information on the Children's Wing as well. Miriam included the newspaper clipping in one of her letters to Saidie.[41]

Notes

1   Saidie A. May to Gertrude Rosenthal, April 22, 1950, Saidie A. May Papers, BMA.

2   Saidie A. May to Belle Boas, April 23, 1950, Saidie A. May Papers, BMA.

3   Lee Hall, *Betty Parsons, Artist, Dealer, Collector*, (New York: Harry N. Abrams, 1991), 99.

4   Hilton Kramer, "The Borgenicht Legacy, The Glory of the 50s—Arts&Entertainment," *The New York Observer*, August 6, 2001.

5   *Ibid.*

6   Press Release for Rose Fried Gallery, May 1, 1964, Rose Fried Gallery records, Roll #N69-37 Archives of American Art, SI.

7   Saidie A. May to Gertrude Rosenthal, April 22, 1950, Saidie A. May Papers, BMA.

8   Saidie A. May to Adelyn Breeskin, May 1, 1950, Saidie A. May Papers, BMA.

9   *Ibid.*

10 http://en.wikipedia.org/wiki/Sidney_Janis.

11 *Ibid.*

12 Adelyn Breeskin to Saidie A. May, May 12, 1950, Saidie A. May Papers, BMA.

13 Saidie A. May to Adelyn Breeskin, May 1, 1950, Saidie A. May Papers, BMA.

14 Saidie A. May to Adelyn Breeskin, May 1, 1950, Saidie A. May Papers, BMA.

15 Obituary, "Richard Lippold, sculptor, dies at 87," *The Detroit News*, August 31, 2002.

16 Saidie A. May to Adelyn Breeskin, May 1, 1950, Saidie A. May Papers, BMA.

17 Saidie A. May to Gertrude Rosenthal, June 17, 1950, Saidie A. May Papers, BMA.

18 Saidie A. May to Belle Boas, April 23, 1950, Saidie A. May Papers, BMA.

19 Saidie A. May to Adelyn Breeskin, May 1, 1950, Saidie A. May Papers, BMA.

20 *Ibid.*

21 Saidie A. May to Gertrude Rosenthal, May 20, 1950, Saidie A. May Papers, BMA.

22 *Ibid.*

23 *Ibid.*

24 *Ibid.*

25 Saidie A. May to Gertrude Rosenthal, June 17, 1950, Saidie A. May Papers, BMA.

26 *Ibid.*

27 Saidie A. May to Gertrude Rosenthal, June 18, 1950, Saidie A. May Papers, BMA.

28 Alfred Barr to Saidie A. May, June 1, 1950, Saidie A. May Papers, BMA.

29 Saidie A. May to Adelyn Breeskin, August 17, 1950, Saidie A. May Papers, BMA.

30 *Ibid.*

31 Michael Loew to Saidie A. May, March 20, 1950, Saidie A. May Papers, BMA.

32 Henry Miller to Saidie A. May, June 28, 1950, Saidie A. May Papers, BMA.

33 Naum Gabo to Saidie A. May, August 20, 1950, Saidie A. May Papers, BMA.

34 Saidie A. May to Gertrude Rosenthal, September 20, 1950, Saidie A. May Papers, BMA.

35 Saidie A. May to Adelyn Breeskin, September 27, 1950, Saidie A. May Papers, BMA.

36 http://americanart.si.edu/collections/exhibits/abstraction/shaw.html.

37 The Baltimore Museum of Art to Saidie A. May, October 20, 1950, Saidie A. May Papers, BMA.

38 Saidie A. May to Adelyn Breeskin, November 15, 1950, Saidie A. May Papers, BMA.

39 Naum Gabo to Saidie A. May, November 21, 1950, Saidie A. May Papers, BMA.

40 Miriam Gabo to Saidie A. May, December 4, 1950, Saidie A. May Papers, BMA.

41 Miriam Gabo to Saidie A. May, January 14, 1951, Saidie A. May Papers, BMA.

262 Saidie May

Saidie's Swan Song

aidie and Al spent the entire winter of 1950 in Daytona Beach at the Sheraton Plaza Hotel, right on the beach. Their apartment had a studio where they could paint. They studied art of the Baroque period together, and walked the beach every day. Al seemed unhappy though; he did not like being in Daytona Beach and felt like a misfit. Struggling, he concentrated on his painting, which Saidie observed was taking on more depth and richness.[1]

In the evening, Al read works by Paul Valery and William Faulkner to Saidie. He especially loved Faulkner's work, and they were enjoying what was considered his best book, *Light in August*. Saidie felt, "He makes you feel the great forces that push and pull us this way and that, and makes us what we are." They also read the book by Max Burchartz, an interior designer and commercial graphic artist (and student of Theo van Doesburg), *Gleichnis der Harmonie* (Graphic Design in Germany).[2] According to Herbert Read, the British poet, literary critic and philosopher of Modern art, it was considered the most thorough treatment of the theoretical aspects of Modern art.[3]

Events at the BMA

Back at the BMA, Gertrude Rosenthal was taking notes on the "doings" at the Saidie May Wing, and sending her findings to Saidie, which Saidie really enjoyed. The museum had been sponsoring various public events: art-related games for children, printing, drawing and pottery classes for both children and adults. On Tuesday evenings, they had chess for older children and adults and "Magnet Master" constructions for children to build. They created a vital, living community out of Saidie's idea, "bringing all of this to a worried and often apathetic Baltimore," as Saidie saw it.[4] Encouraged by all the good news from Baltimore, Saidie and Al sent a package of their most recent paintings to the BMA, planning to show them to the staff when they arrived in Baltimore on April 3.[5]

Marianna Smith and Barbara Samson at exhibit of the Saidie A. May Collection of Surrealist and Abstract Art, Baltimore Museum of Art, April 3, 1950, photo by Frank A. Miller, *Baltimore Sun* Archives, Special Collections, UMBC Library. Reprinted with permission of the *Baltimore Sun* Media Group. All Rights Reserved.

A Visit with Murray

By March 13, 1951, they left Florida to go up to Philadelphia to see Murray, who was ill with complications from his diabetes. He had been taken to the hospital to have his blood sugar stabilized at 270. Mrs. Walker, of the Van Hook School, wrote to Saidie about Murray's condition, reassuring her that he was receiving the best of care. The school's nurse was staying with Murray round the clock while he was in the hospital. But Saidie was worried and wanted to see for herself what was being done for him.[6] They rode the train to Philadelphia, where they spent three weeks at the Penn Sheraton Hotel, near the hospital where Murray was recuperating. As a result of the change in the weather, Saidie caught a cold.

Gabo's Construction Progresses

Miriam Gabo continued writing to Saidie about Gabo's progress with the construction for the new wing. By the beginning of March, he had accumulated most of the materials he needed by traveling around New England to metal foundries and scrapyards. He collected what he could and ordered the rest, hoping that the factories would deliver the materials, even though there were stiff restrictions on metals consumption for non-government use. He had to order the specific "milled" materials from metal workshops in New York. Gabo was so precise about his work that on one trip to a machinist's shop in Brooklyn, he spent an hour trying to convince the iron-craftsman that he could really detect a flaw of one millimeter in a piece of metal three feet long. But he still had to wait for his materials until the foundries had fulfilled government orders.[7]

Gabo loved America, hoping to become an American citizen. He felt strongly about what America stood for, and, most importantly for him, one could hope for change without violence.[8] He had filed an application for citizenship. His brother, Antoine Pevsner, was ill and Gabo wanted to go back to France to visit him, but he couldn't without a U.S. visa.[9] The following year his dream was realized.

In April, 1951, the Whitney Museum opened a show of contemporary American sculpture, in which a work by Naum Gabo was included. Gabo wrote to Al and Saidie, inviting them to New York to see the show.[10] He then planned to go on to Baltimore on May 7 to test the structural strength of the ceiling in the wing's stairwell, from which his sculpture would be suspended.[11] Miriam Gabo wrote to Saidie on May 19 that "Gabo works furiously, and we plan to be in Baltimore in July so that he can supervise the installation of the finished piece."

Saidie continued to correspond with her old friend Elise Donaldson from San Diego.[12] Once Murray recovered from his illness, Saidie and Al made a brief visit to Baltimore and then planned to head to New York for her annual "gallery hopping." Saidie invited Elise to meet them there for another opportunity to introduce her to gallery owners to help her sell her artwork on the East Coast.

Top: Special children's class, Saidie A. May Young People's Art Center, The Baltimore Museum of Art, December 31, 1953. Belle Boas Records, Archives and Manuscripts Collections, The Baltimore Museum of Art. BB3.2.5. Lower: Summer creative art classes, The Baltimore Museum of Art, 1955. Belle Boas Records, Archives and Manuscripts Collections, The Baltimore Museum of Art. BB3.2.6. (Sculpture in the background made by Saidie A. May during the winter of 1949 in her studio near Pineneedles, South Carolina, p. 240).

Saidie's Illness Worsens

Saidie was almost seventy-three. She arrived in Baltimore fighting the cold she caught in Philadelphia and it became more serious. On April 13, she was admitted to the Union Memorial Hospital with what the doctor thought was pneumonia, complicated by her diabetes. Saidie remained hospitalized for five weeks. When she finally was discharged, Al felt that she wasn't ready to leave the hospital.[13]

They left Baltimore May 22, taking the train to New York. Sitting for a prolonged period of time on the train may have worsened her condition and caused a blood clot. When they arrived in the city, they met Elise. The next day, even in her weakened condition, Saidie insisted that the three visit a couple of galleries in the city.

Saidie's Decline

Saidie had a relapse May 24 and was admitted to the Stuyvesant Polyclinic Hospital in New York. Al and Elise stayed by Saidie's side as she struggled for five days. Early on the morning of May 29, 1951, Saidie passed away. Al and Elise were heartbroken. Al felt that the doctors in Baltimore had misdiagnosed the problem, and treated the wrong symptoms. He was very angry, and expressed this in a letter to Gertrude Rosenthal.[14]

Elise immediately returned to San Diego.[15] Al remained in New York for a short time and consulted his friends, Pierre Matisse and J. B. Neumann about how to deal with his grief through his painting. They discussed his work, colors to use, and how to express his loss and loneliness on the canvas. Soon after, he headed to San Diego, following Elise Donaldson, hoping that she could help him through his period of grief.[16]

A Tense Period of Mourning

Elise had studied with Al for a time when he and Saidie had lived in La Jolla. They had all painted together one day a week, but now there was tension between Al and Elise. The animosity between the two had grown to a point where she no longer felt comfortable working with him. He had alienated other artists and art-related people who perceived his knowledge of painting as arrogance. Elise's interest in the couple had been confined to Saidie and she did not provide any hope for consolation to Al.

Al Finds a New Relationship

Al rented a studio apartment in La Jolla on the fringe of Balboa Park, where he continued to work and lament Saidie's death. As he wrote to Adelyn Breeskin in June, "I am getting to work and hope to pour forth a melody of love and suffering in memory of Mrs. May. After a year I might go east or go back to France—who knows."[17] Eventually he met another much younger female painter and fell in love with her. They moved east and married. He was able to concentrate his efforts on

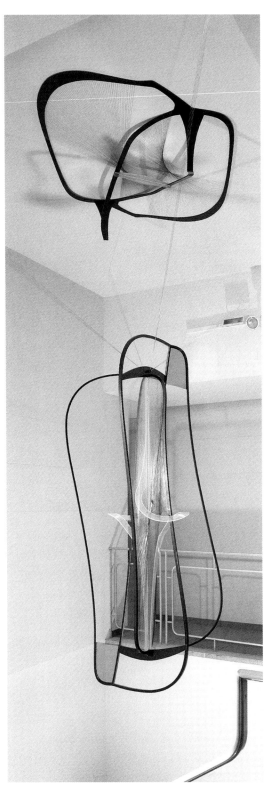

a more modern form of painting, dealing with the science of numbers, and his work was finally appreciated and shown.

Aftermath

The bulk of Saidie's estate and personal effects went to the Baltimore Museum of Art.[18] Nothing was formally left in her will to Al Jensen other than jointly owned personal property and their paintings in the bank's vault which the BMA did not want.[19] The remainder of her personal property went to her niece.

In June of 1951, the Young People's Art Center at the BMA celebrated its first birthday. Many activities were offered, including painting and sculpture classes, as well as lectures and demonstrations of weaving by Pauline Dutterer, oil painting by Edward Rosenfeld, sculptural modeling by Reuben Kramer and jewelry-making by Betty Cooke. The Baltimore Museum of Art had grown in popularity. Visitor attendance by April 30 of that year had increased by 10,000 compared to the preceding year.

Naum Gabo continued working on the construction for the Young People's Art Center. By the end of October, it was finally installed in the stairwell. Its formal presentation came in a ceremony dedicated to Saidie on November 4, 1951. During the installation, Gabo recognized the museum as a "pioneer," presenting his first major work completed in full scale for an architectural setting. The construction made of aluminum, plastic, gold and steel wires and bronze mesh was suspended from the ceiling, fifteen feet into the stairwell of the Art Center.

Naum Gabo, American, born Russia, 1890–1977, *Construction*, 1951, aluminum, plexiglass, gold wire, bronze mesh, steel wire, approx. 180 in. H, The Baltimore Museum of Art: Bequest of Saidie A. May, BMA, 1951.148.1.

"Take it all in," Bobby McDowell, age 7 in the Saidie A. May Young People's Art Center Children's Art Library, March 1, 1955, photo by Wm. Klender, *Baltimore Sun* Archives, Special Collections, UMBC Library. Reprinted with permission of the *Baltimore Sun* Media Group. All Rights Reserved.

In his moving address, Gabo talked about the vitality which he felt while completing the piece, and the camaraderie he felt with the many people involved in the completion and installation of it. He dedicated his work to the memory of Saidie A. May, to the impression she left on the people she knew and on the city of her birth, where she gave so much for the citizens to learn from and enjoy.

Belle Boas and Adelyn Breeskin continued offering classes and activities in the Young People's Art Center. There were art classes for children and adults. In the summer of 1954, there were outdoor sketching classes in the gardens for children ages six to fifteen. In the spring and fall of 1958 to 1961, painting, pottery, sculpture, graphics and an art survey course were offered.

The Legacy of Saidie A. May

With extraordinary foresight, Saidie had bequeathed an endowment fund for the maintenance of her collection and the wing, as well as a purchase fund to acquire new works for the collection.

Over the years, objects in Saidie's collection have been singled out for their rarity or timeliness in relation to other collections all over the world. In the late 1960s, the Saidie A. May collection of over three hundred items was inventoried and catalogued by then BMA Curator Jane Harrison Cone. Highlights from the collection were published by the museum in an illustrated catalogue in 1972.

In 1982, the Baltimore Museum of Art formally rededicated the Saidie A. May Wing in her memory. The many activities she envisioned and supported financially had expanded well beyond the scope of her early conception. The museum gradually developed a formal Education Department and an active docent program. The art-related programs for children and adults were eventually absorbed into the museum's overall programming.

Throughout the museum's renovated permanent collection galleries, her progressive and tireless vision is evident. Visitors are reminded of Saidie's vital contributions as they encounter works bearing her name, whether in the Old Masters' Gallery, the European Decorative Arts galleries, Modern and Print galleries or the wing Saidie created for the public use.

Notes

1 Saidie A. May to Gertrude Rosenthal, February 9, 1951, Saidie A. May Papers, BMA.

2 *Ibid.*

3 Saidie A. May to Gertrude Rosenthal, February 24, 1951, Saidie A. May Papers, BMA.

4 *Ibid.*

5 Saidie A. May to Gertrude Rosenthal, March 6, 1951, Saidie A. May Papers, BMA.

6 *Ibid.*

7 Miriam Gabo to Saidie A. May, March 8, 1951, Saidie A. May Papers, BMA.

8 *Ibid.*

9 *Ibid.*

10 Naum Gabo to Francis H. Jencks, March 21, 1951, Saidie A. May Papers, BMA.

11 Naum Gabo to Alfred Jensen, April 16, 1951, Saidie A. May Papers, BMA.

12 Freda Klapp to Saidie A. May, 1951, Saidie A. May Papers, BMA.

13 Alfred Jensen to Gertrude Rosenthal, June 1, 1951, Saidie A. May Papers, BMA.

14 *Ibid.*

15 *Ibid.*

16 *Ibid.*

17 Alfred Jensen to Gertrude Rosenthal, June 10, 1951, Saidie A. May Archives, BMA.

18 The Baltimore Museum of Art to the Executors of the Estate of the late Mrs. Saidie A. May, June 13, 1951, Saidie A. May Papers, BMA.

19 Safe Deposit and Trust Company to The Baltimore Museum of Art, October 2, 1951, Saidie A. May Papers, BMA.

The Baltimore Museum of Art—
Works Collected by Saidie A. May

AFRO (BASALDELLA) (ITALIAN, 1912–1976)
Abstract Composition, Blue, Black and Orange
1949, Color lithograph, 320.68 x 107.95 mm.
(12-5/8 x 4-1/4 in.)
The Baltimore Museum of Art: The Baltimore
Museum of Art: Gift of Saidie A. May
BMA 1951.222.1

AFRO (BASALDELLA) (ITALIAN, 1912–1976)
Abstract Composition, Blue, Brown and Green
1949, Color lithograph, 321 x 206 mm.
(12-5/8 x 8-1/8 in.)
The Baltimore Museum of Art:
Gift of Saidie A. May
BMA 1951.222.2

PROBABLY MICHEL ANGIER
(FRENCH, 1612–1686)
Neptune
n.d., Bronze, 9-1/2 in. H
The Baltimore Museum of Art: The Baltimore
Museum of Art: Bequest of Saidie A. May
BMA 1951.443

ATTRIBUTED TO SPINELLO ARETINO
(ITALIAN, ACTIVE 1346–1411)
Head of a Saint
c. 1390, Fresco fragment, 235 x 162 mm.
(9-1/4 x 6-3/8 in.)
The Baltimore Museum of Art:
Bequest of Saidie A. May
BMA 1951.395

HANS BALDUNG GRIEN
(GERMAN, 1484/85–1545)
St. Martin Dividing his Cloak with the Beggar
c. 1505-1507, Woodcut, 235 x 162 mm.
(9-1/4 x 6-3/8 in.)
The Baltimore Museum of Art:
Gift of Saidie A. May
BMA 1931.43.3

CULTURE: BAULE PEOPLES
Pendant Head
19th century, Gold, possibly alloyed,
1-15/16 x 1-1/2 x 11/16 in. (4.9 x 3.8 x 1.7 cm.)
The Baltimore Museum of Art:
Bequest of Saidie A. May
BMA 1951.168

WILLIAM BAZIOTES (AMERICAN, 1912–1963)
The Drugged Balloonist
1943, Collage of printed paper, ink, and graphite,
Sheet: 464 x 609 mm. (18-1/4 x 24 in.)
The Baltimore Museum of Art:
Bequest of Saidie A. May
BMA 1951.266

ANDRÉ GUSTAVE BEAUDIN
(FRENCH, 1895–1979)
Le Troupeau
1939, Oil on canvas, 51 x 63-5/8 in.
(129.6 x 161.7 cm.)
The Baltimore Museum of Art:
Bequest of Saidie A. May
BMA 1951.267

Baule peoples, Côte d'Ivoire, Pendant Head, 19th century, gold, possibly alloyed, 2 x 1.5 in. (5.1 x 3.8 cm),
The Baltimore Museum of Art: Bequest of Saidie A. May, BMA 1951.168.

ANDRÉ GUSTAVE BEAUDIN (FRENCH, 1895–1979)
Ermenonville
1940, Watercolor and pen and black ink over graphite,
Sheet: 371 x 265 mm. (14-5/8 x 10-7/16 in.)
The Baltimore Museum of Art:
Bequest of Saidie A. May
BMA 1951.268

HARRISON BEGAY (AMERICAN NAVAJO, BORN 1917)
Antelope Hunt
n.d., Opaque watercolor, Sheet: 191 x 292 mm.
(7-1/2 x 11-1/2 in.)
The Baltimore Museum of Art: Gift of Saidie A. May
BMA 1941.373

SEBALD BEHAM (GERMAN, 1500–1550)
Infortitude
n.d., Engraving, 81 x 52 mm. (3-3/16 x 2-1/16 in.)
The Baltimore Museum of Art: Gift of Saidie A. May
BMA 1931.43.4

WORKSHOP: AFTER BENNEDETTO DA MAIANO
(MODERN COPY) (ITALIAN, 1442–1497)
St. John the Baptist
1856 or later, Terracotta with traces of gilt, 12 in.
(30.5 cm.)
The Baltimore Museum of Art: Gift of Saidie A. May
BMA 1948.125

PIERRE BONNARD (FRENCH, 1867–1947)
Breakfast in the Garden
1916, Oil on canvas, 19-1/4 x 16-1/4 in.
(48.9 x 41.3 cm.)
The Baltimore Museum of Art:
Bequest of Saidie A. May
BMA 1951.269

PIERRE BONNARD (FRENCH, 1867–1947)
The Bath (Le Bain)
c. 1925, Crayon lithograph with scraping,
Sheet: 367 x 276 mm. (14-7/16 x 10-7/8 in.)
Image: 311 x 216 mm. (12-1/4 x 8-1/2 in.)
The Baltimore Museum of Art: Gift of Saidie A. May
BMA 1934.38.1

Woman Dressing, Seated
1925, Lithograph, Sheet: 494 x 322 mm.
(19-7/16 x 12-11/16 in.), Image: 333 x 220 mm.
(13-1/8 x 8-11/16 in.)
The Baltimore Museum of Art: Gift of Saidie A. May
BMA 1934.38.2

E. BORDONI (ITALIAN, DATES UNKNOWN)
Black and White Composition
1949, Lithograph, 321 x 216 mm. (12-5/8 x 8-1/2 in.)
The Baltimore Museum of Art: Gift of Saidie A. May
BMA 1951.222.5

Abstract Composition, Blue, Black and White
1949, Color lithograph, 235 x 152 mm. (9-1/4 x 6 in.)
The Baltimore Museum of Art: Gift of Saidie A. May
BMA 1951.222.6

FRANCISCO BORES (SPANISH, 1898–1972)
Painter's Table
1939, Watercolor and graphite on wove paper,
Sheet: 279 x 349 mm. (27.9 x 34.9 cm.)
The Baltimore Museum of Art:
Bequest of Saidie A. May, 1951
BMA 1997.35

House in the Country
1939, Watercolor, 273 x 349 mm. (10-3/4 x 13-3/4 in.)
The Baltimore Museum of Art:
Bequest of Saidie A. May, 1951
BMA 1997.36

GEORGES BRAQUE (FRENCH, 1882–1963)
PUBLISHER: FERNAND MOURLOT
(FRENCH, 1895–1988)
La Madoline
n.d., Color lithograph, 241 x 171 mm.
(9-1/2 x 6-3/4 in.)
The Baltimore Museum of Art: Gift of Saidie A. May
BMA 1949.33

GEORGES BRAQUE (FRENCH, 1882–1963)
Abstraction, Fruit and Pipe
c. 1928, Sanquine crayon, 203.2 x 441.33 mm.
(8 x 17-3/8 in.)
The Baltimore Museum of Art: Gift of Saidie A. May
1937.24

Still Life: Le Journal
1929, Oil on canvas, 10 x 16 in. (25.4 x 40.6 cm.)
The Baltimore Museum of Art: Gift of Saidie A. May
BMA 1942.64

ANDRÉ BRETON (FRENCH, 1896–1966)
PUBLISHER: *VVV*
 I Saluted at Six Paces Commander Lefebvre des Noettes
 1942, published 1943, Collage of color lithograph
 postcard, colored thread, sequins, brush and silver ink,
 pen and black ink, Sheet: 458 x 356 mm.
 (18-1/16 x 14 in.)
 The Baltimore Museum of Art: Gift of Saidie A. May
 BMA 1948.54.1

ALEXANDER CALDER (AMERICAN, 1898–1976)
PRINTER: KURT SELIGMANN (AMERICAN, BORN
 SWITZERLAND, 1900–1962)
PUBLISHER: *VVV*
 Score for Ballet 0-100
 1942, published 1943, Engraving and drypoint,
 Sheet: 354 x 456 mm. (13-15/16 x 17-15/16 in.)
 Plate: 290 x 378 mm. (11-7/16 x 14-7/8 in.)
 The Baltimore Museum of Art: Gift of Saidie A. May
 BMA 1948.54.2

LEONORA CARRINGTON (BRITISH, BORN 1917)
PRINTER: KURT SELIGMANN (AMERICAN, BORN
 SWITZERLAND, 1900–1962)
PUBLISHER: *VVV*
 Untitled
 1942, published 1943, Etching, Mount: 352 x 455 mm.
 (13-7/8 x 17-15/16 in.)
 Sheet: 302 x 352 mm. (30.2 x 35.2 cm.),
 Plate: 203 x 251 mm. (20.3 x 25.1 cm.)
 The Baltimore Museum of Art: Gift of Saidie A. May
 BMA 1948.54.3

MARC CHAGALL
 (FRENCH, BORN RUSSIA, 1887–1985)
 Reclining Nude with Fan
 1925, Etching and drypoint, 215 x 278 mm.
 (8-7/16 x 10-15/16 in.)
 The Baltimore Museum of Art: Gift of Saidie A. May
 BMA 1941.370

 Flowers in a Dream
 c. 1930, Oil, opaque watercolor, crayon, and pastel,
 Sheet: 686 x 528 mm. (27 x 20-13/16 in.)
 The Baltimore Museum of Art:
 Bequest of Saidie A. May
 BMA 1951.281

MARC CHAGALL
 (FRENCH, BORN RUSSIA, 1887–1985)
PRINTER: KURT SELIGMANN (AMERICAN, BORN
 SWITZERLAND, 1900–1962)
PUBLISHER: *VVV*
 Eiffel Tower
 1942, published 1943, Etching with bitten tone,
 Sheet: 457 x 351 mm. (18 x 13-13/16 in.)
 Plate: 276 x 202 mm. (10-7/8 x 7-15/16 in.)
 The Baltimore Museum of Art: Gift of Saidie A. May
 BMA 1948.54.4

GIORGIO DE CHIRICO (ITALIAN, 1888–1978)
 Reclining Abstract Figure
 1926–1927, Conté crayon, Sheet: 281 x 457 mm.
 (11-1/16 x 18 in.)
 The Baltimore Museum of Art: Gift of Saidie A. May
 BMA 1935.13.1

MAKER: CHRISTIE PAINTER
 (GREEK, ACTIVE C. 450–420 B.C.)
 Bell Krater with Eos and Kephalos
 5th century B.C., Clay, 14-9/16 x 12-13/16 in.
 (37 x 32.5 cm.)
 The Baltimore Museum of Art:
 Bequest of Saidie A. May
 BMA 1951.486

PAUL CORNET (FRENCH, 1892–1977)
 Seated Nude
 n.d., Graphite, Mat Opening: 521 x 356 mm.
 (20-1/2 x 14 in.)
 The Baltimore Museum of Art: Gift of Saidie A. May
 BMA 1934.44.1

 Standing Nude
 n.d., Graphite, Mat opening: 524 x 387 mm.
 (20-5/8 x 15-1/4 in.)
 The Baltimore Museum of Art: Gift of Saidie A. May
 BMA 1934.44.2

 Saidie A. May
 n.d., Bronze, 16 in. (40.6 cm.)
 The Baltimore Museum of Art:
 Bequest of Saidie A. May
 BMA 1951.149

 Algerian Dancer
 n.d., Bronze, 19 in. (48.3 cm.)
 The Baltimore Museum of Art:
 Bequest of Saidie A. May
 BMA 1951.369

Portrait of My Mother
n.d., Bronze, 18-1/2 in. (47 cm.)
The Baltimore Museum of Art:
Bequest of Saidie A. May
BMA 1951.370

Seated Nude
n.d., Bronze, 15-1/4 in. (38.7 cm.)
The Baltimore Museum of Art:
Bequest of Saidie A. May
BMA 1951.371

Standing Figure
n.d., Terracotta, 17-1/4 in. (43.8 cm.)
The Baltimore Museum of Art:
Bequest of Saidie A. May
BMA 1951.373

BELA ADALBERT CZOBEL (HUNGARIAN, 1883–1976)
Nude
n.d., Watercolor, 622 x 470 mm. (24-1/2 x 18-1/2 in.)
The Baltimore Museum of Art:
Bequest of Saidie A. May
BMA 1951.282

CULTURE: DAN PEOPLES
Mask (Tankë Ge/Tanka Gle)
early 20th century, Wood, 9-7/16 x 7-1/16 x 5-1/8 in.
(24 x 18 x 13 cm.)
The Baltimore Museum of Art:
Bequest of Saidie A. May
BMA 1951.388

JEANNE DAOUR (FRENCH, BORN ROMANIA 1914)
Nude
20th Century, Graphite, NO DIMENSION
The Baltimore Museum of Art: Gift of Saidie A. May
BMA 1932.48.3

Akt
1931, Graphite on waxed tracing paper, 260 x 171 mm.
(10-1/4 x 6-3/4 in.)
The Baltimore Museum of Art: Gift of Saidie A. May
BMA 1934.45.1

Nude Leaning Forward
1931, Graphite, 318 x 237 mm. (12-1/2 x 9-5/16 in.)
The Baltimore Museum of Art: Gift of Saidie A. May
BMA 1933.43.1

Standing Nude
1932, Graphite, 318 x 238 mm. (12-1/2 x 9-3/8 in.)
The Baltimore Museum of Art: Gift of Saidie A. May
BMA 1933.43.2

HONORÉ DAUMIER (FRENCH, 1808–1879)
Three Men Laughing
c. 1865–1870, Pen and black ink and brush and wash,
Sheet: 70 x 85 mm. (7 x 8.5 cm.)
The Baltimore Museum of Art: Gift of Saidie A. May in
Honor of Blanche Adler
BMA 1933.59.1

Five Heads
c. 1865–1870, Pen and black ink, brush and wash, and
watercolor, Sheet: 52 x 84 mm. (5.2 x 8.4 cm.)
The Baltimore Museum of Art: Gift of Saidie A. May in
Honor of Blanche Adler
BMA 1933.59.2

EUGÈNE DELACROIX (FRENCH, 1798–1863)
The Source
n.d., Oil on wood panel, 9-7/8 x 6-1/2 in.
(25.1 x 16.5 cm.)
The Baltimore Museum of Art:
Bequest of Saidie A. May
BMA 1951.285

ROBERT DELAUNAY (FRENCH, 1885–1941)
Portuguese Still Life
1915–1916, Oil on muslin, 44-1/4 x 55-1/4 in.
(112.4 x 140.3 cm.)
The Baltimore Museum of Art:
Bequest of Saidie A. May
BMA 1951.286

ANDRÉ DERAIN (FRENCH, 1880–1954)
Landscape with Two Nudes
1909, Oil on composition board, 11-11/16 x 10-5/8 in.
(29.7 x 27 cm.)
The Baltimore Museum of Art:
Bequest of Saidie A. May
BMA 1951.288

Wooded Landscape
1926, Oil on canvas, 21-5/16 x 25-5/8 in.
(54.1 x 65.1 cm.)
The Baltimore Museum of Art:
Bequest of Saidie A. May
BMA 1951.289

CHARLES DESPIAU (FRENCH, 1874–1946)
PUBLISHER: PHILIPPE GONIN

Untitled (standing nude in profile)
n.d., Wood engraving, 56 x 30 mm.
(2-3/16 x 1-3/16 in.)
The Baltimore Museum of Art: Gift of Saidie A. May
BMA 1937.23.1

Baudelaire/Poemes
n.d., Wood engraving, 56 x 30 mm.
(2-3/16 x 1-3/16 in.)
The Baltimore Museum of Art: Gift of Saidie A. May
BMA 1937.23.2

Untitled
n.d., Lithograph, 230 x 167 mm. (9-1/16 x 6-9/16 in.)
The Baltimore Museum of Art: Gift of Saidie A. May
BMA 1937.23.3

J'AIME le souvenie de ces épouques nues,…
n.d., Lithograph, 140 x 193 mm. (5-1/2 x 7-5/8 in.)
The Baltimore Museum of Art: Gift of Saidie A. May
BMA 1937.23.4

Nous avons, il est vrai, nations corrompues,…
n.d., Lithograph, 118 x 118 mm. (4-5/8 x 4-5/8 in.)
The Baltimore Museum of Art: Gift of Saidie A. May
BMA 1937.23.5

Ma pauvre Muse, helás!…
n.d., Lithograph, 201 x 140 mm.
The Baltimore Museum of Art: Gift of Saidie A. May
BMA 1937.23.6

Le succube verdâtre et le rose lutin…
n.d., Lithograph, 90 x 205 mm.
The Baltimore Museum of Art: Gift of Saidie A. May
BMA 1937.23.7

O Muse de mon coeur, amante des palais,…
n.d., Lithograph, 110 x 230 mm.
The Baltimore Museum of Art: Gift of Saidie A. May
BMA 1937.23.8

Il te faut, pour gagner ton pain de chacque soir,…
n.d., Lithograph, 103 x 107 mm.
The Baltimore Museum of Art: Gift of Saidie A. May
BMA 1937.23.9

Je suis belle, o mortels,…
n.d., Lithograph, 160 x 175 mm.
The Baltimore Museum of Art: Gift of Saidie A. May
BMA 1937.23.10

Je trone dans l'azur comme un sphinx incompris,…
n.d., Lithograph, 80 x 55 mm.
The Baltimore Museum of Art: Gift of Saidie A. May
BMA 1937.23.11

Tu mettrais l'univers entier dans ta ruelle,…
n.d., Lithograph, 132 x 230 mm.
The Baltimore Museum of Art: Gift of Saidie A. May
BMA 1937.23.12

Machine aveugle et sourde…
n.d., Lithograph, 122 x 73 mm.
The Baltimore Museum of Art: Gift of Saidie A. May
BMA 1937.23.13

Que l'aime voir, chère indolente,…
n.d., Lithograph, 110 x 225 mm.
The Baltimore Museum of Art: Gift of Saidie A. May
BMA 1937.23.14

Et ton corps se penche et s'allonge…
n.d., Wood engraving, 60 x 62 mm.
The Baltimore Museum of Art: Gift of Saidie A. May
BMA 1937.23.15

Une nuit qui j'etais près d'une affreuse Juive…
n.d., Lithograph, 124 x 220 mm.
The Baltimore Museum of Art: Gift of Saidie A. May
BMA 1937.23.16

Je me représentai se majesté native…
n.d., Wood engraving, 93 x 170 cm.
The Baltimore Museum of Art: Gift of Saidie A. May
BMA 1937.23.17

Le Démon, dans ma chambre haute,…
n.d., Lithograph, 160 x 103 mm.
The Baltimore Museum of Art: Gift of Saidie A. May
BMA 1937.23.18

Parmi toutes les belles choses…
n.d., Lithograph, 100 x 127 mm.
The Baltimore Museum of Art: Gift of Saidie A. May
BMA 1937.23.19

Lorsque tout me ravit,…
n.d., Wood engraving, 60 x 62 mm.
The Baltimore Museum of Art: Gift of Saidie A. May
BMA 1937.23.20

Quoique tes sourcils méchants…
n.d., Lithograph, 208 x 138 mm.
The Baltimore Museum of Art: Gift of Saidie A. May
BMA 1937.23.21

Je t'adore, o ma frivole,…
n.d., Lithograph, 202 x 105 mm.
The Baltimore Museum of Art: Gift of Saidie A. May
BMA 1937.23.22

Tes hanches sont amoureuses…
n.d., Lithograph, 219 x 97 mm.
The Baltimore Museum of Art: Gift of Saidie A. May
BMA 1937.23.23

Mon âme par toi guerie,…
n.d., Lithograph, 198 x 160 mm.
The Baltimore Museum of Art: Gift of Saidie A. May
BMA 1937.23.24

Ils me disent, tes yeux, clairs comme le cristal:…
n.d., Lithograph, 193 x 138 mm.
The Baltimore Museum of Art: Gift of Saidie A. May
BMA 1937.23.25

Ne veut pas te montrer son secret infernel,…
n.d., Wood engraving, 102 x 145 mm.
The Baltimore Museum of Art: Gift of Saidie A. May
BMA 1937.23.26

Que m'importe que tu sois sage?…
n.d., Lithograph, 197 x 92 mm.
The Baltimore Museum of Art: Gift of Saidie A. May
BMA 1937.23.27

Je sais que ton coeur, quie regorge…
n.d., Lithograph, 86 x 210 mm.
The Baltimore Museum of Art: Gift of Saidie A. May
BMA 1937.23.28

N'ouvrant à chacun qu'avec crainte,…
n.d., Wood engraving, 93 x 201 mm.
The Baltimore Museum of Art: Gift of Saidie A. May
BMA 1937.23.29

Vous pouvez mépriser les yeux les plus celebres
n.d., Lithograph, 146 x 165 mm.
The Baltimore Museum of Art: Gift of Saidie A. May
BMA 1937.23.30

Grands yeux de mon enfant,…
n.d., Lithograph, 120 x 220 mm.
The Baltimore Museum of Art: Gift of Saidie A. May
BMA 1937.23.31

C'est ici la case sacrée…
n.d., Lithograph, 135 x 190 mm.
The Baltimore Museum of Art: Gift of Saidie A. May
BMA 1937.23.32

C'est la chambre de Dorothée
n.d., Wood engraving, 112 x 66 mm.
The Baltimore Museum of Art: Gift of Saidie A. May
BMA 1937.23.33

Quand je te vois passer, o ma chère indolente,…
n.d., Lithograph, 188 x 137 mm.
The Baltimore Museum of Art: Gift of Saidie A. May
BMA 1937.23.34

Mais ne suffit-il pas que tu sois l'apparence…
n.d., Lithograph, 177 x 130 mm.
The Baltimore Museum of Art: Gift of Saidie A. May
BMA 1937.23.35

Viens sur mon coeur, âme cruelle et sourde,…
n.d., Lithograph, 180 x 125 mm.
The Baltimore Museum of Art: Gift of Saidie A. May
BMA 1937.23.36

Je sucerai, pour noyer ma rancoeur,…
n.d., Lithograph, 195 x 130 mm.
The Baltimore Museum of Art: Gift of Saidie A. May
BMA 1937.23.37

Ta tête, ton geste, gon air…
n.d., Lithograph, 200 x 133 mm.
The Baltimore Museum of Art: Gift of Saidie A. May
BMA 1937.23.38

Et le printemps et la verdure…
n.d., Lithograph, 207 x 140 cm.
The Baltimore Museum of Art: Gift of Saidie A. May
BMA 1937.23.39

Ainsi je voudrais, une nuit,…
n.d., Lithograph, 55 x 165 mm.
The Baltimore Museum of Art: Gift of Saidie A. May
BMA 1937.23.40

Mère des jeux latins et des voluptés grecques,…
n.d., Lithograph, 135 x 175 mm.
The Baltimore Museum of Art: Gift of Saidie A. May
BMA 1937.23.41

Laisse du vieux Platon se froncer l'oeil austère:…
n.d., Lithograph, 192 x 112 mm.
The Baltimore Museum of Art: Gift of Saidie A. May
BMA 1937.23.42

Et c'est depuis ce temps que Lesbos se lamente
n.d., Lithograph, 118 x 197 mm.
The Baltimore Museum of Art: Gift of Saidie A. May
BMA 1937.23.43

A la pâle clarté des lampes languissantes,…
n.d., Lithograph, 125 x 223 mm.
The Baltimore Museum of Art: Gift of Saidie A. May
BMA 1937.23.44

Hippolyte, cher coeur, que dis-tu de ces choses?
n.d., Lithograph, 197 x 135 mm.
The Baltimore Museum of Art: Gift of Saidie A. May
BMA 1937.23.45

Je sens fondre sur moi de lourdes épouvantes…
n.d., Lithograph, 105 x 217 mm.
The Baltimore Museum of Art: Gift of Saidie A. May
BMA 1937.23.46

Va, si tu veux, chercher un fiancé stupide;…
n.d., Lithograph, 198 x 137 mm.
The Baltimore Museum of Art: Gift of Saidie A. May
BMA 1937.23.47

Bouillonnent pêle-mêle avec un bruit d'orage
n.d., Lithograph, 125 x 170 cm.
The Baltimore Museum of Art: Gift of Saidie A. May
BMA 1937.23.48

L'âpre stérilité de votre jouissance…
n.d., Lithograph, 97 x 72 mm.
The Baltimore Museum of Art: Gift of Saidie A. May
BMA 1937.23.49

Untitled
n.d., Lithograph, 221 x 227 mm.
The Baltimore Museum of Art: Gift of Saidie A. May
BMA 1937.23.50

Colophon
n.d., Lithograph, 22 x 67 mm.
The Baltimore Museum of Art: Gift of Saidie A. May
BMA 1937.23.51

CHARLES DESPIAU (FRENCH, 1874–1946)
Diana
c. 1927, Bronze, 24-7/8"
The Baltimore Museum of Art:
Bequest of Saidie A. May
BMA 1951.374

Mme. X of Lyons (Mme. Vautheret)
1929, Bronze, 13-3/4 in. (34.9 cm.)
The Baltimore Museum of Art:
Bequest of Saidie A. May
BMA 1951.377

CHARLES DESPIAU (FRENCH, 1874–1946)
AUTHOR: CHARLES BAUDELAIRE
(FRENCH, 1821–1867)
PUBLISHER: GONIN
'Poems' by Charles Baudelaire
Published 1933
Bound volume with 51 lithographs and woodcuts
Page: 12-1/2 x 10 in.
The Baltimore Museum of Art: Gift of Saidie A. May
BMA 1937.23.1-51

CHARLES DESPIAU (FRENCH, 1874–1946)
Reclining Nude
c. 1933, Chalk
The Baltimore Museum of Art: Gift of Saidie A. May
BMA 1933.59.5

CHARLES DESPIAU (FRENCH, 1874–1946)
FOUNDRY: VALSUANI
Saidie A. May
1934, Bronze
14-1/4 x 8-1/4 x 22 in. (36.2 x 21 x 55.9 cm.)
The Baltimore Museum of Art:
Bequest of Saidie A. May
BMA 1951.375

THEO VAN DOESBURG (DUTCH, 1883–1931)
Interior
1919, Oil on canvas, 26 x 21-3/4 in. (66 x 55.2 cm.)
The Baltimore Museum of Art:
Bequest of Saidie A. May
BMA 1951.292

GILLO DORFLES (ITALIAN, BORN 1910)
Red, Black and White Composition
1949, Color lithograph, 321 x 206 mm.
(12-5/8 x 8-1/8 in.)
The Baltimore Museum of Art: Gift of Saidie A. May
BMA 1951.222.7

Pink, Brown, Lavender and White Composition
1949, Color lithograph, 178 x 191 mm. (7 x 7 1/2 in.)
The Baltimore Museum of Art: Gift of Saidie A. May
BMA 1951.222.8

GUY PÈNE DU BOIS (AMERICAN, 1884–1958)
Seated Woman
1929, Watercolor, graphite, and pen and ink
Sheet: 465 x 310 mm. (46.5 x 31 cm.)
The Baltimore Museum of Art: Gift of Saidie A. May
BMA 1936.66

Girl in Italian Costume
1934, Graphite
Mat opening: 305 x 254 mm. (12 x 10 in.)
The Baltimore Museum of Art: Gift of Saidie A. May
BMA 1936.145

JEAN DUBUFFET (FRENCH, 1901–1985)
Suite de Visages
n.d., Color lithograph
Sheet: 206 x 336 mm. (8-1/8 x 13-1/4 in.)
The Baltimore Museum of Art: Gift of Saidie A. May
BMA 1948.80

Orator at the Wall
1945, Oil on canvas
38-1/4 x 51-1/4 in. (97.2 x 130.2 cm.)
The Baltimore Museum of Art:
Bequest of Saidie A. May
BMA 1951.293

JEAN DUBUFFET (FRENCH, 1901–1985)
AUTHOR: EUGÈNE GUILLEVIC
(FRENCH, 1907–1997)
PUBLISHER: LE CALLIGRAPHE
Elégies
1946, Bound volume with one two-page color
lithograph
Book: 222 x 171 x 11 mm. (8-3/4 x 6-3/4 x 7/16 in.)
The Baltimore Museum of Art: Gift of Saidie A. May
BMA 1948.81

RAOUL DUFY (FRENCH, 1877–1953)
Le Haras du Pin
1936, Opaque watercolor
Sheet: 505 x 655 mm. (19-7/8 x 25-13/16 in.)
The Baltimore Museum of Art:
Bequest of Saidie A. May
BMA 1951.295

PIERRE DUHENIL (FRENCH, DATES UNKNOWN)
Le Lit
n.d., Engraving, 130 x 175 mm. (5-1/8 x 6-7/8 in.)
The Baltimore Museum of Art: Gift of Saidie A. May
BMA 1934.40.1

POSSIBLY MASTER E.S.
(GERMAN, ACTIVE C. 1450–1467)
St. John the Baptist
late 15th century, Wood (linden or basswood)
31-1/2 in. (80 cm.)
The Baltimore Museum of Art:
Bequest of Saidie A. May
BMA 1951.476

GÉRARD EDELINCK
(FRENCH, BORN FLANDERS, 1640–1707)
Portrait of Jacques Blanchard. Study for an engraving
n.d., Red chalk, 250 x 188 mm. (9-13/16 x 7-3/8 in.)
The Baltimore Museum of Art: Gift of Saidie A. May
BMA 1928.1.2

MAX ERNST (FRENCH, BORN GERMANY, 1891–1976)
Chimeras in the Mountains
1940, Oil on canvas, 9-1/2 x 7-1/2 in. (24.1 x 19.1 cm.)
The Baltimore Museum of Art:
Bequest of Saidie A. May
BMA 1951.296

MAX ERNST (FRENCH, BORN GERMANY, 1891–1976)
PUBLISHER: *VVV*
The Bird People
1942, published 1943
Black crayon frottage reworked with colored crayon
Sheet: 457 x 356 mm. (18 x 14 in.)
The Baltimore Museum of Art: Gift of Saidie A. May
BMA 1948.54.5

MAX ERNST (FRENCH, BORN GERMANY, 1891–1976)
Earthquake, Late Afternoon
1948, Oil on canvas, 10-1/4 x 18-1/4 in. (26 x 46.4 cm.)
The Baltimore Museum of Art:
Bequest of Saidie A. May
BMA 1951.297

ADAM FISCHER (DANISH, 1888–1968)
Head of a Woman
n.d., Limestone, Overall: 8-1/2 in. (21.6 cm.)
The Baltimore Museum of Art:
Bequest of Saidie A. May
BMA 1951.379

Head of a Boy
c. 1920, Bronze, Without Base: 7-3/4 in. (19.7 cm.)
Base (marble): 10 in. (25.4 cm.)
The Baltimore Museum of Art:
Bequest of Saidie A. May
BMA 1951.378

LAVINIA FONTANA (ITALIAN, 1552–1614)
The Birth of ?
c. 1614, Pen, Sheet: 110 x 159 mm. (4-5/16 x 6-1/4 in.)
The Baltimore Museum of Art: Gift of Saidie A. May
BMA 1928.1.4

LUCIO FONTANA (ITALIAN, 1899–1968)
Silver and Purple Composition
1949, Color lithograph, 203.2 x 158.75 mm.
(8 x 6-1/4 in.)
The Baltimore Museum of Art: Gift of Saidie A. May
BMA 1951.222.9

Blue, Red, Black and Gold Composition
1949, Color lithograph, 321 x 210 mm.
(12-5/8 x 8-1/4 in.)
The Baltimore Museum of Art: Gift of Saidie A. May
BMA 1951.222.10

JEAN-LOUIS FORAIN (FRENCH, 1852–1931)
Les Deux Gommeux
n.d., Etching, 156 x 111 mm. (6-1/8 x 4-3/8 in.)
The Baltimore Museum of Art: Gift of Saidie A. May
BMA 1934.39.1

Two Waiters
c. 1876, Watercolor and graphite
Sheet: 313 x 225 mm. (31.3 x 22.5 cm.)
The Baltimore Museum of Art: Gift of Saidie A. May
in Honor of Blanche Adler
BMA 1933.59.3

OTHON FRIESZ (FRENCH, 1879–1949)
The Lake (Annecy)
1933, Oil on canvas, 19 x 28 in. (48.3 x 71.1 cm.)
The Baltimore Museum of Art:
Bequest of Saidie A. May
BMA 1951.299

Portrait of Saidie A. May
1937, Oil on canvas, 25-3/4 x 19-3/4 in.
(65.4 x 50.2 cm.)
The Baltimore Museum of Art:
Bequest of Saidie A. May
BMA 1951.301

NAUM GABO (AMERICAN, BORN RUSSIA, 1890–1977)
Model of May Wing Stair Installation
20th Century, Wood, brass wire, plastic, iron nails,
cardboard, Overall (Sculpture Model): 12 x 10 x 11 in.
(30.5 x 25.4 x 27.9 cm.)
Overall (Diorama): 32-7/8 x 27-7/8 x 27-1/8 in.
(83.5 x 70.8 x 68.9 cm.)
The Baltimore Museum of Art:
Bequest of Saidie A. May
BMA 1951.148.2

Construction with Alabaster Carving
1938–1939, Alabaster, Plexiglas, 15-1/2 in. (39.4 cm.)
The Baltimore Museum of Art:
Bequest of Saidie A. May
BMA 1951.380

Construction
1951, Aluminum, Plexiglas, gold wire, bronze mesh,
steel wire, approx. 180 in. (457.2 cm.)
The Baltimore Museum of Art:
Bequest of Saidie A. May
BMA 1951.148.1

MANNER OF THOMAS GAINSBOROUGH
(ENGLISH, 1727–1788)
Landscape
n.d., Black crayon and gray wash
194 x 259 mm. (7-5/8 x 10-3/16 in.)
The Baltimore Museum of Art: Gift of Saidie A. May
BMA 1928.1.1

GARAU (ITALIAN, DATES UNKNOWN)
Composition in Brown
1949, Lithograph on green paper
286 x 200 mm. (11-1/4 x 7-7/8 in.)
The Baltimore Museum of Art: Gift of Saidie A. May
BMA 1951.222.11

Composition in Green
1949, Lithograph, 286 x 200 mm. (11-1/4 x 7-7/8 in.)
The Baltimore Museum of Art: Gift of Saidie A. May
BMA 1951.222.12

ARTISTS: CIRCLE OF NICCOLO DI PIETRO GERINI
(ITALIAN, ACTIVE 1368–1415)
*Madonna and Child Enthroned with Two Angels and
Four Saints*
c. 1400, Tempera on wood panel, 30-1/4 x 18-1/8 in.
(76.8 x 46 cm.)
The Baltimore Museum of Art:
Bequest of Saidie A. May
BMA 1951.390

ALBERTO GIACOMETTI (SWISS, 1901–1966)
Man Pointing
original model 1947; this cast 1947
Bronze, 70 x 38 x 17 in. (177.8 x 96.5 x 43.2 cm.)
The Baltimore Museum of Art:
Bequest of Saidie A. May
BMA 1951.382

GIOVANNI DAL PONTE (GIOVANNI DI MARCO)
(ITALIAN, 1385–1437)
Saint Anthony Abbot
c. 1430, Tempera on wood panel
52-1/4 x 22-3/4 in. (132.7 x 57.8 cm.)
The Baltimore Museum of Art:
Bequest of Saidie A. May
BMA 1951.391

WILLIAM J. GLACKENS (AMERICAN, 1870–1938)
Study for an Illustration
n.d., Black conté crayon, graphite with gray and blue
wash on tan butchers paper
Sheet: 234 x 361 mm. (9-3/16 x 14-3/16 in.)
The Baltimore Museum of Art: Gift of Saidie A. May
BMA 1935.37.2

FRITZ GLARNER
(AMERICAN, BORN SWITZERLAND, 1899–1972)
Relational Painting Tondo #15
1950, Oil on canvasboard, 25 in. (63.5 cm.) diam.
The Baltimore Museum of Art:
Bequest of Saidie A. May
BMA 1951.303

ALBERT GLEIZES (FRENCH, 1881–1953)
On a Circus Theme
1917, Oil on composition board
39-3/4 x 30-1/8 in. (101 x 76.5 cm.)
The Baltimore Museum of Art:
Bequest of Saidie A. May
BMA 1951.304

HENDRICK GOLTZIUS (DUTCH, 1558–1617)
Head of an Old Man
1606, Black and white chalk on tan paper
Sheet: 192 x 148 mm. (7-9/16 x 5-13/16 in.)
The Baltimore Museum of Art: Gift of Saidie A. May
BMA 1928.1.5

URS GRAF (SWISS, C. 1485–1527/1529)
Knight Seated
1523, Engraving, Sheet: 108 x 80 mm.
(4-1/4 x 3-1/8 in.)
Plate: 105 x 75 mm. (4-1/8 x 2-15/16 in.)
The Baltimore Museum of Art: Gift of Saidie A. May
BMA 1931.43.2

JUAN GRIS (SPANISH, 1887–1927)
Pierrot with Guitar
c. 1922, Pen and black ink with charcoal and stumping
Sheet: 384 x 284 mm. (15-1/8 x 11-3/16 in.)
The Baltimore Museum of Art:
Bequest of Saidie A. May, 1951
BMA 1992.187

Bottle and Glass
1918, Oil on canvas, 21-1/2 x 13 in. (54.6 x 33 cm.)
The Baltimore Museum of Art:
Bequest of Saidie A. May
BMA 1951.305

JUAN GRIS (SPANISH, 1887–1927)
AUTHOR: MAX JACOB (FRENCH, 1876–1944)
PUBLISHER: EDITIONS DE LA GALERIE SIMON
Ne Coupez pas Mademoiselle (ou les erreurs des P.T.T.)
1921, Bound volume with text and lithographs
Book: 327 x 245 x 6 mm. (12-7/8 x 9-5/8 x 1/4 in.)
The Baltimore Museum of Art: Gift of Saidie A. May
BMA 1940.171

JUAN GRIS (SPANISH, 1887–1927)
The Painter's Window
1925, Oil on canvas, 39-1/4 x 31-3/4 in.
(99.7 x 80.6 cm.)
The Baltimore Museum of Art:
Bequest of Saidie A. May
BMA 1951.306

MARCEL GROMAIRE (FRENCH, 1892–1971)
Refugees from Spain
1938, Pen and watercolor, 321 x 429 mm.
(12-5/8 x 16-7/8 in.)
The Baltimore Museum of Art: Gift of Saidie A. May
BMA 1938.815

FRANCIS GRUBER (FRENCH, 1912–1948)
Les Plaisirs de la peche
n.d., Graphite on tracing paper
Sheet: 591 x 406 mm. (23-1/4 x 16 in.)
The Baltimore Museum of Art: Gift of Blanche Adler
and Saidie A. May
BMA 1933.29.1

La Famille
1930, Watercolor over graphite
Sheet: 267 x 216 mm. (10-1/2 x 8-1/2 in.)
The Baltimore Museum of Art: Gift of Saidie A. May
BMA 1941.241

ATTRIBUTED TO GIOVANNI FRANCESCO BARBIERI
GUERCINO (ITALIAN, 1591–1666)
St. John
n.d., Pen and bistre ink, pale blue watercolor, on ivory
paper, 208 x 146 mm. (8-3/16 x 5-3/4 in.)
The Baltimore Museum of Art: Gift of Saidie A. May
1928.1.3

CONSTANTIN GUYS (FRENCH, 1802–1892)
The Hansom Team
c. 1856–1869, Pen and black ink and watercolor over
graphite, Sheet: 275 x 360 mm. (27.5 x 36 cm.)
The Baltimore Museum of Art:
Bequest of Saidie A. May
BMA 2001.279

WADE HADLEY (TO'DACHINE)
(AMERICAN, DATES UNKNOWN)
Deer Hunting
n.d., Opaque watercolor
Sheet: 305 x 381 mm. (12 x 15 in.)
The Baltimore Museum of Art: Gift of Saidie A. May
BMA 1941.377

WILLIAM MELTON HALSEY (AMERICAN, 1915–1999)
Mexican Landscape
1950, Oil on composition board
21-3/4 x 26 in. (55.2 x 66 cm.)
The Baltimore Museum of Art: Gift of Saidie A. May
BMA 1950.58

DAVID HARE (AMERICAN, 1917–1992)
PUBLISHER: *VVV*
Seated Nude
1938, published 1943
Toned gelatin silver print from an altered negative
Mount: 455 x 356 mm. (17-15/16 x 14 in.)
Image/Sheet: 305 x 248 mm. (12 x 9-3/4 in.)
The Baltimore Museum of Art: Gift of Saidie A. May
BMA 1948.54.6

ATTRIBUTED TO CATERINA VAN HEMESSEN
(FLEMISH, 1528–AFTER 1587)
Portrait of a Young Lady
c. 1560, Oil on wood panel, 12 x 9 in. (30.4 x 22.9 cm.)
The Baltimore Museum of Art:
Bequest of Saidie A. May
BMA 1951.397

UTAGAWA HIROSHIGE (JAPANESE, 1797–1858)
Landscape
after 1858, Reduced facsimile reproduction
Sheet: 301 x 197 mm. (30.1 x 19.7 cm.)
The Baltimore Museum of Art: Gift of Saidie A. May
BMA 1932.45.4

HUBER (ITALIAN, DATES UNKNOWN)
Abstraction
1949, Lithograph, 321 x 216 mm. (12-5/8 x 8-1/2 in.)
The Baltimore Museum of Art: Gift of Saidie A. May
BMA 1951.222.13

Abstraction
1949, Lithograph, 321 x 216 mm. (12-5/8 x 8-1/2 in.)
The Baltimore Museum of Art: Gift of Saidie A. May
BMA 1951.222.14

ATTRIBUTED TO HANS JAMNITZER II
(GERMAN, C. 1538–1603)
Plaque: Judgment of Solomon
late 16th century, Bronze, 5-3/4 in. (14.6 cm.)
The Baltimore Museum of Art:
Bequest of Saidie A. May
BMA 1951.457

ALFRED JENSEN
(AMERICAN, BORN GUATEMALA, 1903–1981)
Standing Nude
n.d., Graphite, Sheet: 306 x 226 mm.
(12-1/16 x 8-7/8 in.)
The Baltimore Museum of Art: Gift of Saidie A. May
BMA 1935.37.7

Recto: Nude Leaning on Hand;
Verso: Nude Seated on the Floor
n.d., Graphite, Sheet: 270 x 386 mm.
(10-5/8 x 15-3/16 in.)
The Baltimore Museum of Art: Gift of Saidie A. May
BMA 1935.37.8a-b

Untitled (recto); Untitled (verso)
1920–1951, Watercolor (recto); watercolor (verso)
Sheet: 561 x 761 mm. (22-1/16 x 29-15/16 in.)
The Baltimore Museum of Art:
Bequest of Saidie A. May
BMA 2008.67

WASSILY KANDINSKY (RUSSIAN, 1866–1944)
Penetrating Green
1938, Oil on canvas, 29-3/16 x 49-3/8 in.
(74.1 x 125.4 cm.)
The Baltimore Museum of Art:
Bequest of Saidie A. May
BMA 1951.310

EDMOND KAYSER (FRENCH, 1882–1965)
The Rhone at Avignon
n.d., Watercolor
Mat opening: 248 x 362 mm. (9-3/4 x 14-1/4 in.)
The Baltimore Museum of Art: Bequest of
Saidie A. May
BMA 1951.313

Au bord de l'eau
n.d., Brass plate (cancelled)
270 x 327 mm. (10-5/8 x 12-7/8 in.)
The Baltimore Museum of Art: Gift of Blanche Adler
and Saidie A. May
BMA 1931.47.9a

Ramparts of the Town
1913, Copperplate (cancelled)
254 x 419 mm. (10 x 16-1/2 in.)
The Baltimore Museum of Art: Gift of Blanche Adler
and Saidie A. May
BMA 1931.47.8a

EUGENE-NESTOR DE KERMADEC
(FRENCH, 1899–1976)
Nocturne Blanc
n.d., Oil on canvas, 38-1/4 x 57-9/16 in.
(97.2 x 146.2 cm.)
The Baltimore Museum of Art:
Bequest of Saidie A. May
BMA 1951.316

PAUL KLEE (SWISS, 1879–1940)
Traveling Circus
1937, Mixed media on canvas
25-1/2 x 19-3/4 in. (64.8 x 50.2 cm.)
The Baltimore Museum of Art:
Bequest of Saidie A. May
BMA 1951.317

GASTON LACHAISE
(AMERICAN, BORN FRANCE, 1882–1935)
Augusta Hartman
1923, Bronze, Without Base: 14-1/8 x 6-1/4 x 6-1/2 in.
(35.9 x 15.9 x 16.5 cm.), Base: 7/8 in. (2.2 cm.)
The Baltimore Museum of Art: Gift of Saidie A. May
BMA 1936.65

WIFREDO LAM (CUBAN, 1902–1982)
Deity
1942, Opaque watercolor and charcoal
Sheet: 1048 x 845 mm. (41-1/4 33-1/4 in.)
Framed: 50-13/16 x 41-1/8 x 1-15/16 in.
(129 x 104.5 x 5 cm.)
The Baltimore Museum of Art:
Bequest of Saidie A. May
BMA 1951.318

ELIE LASCAUX (FRENCH, 1888–1968)
Le Moulin de Pont Au
1940, Pen and ink, Sheet: 479 x 630 mm.
(47.9 x 63 cm.)
The Baltimore Museum of Art:
Bequest of Saidie A. May, 1951
BMA 1999.247

Saint Léonard Vue des Hauteurs de l'Abesse
1940, Pen and ink
Sheet: 480 x 629 mm. (48 x 62.9 cm.)
Image: 480 x 629 mm. (48 x 62.9 cm.)
The Baltimore Museum of Art:
Bequest of Saidie A. May, 1951
BMA 1999.248

MARIE LAURENCIN (FRENCH, 1885–1956)
Young Girl
1938, Watercolor, 324 x 244 mm. (12-3/4 x 9-5/8 in.)
The Baltimore Museum of Art:
Bequest of Saidie A. May
BMA 1951.321

HENRI LAURENS (FRENCH, 1885–1954)
Two Women Reclining
1930, Terracotta
Base (with): 4-1/4 x 13 in. (10.8 x 33 cm.)
The Baltimore Museum of Art:
Bequest of Saidie A. May
BMA 1951.383

ATTRIBUTED TO JUSTE LE COUR
(FLEMISH, 1627–1679)
Prophet
mid-17th century, Terracotta, 13-3/8 in. (34 cm.)
The Baltimore Museum of Art: Gift of Saidie A. May
BMA 1930.47.1a

Prophet
mid-17th century, Terracotta, 13-1/4 in. (33.7 cm.)
The Baltimore Museum of Art: Gift of Saidie A. May
BMA 1930.47.1b

FERNAND LÉGER (FRENCH, 1881–1955)
Yellow Composition
1928, Oil on canvas, 36 x 29 in. (91.4 x 73.7 cm.)
The Baltimore Museum of Art:
Bequest of Saidie A. May
BMA 1951.322

Study for "Acrobats and Musicians"
1939, Opaque and transparent watercolor with ink
over graphite, squared for transfer
Sheet: 1011 x 1347 mm. (39-13/16 x 53-1/16 in.)
The Baltimore Museum of Art:
Bequest of Saidie A. May
BMA 1951.324

ALPHONSE LEGROS
(ENGLISH, BORN FRANCE, 1837–1911)
Old Traveller Resting
n.d., Etching, 101 x 135 mm. (4 x 5-5/16 in.)
The Baltimore Museum of Art: Gift of Saidie A. May
BMA 1931.43.5

AUGUSTE LEPÈRE (FRENCH, 1849-1918)
Beggars at the Last House
n.d., Wood engraving
95 x 111 mm. (3-3/4 x 4-3/8 in.)
The Baltimore Museum of Art: Gift of Saidie A. May
BMA 1931.43.1

RICHARD HAYLEY LEVER (AMERICAN, 1876–1958)
Four Sailboats
before 1941, Watercolor and graphite
Mat opening: 168 x 276 mm. (6-5/8 x 10-7/8 in.)
The Baltimore Museum of Art: Gift of Saidie A. May
BMA 1941.242

CHARLES MALFRAY (FRENCH, 1885–1940)
Seated Nude
1928, Terracotta, 7-3/4 in. (19.7 cm.)
The Baltimore Museum of Art:
Bequest of Saidie A. May
BMA 1951.384

ÉDOUARD MANET (FRENCH, 1832–1883)
Olympia
before 1923, Color woodcut
Sheet: 130 x 203 mm. (5-1/8 x 8 in.)
The Baltimore Museum of Art: Gift of Saidie A. May
BMA 1949.6

MANUEL MANOLO (SPANISH, 1872–1945)
Seated Catalan Woman
late 19th-early 20th century, Terracotta
Overall: 6-3/4 in. (17.1 cm.)
The Baltimore Museum of Art:
Bequest of Saidie A. May
BMA 1951.385

ATTRIBUTED TO FRANZ MARC
(GERMAN, 1880–1916)
Antelopes
n.d., Watercolor
Sheet: 318 x 495 mm. (12-1/2 x 19-1/2 in.)
The Baltimore Museum of Art:
Bequest of Saidie A. May
BMA 1951.326

FRANZ MARC (GERMAN, 1880–1916)
Deer at the Edge of the Forest
1907, Opaque and transparent watercolor and crayon
over graphite
Sheet: 111 x 295 mm. (4-3/8 x 11-5/8 in.)
The Baltimore Museum of Art:
Bequest of Saidie A. May
BMA 1951.325

TONY MARTINEZ (AMERICAN, 1921–1971)
Man Carrying Baby
n.d., Opaque watercolor
Sheet: 280 x 241 mm. (11 x 9-1/2 in.)
The Baltimore Museum of Art: Gift of Saidie A. May
BMA 1941.374

ANDRÉ MASSON (FRENCH, 1896–1987)
Ophelia
1937, Oil on canvas, 44-3/4 x 57-3/4 in.
(113.7 x 146.7 cm.)
The Baltimore Museum of Art:
Bequest of Saidie A. May
BMA 1951.328

In the Tower of Sleep
1938, Oil on canvas, 32 x 39-1/2 in. (81.3 x 100.3 cm.)
The Baltimore Museum of Art:
Bequest of Saidie A. May
BMA 1951.329

The Metaphysical Wall
1940, Watercolor with pen and black ink over traces of graphite, Sheet: 474 x 614 mm. (18-11/16 x 24-3/16 in.)
Framed: 28-3/4 x 32-11/16 x 1-3/8 in. (73 x 83 x 3.5 cm.)
The Baltimore Museum of Art:
Bequest of Saidie A. May
BMA 1951.331

Self-Portrait
1940, Pen and ink, 505 x 2 mm. (19-7/8 x 14-1/4 in.)
The Baltimore Museum of Art:
Bequest of Saidie A. May
BMA 1951.484

There is No Finished World
1942, Oil on canvas, 53 x 68 in. (134.6 x 172.7 cm.)
The Baltimore Museum of Art:
Bequest of Saidie A. May
BMA 1951.333

Diagram Explaining the Artist's Painting, 'There Is No Finished World.' Consists of two diagrams, one with text in French, the other in English
1942, Pen and black ink over traces of graphite
Sheet (each): 279 x 760 mm. (11 x 29-15/16 in.)
The Baltimore Museum of Art: Gift of Saidie A. May
BMA 1947.138

ANDRÉ MASSON (FRENCH, 1896–1987)
PRINTER: KURT SELIGMANN (AMERICAN, BORN SWITZERLAND, 1900–1962)
PUBLISHER: *VVV*
Fruits of the Abyss
1942, published 1943, Etching and softground etching
Mount: 458 x 355 mm. (18-1/16 x 14 in.)
Sheet: 429 x 309 mm. (16-7/8 x 12-3/16 in.)
Plate: 302 x 202 mm. (11-7/8 x 7-15/16 in.)
The Baltimore Museum of Art: Gift of Saidie A. May
BMA 1948.54.7

MASTER OF THE VIEW OF ST. GUDULE
(FLEMISH, ACTIVE 1480–1500)
The Adoration of the Magi
n.d., Oil on wood panel
22-3/4 x 16-1/4 in. (57.8 x 41.3 cm.)
The Baltimore Museum of Art:
Bequest of Saidie A. May
BMA 1951.398

HENRI MATISSE (FRENCH, 1869–1954)
Sleeping Man (L'homme endormi)
1936, Aquatint
Sheet: 333 x 257 mm. (13-1/8 x 10-1/8 in.)
Plate: 247 x 175 mm. (9-3/4 x 6-7/8 in.)
The Baltimore Museum of Art: Gift of Saidie A. May
BMA 1941.371

MATTA (CHILEAN, 1911–2002)
Forms in a Landscape
1937, Crayon and graphite
Sheet: 500 x 651 mm. (19-11/16 x 25-5/8 in.)
The Baltimore Museum of Art: Gift of Saidie A. May
BMA 1938.819

Rocks
1940, Oil on canvas, 38-1/8 x 60-1/8 in.
(96.8 x 152.7 cm.)
The Baltimore Museum of Art:
Bequest of Saidie A. May
BMA 1951.335

MATTA (CHILEAN, 1911–2002)
PUBLISHER: *VVV*
Untitled
1942, published 1943, Colored inks and graphite
Mount: 456 x 355 mm. (17-15/16 x 14 in.)
Sheet: 426 x 348 mm. (16-3/4 x 13-11/16 in.)
The Baltimore Museum of Art: Gift of Saidie A. May
BMA 1948.54.8

SAIDIE A. MAY (AMERICAN, 1879–1951)
House Among Trees
n.d., Oil on canvas, 20 x 24 in.
The Baltimore Museum of Art:
Bequest of Saidie A. May, 1951
BMA L.1943.101

Seated Nude
n.d., Crayon, with scraping
Sheet: 303 x 227 mm. (30.3 x 22.7 cm.)
Image: 303 x 227 mm. (30.3 x 22.7 cm.)
The Baltimore Museum of Art: Gift of Saidie A. May
BMA 1935.37.5

Man at Piano
n.d., Graphite
Sheet: 226 x 306 mm. (22.6 x 30.6 cm.)
Image: 226 x 306 mm. (22.6 x 30.6 cm.)
The Baltimore Museum of Art: Gift of Saidie A. May
BMA 1935.37.6

GALLIANO MAZZON (ITALIAN, 1896–1978)
Pink, Blue, Black and White Composition
1949, Color lithograph, 21 x 216 mm.
(12-5/8 x 8-1/2 in.)
The Baltimore Museum of Art: Gift of Saidie A. May
BMA 1951.222.15

Red, Blue, Black and White Composition
1949, Color lithograph, 21 x 216 mm.
(12-5/8 x 8-1/2 in.)
The Baltimore Museum of Art: Gift of Saidie A. May
BMA 1951.222.16

MELIUS (FRENCH, DATES UNKNOWN)
Seated Nude with Hidden Face
n.d., Sanguine on board
413 x 241 mm. (16-1/4 x 9-1/2 in.)
The Baltimore Museum of Art: Gift of Saidie A. May
BMA 1932.48.7

Two Nudes
n.d., Sanguine on cream paper
356 x 241 mm. (14 x 9-1/2 in.)
The Baltimore Museum of Art: Gift of Saidie A. May
BMA 1932.48.8

Seated Nude
n.d., Red chalk, NO DIMENSIONS
The Baltimore Museum of Art: Gift of Saidie A. May
BMA 1930.41.1

Action Drawings
n.d., Sanguine on brown paper
381 x 267 mm. (15 x 10-1/2 in.)
The Baltimore Museum of Art: Gift of Saidie A. May
BMA 1932.48.2

VICENTI MIRABAL (CHIU TAU, DANCING BIRD)
(AMERICAN, TAOS PUEBLO, 1917–1945)
Taos Indian War Dancer
c. 1940, Brush and opaque watercolor over graphite
Sheet: 324 x 250 mm. (12-3/4 x 9-13/16 in.)
The Baltimore Museum of Art: Gift of Saidie A. May
BMA 1941.378

JOAN MIRÓ (SPANISH, 1893–1983)
Figures and Birds in a Landscape
1935, Opaque watercolor over graphite on masonite
10-7/8 x 19-1/2 in. (27.6 x 49.5 cm.)
The Baltimore Museum of Art:
Bequest of Saidie A. May
BMA 1951.340

Personages Attracted by the Forms of a Mountain
1936, Tempera over graphite on masonite
13 x 19-3/4 in. (33 x 50.2 cm.)
The Baltimore Museum of Art:
Bequest of Saidie A. May
BMA 1951.338

A Night Scene
1937, Brush and tempera with collage of printed
papers and thin wood veneer with graphite
underdrawing, Sheet: 640 x 407 mm. (25-3/16 x 16 in.)
The Baltimore Museum of Art:
Bequest of Saidie A. May
BMA 1951.337

Reclining Nude
1937, Graphite, 232 x 308 mm. (9-1/8 x 12-1/8 in.)
The Baltimore Museum of Art:
Bequest of Saidie A. May
BMA 1951.485

JOAN MIRÓ (SPANISH, 1893–1983)
PUBLISHER: PIERRE MATISSE, NEW YORK
PUBLISHER: PIERRE LOEB
PRINTER: L'ATELIER LACOURIÈRE
The Giantess (La géante)
1938, Etching and drypoint
Sheet: 442 x 324 mm. (17-3/8 x 12-3/4 in.)
Plate: 347 x 235 mm. (13-11/16 x 9-1/4 in.)
The Baltimore Museum of Art:
Bequest of Saidie A. May, 1951
BMA 1995.64

Summer
1938, Opaque watercolor
Sheet: 362 x 273 mm. (14-1/4 x 10-3/4 in.)
The Baltimore Museum of Art:
Bequest of Saidie A. May
BMA 1951.341

Portrait No. 1
1938, Oil on canvas
64-1/4 x 51-1/4 in. (163.2 x 130.2 cm.)
The Baltimore Museum of Art:
Bequest of Saidie A. May
BMA 1951.339

Women and Bird in Front of the Moon
1944, Oil on burlap, 8-5/8 x 6-1/2 in. (21.9 x 16.5 cm.)
The Baltimore Museum of Art:
Bequest of Saidie A. May
BMA 1951.342

Bird
1946, Bronze, 5 in. H (12.7 cm.)
The Baltimore Museum of Art:
Bequest of Saidie A. May
BMA 1951.386

JOAN MIRÓ (SPANISH, 1893–1983)
PRINTER: ATELIER 17
Composition II
1947, Etching printed in black (intaglio) and
red (relief)
Sheet: 280 x 211 mm. (11 x 8-5/16 in.)
Plate: 126 x 150 mm. (4-15/16 x 5-7/8 in.)
The Baltimore Museum of Art: Gift of Saidie A. May
BMA 1948.82

Composition I
1947, Etching printed in black (intaglio) and color
stencil (pochoir)
Sheet: 281 x 208 mm. (11-1/16 x 8-3/16 in.)
Plate: 125 x 149 mm. (4-15/16 x 5-7/8 in.)
The Baltimore Museum of Art: Gift of Saidie A. May
BMA 1948.83

PIET MONDRIAN (DUTCH, 1872–1944)
Composition V
1927, Oil on canvas, 15-1/8 x 14 in. (38.4 x 35.6 cm.)
The Baltimore Museum of Art:
Bequest of Saidie A. May
BMA 1951.343

GIANNI MONNET (ITALIAN, 1912–1958)
Purple, Brown and White Composition
1949, Color lithograph, 321 x 216 mm.
(12-5/8 x 8-1/2 in.)
The Baltimore Museum of Art: Gift of Saidie A. May
BMA 1951.222.17

Blue, Orange, Black and White Composition
1949, Color lithograph, 321 x 216 mm.
(12-5/8 x 8-1/2 in.)
The Baltimore Museum of Art: Gift of Saidie A. May
BMA 1951.222.18

IGNACIO MOQUINO (WAKA)
(AMERICAN, 1917–1982)
Hunters Luck
n.d., Opaque watercolor, Sheet: 305 x 559 mm.
(12 x 22 in.)
The Baltimore Museum of Art: Gift of Saidie A. May
BMA 1941.376

ROBERT MOTHERWELL (AMERICAN, 1915–1991)
PUBLISHER: *VVV*
Yellow Abstract Composition
1942, published 1943
Pen and black ink and watercolor
Mount: 457 x 355 mm. (18 x 14 in.)
Sheet: 224 x 151 mm. (8-13/16 x 5-15/16 in.)
The Baltimore Museum of Art: Gift of Saidie A. May
BMA 1948.54.9

The Joy of Living
1943, Collage of construction paper, mulberry paper,
fabric, and printed map with tempera, ink, crayon, oil,
and graphite, Sheet: 1105 x 854 mm. (43-1/2 x 33-5/8 in.)
The Baltimore Museum of Art:
Bequest of Saidie A. May
BMA 1951.344

BRUNO MUNARI (ITALIAN, 1907–1998)
Black, Purple, Green and White Composition
1949, Color lithograph
321 x 216 mm. (12-5/8 x 8-1/2 in.)
The Baltimore Museum of Art: Gift of Saidie A. May
BMA 1951.222.19

Lines and Dots
1949, Color lithograph
321 x 216 mm. (12-5/8 x 8-1/2 in.)
The Baltimore Museum of Art: Gift of Saidie A. May
BMA 1951.222.20

ADRIAEN VAN OSTADE (DUTCH, 1610–1685)
Peasant Holding a Glass and a Jug
n.d., Pen and brown ink with gray wash
Sheet: 127 x 85 mm. (12.7 x 8.5 cm.)
The Baltimore Museum of Art:
Bequest of Saidie A. May, 1951
BMA 1985.5

GEORGES PAPAZOFF (BULGARIAN, 1894–1972)
Papillons
1924, Oil on canvas, 15 x 18 in. (38.1 x 45.7 cm.)
The Baltimore Museum of Art:
Bequest of Saidie A. May
BMA 1951.345

ANTOINE PEVSNER
(FRENCH, BORN RUSSIA, 1886–1962)
Projection in Space
1927, Copper alloy
Overall: 12 x 21-1/2 in. (30.5 x 54.6 cm.)
The Baltimore Museum of Art:
Bequest of Saidie A. May
BMA 1951.387

FRANCIS PICABIA (FRENCH, 1879–1953)
Reverence
1915, Oil and metallic paint on paperboard
39 x 39 in. (99.1 x 99.1 cm.)
The Baltimore Museum of Art:
Bequest of Saidie A. May
BMA 1951.347

PABLO PICASSO (SPANISH, 1881–1973)
Still Life
1924, Oil on canvas, 15 x 18 in. (38.1 x 45.7 cm.)
The Baltimore Museum of Art:
Bequest of Saidie A. May
BMA 1951.348

PABLO PICASSO (SPANISH, 1881–1973)
PUBLISHER: EDITIONS DE QUATRE CHEMINS
Head of a Woman, Face and Profile
1925 image, published 1926
Crayon lithograph with scraping
Sheet: 261 x 209 mm. (26.1 x 20.9 cm.)
Image: 128 x 116 mm. (12.8 x 11.6 cm.)
The Baltimore Museum of Art:
Gift of Blanche Adler and Saidie A. May
BMA 1977.54

PETE PINO, JR. (TA-MU-YU-WA)
(AMERICAN, DATES UNKNOWN)
Deers n N'to'lopes wun'ders o'er the mount'een C'neri
1940, Watercolor and ink
Sheet: 11-1/4 x 14-1/4 in. (28.6 x 36.2 cm.)
The Baltimore Museum of Art: Gift of Saidie A. May
BMA 1941.372

CAMILLE PISSARRO (FRENCH, 1830–1903)
Rouen, rue de Arpente, No. 83
n.d., Pen and black ink
Sheet: 225 x 211 mm. (22.5 x 21.1 cm.)
The Baltimore Museum of Art: Gift of Saidie A. May
BMA 1928.1.9

ANTONIO POLLAIUOLO (ITALIAN, C. 1431/32–1498)
Battle of the Naked Men
c. 1470–1475, Engraving
Sheet: 405 x 584 mm. (40.5 x 58.4 cm.)
The Baltimore Museum of Art:
Gift of Blanche Adler and Saidie A. May
BMA 1933.66.1

JACKSON POLLOCK (AMERICAN, 1912–1956)
Water Birds
1943, Oil on canvas, 26-1/8 x 21-3/16 in.
(66.4 x 53.8 cm.)
The Baltimore Museum of Art:
Bequest of Saidie A. May
BMA 1951.349

JOE A. QUINTANA (COCHITÍ, DATES UNKNOWN)
Buffalo Dancer
1941, Opaque watercolor over graphite
Plate: 425 x 356 mm. (16-3/4 x 14 in.)
Plate: 425 x 356 mm. (16-3/4 x 14 in.)
The Baltimore Museum of Art: Gift of Saidie A. May
BMA 1941.375

MARCANTONIO RAIMONDI
(ITALIAN, C. 1470/82–C. 1527/34)
AFTER ALBRECHT DÜRER (GERMAN, 1471–1528)
The Crucifixion
n.d., Engraving, Sheet: 268 x 168 mm.
(10-9/16 x 6-5/8 in.)
The Baltimore Museum of Art: Gift of Saidie A. May
BMA 1932.50.2

MARIUS ROCHE (AMERICAN, DATES UNKNOWN)
Home Brew
n.d., Lithograph, 210 x 248 mm. (8-1/4 x 9-3/4 in.)
The Baltimore Museum of Art: Gift of Saidie A. May
BMA 1935.7.2

MARGOT ROCLE (AMERICAN, 1893–1981)
Horseplay
n.d., Lithograph, 254 x 216 mm. (10 x 8-1/2 in.)
The Baltimore Museum of Art: Gift of Saidie A. May
BMA 1935.7.1

J. ROSEMAN (FRENCH, DATES UNKNOWN)
A Portrait of Emile Othon Friesz
n.d., Gelatin silver print
Sheet: 240 x 171 mm. (24 x 17.1 cm.)
Image: 222 x 165 mm. (22.2 x 16.5 cm.)
The Baltimore Museum of Art:
Bequest of Saidie A. May, 1951
BMA 1977.15

GEORGES ROUAULT (FRENCH, 1871–1958)
PUBLISHER: AMBROISE VOLLARD
Réincarnations du Père Ubu
published 1932, Bound volume with text, etchings
and wood engravings, plus extra loose copy of print
(frontispiece)
Book: 442 x 330 x 50 mm. (17-3/8 x 13 x 1-15/16 in.)
The Baltimore Museum of Art: Gift of Saidie A. May
BMA 1936.144

JACOB VAN RUISDAEL (DUTCH, 1628/29–1682)
Landscape, with Towered Moat (recto);
Unfinished Sketch (verso)
n.d., Graphite heightened with white
196 x 281 mm. (7-11/16 x 11-1/16 in.)
The Baltimore Museum of Art: Gift of Saidie A. May
BMA 1928.1.7

BASTIANO DA SANGALLO (ITALIAN, 1482–1551)
Massacre of the Innocents
n.d., Ink wash, 305 x 440 mm. (12 x 17-5/16 in.)
The Baltimore Museum of Art: Gift of Saidie A. May
1928.1.8

M. SCHNITZLER (FRENCH, DATES UNKNOWN)
Seated Nude
n.d., Graphite, 337 x 260 mm. (13-1/4 x 10-1/4 in.)
The Baltimore Museum of Art: Gift of Saidie A. May
BMA 1932.48.4

Nude Seated on Stool
n.d., Graphite, 343 x 264 mm. (13-1/2 x 10-3/8 in.)
The Baltimore Museum of Art: Gift of Saidie A. May
BMA 1932.48.5

MAX SCHNITZLER (AMERICAN, BORN 1902)
Composition
n.d., Oil on canvas, 24-1/8 x 30 in. (61.3 x 76.2 cm.)
The Baltimore Museum of Art:
Bequest of Saidie A. May
BMA 1951.356

ARTIST AND PRINTER: KURT SELIGMANN
(AMERICAN, BORN SWITZERLAND, 1900–1962)
PUBLISHER: *VVV*
Phantom of the Past
1942, published 1943, Etching and aquatint
Sheet: 446 x 341 mm. (17-9/16 x 13-7/16 in.)
Plate: 352 x 295 mm. (13-7/8 x 11-5/8 in.)
Mount: 457 x 355 mm. (18 x 14 in.)
The Baltimore Museum of Art: Gift of Saidie A. May
BMA 1948.54.10

GEORGES SEURAT (FRENCH, 1859–1891)
Preparatory Sketch for the Painting "La Grève du
Bas-Butin, Honfleur"
1886, Oil on wood panel
6-3/4 x 10-1/4 in. (17.1 x 26 cm.)
The Baltimore Museum of Art:
Bequest of Saidie A. May
BMA 1951.357

CHARLES GREEN SHAW (AMERICAN, 1892–1974)
Figure in Space
1950, Oil on composition board
35-7/8 x 24-7/8 in. (91.1 x 63.2 cm.)
The Baltimore Museum of Art:
Bequest of Saidie A. May
BMA 1951.358

ATANASIO SOLDATI (ITALIAN, 1896–1953)
Brown, Red and Blue Composition
1949, Color lithograph
321 x 216 mm. (12-5/8 x 8-1/2 in.)
The Baltimore Museum of Art: Gift of Saidie A. May
BMA 1951.222.21

Blue, Red and Green Composition
1949, Color lithograph
321 x 216 mm. (12-5/8 x 8-1/2 in.)
The Baltimore Museum of Art: Gift of Saidie A. May
BMA 1951.222.22

SOPHIE HENRIETTE TAEUBER-ARP
(SWISS, 1889–1943)
Cercles et demi-cercles sur fond noir
n.d., Opaque watercolor
Sheet: 270 x 350 mm. (10-5/8 x 13-3/4 in.)
The Baltimore Museum of Art:
Bequest of Saidie A. May
BMA 1951.364

Disjointed Forms
1928, Opaque watercolor
Sheet: 300 x 259 mm. (11-13/16 x 10-3/16 in.)
The Baltimore Museum of Art:
Bequest of Saidie A. May
BMA 1951.365

FRANCIS TAILLEUX (FRENCH, 1913–1981)
Nude
1931, Oil on canvas
28-3/4 x 23-5/8 in. (73 x 60 cm.)
The Baltimore Museum of Art:
Bequest of Saidie A. May
BMA 1951.359

Bending Nude
1935, NO MEDIUM
546 x 381 mm. (21-1/2 x 15 in.)
The Baltimore Museum of Art: Gift of Saidie A. May
BMA 1937.25

PIERRE TAL-COAT (FRENCH, 1905–1985)
Birds
n.d., Oil on wood panel
6-1/8 x 8-5/8 in. (15.6 x 21.9 cm.)
The Baltimore Museum of Art:
Bequest of Saidie A. May
BMA 1951.361

Gertrude Stein
1937, Oil on canvas
29 x 23-1/8 in. (73.7 x 58.7 cm.)
The Baltimore Museum of Art:
Bequest of Saidie A. May
BMA 1951.360

YVES TANGUY
(AMERICAN, BORN FRANCE, 1900–1955)
The Earth and the Air
1941, Oil on canvas, 45 x 36 in. (114.3 x 91.4 cm.)
The Baltimore Museum of Art:
Bequest of Saidie A. May
BMA 1951.363

YVES TANGUY
(AMERICAN, BORN FRANCE, 1900–1955)
PRINTER: KURT SELIGMANN
(AMERICAN, BORN SWITZERLAND, 1900–1962)
PUBLISHER: *VVV*
Composition
1942, published 1943, Etching
Mount: 457 x 355 mm. (18 x 14 in.)
Sheet: 408 x 311 mm. (40.8 x 31.1 cm.)
Plate: 326 x 252 mm. (32.6 x 25.2 cm.)
The Baltimore Museum of Art: Gift of Saidie A. May
BMA 1948.54.11

ERNEST THURN (AMERICAN, BORN 1889)
Standing Nude
n.d., Graphite, 12 x 9 in.
The Baltimore Museum of Art: Gift of Saidie A. May
BMA 1934.46.1

LANFRANCO BOMBELLI TIRAVANTI
(ITALIAN, DATES UNKNOWN)
Circles
1949, Lithograph
318 x 216 mm. (12-1/2 x 8-1/2 in.)
The Baltimore Museum of Art: Gift of Saidie A. May
BMA 1951.222.3

Purple and Green Design
1949, Color lithograph
318 x 216 mm. (12-1/2 x 8-1/2 in.)
The Baltimore Museum of Art: Gift of Saidie A. May
BMA 1951.222.4

MARIO TOPPI (ITALIAN, DATES UNKNOWN)
Madonna and Child in a Landscape with a Shepherd
n.d., Graphite, ink, watercolor and gold plaint
Sheet: 346 x 234 mm. (34.6 x 23.4 cm.)
The Baltimore Museum of Art:
Bequest of Saidie A. May
2003.9

CULTURE: UNKNOWN
Head of Kefram (Chephren)
probably 4th dynasty, Diorite, 4 in. (10.2 cm.)
The Baltimore Museum of Art:
Bequest of Saidie A. May
BMA 1951.401

CULTURE: UNKNOWN
Vase
12th dynasty, Anhydrite
4 x 3-1/2 in. (10.2 x 8.9 cm.)
The Baltimore Museum of Art:
Bequest of Saidie A. May
BMA 1951.264

CULTURE: UNKNOWN
Necklace
1991–1778 B.C., Carnelian beads and pendants (15),
gold, 17-1/2 in.(44.4 cm.)
The Baltimore Museum of Art: Gift of Saidie A. May
BMA 1941.389

CULTURE: UNKNOWN
Votive Figure of a Man
c. 1773–1650 B.C., Granodiorite, 8-1/2 in. (21.6 cm.)
The Baltimore Museum of Art:
Bequest of Saidie A. May
BMA 1951.263

CULTURE: UNKNOWN
Seated Figure of Imhotep
9th–2nd century BC, Bronze, 5 in. (12.7 cm.)
The Baltimore Museum of Art:
Bequest of Saidie A. May
BMA 1951.261

CULTURE: UNKNOWN
Figure of a Man
664–525 B.C., Brown quartzite, 6 in. (15.2 cm.)
The Baltimore Museum of Art:
Bequest of Saidie A. May
BMA 1951.258

CULTURE: UNKNOWN
Isis Holding the Child Horus
26th dynasty, Faïence, 5-3/8 in. (13.6 cm.)
The Baltimore Museum of Art:
Bequest of Saidie A. May
BMA 1951.259

CULTURE: UNKNOWN
Profile Bust of Youth [Sculptor's Model]
332–30 B.C., Limestone
8-1/2 x 6-5/8 in. (21.6 x 16.8 cm.)
The Baltimore Museum of Art:
Bequest of Saidie A. May
BMA 1951.260

CULTURE: UNKNOWN
Head of a Man
early Ptolemaic, Limestone, 7 in. (17.8 cm.)
The Baltimore Museum of Art:
Bequest of Saidie A. May
BMA 1951.257

CULTURE: UNKNOWN
Spoon Ornamented with Figures
Blackstone (soapstone), 4 in. (10.2 cm.)
The Baltimore Museum of Art:
Bequest of Saidie A. May
BMA 1951.262

CULTURE: UNKNOWN
Basket
early 20th century, Leather, polychrome
5-7/8 x 9-13/16 in. (15 x 25 cm.)
The Baltimore Museum of Art:
Bequest of Saidie A. May, 1951
BMA 1985.45.33

UNKNOWN ARTIST (AMERICAN)
AFTER ANDRÉ DERAIN (FRENCH, 1880–1954)
Nude Bending Over
1921, Sanguine
Sheet: 606 x 507 mm. (60.6 x 50.7 cm.)
The Baltimore Museum of Art:
Bequest of Saidie A. May, 1951
BMA 1999.270

UNKNOWN ARTIST (DUTCH)
Half Book Cover
16th Century, Leather on wood panel
13-1/2 x 8-3/4 in. (34.3 x 22.2 cm.)
The Baltimore Museum of Art:
Bequest of Saidie A. May
1951.462

UNKNOWN ARTIST (ENGLISH)
Tomb Figure of Kneeling Knight
first quarter 17th century, Alabaster, 26 in. (66 cm.)
The Baltimore Museum of Art: Gift of Saidie A. May
BMA 1941.388

UNKNOWN ARTIST (EUROPEAN)
AFTER TILMAN RIEMENSCHNEIDER
(GERMAN, C.1460–1531)
UNKNOWN ARTIST (GERMAN)
St. Anne and the Virgin
possibly 15th century, Wood, 28 in. (71.1 cm.)
The Baltimore Museum of Art:
Bequest of Saidie A. May
BMA 1951.410

UNKNOWN ARTIST (EUROPEAN)
Plaque: Four Putti Dancing
19th century, Bronze, 9-1/4 in. (23.5 cm.)
The Baltimore Museum of Art:
Bequest of Saidie A. May
BMA 1951.475

UNKNOWN ARTIST (FLEMISH)
Madonna and Child
14th century style, 15th century work, Dinanderie
6-5/8 in. (16.8 cm.)
The Baltimore Museum of Art:
Bequest of Saidie A. May
BMA 1951.437

UNKNOWN ARTIST (FLEMISH)
Sleeping Apostle from Gethsemane Group
mid-15th century, Oak, 9-1/2 in. (24.1 cm.)
The Baltimore Museum of Art:
Bequest of Saidie A. May
BMA 1951.464

UNKNOWN ARTIST (FLEMISH)
St. Margaret of Antioch
late 15th century, Carved wood
17-1/8 in. (43.5 cm.)
The Baltimore Museum of Art: Gift of Saidie A. May
BMA 1948.126

UNKNOWN ARTIST (FRENCH)
Madonna and Child
possibly late 13th century, Ivory, silver, and traces of
pigment, 6-3/4 in. (17.1 cm.)
The Baltimore Museum of Art:
Bequest of Saidie A. May
BMA 1951.452

UNKNOWN ARTIST (FRENCH)
Virgin and Child
c. 1330-1350, Limestone with traces of paint
69-1/2 x 21-1/2 x 11-1/4 in. (176.5 x 54.6 x 28.6 cm.)
The Baltimore Museum of Art: Gift of Saidie A. May
BMA 1942.46

UNKNOWN ARTIST (FRENCH)
Bust of a Nobleman
possibly 15th century, Oak corbel
3-1/2 x 4 in. (8.9 x 10.2 cm.)
The Baltimore Museum of Art:
Bequest of Saidie A. May
BMA 1951.422a

UNKNOWN ARTIST (FRENCH)
Bust of a Man
possibly 15th century, Oak corbel
3-1/2 x 4 in. (8.9 x 10.2 cm.)
The Baltimore Museum of Art:
Bequest of Saidie A. May
BMA 1951.422b

UNKNOWN ARTIST (FRENCH)
Bust of a Female Saint
15th century, Limestone with polychrome
17-3/4 in. (45.1 cm.)
The Baltimore Museum of Art:
Bequest of Saidie A. May
BMA L.1933.39.81

UNKNOWN ARTIST (FRENCH)
*Illuminated Page from a Book of Hours: Holy Family
Kneeling in Adoration of the Christ Child*
c. 1480, on vellum, 4-3/8 x 6-1/8 in. (11.1 x 15.6 cm.)
The Baltimore Museum of Art:
Bequest of Saidie A. May
BMA 1951.478

UNKNOWN ARTIST (FRENCH)
Plaque
early 16th century, Wood, No dimensions
The Baltimore Museum of Art:
Bequest of Saidie A. May
BMA 1951.407

UNKNOWN ARTIST (FRENCH)
Mourning Virgin from Crucifixion Group
c. 1560, Dinanderie, 7-3/8 in. (18.7 cm.)
The Baltimore Museum of Art:
Bequest of Saidie A. May
BMA 1951.435

UNKNOWN ARTIST (FRENCH)
Rearing Horse
c. 1700, Dinanderie, 6 in. (15.2 cm.)
The Baltimore Museum of Art: Gift of Saidie A. May
BMA 1945.11

UNKNOWN ARTIST (FRENCH)
AFTER AUGUSTE RODIN (FRENCH, 1840–1917)
Two Nudes
n.d., Watercolor over graphite
Sheet: 299 x 468 mm. (11-3/4 x 18-7/16 in.)
The Baltimore Museum of Art: Gift of Saidie A. May
BMA 1933.59.4

UNKNOWN ARTIST (FRENCH OR GERMAN)
Venus
19th century, 16th century form, Bronze
10-1/2 in. (26.7 cm.)
The Baltimore Museum of Art:
Bequest of Saidie A. May
BMA 1951.393a

UNKNOWN ARTIST (FRENCH OR GERMAN)
Paris
19th century, 16th century form, Bronze
10 in. (25.4 cm.)
The Baltimore Museum of Art:
Bequest of Saidie A. May
BMA 1951.393b

UNKNOWN ARTIST (GERMAN)
St. Florian with Burning Church
15th–16th century, Wood, 29-1/2 in. (74.9 cm.)
The Baltimore Museum of Art:
Bequest of Saidie A. May
BMA 1951.409

UNKNOWN ARTIST (GERMAN)
Pieta
possibly 15th century, Boxwood, 5-1/4 in. (13.3 cm.)
The Baltimore Museum of Art:
Bequest of Saidie A. May
BMA 1951.450

UNKNOWN ARTIST (GERMAN)
Angel or Saint (Candlestick)
15th century, Wood, 16-1/2 in. (41.9 cm.)
The Baltimore Museum of Art:
Bequest of Saidie A. May
BMA 1948.115

UNKNOWN ARTIST (GERMAN)
Madonna and Child
early 15th century, Boxwood with traces of pigment
and gold, 10-1/2 in. (26.7 cm.)
The Baltimore Museum of Art:
Bequest of Saidie A. May
BMA 1951.458

UNKNOWN ARTIST (GERMAN)
St. Catherine of Alexandria
c. 1490–1500, Linden wood, polychrome, 40-1/2 in.
(102.9 cm.)
The Baltimore Museum of Art: Gift of Saidie A. May
BMA 1946.175a-b

UNKNOWN ARTIST (GERMAN)
Hercules and the Lion
late 16th century, Bronze, 7-1/8 in. (18.1 cm.)
The Baltimore Museum of Art:
Bequest of Saidie A. May
BMA 1951.444

AFTER UNKNOWN ARTIST (GERMAN)
HANS HOLBEIN THE YOUNGER
(GERMAN, 1497–1543)
Plaque: Death and the Knight.
After Holbein's "Dance of Death" Series.
late 16th-early 17th century, Gilt bronze
2 x 1-1/2 in. (5.1 x 3.8 cm.)
The Baltimore Museum of Art:
Bequest of Saidie A. May
BMA 1951.451

UNKNOWN ARTIST, ITALIAN
Crucifixion
14th century, Oil on wood panel
19-1/2 x 14-1/2 in. (49.5 x 36.7 cm.)
The Baltimore Museum of Art:
Bequest of Saidie A. May
BMA 1951.394

UNKNOWN ARTIST, ITALIAN, POSSIBLY AREZZO
PREVIOUSLY ATTRIBUTED TO: AREZZO
(14TH CENTURY)
Madonna and Child Enthroned with Four Saints
early 14th century, Tempera on wood panel
16-1/2 x 12-3/4 in. (41.9 x 32.4 cm.)
The Baltimore Museum of Art:
Bequest of Saidie A. May
BMA 1951.392

UNKNOWN ARTIST, JAPANESE
AFTER KATSUKAWA SHUNSHO
(JAPANESE, 1726–1792)
Woman with a Writing Brush
late 19th century, Color woodcut
Sheet: 195 x 300 mm. (19.5 x 30 cm.)
The Baltimore Museum of Art: Gift of Saidie A. May
BMA 1932.45.1

UNKNOWN ARTIST (PERSIAN)
Book Cover
n.d., Lacquered, 178 x 114 mm. (7 x 4-1/2 in.)
The Baltimore Museum of Art: Gift of Saidie A. May
BMA 1932.56.6a

Book Cover
n.d., Lacquered, 178 x 114 mm. (7 x 4-1/2 in.)
The Baltimore Museum of Art: Gift of Saidie A. May
BMA 1932.56.6b

UNKNOWN ARTIST (PROBABLY GERMAN)
Illuminated Leaf from Manuscript
first half 14th century, 448 x 273 mm.
(17-5/8 x 10-3/4 in.)
The Baltimore Museum of Art:
Bequest of Saidie A. May
BMA 1951.465

UNKNOWN ARTIST (PROBABLY GERMAN)
Illuminated Leaf from Manuscript
first 1st half 14th century
448 x 270 mm. (17-5/8 x 10-5/8 in.)
The Baltimore Museum of Art:
Bequest of Saidie A. May
BMA 1951.466

UNKNOWN ARTIST (PROBABLY GERMAN)
Giovanni Villanni
14th century, Ivory, 4 x 3-1/4 in. (10.2 x 8.3 cm.)
The Baltimore Museum of Art: Gift of Saidie A. May
BMA 1932.56.4

UNKNOWN ARTIST (PROBABLY GERMAN)
Walking Man
15th-16th century, Bronze, 6 in. (15.2 cm.)
The Baltimore Museum of Art:
Bequest of Saidie A. May
BMA 1951.405

UNKNOWN ARTIST (PROBABLY GERMAN)
Plaque: Figure of Christ
16th century, Gilded bronze
6-1/2 x 4-1/16 in. (16.5 x 10.3 cm.)
The Baltimore Museum of Art:
Bequest of Saidie A. May
BMA 1951.402

UNKNOWN ARTIST (PROBABLY GERMAN)
Hercules
16th–18th century, Green marble, 21 in. (53.3 cm.)
The Baltimore Museum of Art: Gift of Saidie A. May
BMA 1941.387

UNKNOWN ARTIST (PROBABLY GERMAN)
Pope Blessing
n.d., Pen and brown ink and brush and brown wash
heightened with white opaque watercolor over black
chalk, Sheet: 268 x 249 mm. (10-9/16 x 9-13/16 in.)
The Baltimore Museum of Art:
Bequest of Saidie A. May, 1951
BMA 1994.195

UNKNOWN ARTIST (PROBABLY GERMAN)
Head of a Fauness
late 16th-early 17th century, Bronze
4-3/4 in. (12.1 cm.)
The Baltimore Museum of Art: Gift of Saidie A. May
BMA 1948.127

UNKNOWN ARTIST (PROBABLY GERMAN)
Madonna and Child
17th century, Polychromed wood, 18 in. (45.7 cm.)
The Baltimore Museum of Art:
Bequest of Saidie A. May
BMA 1951.426

UNKNOWN ARTIST (PROBABLY GERMAN)
Diana (possibly Amazon)
possibly 18th century, Bronze, 9-1/4 in. (23.5 cm.)
The Baltimore Museum of Art:
Bequest of Saidie A. May
BMA 1951.406

UNKNOWN ARTIST (PROBABLY GERMAN)
Gladiator
n.d., Bronze, 2-1/2 in. H
The Baltimore Museum of Art:
Bequest of Saidie A. May
BMA 1951.400

UNKNOWN ARTIST (RUSSIAN)
Icon: Madonna and Child
18th century, copy after a 14th century piece
Tempera on wood panel
11-1/4 x 8-1/2 in. (28.6 x 21.6 cm.)
The Baltimore Museum of Art: Gift of Saidie A. May
BMA 1932.56.3

LUIGI VERONESI (ITALIAN, 1908–1998)
Red and Blue Composition
1949, Color lithograph, 321 x 216 mm.
(12-5/8 x 8-1/2 in.)
The Baltimore Museum of Art: Gift of Saidie A. May
BMA 1951.222.23

Abstraction
1949, Lithograph, 321 x 216 mm. (12-5/8 x 8-1/2 in.)
The Baltimore Museum of Art: Gift of Saidie A. May
BMA 1951.222.24

ENEA VICO (ITALIAN, 1523–1567)
AFTER MARCANTONIO
OR AFTER RAPHAEL [RAFFAELLO SANTI]
(ITALIAN, 1483–1520)
The Death of Lucretia
1541, Engraving, 204 x 130 mm. (8-1/16 x 5-1/8 in.)
The Baltimore Museum of Art: Gift of Saidie A. May
BMA 1932.50.3

EMMANUEL VIVIANO
(AMERICAN, DATES UNKNOWN)
Fish
20th century, Stained glass and lead
without Base: 15 x 16-1/2 in. (38.1 x 41.9 cm.)
The Baltimore Museum of Art: Gift of Saidie A. May
BMA 1950.83

MAURICE DE VLAMINCK (FRENCH, 1876–1958)
Landscape
n.d., Woodcut, 257 x 337 mm. (10-1/8 x 13-1/4 in.)
The Baltimore Museum of Art: Gift of Saidie A. May
BMA 1933.56.1

PUBLISHER: *VVV*
Cover for the "VVV Portfolio"
Published 1943, Letterpress and relief print
Overall: 460 x 358 x 8 mm. (18-1/8 x 14-1/8 x 5/16 in.)
The Baltimore Museum of Art: Gift of Saidie A. May
BMA 1948.54.1-11

WILFRED ZOGBAUM (AMERICAN, 1915–1965)
Portrait of Hans Hofmann
c. 1960, Gelatin silver print
Sheet: 352 x 273 mm. (35.2 x 27.3 cm.)
Image: 330 x 269 mm. (33 x 26.9 cm.)
The Baltimore Museum of Art:
Bequest of Saidie A. May, 1951
BMA 1976.18

FEDERICO ZUCCARO (ITALIAN, C. 1541–1609)
St. Paul
n.d., Pen and ink with brown wash heightened with
white on blue paper, squared for transfer in black
chalk; black chalk
Sheet: 367 x 191 mm. (36.7 x 19.1 cm.)
The Baltimore Museum of Art: Gift of Saidie A. May
BMA 1928.1.6

Deaccessioned Objects

ALFREDO BARTOLETTI (ITALIAN)
Seated Nude
n.d., Oil on composition board, 15-1/4 x 18 in.
Bequest of Saidie A. May
1951.265

FRANCISCO BORES (SPANISH, 1898–1972)
Blonde Woman
1937, Oil on canvas, 35 x 46 in.
Bequest of Saidie A. May
1951.270

Girl Reading
1938, Oil on canvas, 35 x 45-3/4 in.
Bequest of Saidie A. May
1951.271

Slice of Watermelon
1939, Oil on canvas
Bequest of Saidie A. May
1951.272

ETIENNE BOUCHAUD (FRENCH, BORN 1898)
The Bridge at Nantes
n.d., Oil on canvas, 17-1/4 x 32-1/2 in.
Bequest of Saidie A. May
1951.273

SERGE BRIGNONI (SWISS, 1903–2002)
Germination
1937, Oil on canvas
Bequest of Saidie A. May
1951.274

PIERRE BRUNE (FRENCH, 1887–1956)
Landscape
n.d., Oil on composition board, 6-3/4 x 10-1/2 in.
Bequest of Saidie A. May
1951.276

Notre Dame
n.d., Oil on canvas, 21-1/2 x 18 in.
Bequest of Saidie A. May
1951.277

Fall Flowers in a Vase
n.d., Oil on canvas, 18-1/8 x 15 in.
Bequest of Saidie A. May
1951.278

Head of a Man
n.d., Oil on canvas, 16-1/4 x 13 in.
Bequest of Saidie A. May
1951.275

MARY CASSATT (AMERICAN, 1844–1926)
Portrait Sketch of a Lady in a Black Hat
n.d., Pastel, 18-1/2 x 14-7/8 in.
Bequest of Saidie A. May
1951.279

PAUL CÉZANNE (FRENCH, 1839–1906)
Still Life with Fruit
n.d., Oil on canvas, 8 x 9-1/2 in.
Bequest of Saidie A. May
1951.280

PAUL CORNET (FRENCH, 1892–1977)
Standing Nude
n.d., Bronze, 20-3/4 in. H
Bequest of Saidie A. May
1951.372

JEANNE DAOUR (FRENCH, BORN ROMANIA 1914)
The Seine
1930, Oil on composition board
Bequest of Saidie A. May
1951.283

HERMINE DAVID (FRENCH, 1886–1971)
Rue à Versailler
n.d., Oil on composition board, 27-1/2 x 20 in.
Bequest of Saidie A. May
1951.284

JACQUES DENIER (FRENCH, BORN 1894)
Mantelpiece
n.d., Oil on canvas, 24-3/4 x 46 in.
Bequest of Saidie A. May
1951.287

ANDRÉ DERAIN (FRENCH, 1880–1954)
Girl Leaning on her Elbow
n.d., Oil on canvas, 15 x 18-1/2 in.
Bequest of Saidie A. May
1951.290

Head of a Girl
n.d., Oil on canvas, 14 x 10-3/4 in.
Bequest of Saidie A. May
1951.291

CHARLES DESPIAU (FRENCH, 1874–1946)
Spring
n.d., Bronze, 13-1/2 in. H
Bequest of Saidie A. May
1951.376

CHARLES GEORGES DUFRESNE
(FRENCH, 1876–1938)
Still Life with Fish
n.d, Oil on canvas, 25-1/2 x 21-1/4
Bequest of Saidie A. May
1951.294

OTHON FRIESZ (FRENCH, 1879–1949)
Reclining Woman
1931, Oil on canvas, 37-1/2 x 50-1/2 in.
Bequest of Saidie A. May
1951.298

Landscape at Toulon
1932, Oil on canvas, 5-3/8 x 9-1/4 in.
Bequest of Saidie A. May
1951.302

Bather
1935, Oil on canvas, 25-5/8 x 21-1/4 in.
Bequest of Saidie A. May
1951.300

ALBERTO GIACOMETTI (SWISS, 1901–1966)
A Man
1930, Polychrome plaster, 26 in. H
Bequest of Saidie A. May
1951.381

FRANCIS GRUBER (FRENCH, 1912–1948)
Shipwreck
1937, Oil on canvas, 16 x 13 in.
Bequest of Saidie A. May
1951.307

HANS HARTUNG (GERMAN, 1904–1989)
Peinture
1950, Oil on canvas, 19-3/4 x 28-3/4 in.
Bequest of Saidie A. May
1951.308

ALFRED JENSEN
(AMERICAN, BORN GUATEMALA, 1903–1981)
Still Life
1930, Oil on canvas, 25-1/2 x 32 in.
Bequest of Saidie A. May
1951.309

BERNARD KARFIOL (AMERICAN, 1886–1952)
Three Young Women
1927, Oil on canvas
Gift of Saidie A. May
1935.34.5

EDMOND KAYSER (FRENCH, 1882–1965)
Woman in Landscape
n.d., Oil on canvas, 18 x 21-3/4 in.
Bequest of Saidie A. May
1951.311

Landscape with Castle
n.d., Oil on canvas, 15 x 18-1/4 in.
Bequest of Saidie A. May
1951.312

Head of a Young Girl
n.d., Oil on board, 15-3/4 x 12-1/2 in.
Bequest of Saidie A. May
1951.315

Man in a Blue Smock
n.d., Oil on board, 17 x 14-3/4 in.
Bequest of Saidie A. May
1951.314

ELIE LASCAUX (FRENCH, 1888–1968)
Le Robec, Rouen
1937, Oil on canvas, 18-1/4 x 21-1/2 in.
Bequest of Saidie A. May
1951.319

Rue de l'hopital à Rouen
1938, Oil on canvas
Bequest of Saidie A. May
1951.320

FERNAND LÉGER (FRENCH, 1881–1955)
Abstraction
1931, Watercolor, 18 x 15 in. (mat opening)
Bequest of Saidie A. May
1951.323

ANDRÉ MASSON (FRENCH, 1896–1987)
City of the Skull
1938
Bequest of Saidie A. May
1951.330

Cascatelles (1949)
n.d.
Bequest of Saidie A. May
1951.334

Les Amoureux
1930, Oil, pastel and charcoal on canvas, 15 x 18-1/4 in.
Bequest of Saidie A. May
1951.327

Birds Fighting
1941, Pastel on paper, 24-1/2 x 18-3/4 in.
Bequest of Saidie A. May
1951.332

MELIUS (FRENCH, DATES UNKNOWN)
View of Turin
n.d., Oil on canvas, 24-1/4 x 30-3/4 in.
Bequest of Saidie A. May
1951.336

JULES PASCIN
(AMERICAN, BORN BULGARIA, 1885–1930)
Girl Reading
1923, Oil on canvas, 29 x 23-1/2 in.
Bequest of Saidie A. May
1951.346

PIERRE-AUGUSTE RENOIR (FRENCH, 1841–1919)
Washerwomen
n.d., Oil on canvas, 6-3/4 x 9-1/4 in.
Bequest of Saidie A. May
1951.350

Seated Nude
c. 1909, Oil on canvas, 11 x 10-3/4 in.
Bequest of Saidie A. May
1951.352

The Bowl
c. 1910, Oil on canvas, 6-1/4 x 8-1/4 in.
Bequest of Saidie A. May
1951.351

SUZANNE ROGER (FRENCH, BORN 1899)
Serpents
n.d., Oil on canvas, 18 x 15 in.
Bequest of Saidie A. May
1951.353

GEORGES ROUAULT (FRENCH, 1871–1958)
Head of a Woman
n.d., Oil on composition board, 10-3/4 x 8-3/4 in.
Bequest of Saidie A. May
1951.354

THEODORE SCHEMPP (AMERICAN, BORN 1904)
Still Life
n.d., Oil on canvas, 13-1/8 x 11 in.
Bequest of Saidie A. May
1951.355

PIERRE TAL-COAT (FRENCH, 1905–1985)
Woman with Dishevelled Hair
n.d., Oil on canvas, 28-1/8 x 23-1/8 in.
Bequest of Saidie A. May
1951.362

MAURICE UTRILLO (FRENCH, 1883–1955)
Gênet Facing Mont St. Michel
1922, Oil on canvas, 18 x 22-1/4 in.
Bequest of Saidie A. May
1951.366

LOUIS VIVIN (FRENCH, 1861–1936)
View of Nantes Cathedral
n.d., Oil on canvas, 12-3/4 x 19-1/2 in.
Bequest of Saidie A. May
1951.367

MAURICE DE VLAMINCK (FRENCH, 1876–1958)
Flowers in a Vase
n.d., Oil on canvas, 21-3/4 x 18 in.
Bequest of Saidie A. May
1951.368

Artworks in Other American Museums from the Saidie A. May Collection

BERTOIA, HARRY (ITALIAN, 1915–1978)
Abstraction
undated, monotype, 26 x 40 in.
1948:84 SD deaccessioned

BONNARD, PIERRE (FRENCH, 1867–1947)
Fruit Bowl and Dish
1925, lithograph,
7 x 9 7/8 in., 1935:10 SD

Arc de Triomphe
1895, transfer lithograph printed in 5 colors,
comp., 12-5/8 x 18-1/4 in.,
30.1932 MOMA

BORÈS, FRANCISCO (SPANISH, 1898–1972)
The Card Players
1934, oil on canvas, 35 x 46 in.
1940:15 SD deaccessioned

BRAQUE, GEORGES (FRENCH, 1882–1963)
Still Life
1932, lithograph printed in color, comp.
8 x 15-5/8 in.
31.1932 MOMA

BRUNE, PIERRE (FRENCH, 1887–1956)
Portrait de Mon. T
oil on canvas, 18-1/4 x 15 in.
N. Adkins deaccessioned

BUFF, CONRAD (AMERICAN, 1886–1975)
Forest Folk
undated, lithograph (12 x15 in.)
1935:21 SD

CORINTH, LOVIS (GERMAN, 1858–1925)
Reclining Woman
1912, etching, 8 x 11-1/2 in.
28.10.10 CAR

DE CHIRICO, GIORGIO (GREEK, 1888–1978)
Warriors
undated, oil on canvas, 18 x 22 in.
1937:4 SD deaccessioned

Horses
1930–32, lithographic crayon, sheet
13-5/8 x 17 in.
SC32.1932 MOMA deaccessioned

Horses
1930–35, gouache on paper over cardboard
9-3/4 x 13-1/4 in.
SC2.1935 MOMA

Conversation
1926, oil on wood, 13-1/4 x 10-1.4 in.
1.35 MOMA

CORNET, PAUL (FRENCH, 1892–1977)
Mother and Child
undated, bronze,
22-1/4 x 6-1/2 x 8-1/2 in.
1935:4 SD deaccessioned

DAVIES, ARTHUR BOWEN
(AMERICAN, 1862–1928)
Nocturne
etching & aquatint
7-5/8 x 5-5/8 in.
21.3.1 CAR

DERAIN, ANDRÉ (FRENCH, 1880–1954)
Head of a Girl
1928, oil on canvas,
14-1/8 x 10-7/8 in.
1936.44 SD

Head of a Woman
1927, lithograph, printed in black, comp.
14-1/4 x 11-5/8 in.
33.32 MOMA

Head of a Girl with Black Hair
1927, lithograph, printed in black, comp.
17-13/16 x 14-1/2 in.
34.1932 MOMA

DESPIAU, CHARLES (FRENCH, 1874–1946)
Seated Nude
red crayon, sheet, 11-3/4 x 7-3/4 in.
35.1932 MOMA

DUBUFFET, JEAN (FRENCH, 1901–1985)
Snack for Two
1945, oil on canvas,
29-1/8 x 24-1/8 in.
280.1949 MOMA

North African Wall
1948, watercolor, gouache & distemper
18 x 21-1/2 in.
1949.40 SD

DUFRESNE, CHARLES GEORGES
(FRENCH, 1876–1938)
Studio
brown ink & wash, sheet, 10-1/8 x 9-3/8 in.
3.1935 MOMA

DUFY, RAOUL (FRENCH, 1887–1953)
The Promenade
1913, oil on canvas,
25-1/2 x 31-3/4 in.
1935.12 SD

The Palm
1923, watercolor on paper mounted on cardboard
19-3/4 x 25 in.
140.34 MOMA

FRIESZ, ACHILLE-ÉMILE-OTHON
(FRENCH, 1879–1949)
The Creek
oil on canvas, 36-1/4 x 25-1/2 in.
1935.13 SD

Landscape with Figures (Bathers)
1909, oil on canvas, 25-5/8 x 32 in.
5.1935 MOMA

Standing Nude
1929, watercolor sheet, 20-1/8 x 12-7/8 in.
17.1932 MOMA deaccessioned

The Garden
1930, oil on canvas, 23-5/8 x 28-3/4 in.
16.1932 MOMA

Lovers
1930, watercolor
18-3/4 x 12-1/4 in.
18.1932 MOMA deaccessioned

Les Baigneuses au Lac/Nudes in Landscape
oil on canvas, 15 x 18 in.
N. Adkins deaccessioned

GRUBER, FRANCIS (FRENCH, 1912–1948)
Le Promenade
undated, oil on canvas, 8-7/8 x 13 in.
1936.10 SD

HADEN, SIR FRANCIS SEYMOUR
(ENGLISH, 1818–1910)
On the Test at Longparish
1896, watercolor with charcoal on paper
10-1/4 x 14-5/16 in.
28.10.2 CAR

HALLER, HERMANN (SWISS, 1880–1950)
Standing Girl
1926, bronze, 14 in. H
13.30 MOMA

KOLLWITZ, KATHE SCHMIDT (GERMAN, 1867–1945)
Head of Man
etching, 12-5/8 x 9-3/8 in.
28.10.3 CAR

You Bleed from Many Wounds, Oh, People
1896, etching & aquatint, 4-3/4 x 12-13/16 in.
28.10.5 CAR

Mothers
1920, lithograph on paper,
11-3/4 x 15-3/4 in.
28.10.11 CAR

LANKES, JULIUS J. (AMERICAN, 1884–1960)
The Sleigh Ride
1919, woodcut on paper, 4 x 6 in.
21.3.2 CAR

LEGROS, ALPHONSE
(ENGLISH, BORN FRANCE, 1837–1911)
Priests Celebrating Mass
watercolor on paper,
7-1/8 x 9-11/16 in.
28.10.1 CAR

LEVER, HAYLEY (AMERICAN, 1883–1959)
Tunny Boats
1926, watercolor on paper,
19-11/16 x 14-9/16 in.
27.73 MET

Gamrie
1925, cancelled copper plate for etching,
14-3/8 x 8-15/16 in.
25.57 MET

Fishing Boats
watercolor MONT

LOVIS, CORINTH (GERMAN, 1858–1925)
Reclining Woman
CAR

MAILLOL, ARISTIDE (FRENCH, 1861–1944)
Crouching Woman
1927, etching, printed in black, plate
8-1/4 x 10-3/4 in.
37.1932 MOMA

Seated Figure
c.1930, terracotta (9"h) including bronze base
2-3/8 x 5-3/8 in.
391.1942 MOMA

MANOLO, MANUEL (CUBAN, 1872–1945)
Dancer with a Fan
1928, terracotta,
11-3/8 x 5-3/16 in.
1935:2 SD

MASSON, ANDRÉ (FRENCH, 1896–1987)
The Germ of the Cosmos
1942, gouache & pastel on canvas, 40 x 33 in.
1946.30 SD

The Little Tragedy
1933, oil on canvas, 10-3/4 x 18 in.
N. Adkins

MATISSE, HENRI (FRENCH, 1869–1954)
Bust of a Woman Wearing Necklace & Bracelet
1926, etching, 7 x 4-7/8 in.
1935.5 SD

Reader with Bouquet of Roses
1925, lithograph,
6-5/16 x 9-5/8 in.
1935.6 SD

Nude Seated on a Stool
1936, ink drawing,
20-3/4 x 15-1/8 in.
1938.14 SD

Sleeping Figure with Turkish Slippers
1929, lithograph, 10-3/4 x 14-1/2 in.
1935.7 SD

Ten Dancers
1927, transfer lithographs, printed in black, portfolio,
19-15/16 x 13-1/8 in.
19.1932.1–10 MOMA

Reclining Nude
1926, transfer lithograph printed in black, comp.
17-5/16 x 31-1/4 in.
38.1932 MOMA

Black Eyes
1913, transfer lithograph, printed in black, comp.
17-7/8 x 12-3/4 in.
39.1932 MOMA

MIRÓ, JOAN (SPANISH, 1893–1983)
Untitled
1934, ink & pastel, 24-1/4 x 18 in.
1940:16 SD

MODIGLIANI, AMEDEO (ITALIAN, 1884–1920)
Caryatid
1914, pencil & wash sheet
21-1/4 x 16-3/8 in.
29.1932 MOMA

MCBEY, JAMES (SCOTTISH, 1884–1959)
Cancelled copper plate for the etching Gamrie
MET

NIGHTINGALE, CHARLES THRUPP
(ENGLISH, 1878–UNKNOWN)
Arcadia
1923, woodcut on paper, 2-13/16 x 4-1/16 in.
28.10.12 CAR

PICASSO, PABLO (SPANISH, 1881–1973)
The Three Graces II
1922–23 etching,
12-27/32 x 7-25/32 in.
1935:9 SD

Head
1909, gouache, 24 x18 in.
12.30 MOMA

On the Beach II
1921, lithograph, printed in black, comp.
3-1/2 x 7-1/2 in.
40.32 MOMA

The Wrestlers
1921, lithograph, printed in black, comp.
4-1/2 x 7-3/4 in.
41.32 MOMA

The Horseman
1921, lithograph, printed in black, comp.
7-9/16 x 10-3/4 in.
42.32 MOMA

Nude Model
1927, etching on copper, printed in black
plate, 11 x 7-1/2 in.
43.32 MOMA

ROSENFELD, EDWARD (AMERICAN, 1906–1963)
Flowers
undated, oil on canvas, 24-1/2 x 12-7/16 in.
1948:16 SD deaccessioned

ROUAULT, GEORGES (FRENCH, 1871–1958)
The Dictator (Left); The Favorite (Right)
1928, collotype with hand-coloring, 8-3/4 x 6 in.
1935:8 SD

SCHONGAUER, MARTIN (GERMAN, 1445–1491)
Death of the Virgin
c.1470, engraving, 9-27/32 x6-1/2 in.
1935.11 SD

SOPHER, AARON (AMERICAN, 1905–1972)
Archbishop Athenagoras
undated, ink
1949:39 SD

TIEPOLO, GIOVANNI BATTISTA (ITALIAN, 1696–1770)
Nymph with Satyr
28.10.6 CAR

Untitled
28.10.7 CAR

Untitled
28.10.8 CAR

UNKNOWN, 3RD CENTURY B.C. (GREEK)
Woman with Sun Hat
3rd century B.C., terracotta
30.117 MET

UTRILLO, MAURICE (FRENCH, 1883–1955)
La Place du Tertre
1919, lithograph, printed in black, comp.
7-3/8 x 10-11/16 in.
44.1932 MOMA

VILLON, JACQUES (FRENCH, 1875–1963)
Dancer in Repose
undated, oil on canvas,
13-3/4 x 10-1/2 in.
1937:5 SD deaccessioned

VIVIN, LOUIS (FRENCH, 1861–1934)
Church of St. Laurent & the Gare de l'Est
1920–30, oil on canvas, 18 x 24 in.
4.35 MOMA (destroyed by fire in 1949 while being
restored outside the museum)

DE VLAMINCK, MAURICE (FRENCH, 1876–1958)
Factory
1920, watercolor and gouache on board
16-1/2 x 19-1/2 in.
1935.3 SD

Le Promenade
1913, oil on canvas, 25-1/2 x 31-3/4 in.
1935.12 SD

VUILLARD, EDOUARD (FRENCH, 1868–1940)
Mother and Sister of the Artist
1893, oil on canvas,
18-1/4 x 22-1/4 in.
141.1934 MOMA

VYTLACIL, VACLAV (AMERICAN, 1892–1984)
Still Life
1929, monotype, printed in color, sheet
17-1/4 x 22-5/8 in.
45.1932 MOMA

Still Life
monotype, sheet, 13-1/4 x 19-1/2 in.
46.1932 MOMA

WATERLOO, ANTHONY (DUTCH, 1609–1676/1695)
Le Berger Sur le Petit Pont
etching, 5-1/4 x 6-3/16 in.
28.10.9 CAR

Index